England's Population

A History Since the Domesday Survey

ANDREW HINDE

Senior Lecturer in Population Studies,
University of Southampton

A Member of the Hodder Headline Group
London
Distributed in the United States of America by
Oxford University Press Inc., New York

First published in Great Britain in 2003 by
Hodder Arnold, a member of the Hodder Headline Group,
338 Euston Road, London NW1 3BH

http://www.arnoldpublishers.com

Distributed in the Unitied States of America by
Oxford University Press Inc.
198 Madison Avenue, New York, NY10016

© 2003 Andrew Hinde

The advice and information in this book are believed to be true and accurate at the date of
going to press, but neither the author nor the publisher can accept any legal responsibility or
liability for any errors or omissions.

British Library Cataloguing in Publication Data
A catalogue record for this book is available from the British Library

Library of Congress Cataloging-in-Publication Data
A catalog record for this book is available from the Library of Congress

ISBN 0 340 76189 X (hb)
ISBN 0 340 76190 3 (pb)

1 2 3 4 5 6 7 8 9 10

Typeset in 10/12 Sabon by Phoenix Photosetting, Chatham, Kent
Printed and bound in Great Britain by Bath Press

What do you think about this book? Or any other Arnold title?
Please send your comments to feedback.arnold@hodder.co.uk

Table of Contents

List of Tables

List of Figures

List of Boxes

Preface

It is now more than ten years since I started to teach an undergraduate course in the population history of England, at the University of Southampton. From the start, this course had to overcome the lack of a single textbook that told the story of the evolution of England's population for the whole period since the time of the Norman Conquest. Even the compilation of a series of estimates of such a basic quantity as the total number of people in the country required a search through several different sources. There were, of course, excellent summaries of what was known about certain periods: John Hatcher's *Plague, Population and the English Economy 1348–1530* (London, Macmillan, 1977) and Robert Woods' *The Population of Britain in the Nineteenth Century* (London, Macmillan, 1992) were two.

The lack of a unified treatment was probably the impetus behind the publication of Michael Anderson's edited volume entitled *British Population History: from the Black Death to the Present Day* (Cambridge, Cambridge University Press, 1995). This was, in effect, the repackaging of several shorter books dealing with particular time periods (including those by Hatcher and Woods mentioned above), with some new material written by Anderson on the twentieth century. It was a good 'quick fix', and remains a very useful resource. However, its mode of creation means that some parts of the book deal with England, others include Wales and Scotland; the contributions were written at different times – that by Hatcher was nearly 20 years old in 1995; and there are gaps in the coverage – the crucial period around the turn of the fourteenth century, for example, is omitted. Moreover, research into England's population history has proceeded apace during the last ten or fifteen years, and many 'new orthodoxies' have come under attack. For all these reasons, it seemed worth trying to write a single-volume history of England's population since the time of Domesday Book. This is the result.

The history of population has tended, in England, to be written by non-historians, at least until the last decade or so. I was not trained as a historian, and *England's Population: a History since the Domesday Survey* reflects my background in the social sciences. The book is written from a demographic perspective, being principally concerned with describing and accounting for changes in the number of people in England over time. However, I have tried to recognize some of the shortcomings of the social scientific perspective that suffuses much historical demography (as it has usually been known), and to recognize that the historians, anthropologists and others have begun to make serious inroads into territory previously occupied by social scientists, bringing with them alternative approaches to the generation of new knowledge.

Demography can be a technical subject, and the measurement of the impact of the factors that affect population size does involve some arithmetic. However, I have assumed that readers will have no knowledge of demographic methods. The various bits of technical apparatus necessary to understand the issues are presented in 'boxes' separated from the main text at the points where they are first needed.

In writing the book, I have tried not to privilege certain periods over others. Thus the three parts, dealing respectively with the medieval period, the early modern era and the post-1750 period, are roughly the same length. Since more material has been published on certain periods (for example, the seventeenth century and the late nineteenth century) than others, this means that some research on the more popular periods has been glossed over. The twentieth century also receives rather less detailed treatment than preceding periods, mainly because there are other books that cover this period much more fully (such as D. Coleman and J. Salt, *The British Population: Patterns, Trends and Processes* (Oxford, Oxford University Press, 1992)).

My interest in the population history of England began in 1980 when I attended a series of lectures given in the Department of Geography at the University of Cambridge by Richard Smith. That year was an exciting time to be studying population history in Cambridge. E.A. Wrigley and R.S. Schofield's *The Population History of England 1541–1871: a Reconstruction* (London, Edward Arnold, 1981) was in press, and the Cambridge Group for the History of Population and Social Structure at 27 Trumpington Street was filled with the anticipation of a major research project about to come to fruition. Since then, I have incurred many debts: to Robert Woods for his excellent supervision at the University of Sheffield, to successive sets of colleagues in Oxford, London and Southampton, to the other members of the Editorial Board of *Local Population Studies* and to the doctoral students I have supervised during the past ten years or so. Finally, Jane, Luke, Dominic, Joel and Susanna have been wonderfully supportive, but I know that they are relieved that 'England's population history' has, finally, come to an end.

Alton, Hampshire
October 2002

Acknowledgements

Many people have helped with the preparation of this book, either directly, or indirectly (through conversations, or participation in seminars). Some of these may not know they helped, but they did, and I should like to acknowledge them here. Richard Smith led me to clarify my thinking about the demography of medieval England. Conversations with Bernard Harris about the mortality decline after 1750, and with Eilidh Garrett about the history of English fertility informed Chapters 11, 12 and 13. David Coleman, Briony Eckstein, Martin Ecclestone, Michael Edgar, Nigel Goose, Violetta Hionidou, Steven King, Dennis Mills, Jim Oeppen, Roger Schofield, Kevin Schürer, Wendy Sigle-Rushton, Bob Woods and Matthew Woollard all provided informal input at various stages. These good people, of course, are not responsible for any errors in this book, or for things which have been omitted.

The author and the publisher would like to thank Cambridge University Press for permission to reproduce a substantial extract from a table in D. Baines, *Migration in a Mature Economy: Emigration and Internal Migration in England and Wales, 1861–1900* (Cambridge, Cambridge University Press, 1985), p. 61.

1

Introduction

1.1 The number of people in England, 1086–2000

According to the Office for National Statistics, on 30 June 2000 there were just 2900 short of 50 million people resident in England.[1] Yet a thousand years earlier, the population probably numbered less than one-thirtieth of that total. The earliest date at which an estimate with some credibility can be made is 1086, the year of the Domesday survey. Though historians disagree, for a number of good reasons, about the exact figure (see Chapter 2), it seems unlikely that the population of Domesday England was less than 1.4 million, or more than 1.9 million. This book is an attempt to describe and account for the growth of the English population during the 900-plus years since William the Conqueror instructed his administrators to survey his recently acquired realm.

The analysis of the growth (or decline) of human populations is the domain of the academic discipline of demography.[2] The study of population change in the past is a sub-discipline of demography, known as *historical demography*. During the past 35 years, the work of historical demographers has led to enormous advances in our knowledge of the evolution of the English population. Progress has been greatest for the early modern period, largely because of the exploitation of the Church of England parish registers by members and associates of the Cambridge Group for the History of Population and Social Structure. In 1981 the publication of E.A. Wrigley and R.S. Schofield's *The Population History of England, 1541–1871: a Reconstruction* made available for the first time accurate estimates of the number of people living in England from the mid-sixteenth century

---

[1] http://www.statistics.gov.uk/statbase.
[2] To demographers, a *population* consists of any group of persons who can be delimited on the basis of some observable characteristic, most commonly residence within a given geographical area. Thus the population of England at a given time refers to those persons resident in England at that time. 'Residents', in this context, normally exclude temporary visitors and holiday-makers; they are taken to include those who live in England but who are temporarily abroad.

onwards.[3] When taken together with the figures that have long been available for the nineteenth and twentieth centuries from population censuses (the first census was held in 1801), these provide a consistent series of population totals more than 460 years long.

For earlier periods knowledge is inevitably more sketchy and there is room for substantial disagreement even about such a fundamental quantity as the number of people living in the country (see Chapter 3). Nevertheless, enough is probably known to make it worth presenting a 'best guess' scenario for the years before the 1540s, which can be combined with the aforementioned 460-year series to chart changes in the English population over the entire period since 1086 (Figure 1.1).

The result is striking, for the population history of England seems to fall into two parts. Before about 1750, periods of growth (for example, in the twelfth, thirteenth and sixteenth centuries) alternated with periods of stagnation (the fifteenth and seventeenth centuries) and one period of spectacular decline (the fourteenth century). The overall expansion of the population during this period of more than 650 years was very modest. Even as late as 1750, the population of England was only one-tenth of its 2000 figure. Indeed, it is quite possible that there were fewer

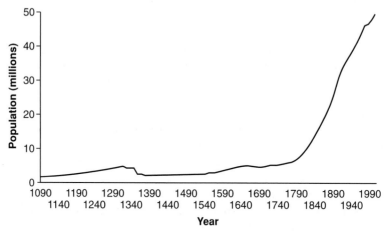

Figure 1.1 The population of England, 1086–2000
Sources: Table 2.1; E.A. Wrigley and R.S. Schofield, *The Population History of England 1541–1871: a Reconstruction* (London, Arnold, 1981), pp. 531–5; Census of England and Wales, 1901, *General Report with Appendices* (London, Her Majesty's Stationery Office, 1904), pp. 195–6; Office of Population Censuses and Surveys, *Census 1981: Historical Tables 1801–1901, England and Wales* (London, Her Majesty's Stationery Office, 1982), p. 2; *Population Trends*, 83 (1996), p. 55; http://www.statistics.gov.uk/statbase.

---

3   E.A. Wrigley and R.S. Schofield, *The Population History of England, 1541–1871: a Reconstruction* (London, Edward Arnold, 1981).

inhabitants in the country in 1750 than there were in 1300. Much of Parts I and II of this book will be devoted to trying to account for the apparent lack of progress that population growth made during this period.

Whatever the nature of the checks to growth before 1750, there can be no doubt that the mid-eighteenth century marked a turning point, when the population of England entered a period of spectacular and uninterrupted growth that lasted until the beginning of the twentieth century. Indeed, of the 48 million or so added to the English population between 1086 and 2000, more than half were added in the 150-year period between 1750 and 1900. This phenomenon will be familiar to many readers as the *demographic transition*, and Part III of this book is principally concerned with charting its course in England, and attempting to explain how and why it happened.

1.2 The components of population change

Populations can only change in size because of a limited range of events: births, deaths and migration. The difference between the number of births and the number of deaths over a period is known as *natural increase* (or *decrease* if deaths exceed births) and the difference between the number of immigrants and the number of emigrants is known as *net migration*. Understanding the reasons for changes in the size of human populations, therefore, involves an analysis of the processes by which births, deaths and migration events come about. The process that produces births is known as *fertility*, the corresponding process that results in deaths is called *mortality*. The three processes of fertility, mortality and migration are known as the *components of population change*.

Although there are many examples of populations that have grown or declined by large amounts through migration, over many generations natural increase almost invariably dominates. If migration is ignored completely, population growth depends just on fertility and mortality. A convenient way of showing the growth rates that arise from different combinations of fertility and mortality in the absence of migration is to draw a picture of *fertility–mortality space* (Figure 1.2). This takes the form of a chart with some measure of fertility on the vertical axis, and a measure of mortality on the horizontal axis. Every population may then be placed somewhere in the resulting two-dimensional area. The scales of the axes are chosen so that the normal range of human fertility and mortality experience is covered. The space is divided into two by a line representing zero population growth: above and to the right of this line populations will grow in size; below and to the left they will decline. The further a population is located from the zero growth line, the more rapid the growth or decline.

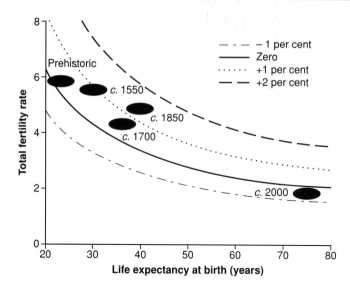

Figure 1.2 Fertility–mortality space, showing the position of the population of England at selected dates
Notes: The curved solid line is the 'zero growth line' that divides the zone of population growth (above and to the right) from the zone of population decline (below and to the left). Lines joining combinations of fertility and mortality that lead to population growth at rates of 1.0 and 2.0 per cent per year, and to decline at a rate of 1.0 per cent per year, are also shown.
Sources: The structure of the diagram is based on that in M. Livi-Bacci, *A Concise History of World Population* (Oxford, Blackwell, 1992), pp. 21–3, 151. Apart from the prehistoric period, the position of English population at various dates is taken from Figure 1.3.

In order to place real populations in this fertility–mortality space, measures of fertility and mortality need to be chosen. Annual growth rates implied by different combinations of fertility and mortality can then be worked out and lines drawn that join combinations of fertility and mortality leading to equal rates of growth. Figure 1.2 uses the *total fertility rate* (TFR) and the *life expectancy at birth*.[4] With a life expectancy at birth of 25 years, for example, a TFR of about five births per woman is required in order to achieve zero population growth, or, in other words, to ensure that each generation just replaces itself. As mortality falls, and life expectancy rises, the TFR required to replace the population falls towards 2.0 (an average of two children per woman).

---

[4]   In this we follow M. Livi-Bacci, *A Concise History of World Population* (Oxford, Blackwell, 1992), pp. 21–3 and 151. The total fertility rate is defined and discussed further in Box 3.1 and Box 8.1. It is an estimate of the average completed family size (or the average number of children born to each woman). The life expectancy, or expectation of life, is defined and discussed further in Box 7.1.

Figure 1.2 also shows the population of England at different periods placed in this calibrated fertility–mortality space. The prehistoric population, in so far as anything is known about its demography, appears to have had a life expectancy at birth of 25 years or less. Assuming that it managed at least to maintain its numbers, it must have occupied a zone at the top left-hand corner. The population of England at the beginning of the twenty-first century is close to the zero growth line in the 'south-east' corner of the chart, with a TFR of 1.8 and a life expectancy at birth of between 75 and 80 years. The population history of England, therefore, can be seen as a story about how English society moved from the 'north-west' to the 'south-east' corner of Figure 1.2.

Since, overall, the English population has grown substantially since 1086, its route through fertility–mortality space must have taken it, on balance, above and to the right of the zero growth line. However, the power of population growth is such that it cannot have spent a large proportion of the intervening period very far from that line. A population that grows at 2 per cent per year will double in size every 35 years. Continuous growth at 2 per cent per year will, therefore, cause a population to multiply by 32 times in 175 years.[5] In other words, the entire increase in the number of people living in England between 1086 and 2000 could have been accomplished by 175 years of growth at 2 per cent per year (a rate, incidentally, that is rather less than that of many African and Asian countries during the second half of the twentieth century).

Figure 1.3 attempts to plot the route taken by the population of England between 1086 and 2000. As Chapters 3 and 5 will explain, knowledge of fertility and mortality prior to the mid-sixteenth century is at least as sketchy as our knowledge of the population size. For the period before the mid-sixteenth century, therefore, the line drawn in Figure 1.3 assumes an average family size of six children per woman. The rate of population growth is then determined by the level of mortality, the position of the population moving back and forth along a line parallel to the horizontal axis. The twelfth and thirteenth centuries were characterized by steady, if unspectacular, growth and the demographic disasters of the fourteenth century are marked by a series of excursions into the zone of population decline. By the early sixteenth century, the population of England had probably made some progress, though not a great deal, away from the north-western corner of the fertility–mortality space.

For the period from 1541 until the nineteenth century, however, the work of the Cambridge Group for the History of Population and Social Structure has produced reliable estimates of both the TFR and the

---

[5] It is, of course, this 'power of population' to grow that was recognized by T.R. Malthus. See, for example, T.R. Malthus, *An Essay on the Principle of Population and a Summary View of the Principle of Population*, ed. A. Flew (Harmondsworth, Penguin, 1970), pp. 71–2.

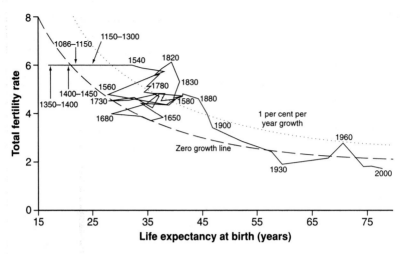

Figure 1.3 Route taken by the population of England through fertility–mortality space, 1086–2000
Sources: The structure of the diagram is based on that in M. Livi-Bacci, *A Concise History of World Population* (Oxford, Blackwell, 1992), pp. 21–3, 151. Data from E.A. Wrigley and R.S. Schofield, *The Population History of England 1541–1871: a Reconstruction* (London, Arnold, 1981), pp. 528–9; R.I. Woods and P.R.A. Hinde, 'Mortality in Victorian England: Models and Patterns', *Journal of Interdisciplinary History* XVIII (1987), p. 33; Office of Population Censuses and Surveys, *Birth Statistics, 1837–1983* (series FM1, no. 13) (London, Her Majesty's Stationery Office, 1987), pp. 26–8; http://www.statistics.gov.uk/statbase.

expectation of life at birth.[6] These may be continued from the mid-nineteenth century up to 2000 using statistics derived from the civil registers of births and deaths (see Appendix III). The delineation of the route taken by the population through fertility–mortality space through the second half of the period is, therefore, much more accurate. Between 1540 and 1750 the population moved rather erratically within an area just above the zero growth line. After 1750, however, it made a pronounced detour into the zone of population growth, though the annual growth rate only exceeded 1.5 per cent for a short period between 1800 and 1830 (and even then not by much). After 1830, the population of England gradually returned to the zero growth line, reaching it early in the twentieth century and remaining close to it since then.

1.3 Explaining population change

Recent developments in English population history or historical demography have, indeed, been spectacular, and are acknowledged as such across the

---

[6]   Wrigley and Schofield, *Population History*, pp. 528–35.

academic community in both disciplines. Yet certain characteristics of what has so far been done are worth highlighting before beginning the story of the evolution of England's population since 1086. First, work has concentrated much more on the 'how' of population change rather than on the 'why'. The chief reason for this is that most of it has been carried out within a demographic, social scientific tradition, in which the rigorous quantitative description of demographic processes has taken centre stage.[7] Because demographers account for population change in terms of fertility, mortality and migration, historical demographers tend to start by estimating or measuring these three components and then seek to understand population change as a consequence of their evolution and interaction over time. The history of fertility and mortality is then analysed in terms of changes in a small number of quantifiable 'determinants' (notably, in the case of fertility, the proportions of women married). Demographers tend to be reluctant to venture beyond the quantifiable, which restricts their ability to answer 'why' questions.

Second, being a social science, demography tends to seek general 'laws' or regularities governing human behaviour. To discover these 'laws' it applies a broadly scientific method that involves the formulation and testing of hypotheses. In this process, demographers make use of models (simplified representations of reality) that involve the deliberate abstraction of certain elements of human behaviour or biological processes from their broader context. The analytical part of Wrigley and Schofield's *Population History of England* (as opposed to the first section describing the exploitation and limitations of parish register data) is built around the Malthusian model of positive and preventive checks (see Chapter 6). Key themes of their book are the description of how the Malthusian preventive check operated in England between 1540 and 1750, and an analysis of how and why it began to break apart thereafter. In order to demonstrate the working of the model, Wrigley and Schofield are obliged to strip the demography of pre-industrial England down to its bare essentials. Regional and local variations, for example, are minimized or glossed over. In a later volume, the members of the Cambridge Group used much more detailed data on a small number of parishes to add demographic depth to the story told in *The Population History of England*.[8] Even in this later work, though, the local context of each of the parishes being studied was not given a great deal of attention.

---

[7] Important among the proponents of this approach have been the members and associates of the Cambridge Group for the History of Population and Social Structure. Their three most important contributions are P. Laslett and R. Wall (eds), *Household and Family in Past Time* (Cambridge, Cambridge University Press, 1972); Wrigley and Schofield, *Population History*; and E.A. Wrigley, R.S. Davies, J.E. Oeppen and R.S. Schofield, *English Population History from Family Reconstitution, 1580–1837* (Cambridge, Cambridge University Press, 1997). Others, notably Robert Woods and his colleagues at the University of Liverpool, work within a similar tradition; see R. Woods, *The Demography of Victorian England and Wales* (Cambridge, Cambridge University Press, 2000).

[8] Wrigley *et al.*, *English Population History from Family Reconstitution*.

History, on the other hand, emphases the unique or particular. It primarily uses a narrative method to construct 'true stories' about people's actions in the past, stories that acknowledge the contingent nature of these actions – in other words that what a person does will depend on the particular situation facing him or her at a given moment in time.[9]

The contrast between the two approaches is clearly illustrated by the development of research on the decline of fertility in the nineteenth and early twentieth centuries (see Chapter 13). For several decades after the elaboration of the theory of the demographic transition in the 1940s, research on this issue was carried out by social scientists who subscribed, for the most part, to the view that the decline in fertility was the result of a falling demand for children caused, in turn, by economic development. This explanation was believed to apply to all societies. When the validity of this 'demand for children' account was called into question in the 1980s, on the basis, substantially, of evidence from historical Europe, and specifically from early modern England (see Chapter 9), the demographers' reaction was to discard it and to replace it by another universal explanation, this time based around a rather ill-defined notion of 'culture'.[10] What is important here is that demographers privileged the universality of the explanation over its content. When the historians entered the fray in the early 1990s, their main objection was not that demographers were wrong about the relative importance of 'economics' and 'culture', but that they were wrong to think that any universal explanation could be found. The historians viewed their main task as being to show that different accounts of the decline of fertility were possible in different contexts.[11]

Since this book draws heavily on recent research by historical demographers, it reflects the strengths and limitations of that body of work. Consequently, there is a lot in the following chapters about the effect of fertility, mortality and migration on population growth, and rather less on the reasons for changes in the components of fertility. There is also much less than there ought to be on regional and local variations, and this omission is not entirely because of space constraints. Despite these limitations, it is hoped that the book describes the demographic experience of England as a whole in a coherent and integrated way, and that it accurately summarizes what is known and identifies what is still to be discovered about the country's population history.

---

[9] J.H. Arnold, *History: a Very Short Introduction* (Oxford, Oxford University Press, 2000), p. 13.

[10] For a good summary of this evidence, see J. Cleland and C. Wilson, 'Demand Theories of the Fertility Transition: an Iconoclastic View', *Population Studies* XLI (1987), pp. 5–30.

[11] The key contribution here is J.R. Gillis, L.A. Tilly and D. Levine (eds), *The European Experience of Declining Fertility, 1850–1970: the Quiet Revolution* (Cambridge, Mass., Blackwell, 1992). However, see also D. Levine, *Reproducing Families: the Political Economy of English Population History* (Cambridge, Cambridge University Press, 1987).

PART

I

THE MEDIEVAL PERIOD

|2|

Domesday England

2.1 Introduction

The population history of England began when the first humans set foot on the soil that was to become English. However, it is hard to write meaningful history without source materials, and prior to the compilation of Domesday Book in 1086, there really were no systematic data on which to base any kind of quantitative analysis of the English population. For this reason alone, the Domesday survey would form a logical starting point for the population historian. However, the period just after the Norman Conquest of 1066 is a good place to start for another reason, which is that since that time England has never been successfully invaded by a hostile power, so that its demographic development has been free of the inevitable dislocation caused by such events. There is a sense, therefore, in which 1066 marked the end of a series of settlements and withdrawals (including those of the Romans, the Saxons and various Scandinavian peoples) and the start of a long period of stability.

The purpose of this chapter is to describe the population in England as it is revealed to us by the Domesday inquest. Nevertheless, England in 1086 was, as historians often remind us, an 'old country', and so Section 2.2 will briefly describe the evolution of the population prior to that date. Section 2.3 discusses how the information in Domesday Book can be used to estimate the population of the country in 1086, stressing the major alternative interpretations of the data that lead to a range of plausible estimates. Sections 2.4 and 2.5 look, respectively, at the geographical distribution and the social structure of the Domesday population.

2.2 England's population before the Norman Conquest

The period before 1086 can be simply divided into the pre-Roman era, the Roman era, and the era of the Anglo-Saxon and Scandinavian invasions. Hard facts about England's population at any of these distant times are virtually absent. Various ingenious arguments and approaches, however, have been used to make the most of the scanty evidence available.

The most fundamental statistic about the population is how many people there were. Fundamental though this is, it is an aspect about which solid evidence is lacking for this period. It seems unlikely, however, that the population of England during any part of the pre-Roman era exceeded one million.[1] Archaeological evidence, based on the analysis of bones from burial sites, reveals a very high proportion of babies and children among the dead, suggesting that at least one out of every five babies born failed to survive more than a year. Studies of other populations with more complete data on mortality have shown that such a high death rate among infants normally indicates an expectation of life at birth of 30 to 35 years.[2] Since the archaeological evidence probably underestimates the proportion of babies who died in infancy, the true expectation of life is likely to have been lower than this. If we assume that, despite such high mortality, the number of births was, under normal circumstances, close to the number of deaths, then it can also be shown (see Box 2.1) that the average woman must have given birth to at least five children.

Box 2.1 Fertility, mortality and population growth

In the absence of migration, population growth depends only on fertility and mortality. It turns out that the critical determinant of the rate of growth is the average number of daughters a woman has who survive to have children themselves. If the average woman has more than one daughter who herself bears children, each generation will be larger in size than its progenitor and the population will grow. Viewed in this way, the rate of population growth depends on three factors:

1. the number of children the average woman has
2. the proportion of these children that are girls (the *sex ratio of births*), and
3. the mortality of the female population.

Basing the analysis on daughters alone is attractive because the child-bearing age range of women is narrower than that of men, and the average age at which women bear children varies rather little

---

[1] For a recent review of the evidence, see D. Coleman and J. Salt, *The British Population: Patterns, Trends and Processes* (Oxford, Oxford University Press, 1992), p. 5.

[2] For example, according to A.J. Coale and P. Demeny, *Regional Model Life Tables and Stable Populations* (2nd edn) (New York, Academic Press, 1983), p. 45, if the proportions of male and female babies dying before their first birthday were 0.249 and 0.214 respectively, the expectation of life at birth would be 35 years for females and 32.5 years for males.

from population to population, being typically between 26 and 30 years of age. The number of years between successive generations is therefore normally about 28. This means that the chance that a daughter will survive to have children herself can be estimated reliably by the probability that a female will survive to age 28 years. It is also true that the potential fertility of women is much less than that of men, and so the number of women tends to be the limiting factor.

In most human populations, there are about 100 girls born for every 105 boys, so the proportion of babies born that are girls is about 100/205 = 0.488. Assuming this value for the sex ratio of births, the table below gives the number of children (including boys) the average woman must have in order to produce different rates of population growth at different levels of mortality. For example, if only half of all daughters born survive to age 28, an average of more than five children per woman is required to sustain even a modest rate of growth of 1 per cent per year.

Rate of growth (per cent per year)	Probability of a woman surviving to age 28 years				
	0.4	0.5	0.7	0.9	0.98
0	5.1	4.1	2.9	2.3	2.1
1	6.8	5.4	3.9	3.0	2.8
2	9.0	7.2	5.1	4.0	3.7
3	11.8	9.5	6.8	5.3	4.8

The expectation of life at birth in England before, or at the time of, the Domesday inquest is unlikely to have been more than 30 to 35 years and may have been considerably less. Studies of more recent populations suggest that such an expectation of life at birth implies that no more than 45–50 per cent of girls born will survive to age 28 years. Under such fierce mortality conditions, the table above reveals that an average family size of at least five children would have been required in order to maintain population growth rates above zero.

The arrival of the Romans in AD 43 is thought to have led to an increase in the rate of population growth. No written records of population size survive from the Roman occupation, but if assumptions are made about the number of houses per settlement and the average number of persons per house, then a multiplier can be derived to convert the number of settlements into an estimated population total. Using this method, a total population of between four and six million persons for Roman Britain at the peak of the occupation has been arrived at, the vast majority of whom must have lived in England.[3] There is also indirect evidence, based on abandoned land and records indicating a labour shortage, which suggests that there might have been a gradual decline in the population after AD 300. By the time the Romans departed in the fifth century, the population was probably reduced to fewer than one or two million.

There had been Saxon mercenaries in eastern England for a substantial part of the Roman occupation. During the centuries following the Romans' departure, a gradual flow of migrants from what are now Germany and Denmark arrived in lowland areas. These were economic migrants, encouraged to leave their native lands by a combination of population pressure, climatic change and economic depression caused by a decline in trade with Rome. Over a period of several centuries they settled in much of lowland England. The distinctive Anglo-Saxon place-name endings, such as -ing, -ton and -ham, reveal that by the tenth century they had populated most of the region south of a line joining the Humber and Mersey estuaries.[4]

Our knowledge of Anglo-Saxon settlement patterns is in stark contrast to our ignorance about population numbers and trends during this period. The limited evidence that we do have mainly relates to trends. For example, it is known that the sixth century saw major epidemics, including the so-called 'plague of Justinian', which may have been bubonic plague. It is likely that these epidemics meant that the overall population of the country did not rise. The seventh century saw more plague epidemics, though these did not prevent a general recovery in the population.[5] It is likely that the population rose during the eighth century, as there is evidence of increasing pressure on land resources towards 800. During the ninth and tenth centuries there are reports of occasional famines and plagues, but it seems that in normal years slow growth took place. What is certainly not clear is the extent to which changes in the population size were the result of migration or of the changing balance between births and deaths. The available documentary evidence naturally highlights short-term increases in the death rate, whether caused by epidemics, famine or 'the harrying of the heathen', but it is virtually impossible to come to any overall judgement about the importance of such 'mortality crises' in keeping population growth rates low.[6]

[3]   P. Salway, *Roman Britain* (Oxford, Oxford University Press, 1981), pp. 542–4.
[4]   D. Hill, *An Atlas of Anglo-Saxon England* (Oxford, Blackwell, 1981), p. 20.
[5]   See J.R. Maddicott, 'Plague in Seventh-Century England', *Past and Present* CLVI (1997), pp. 7–54. The apparently rapid recovery from the epidemics of the seventh century contrasts with the situation in the fourteenth and fifteenth centuries described in Chapters 4 and 5 below.
[6]   G.N. Garmonsway (ed.), *The Anglo-Saxon Chronicle* (London, Dent, 1972) is a valuable source of information about the frequency of epidemics and famines. The quotation comes from the entry for the year 793 on pp. 54–6.

The Anglo-Saxon period did leave an enduring legacy for the English landscape, however, which it is worth pausing to describe. The Saxons tended to live in villages, and the location and spacing of these villages reflected the need for each settlement to have access to water, pasture, arable land and forest for fuel and rough grazing. In major river valleys, these requirements led to villages being sited on river terraces (close to the river but above flood-prone areas), and to each village being associated with a hinterland stretching back from the river up the valley side to the watershed. An excellent example of this is seen in the Wylye valley in Wiltshire between Salisbury and Warminster. The parishes of villages like Steeple Langford, Wylye and Fisherton Delamere are arranged in two sets of approximately rectangular areas on either side of the river, with the river itself forming one of the 'short' sides of each rectangle, reflecting the boundaries of Anglo-Saxon hinterlands.

The last major immigration to and settlement of England prior to the Norman Conquest was the arrival of various Scandinavian peoples in the north and east, principally Danes in the east during the 870s and Norwegians in Lancashire and Cumberland during the first half of the tenth century.[7] The Scandinavian settlement extended southwards as far as a line drawn roughly from the Thames estuary to the Dee estuary (the border between England and North Wales), overlapping with the area of Anglo-Saxon settlement in East Anglia, Lincolnshire and Yorkshire. Like Anglo-Saxon settlements, places of Scandinavian origin have distinctive place-name endings, such as -by and -thorpe.

2.3 Estimating the population of Domesday England

The survey we know as the Domesday inquest, the results of which were written in Domesday Book, took place in 1086. Its value to historians of population is that it allows the estimation, within a certain range, of the population of almost the whole of England, together with its geographical distribution and social structure. However, as with many of the sources used by population historians, the primary purpose of the Domesday survey was not to collect information about numbers of people. Even today scholars are not sure exactly why it was compiled, but it seems that it may have had several aims, including providing a record of tax payments, quantifying the resources of the English feudal order, and summarizing and legalizing the great changes in landownership that had taken place since 1066.[8] Population historians, therefore, recognize that, in using the data to esti-

---

[7] H.R. Loyn, *The Vikings in Britain* (London, Batsford, 1977), p. 119.
[8] M. Wood, *Domesday: a Search for the Roots of England* (London, Guild Publishing, 1986), pp. 22–4.

mate population totals, they are putting the survey to a use for which it was not designed. Despite this, Domesday Book's early date and the fact that data on population are relatively straightforward to extract have meant that it has been widely used to provide a starting point for the population history of England in the Middle Ages. This section describes how population estimates may be obtained from the data in Domesday Book, and explains the range of plausible figures that might result. (Further details about the Domesday data themselves are provided in Appendix I.)

The people described in Domesday Book fall into a number of distinct categories that need to be treated separately in the analysis. First, there are those called *tenants-in-chief* or *sub-tenants* (popularly known as 'lords of the manor'). Domesday Book records the name of the tenant of each place that is mentioned but, because a tenant might hold land in several different places, it is important to guard against the possibility of multiple counting. This is done by simply enumerating separately the different tenants-in-chief and sub-tenants who are mentioned in the survey (1100 and 6000 respectively).[9] Second, there are the 'peasants', who were mainly farmers and farm workers (though there were some other rural workers). For this group, the number of heads of household in each place is recorded, totalling 240,135. The third group consists of 28,144 *servi*, or 'slaves'; these were mainly to be found in south-west England and were 'chattels of their lords'.[10] It is not clear whether 'slaves' were recorded as heads of household or as individuals.

The first stage in the estimation is therefore to work out the population represented by those actually recorded. There are two elements of uncertainty: the average number of persons per household, and whether 'slaves' are to be counted as heads of household or as individuals. Assuming an average household size of 4.5, and that 'slaves' are heads of household, produces the following estimate.

Tenants-in-chief	1,100 x 4.5	=	4,950
Sub-tenants	6,000 x 4.5	=	27,000
'Peasants'	240,135 x 4.5	=	1,080,608
'Slaves'	28,144 x 4.5	=	126,648
Total			1,239,206

To this figure must be added an allowance for persons not recorded in Domesday Book. These include the populations of towns (including London, which is not mentioned in the survey at all), and the populations of the northern counties of Cumberland, Westmorland, Northumberland and Durham, and part of Lancashire, which were omitted. Even in those areas that were surveyed, it is likely that not everyone was counted. H.C. Darby

---

[9]   H.C. Darby, *Domesday England* (Cambridge, Cambridge University Press, 1977), p. 89.
[10]   Ibid., p. 26.

suggested adding 120,000 to represent the populations of towns and 32,200 for the omitted northern areas, and allowing 5 per cent for omissions.[11] However, Michael Wood points out that Domesday Book's own population figures for the urban places it does mention 'suggest a "real" total of about 111,500', and to this should be added at least 25,000 for London.[12] He concludes that 175,000 is a reasonable estimate for the urban population.[13] Darby's allowance of 5 per cent for omissions may also be optimistic, but we have no evidence with which to challenge it. Adding on these persons produces a final estimate of just over 1.5 million, as shown below.[14]

Total based on recorded persons	1,239,206
Add 5 per cent for omissions	60,363
Addition for towns	175,000
Addition for northern counties	32,200
Final total	1,506,769

Recall that this figure assumes that 'slaves' were counted as heads of households. If this were not the case, and 'slaves' were recorded as individuals, then it should be reduced by 28,144 x 1.05 x 3.5 = 103,429, giving a slightly lower total of 1,403,340. The uncertainty about whether 'slaves' were heads of households or individuals produces a difference of about 100,000 in the estimated population.

Potentially more serious as a source of uncertainty is the assumption about average household size. Historians have used various estimates, ranging from a low of 3.5 to a high of 5.0. The effect of different assumptions here is quite large (Table 2.1). A value of 3.5 produces a total estimated population more than 400,000 (or 25 per cent) less than a value of 5.0. Since this would seem to be the most important source of uncertainty about the population of Domesday England, it is worth discussing the issue more fully. We might ask two questions. First, is there any independent evidence about average household size in medieval England? Second, based on what we know about fertility, mortality and social life, can we identify the most plausible values?

The answer to the first question is, in short, not very much. However, such evidence as there is (for example, from twelfth-century Lincolnshire) suggests a value between 4.5 and 5.0.[15] This range is also consistent with the average household size in England from the sixteenth to the nineteenth centuries, a topic that will be considered in Chapter 8. This suggests that a

---

[11] Darby, *Domesday England*, p. 89.
[12] Wood, *Domesday*, p. 26.
[13] Ibid., p. 28.
[14] The figures presented here assume no omissions among the tenants-in-chief and sub-tenants. In view of the purposes of the Domesday survey, it seems likely that their numbers were accurately recorded.
[15] Wood, *Domesday*, p. 26.

Table 2.1 Estimates of the population of Domesday England

	Household size multiplier			
	3.5	4.0	4.5	5.0
Recorded 'peasantry'	840,473	960,540	1,080,608	1,200,675
Tenants-in-chief	3,850	4,400	4,950	5,500
Sub-tenants	21,000	24,000	27,000	30,000
Population of towns	175,000	175,000	175,000	175,000
Addition for northern counties	32,200	32,200	32,200	32,200
'Slaves'	98,504	112,576	126,648	140,720
Addition of 5 per cent for omissions	46,949	53,656	60,363	67,070
Total	1,217,976	1,362,372	1,506,769	1,651,165
Subtraction if 'slaves' are counted as individuals	73,878	88,654	103,429	118,205
Total counting 'slaves' as individuals	1,144,098	1,273,718	1,403,340	1,532,960

Notes: The addition for omissions is calculated as 5 per cent of the total of the 'peasantry' and the 'slaves'. The subtraction if 'slaves' are counted as individuals is calculated as 28,144 x $(h-1)$ x 1.05, where h is the average household size, and the factor of 1.05 is used to account for the 5 per cent of omissions.

Sources: The structure of the table is based on that in H.C. Darby, *Domesday England* (Cambridge, Cambridge University Press, 1977), p. 89, although I have assumed a larger urban population than Darby did.

value closer to 5.0 than to 3.5 is the most plausible. In answer to the second question, if we suppose that the population of eleventh-century England was growing at a rate of 0.5 per cent per year (see Chapter 3 for further discussion of this) and that fewer than half of all girls born survived to reproductive age, this implies that the average woman had around five children (Box 2.1), with just under 2.5 surviving to adulthood. Though there are many imponderables to consider, such as the age at leaving home and the extent to which the elderly lived alone or with their offspring, this population growth rate seems consistent with an average household size of around 4.5–5.0. Using the value 4.5 produces, as shown earlier, a total population of 1.4–1.5 million; a value of 5.0 gives about 1.53–1.65 million inhabitants (Table 2.1).

The other aspect of uncertainty it is worth commenting on is Darby's allowance of 5 per cent for omissions. This may be too low. Allowing 10 per cent for omissions would increase the estimate of the total population by about 60,000, and it is possible that 10 per cent is on the low side.

In conclusion, it seems that the number of people living in England in 1086 is unlikely to have been less than 1.4 million. On the other hand, assuming a generous 20 per cent for omissions and an average household size of 5.0 persons (and counting 'slaves' as heads of households) produces an estimate of almost 1.9 million.[16] A reasonable 'mid-range' estimate of the population might be, say, 1.6–1.7 million.

2.4 Geographical distribution of the population in 1086

The inhabitants of England in 1086 were not evenly distributed across the country. Though the average population density was about six persons per square mile, by far the heaviest concentrations of people were to be found in East Anglia – an area where both Saxons and Scandinavians had settled. Most of Norfolk and Suffolk had more than ten persons per square mile, with the highest densities (over 20) being found in east Norfolk. Other densely settled areas included the Sussex coast, parts of north Lincolnshire, east Kent, the Somerset plain between Bridgwater and Taunton, and the Oxford region. By contrast, the whole of Lancashire, and most of Cheshire, Derbyshire and Yorkshire had population densities of fewer than three persons per square mile. These were areas that had been 'laid waste' by William the Conqueror during the period since 1066. In general, the population density decreased from south-east to north-west.[17]

Land that was unsuitable for agriculture was sparsely settled. Even in the south and east of England, areas such as the Weald of Sussex and Kent, with its heavy soils, the infertile sandy heaths along the Surrey–Hampshire border, the marshy fens around the Wash, and Dartmoor in Devon had fewer than 2.5 persons per square mile. The population geography of Domesday England reminds us that in medieval times people were heavily dependent upon the land on which they lived for subsistence. Local variations in geology and climate were reflected in population density, and their importance will re-emerge in Chapter 3 in the context of demographic change between 1086 and 1348.

2.5 Social structure of the Domesday population

The system of government that William the Conqueror introduced in England was strongly hierarchical. Legally, all land belonged ultimately to the king.

---

[16]   M.M. Postan has argued that there might have been a large number of landless people or 'tenants' tenants' who went unrecorded in the Domesday survey. If this is true, then it could be that the number of households should be inflated by more than 20 per cent, and that the total population of Domesday England was as high as 2.2 or 2.3 million. See M.M. Postan, *The Medieval Economy and Society: an Economic History of Britain in the Middle Ages* (Harmondsworth, Pelican, 1975), p. 31.

[17]   See the excellent map in H.C. Darby, 'Domesday England', in H.C. Darby (ed.), *A New Historical Geography of England* (Cambridge, Cambridge University Press, 1973), p. 46.

The king leased land to tenants-in-chief in return for feudal services, principally the tenants agreeing to provide a number of soldiers to fight on the king's behalf in the event of war. Tenants-in-chief could, and did, sub-let their lands to sub-tenants or 'under-tenants'. The tenants-in-chief and the sub-tenants together formed an aristocracy, or the class of 'lords of the manor'.

These 'lords of the manor' managed their lands either by farming them directly, or by letting them out to the 'peasantry'. The directly farmed lands were known as *demesne*. The people who farmed the rest fell into several groups, distinguished by the nature of their agreement with the lord (Table 2.2). The so-called 'free peasantry' (referred to in Domesday Book as *freemen* and *sokemen*), comprising about 15 per cent of the total, occupied land by virtue of a more or less commercial arrangement, normally paying rents to the lord. The majority of 'peasants' in eleventh-century England, however, were not free. Around 45 per cent were described in Domesday Book as *villeins*. These occupied land in return for various payments in kind or labour services owed to the lord (typically obligations to provide so many days' labour on the demesne per year). Finally, there was a large class of persons, comprising almost 40 per cent of the 'peasantry', who held little or no land, and who were described in Domesday Book as *bordars* or *cottars*.

The national social structure, however, hides important regional variations. For example, the 'free peasantry' were heavily concentrated in Lincolnshire, Norfolk and Suffolk. More than four-fifths of the total number of freemen and sokemen mentioned in Domesday Book came from these

Table 2.2 Social structure of the recorded Domesday population

Class	Description in Domesday Book	Number recorded (thousands)	Percentage of total
'Lords'	Tenants-in-chief	1.1	0.4
	Sub-tenants	6.0	2.2
'Free peasantry'	Freemen	13.6	4.9
	Sokemen	23.3	8.5
'Unfree peasantry'	Villeins	109.0	39.6
	Bordars	81.6	29.6
	Cottars	5.2	1.9
	Coscets	1.7	0.6
'Slaves'		28.1	10.2
Others	Priests	1.0	0.4
	Miscellaneous	4.8	1.7
Total		275.4	100.0

Notes: The percentages are calculated treating 'slaves' in the same way as other members of the recorded population. This effectively means assuming that 'slaves' are recorded as heads of household. The 'miscellaneous' category included *coliberts* (remnants of an old servile class in the south), *oxmen*, *swineherds*, etc.

Source: Based on H.C. Darby, *Domesday England* (Cambridge, Cambridge University Press, 1977), p. 63.

three counties, where they accounted for one-third to one-half of the population.[18] These areas coincided with those areas settled by Danes during the ninth and tenth centuries, and operating under so-called 'Danelaw'.[19] The 'free peasantry' were distinguished from villeins by being able to buy and sell land. Because they were not constrained by onerous labour services, they were also able to diversify their activities into the non-agricultural sector. This may have enabled them better to withstand climatic fluctuations, and to cope with population pressure.

The largest group among the peasantry, the villeins, were to be found throughout England, but their relative importance varied regionally. In East Anglia they constituted under 20 per cent of the recorded population, whereas throughout most of the Midlands, and a belt stretching from there through Middlesex and Surrey to Kent they formed more than half of those mentioned in the Domesday survey.[20] Unlike the 'free peasantry', villeins were very much subject to the conditions of service imposed by their lords. Moreover, lords could and did change these conditions unilaterally.

Like the 'free peasantry', the 'slave' population was also geographically concentrated, but in their case the greatest numbers were to be found in the south-west, especially in Gloucestershire and Devon.[21] Appreciable numbers of 'slaves', however, were recorded throughout the south of England. North of a line stretching roughly from the Wash to the Mersey, 'slaves' were very rare.

18 Wood, *Domesday*, p. 26; Darby, 'Domesday England', p. 67.
19 Wood, *Domesday*, p. 27.
20 Darby, 'Domesday England', p. 68.
21 Wood, *Domesday*, p. 27.

|3|

Population change between 1086 and the Black Death

3.1 Introduction

For almost three centuries after the compilation of Domesday Book, there is no convenient source of data about the number of people living in England. Only in 1377, with the first of a series of three Poll Taxes, does the historian find a source that can be made to reveal by fairly simple calculations both the number of persons alive and their geographical distribution over the majority of the country.[1] In order to trace the evolution of population numbers during the intervening three centuries, historians have therefore been obliged to work both forwards from the time of the Domesday survey and backwards from 1377. There are a number of landmarks on the way to guide the estimation process, but there is a substantial amount of room for disagreement, and rather little hard evidence to use to resolve the ensuing debates.

The most important of these landmarks is the Black Death of 1348–50, the single most catastrophic event ever to have happened to the population of England. Because of the scale of the calamity, it and its aftermath deserve a chapter to themselves and will, accordingly, be made the subject of Chapter 4. The present chapter considers the period from 1086–1348, although, for the reason just given, an analysis of the data in the Poll Tax returns of 1377 is necessary to shed light on this period.

Section 3.2 describes the procedure of working 'in from both ends' in order to identify a range of reasonable estimates of England's population between 1086 and 1348. Section 3.3 relates these estimates to the long-running debate about the number of people in medieval England. In

---

[1] There are many other documentary sources relating to the intervening period that can be made to provide some information about population totals, but they are generally much more difficult to work with. Normally they either only cover a part of the country, or are local-level sources that are very labour-intensive to use to produce national-level population estimates.

Section 3.4, it is argued that this debate involves the fundamental question of whether the size of the population was limited by resource constraints (in other words, whether the 'carrying capacity' was reached) or whether 'exogenous' factors such as epidemic disease were mainly responsible. This question has profound implications for what the lives of the majority of the population were like. Section 3.5 is devoted to a particular demographic episode that led to increased mortality: the agrarian crisis of 1315–22. Throughout most of the chapter, emphasis is placed on mortality as the limiting factor for population growth, reflecting the view of most historians that the prevailing technological levels meant that mortality was bound to have a dominant influence. However, Section 3.6 asks whether checks to population growth due to reduced fertility might also have been operating. Section 3.7 summarizes the argument of the chapter and essays a conclusion.

3.2 Population numbers

In Chapter 2 it was shown that different assumptions could be made to produce a range of estimates for the population of England in 1086 from as low as 1.4 million to upwards of 1.9 million, with perhaps 1.6 or 1.7 million as the most likely figure. These estimates form the starting point for the analysis described in this section. The next point in time at which a reasonably reliable national-level estimate of the total population can be obtained is 1377. In that year, a Poll Tax was collected by Edward III in order to fund wars with France. Because the Poll Tax was levied at a flat rate of one groat per person aged 14 or over, the number of persons contributing can readily be calculated from records of the amount of money collected. Three groups of people, however, did not pay the Poll Tax. The least important was a small group of persons who were exempt on account of their occupation – for example, 'mendicant friars'. Much more significant were the other two groups: those aged under 14 years, and those who were eligible but who managed to evade payment. Only after making assumptions about the size of these three groups can the population of England in 1377 be estimated. Appendix I (especially Table AI.2) provides details of a range of estimates that might plausibly be produced under different assumptions. The lowest estimate, based on a relatively small proportion of children and a low evasion rate, is 2.2 million, and the highest is about 3.1 million.

In order to delimit possible population scenarios between 1086 and 1348 from these 'end-point' estimates, it would be helpful to establish the population growth rate in an 'average' year. In the very long run, the natural tendency for populations is to grow slowly. Evidence of land reclamation and the decline in the average size of peasant holdings suggests that during the two centuries after 1086, growth was somewhat faster than the very long-run average.[2] Let us, then, make a generous assumption of 0.5 per cent per year over the whole period.[3] The next step is to work out what the likely losses from plague were between 1348 and 1377. There is still a considerable amount of disagreement about the proportion of the population that died in the first great plague epidemic of 1348–50. In Chapter 4, it is shown that a figure of one-third of the population of England in 1348 perishing in the 1348–50 epidemic falls towards the low end of the range of estimates, and a figure of 45 per cent may be considered perhaps on the high side. There were further serious epidemics in 1361 and 1369. It is reckoned that the excess mortality in 1361–62 and 1369 may have been, perhaps, 15 per cent and 10 per cent respectively of those alive at the start of each of those epidemics. It is straightforward to show that these estimates imply a mortality from plague of around 50 per cent of the 1348 population.[4]

In normal years between 1348 and 1377, however, there would have been population growth at around 0.5 per cent per year. This annual growth rate means that each successive generation would be about 15 per cent larger than its predecessor.[5] Since each generation is about 28 years apart (see Box 2.1), almost exactly one generation elapsed between 1348 and 1377. Therefore, in the absence of the series of plague epidemics, the population of 1377 would have been about 15 per cent larger than that of 1348. Combining the losses from plague epidemics with the natural growth, therefore, would suggest that the population of England in 1377 was 35–45 per cent less than it was in 1348 or, equivalently, that the population in England in 1348 was between 55 and 80 per cent greater than the population in 1377.[6] The lowest plausible estimate of the population in 1377 is 2.2 million. By combining this with a low estimate of plague mortality between 1348 and 1377, we obtain a lowest plausible population in 1348 of 1.55 x 2.2 million, which is 3.4 million.

[2]   M.M. Postan, *The Medieval Economy and Society: an Economic History of Britain in the Middle Ages* (Harmondsworth, Pelican, 1975), p. 35.
[3]   As D. Coleman and J. Salt, *The British Population: Patterns, Trends and Processes* (Oxford, Oxford University Press, 1992), p. 6, point out, it is likely that growth was slower than this during the first few decades after the Norman Conquest and rather more rapid between 1150 and 1250.
[4]   If one-third of the population in 1348 died in the 1348–50 epidemic, this leaves two-thirds left. If 15 per cent of the survivors died in the 1361–62 epidemic, this means that 85 per cent of the two-thirds survived this second epidemic, leaving 57 per cent. Finally, if the epidemic of 1369 killed 10 per cent of these survivors, this leaves (57 – 5.7) per cent, or 51 per cent, alive after this third epidemic. Repeating this exercise assuming that 45 per cent perished in 1348–50 produces a gross loss over the three epidemics of 58 per cent.
[5]   A constant annual growth rate of r per cent per year means that the population in t years' time, P_t, is related to the current population, P_0, by the formula $P_t = P_0 e^{rt}$ (see Box 6.1) where e is the root of natural logarithms, or 2.718. A growth rate of 0.5 per cent per year means that $r = 0.005$. For $t = 28$ years, therefore, $P_{28} = P_0 e^{(0.005 \times 28)} = 1.15 P_0$.
[6]   If we denote the population in 1348 by P_{1348} and that in 1377 by P_{1377}, then the 35 per cent decline means that $P_{1377} = 0.65 \times P_{1348}$. This implies that $P_{1348} = P_{1377}/0.65 = 1.54 \times P_{1377}$.

Turning now to a 'low' Domesday survey estimate of 1.4 million, and assuming a population growth rate of 0.5 per cent per year between 1086 and 1348, we obtain an estimate for 1348 of about 5.2 million. However, from this must be subtracted those lost during the period 1086–1348 to exceptional 'mortality crises' caused by epidemic diseases and famine. As described in Section 3.5, there was a serious agrarian crisis during the decade 1310–19, which may have accounted for 10 per cent of the population, and it is almost certain that there were other, less serious, crises during the twelfth and thirteenth centuries.[7] Let us suppose that because of these crises about 20 per cent should be subtracted from the estimated total for 1348; 20 per cent of 5.2 million is 1.04 million, leaving an estimated population in 1348 of around 4.2 million. This is rather higher than the earlier estimate obtained by working backwards from 1377. The two figures could be reconciled, however, in a number of ways. An average household size of 3.5–4.0 in 1086, giving a Domesday population of 1.15–1.25 million, would suffice, as would the assumption that the population in 1377 was 2.7 million. Given what we know of the Domesday population, the second of these possibilities is perhaps more likely. Therefore, a 'lowest plausible' estimate of the population of England on the eve of the Black Death is around 4.0 million (Figure 3.1).

Repeating the exercise using the highest plausible population from the 1377 Poll Tax (3.1 million – see Appendix I, Table AI.2) and a 45 per cent

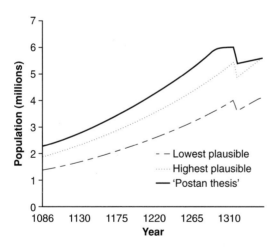

Figure 3.1 Range of estimates of the English population, 1086–1348
Notes: For explanation, see text.

---

[7] Using an abrupt rise in wheat prices to indicate a shortage of food, it seems likely that on the manors of the Bishops of Winchester in Hampshire, there were crises in 1202–03, 1247, 1257–58 and 1272. See J.Z. Titow, *English Rural Society 1200–1350* (London, George Allen and Unwin, 1969), p. 101.

mortality in 1348–50 produces an estimate of 5.6 million for 1348. Working forwards from a high figure of 1.9 million for 1086 produces an almost identical figure in 1348 (after subtracting 20 per cent).[8] These estimates must be regarded as being close to the 'highest plausible' ones (Figure 3.1). A final point to note about both the 'high' and 'low' estimates is that because the 'difficult decade' of 1310–19 carried off probably 10 per cent of the population, we can say even at this stage that the population total achieved by 1310 was, at a minimum, within 5 per cent of the 1348 figure. In other words, a population close to its pre-plague peak had been achieved by the first decade of the fourteenth century.

3.3 The Russell–Postan debate

In 1948, in his book *British Medieval Population*, J.C. Russell presented estimates of population change between 1086 and 1377 that were close to the 'lowest possible' scenario described in the previous section.[9] Taking the figure of 2.2 million for 1377, Russell assumed, in fact, that the population in 1377 was 40 per cent less than it had been in 1348, which gave a population in 1348 of 3.7 million.[10] When working forward from 1086, he achieved consistency with this figure by using a small household size multiplier of 3.5 at the time of Domesday Book, and making a rather smaller deduction than was made in the previous section for epidemic disease and famine during the twelfth and thirteenth centuries, and especially in the decade 1310–19.

Russell's interpretation of the evidence was challenged by M.M. Postan, whose interpretation was close to the 'highest plausible' scenario outlined above (see Appendix I, for further details). Indeed, Postan went further than this, for he argued that in 1086 there might have been a large number of landless people or 'tenants' tenants' who were unrecorded in the Domesday survey, and who might have inflated the number of households by as much as 50 per cent.[11] If this were true, then the Domesday population of England might have been as high as 2.2 or 2.3 million. Assuming a growth rate of 0.5 per cent per year between 1086 and 1348 would produce a population on the eve of the Black Death of 6.7 million (assuming, again, a deduction of 20 per cent for mortality 'crises'). This is much higher than the 'highest

[8]   It is perhaps worth pointing out that some independent support for this scenario comes from a figure of 2.9 million for 1164 quoted in Coleman and Salt, *British Population*, p. 6. A Domesday population of 1.9 million, which grew at 0.5 per cent per year would have increased to 2.8 million by 1164.

[9]   J.C. Russell, *British Medieval Population* (Albuquerque, University of New Mexico Press, 1948); see also J.C. Russell, 'The Preplague Population of England', *Journal of British Studies* V, Pt 2 (1966), pp. 1–21.

[10] Russell, 'Preplague population', pp. 16–21.

[11] Postan, *Medieval Economy*, p. 31.

plausible' estimate of 5.6 million, which can be obtained by working backwards from 1377. It is really the reconciliation of this inconsistency that lies at the heart of the so-called 'Postan thesis'. The key point is that the population of medieval England could not grow without limit. The level of agricultural technology, coupled with the finite land area, meant that there was some maximum that could not be exceeded. Although it is not possible to put a figure on this maximum, Postan's argument hinges on its being somewhere at or close to six million. If Postan is right about the Domesday population, and assuming a growth rate of 0.5 per cent per year, then a population of six million would have been achieved by the last two decades of the thirteenth century (Figure 3.1). This approach to the 'carrying capacity' should, of course, have been accompanied by evidence of land hunger and declining yields caused by overcropping and a reduction in soil fertility.

Using evidence on rents, land reclamation and agricultural yields drawn principally from the manors of the Bishops of Winchester, Postan and his colleague J.Z. Titow attempted to demonstrate that this was indeed the case.[12] Their argument was that the evidence about the state of the agrarian economy on the Winchester manors showed clearly that the English population reached some kind of subsistence-induced plateau at around six million inhabitants at the end of the thirteenth century, and began to decline during the first half of the fourteenth century, not only because of the very definite crisis of the second decade of the century, but because of increased mortality in general brought about by the difficulty of subsistence even in normal years. Titow also presents a more detailed argument that the size of agricultural holdings had fallen by the end of the thirteenth century to the extent that a large proportion of households did not have enough arable land on which to subsist, given prevailing yields.[13] Examining the same data, Martin Ecclestone has recently shown that even 'middling' peasants on the Winchester manors would have struggled to make ends meet in almost half of the years between 1277 and 1348.[14]

Yet serious questions may be raised about the evidence marshalled by Postan and Titow. The first objection is that although the manors of the Bishops of Winchester may indeed have been in distress, they were not representative of England as a whole. The Winchester estates were in southern and south-west England, but Barbara Harvey cites evidence from Yorkshire, the Midlands and Lincolnshire showing that rents and 'entry fines' in those parts of the country were not excessive.[15] Indeed, recent studies of other

[12] Postan, *Medieval Economy*, pp. 39–40; Titow, *English Rural Society*.

[13] Titow, *English Rural Society*, pp. 78–93.

[14] M. Ecclestone, 'Life on a Knife Edge?' *Local Population Studies Society Newsletter* XXVII (2000), pp. 10–12.

[15] B.F. Harvey, 'The Population Trend in England between 1300 and 1348', *Transactions of the Royal Historical Society* XVI (1966), pp. 25–6. 'Entry fines' were one-off payments made by the new tenant of a piece of land.

parts of early fourteenth-century England have painted a picture of prosperity rather than poverty. For example, Peter Franklin shows that, in the manor of Thornbury in Gloucestershire, 86 per cent of villein tenants in the early fourteenth century owned livestock, compared with fewer than half of those on the manors owned by the Bishops of Winchester.[16] Harvey also casts doubt on the use of the size of arable holdings as evidence, for she argues plausibly that families could have obtained part of their living from other activities, and indeed it is clear that in areas where smallholdings were common, this is what happened.[17] Eastern England, for example, 'was a land of smallholders, many of whom were craftsmen, traders or men who lived on the resources of woodland, fen or saltmarsh'.[18] Probably for this reason, areas in which smallholdings proliferated, such as the fenlands, showed little evidence of obvious distress.[19]

Box 3.1 Reproduction rates

As described in Box 2.1, the rate of population growth depends on the number of children the average woman has, the proportion of these children that are girls, and the chance that a daughter will survive to have children herself. The number of children the average woman has is known to demographers as the *total fertility rate* (TFR). In most populations, about 100 out of every 205 babies born are girls. The number of girls the average woman has is termed the *gross reproduction rate* (GRR). The GRR is (to a very close approximation) equal to the TFR x (100/205).

Survival to child-bearing age can be estimated by the probability of a new born girl surviving to age 28 years. If we denote this last quantity by the symbol l_{28}, then the number of daughters the average woman has who survive to have children themselves is approximately equal to TFR x (100/205) x l_{28}. Demographers call this quantity the *net reproduction rate* (NRR). The NRR measures the size of the next generation relative to the size of the present one. An NRR of 1.0 means that the average woman has exactly one daughter who will

---

[16] P. Franklin, 'Peasant Prosperity before the Plague', *Local Population Studies Society Newsletter* XX (1997), p. 8.

[17] Harvey, 'Population Trend', pp. 27–30. Non-agricultural employments may not just have been important in areas where holdings were small, but also in other areas when conditions were difficult, such as on the Winchester manors in the late thirteenth and early fourteenth centuries (see P. Franklin, 'Multiple Occupations and the Middle Peasant, or, the real Eddie Grundy', *Local Population Studies Society Newsletter* XXVII (2000), pp. 12–13).

[18] H.E. Hallam, *Rural England 1066–1348* (London, Fontana, 1981), p. 62.

[19] Harvey, 'Population Trend', p. 28.

herself survive to reproductive age. Therefore the next generation will be the same size as the present one, and the population size will not change. An NRR greater than 1.0 implies a growing population, and an NRR less than 1.0 indicates a declining population. The NRR is related to the average annual rate of population growth, as shown below.

Net reproduction rate	Average annual growth rate (per cent per year)
2.5	3.2
2.0	2.5
1.5	1.4
1.2	0.6
1.0	0.0
0.8	−0.8
0.5	−2.4

The 'male replacement rates' shown in Table 3.1 are estimates of the average number of male heirs that men had when they died. Thus they are analogous to the net reproduction rate, except that they relate to males and not females.

There is some very limited direct evidence from a few places about the population trend during the late thirteenth and early fourteenth centuries. For example, estimates of the population of Halesowen in the Midlands show a growth rate of almost 1 per cent per year between about 1270 and about 1315, followed by a decline of 15 per cent or so between 1311–15 and 1321–25, and then a modest recovery (Table 3.1). This pattern is confirmed by the so-called 'male replacement rates' (see Box 3.1), which may be estimated from surviving manorial records (Table 3.1).

3.4 Internal or external checks to population growth?

In the previous section, the different views held by historians about the evolution of the size of the English population between 1086 and 1348 were outlined. In this section, it is argued that, far from being a dry and rather arcane squabble over numbers, the debate raises fundamental and important issues that relate to the kind of economy and society England was at that time. In a recent review of the population history of England between 1300 and 1348, Richard Smith sets the question out clearly: 'did long-run trends and swings in population and living standards primarily reflect variations in the demand for labour or did they instead largely reflect disturbance in the relative natural powers of increase independent of economic

Table 3.1 Population growth in Halesowen, 1270–1348

Period	Number of males	Male replacement rate
1271–75	331	1.447
1280–82	392	
1293–95	435	1.500
1301–05	457	1.454
1311–15	485	0.989
1321–25	412	1.173
1331–35	433	1.351
1345–49	470	1.093

Notes: Figures for numbers of males are based on the number of different persons recorded in the manorial court rolls during the periods indicated. The male replacement rates relate to the following periods: 1270–82, 1293–99, 1300–09, 1310–19, 1320–29, 1330–39 and 1340–48.
Source: Z. Razi, *Life, Marriage and Death in a Medieval Parish* (Cambridge, Cambridge University Press, 1980), pp. 31, 33.

progress?'[20] If Russell is correct, then the natural slow growth of the population of medieval England was curtailed only by dramatic, external shocks, such as the agrarian crisis during the second decade of the fourteenth century and the appearance of the Black Death in 1348. On the other hand, the 'Postan thesis' holds that the turning point in England's population history was reached around 1300, for reasons internal to the demographic-economic system: that the people had simply become too many for the land to support.[21]

The two views of England's demographic development during the thirteenth and early fourteenth centuries also imply different living standards for many, probably a majority of the population. Titow, a supporter of the 'Postan thesis', paints a 'picture of the thirteenth-century English peasantry, as consisting largely of smallholders leading a wretched existence on an inadequate number of acres'.[22] The thesis implies a standard of living for most people so low that a systematic increase in mortality, even in relatively normal years, took place.[23] If Russell's story is nearer to the truth, however, the implication is that in normal years the standard of living of most people

[20] R.M. Smith, 'Demographic Developments in Rural England, 1300–48: a Survey', in B.M.S. Campbell (ed.), *Before the Black Death: Studies in the 'Crisis' of the Early Fourteenth Century* (Manchester, Manchester University Press, 1991), p. 77.

[21] For an excellent discussion of the issues raised in this paragraph, see B.F. Harvey, 'Introduction: the "Crisis" of the Early Fourteenth Century', in Campbell, *Before the Black Death*, pp. 1–24.

[22] Titow, *English Rural Society*, p. 93.

[23] Postan, *Medieval Economy*, p. 38, says that 'the relative over-population was so great as to push the death-rates to a punishing height' and 'the behaviour of the death-rates would by itself have been sufficient sooner or later to prevent the population from continuing its growth'.

was 'more than a minimal subsistence', and only in the worst years, such as those during the second decade of the fourteenth century, were death rates temporarily inflated by malnutrition.[24] We can take this argument a little further by recalling that Postan assumed a larger proportion of children in the population in 1377 than did Russell (and a larger mean household size in 1086, which is also consistent with a higher proportion of children). Yet both views are based on a similar population growth rate in normal years. It follows from demographic theory that the 'Postan thesis' implies both higher fertility and higher mortality than Russell's scenario. In other words, Postan is arguing for a *higher-pressure* demographic regime than is Russell.

But what kind of levels of mortality are we talking about? Postan and Titow used heriots (death duties) to estimate the expectation of life at age 20 years on the Winchester manors, and came up with a figure of just over 20 years.[25] This is exceptionally heavy mortality by any standards, implying an expectation of life at birth of well below 20 years.[26] Yet other historians who have managed to use manorial and other sources to estimate adult mortality are less pessimistic. Zui Razi presented estimates of the expectation of life at age 20 years for richer tenants in the Worcestershire manor of Halesowen between 1300 and 1348 of 30.2 years, a figure that fell to 25.3 years when adjusted to give more weight to the experience of poorer tenants.[27] Ecclestone used the Glastonbury Abbey head-tax lists to derive an estimate of 27 to 28 years for landless men in Longbridge Deverill and Monckton Deverill in Wiltshire between 1295 and 1345.[28] Even these figures, though, imply an expectation of life at birth of only 20 years for males.[29] Under such mortality conditions, it would have been hard for the population to maintain its numbers, as it would have required the average woman to have almost six children.[30] It seems likely, therefore, that the population of England was in slow decline even in 'normal' years during the 50 or so years before the Black Death.

[24] Russell, 'Preplague Population', p. 10.
[25] M.M. Postan and J.Z. Titow, 'Heriots and Prices on Winchester Manors', *Economic History Review*, 2nd series XI (1958–59), p. 395; J. Longden, 'Statistical Notes on Winchester Heriots', *Economic History Review*, 2nd series XI (1958–59), pp. 414–15.
[26] A.J. Coale and P. Demeny, *Regional Model Life Tables and Stable Populations* (2nd edn) (New York, Academic Press, 1983), p. 42.
[27] Z. Razi, *Life, Marriage and Death in a Medieval Parish: Economy, Society and Demography in Halesowen 1270–1400* (Cambridge, Cambridge University Press, 1980), pp. 43–5.
[28] M. Ecclestone, 'Mortality of Rural Landless Men before the Black Death: the Glastonbury Head-Tax Lists', *Local Population Studies* LXIII (1999), pp. 22–3.
[29] Coale and Demeny, *Regional Model Life Tables*, p. 42, show that an expectation of life at age 20 years for males of 28.1 years is consistent with an expectation of life at birth of 20.4 years. In order to make this inference, it is necessary to assume that the pattern of mortality by age in medieval England was similar to that used by Coale and Demeny in their calculations, which was based on the experience of several populations from different parts of the world during the nineteenth and twentieth centuries.
[30] According to Coale and Demeny, *Regional Model Life Tables*, p. 42, an expectation of life at birth of 20 years implies that only about 35 per cent of women would survive to age 28 years. Using the method described in Box 2.1, this means that the average woman would need to have 5.9 children just to achieve replacement (that is, a growth rate of zero).

3.5 The agrarian crisis of 1315–1322

Whatever their differences of opinion about its significance, historians seem in general agreement that the second decade of the fourteenth century saw an agricultural crisis of dramatic proportions. Even Russell, who is inclined to minimize its impact, admits that there was a net loss of population of 'perhaps a few per cent' during this decade.[31] Postan, on the other hand, argues for a mortality of 10–15 per cent and accords the event more demographic significance, though Harvey's claim that, according to the Postan thesis, '[t]he Great Famine of the years 1315–17 marked, not a fluctuation in demographic history of a familiar, though unusually severe kind, but the turning-point between the early medieval rise in population and the late medieval decline' is probably exaggerated.[32] The Halesowen data (Table 3.1) would seem to support Postan's case, as they indicate a fall in the male population of 15 per cent between 1311–15 and 1321–25.

The crisis began in 1315 when torrential rain ruined the harvest. The poor harvest did not have an immediate impact on nutritional levels, for people could manage for a while on what they did manage to salvage. However, by the late spring of 1316, supplies ran out and 'England was in the throes of a famine of major dimensions' accompanied by an epidemic 'of an enteric type – perhaps typhoid'.[33] Wheat prices rose dramatically, more than doubling, for example, on the Bishop of Winchester's manors in Hampshire.[34] Had the harvest of 1316 been a good one, the period of acute distress might have been short, but it was, if anything, worse than that of 1315.[35] Although the harvest of 1317 was adequate, it was not until a good harvest in 1318 that grain became abundant once more.[36] During the famine period, England was also hit by sheep murrain, and epidemics among cows continued during 1319–21.[37] The year 1321 saw a further bad harvest, and only in 1322 was normality restored to the agrarian economy.[38] The crisis, therefore, had two features that marked it out from other 'bad' years, such as 1258: first, there were consecutive years of deficient harvests; second, it affected all sectors of agriculture, so that the efforts of people to recover 'were rendered vain by the destruction on all sides of their means of production and livelihood'.[39]

---

[31] Russell, 'Preplague Population', p. 10.
[32] Postan, *Medieval Economy*, p. 41; Harvey, 'Introduction', pp. 4–5.
[33] I. Kershaw, 'The Great Famine and Agrarian Crisis in England 1315–1322', *Past and Present* LIX (1973), pp. 10–11.
[34] Titow, *English Rural Society*, p. 102.
[35] Kershaw, 'Great Famine', p. 13.
[36] Ibid., p. 13.
[37] Ibid., pp. 14–15.
[38] Ibid., p. 15.
[39] Ibid., p. 29.

There is no doubting the severity of the crisis, which appears to have been the most serious during the period between 1086 and 1348.[40] The most interesting question from our point of view is whether it was a demographic turning point. It is clear that major agrarian crises of this kind can have long-term impacts on population change: the Great Irish Famine of the 1840s is a case in point. Yet it is curious to note that neither Russell's nor Postan's views are consistent with ascribing this kind of significance to the crisis. For Russell, it was merely a hiatus in a generally rising population trend, which was only brought to a halt in 1348. For Postan, it was just one manifestation (albeit a massive one) of a more fundamental imbalance between population and resources, which had been evident for a few decades before. In other words, population growth would still have slowed down, and perhaps stopped altogether, around 1300 even if the crisis of 1315–22 had not occurred. Nevertheless, I. Kershaw is right to point out that the high famine-induced mortality of 1315–17 has a symbolic significance as a turning point even if this was only strictly true of certain parts of the country.[41]

3.6 Marriage patterns, fertility and population growth

It was pointed out in the Introduction (Chapter 1) that population change depends on three components: fertility, mortality and migration. So far, the questions of whether population growth slowed at the end of the thirteenth century, and possibly stopped altogether half a century before the Black Death, and, if so, why, have been discussed solely in terms of increased mortality. Now there is no doubt that in certain years, such as 1315–17, mortality did increase greatly. However, it is possible, at least in theory, that, if there was a slower rate of population growth in normal years after 1300 than before, this was the result of reduced fertility or changes in migration patterns. It seems most unlikely that, at the national level, increased emigration or reduced immigration was responsible for the slowdown in population growth and so the discussion here will focus on fertility.

When seeking to understand fertility change, demographers often consider changes in the so-called 'proximate determinants' of fertility.[42] There

---

40 This cannot be said for certain, as data are lacking for the earlier part of the period before 1200. Using the proportionate increase in wheat prices as an indicator of the severity of a crisis, on the Winchester manors in Hampshire the years 1316 and 1317 were the most difficult of any between 1163 and 1348, although 1203 and 1204 were also very difficult; see Titow, *English Rural Society*, pp. 101–2.

41 Kershaw, 'Great Famine', p. 50. Kershaw argues that in less densely populated and poorer parts of the country the crisis marked a genuine turning point, in that in the short to medium term the agrarian economy did not recover; but that 'in many of the wealthier and more densely populated parts of the country there is no indication that the agrarian crisis initiated a lasting decline in production and occupation of the land' (p. 49).

42 J. Bongaarts and R.G. Potter, *Fertility, Biology and Behaviour: an Analysis of the Proximate Determinants* (New York, Academic Press, 1983).

are, principally, four of these: the proportion of women who are married; the extent to which contraception or induced abortion are practised; the length of customary periods of breast-feeding or culturally prescribed periods of abstinence from sexual intercourse after the birth of each child; and physiological fecundity.

Let us consider these in reverse order. It is very likely that during severe subsistence 'crises', women's ability to conceive and carry pregnancies to term was compromised. A reduced conception rate has commonly been observed in subsistence crises during later periods when more data are available, and is a tell-tale feature of such crises. However, it is less certain to what extent a reduced standard of living in 'normal' years might have reduced underlying fecundity.

Very little can be said about breast-feeding or abstinence from sexual intercourse after a birth in England in medieval times, though it seems rather unlikely that either practice underwent a secular change around the end of the thirteenth century. The more general question of abstinence, however, does become an issue when we consider the possibility that couples began to take steps to prevent conceptions (or births) occurring. It is commonly supposed by historical demographers ('assumed' might be a better word, since little evidence is provided) that birth control was not practised to any great extent in England prior to the nineteenth century. However, there are isolated references in documentary sources from the early fourteenth century that are suggestive. For example, during the 1320s John Bromyard, in the diocese of Hereford, wrote that 'quite a few people are in wonderment at the barrenness of marriages'.[43] Around the same time William of Pagula, a vicar in the diocese of Salisbury, wrote a work entitled *Oculus Sacerdotus*, in which he expressed concern at *coitus interruptus*, or withdrawal, being practised 'in order not to have more children', and instructed that 'a man knowing his wife or another woman carnally should do nothing – nor should his wife do anything – whereby conception may be impeded'.[44] This evidence is very far from being sufficient to underpin a credible case that birth control did play a part in the slowing of population growth in the early fourteenth century, but it would be unwise to dismiss the notion entirely.

Finally, we turn to marriage patterns. Intuitively, it seems more plausible that changes in marriage patterns might have taken place in the late thirteenth and early fourteenth centuries. Not only do we approach the medieval period in the knowledge that changes in marriage patterns were closely related to the rate of population growth in later centuries (see Chapters 6 and 8), but there is abundant evidence that in times of severe agrarian crises mar-

[43] P.P.A. Biller, 'Birth Control in the West in the Thirteenth and Early Fourteenth Centuries', *Past and Present* XCIV (1982), pp. 24–5.
[44] Ibid., pp. 5, 21, 25.

riage patterns often undergo abrupt short-term changes. The marriage rate is first reduced because of the economic disruption caused by the crisis. Indeed, a reduction in the marriage rate probably contributes to the reduction in conceptions that typically accompanies such crises. After the crisis, the marriage rate increases because the increased mortality has created a supply of eligible widowed persons.[45] What is much less certain is whether longer-term more systematic changes in marriage patterns were happening around the time period of interest. The potential impact of changes in female marriages on population growth rates is considerable (see Box 3.2). However, as Richard Smith points out, 'we still lack studies that have demonstrated that female marriage was either static or shifted in age of incidence in the half century before 1348'.[46] In other words, though it is possible that marriage patterns changed, we simply do not know. The clearest identifiable trend seems to be that widow remarriage, which had formed a high proportion of all marriages around 1300, declined as the Black Death approached.[47] Curiously, this trend, while providing no evidence about the reasons for the slowing of population growth, is usually interpreted as evidence that the pressure of population on resources was declining, and hence might be thought of as supporting the 'Postan thesis'. This is because in medieval society entry into marriage generally relied upon possession of an economic niche conferring economic independence. Widows necessarily possessed such a niche, and therefore the proportion of all marriages that are remarriages of widows is a measure of the proportion of marriages that rely on the recycling of existing niches, as opposed to the creation of new ones.

Box 3.2 Marriage patterns and population growth

Two aspects of marriage patterns can influence population growth rates. The first is the age at marriage of those who do marry, and the second is the proportion of women who remain celibate. Consider first the proportion remaining celibate. Suppose that women bear no children outside marriage. To work out the net reproduction rate (NRR) (see Box 3.1), we need to know how many children the 'average' woman has. Now, in fact, there is no 'average woman': there are women who do marry and women who do not. Suppose, for the purposes of illustration, that women who do marry have, on average, six

---

[45] Precisely this pattern is observed in Halesowen during the great crisis of 1315–22. The number of marriages fell in 1316, and did not recover until the end of the crisis in the 1320s; see Razi, *Life, Marriage and Death*, p. 47.

[46] Smith, 'Demographic Developments', p. 73.

[47] Ibid., pp. 68–71.

children, and that those who never marry have none. Then, if all women marry, the total fertility rate (TFR) will be 6.0, and the NRR will be 6.0 x 100/205 x l_{28}. If 10 per cent of women remain celibate, the TFR will be (6 x 0.9) + (0 x 0.1) = 5.4 (that is, 10 per cent lower) and the NRR will also fall by 10 per cent. The effect on the rate of growth is greater than this, however. Supposing that the NRR is 1.15, a value compatible with a rate of population growth of 0.5 per cent per year, a fall of 10 per cent would reduce the NRR to 1.03, which implies an annual rate of population growth of only 0.1 per cent per year.

The effects of changes in the average age at marriage gain much of their force from the fact that they primarily affect the exposure of women in their twenties to the risk of conception, and this is the age at which women are most fecund. Suppose, for example, that women who marry have a TFR of 6.0, and that the average age at marriage is 20 years. Under normal age patterns of fertility, an increase in the average age of marriage to 22.5 years would reduce the TFR of married women to 5.3 and an increase to 25 years would reduce it to 4.6. Therefore a 2.5-year increase in the average age of marriage would reduce the TFR, and hence the NRR, by 12 per cent. If the NRR were 1.15, a reduction of 12 per cent would mean a new NRR of 1.01, which implies that population growth would almost cease.

3.7 Conclusion

There is no escaping the fact that much of the debate about the population trend in England between 1086 and 1348 arises because of the paucity of reliable data. Moreover, it seems rather unlikely that data of a kind that will provide definitive answers to the questions of whether the English population peaked in 1348 or earlier (around 1300) and, if the peak was earlier, what caused the slowdown in population growth, will be discovered in the near future.[48] However, in the light of the discussion in this chapter, a few conclusions can be drawn.

First, it seems almost certain that the two centuries after 1086 saw a sustained, if modest, level of population growth in normal years. Of course there were individual years when epidemic disease or harvest failure led to short-term setbacks, but overall, the growth was maintained. The disagreement among historians during this period concerns the absolute number of people, not its rate of increase. By the end of the thirteenth century the population of England had reached a level that might have been anything from

---

[48]   This is not to say that such evidence cannot be produced, but that the effort (not to mention the funding) that would be required is prodigious.

about four million to over six million. However, if it approached the latter figure, it is likely that the growth rate was slowing down because of the increased pressure of population on resources. During the period 1315–22 there was a sustained and catastrophic agrarian crisis, which included three years of severe famine, and which probably led to a reduction in the population of over 10 per cent. Thereafter population growth may have resumed, though it seems on the balance of evidence that it was considerably slower than it had been during the twelfth and thirteenth centuries.

Of the two views of England's population history outlined in Section 3.3, recent research tends to support the 'Postan thesis'. By around 1300, English mortality levels appear to have risen to such an extent that population growth was well nigh impossible, and a slow decline more likely. It is worth remembering, however, that just as the 'average woman' does not exist, the 'average English manor' probably did not exist, and the English national pattern almost certainly conceals different demographic developments in different places.

4

The Black Death and its aftermath

4.1 Introduction

The previous chapter suggested that the preponderance of the historical evidence indicates that the population of England during the first half of the fourteenth century was struggling against punishing mortality levels induced, in large part, by the difficulty of securing subsistence. Yet even the disastrous famine of 1315–22 is dwarfed by the calamity that was to strike the country three decades later. In 1348 a deadly new disease appeared on the south coast of England. Within two years this 'Black Death' had spread to the whole of the country, killing at least one in three of the inhabitants. The death toll alone would make the epidemic the single most dramatic demographic event in England's history since 1086. However, its significance extends further, for it now seems that the 1348–50 epidemic marked the appearance of a disease regime that was to be a fundamental feature of England's population history for more than 300 years. The England of the final third of the fourteenth century was, demographically, very different from the England of the thirteenth century, or even of the period between 1300 and 1348.[1]

It is generally acknowledged by most (but not all) historians that the disease responsible for the Black Death was plague, a virulent bacterial infection with a case fatality rate of well over 50 per cent.[2] Plague is

---

[1] R.M. Smith, 'Plagues and Peoples: the Long Demographic Cycle, 1250–1670', in P. Slack and R. Ward (eds), *The Peopling of Britain: the Shaping of a Human Landscape* (Oxford, Oxford University Press, 2002), pp. 177–84, describes the emergence of this changed demographic regime in several English localities.

[2] There are a number of recent contributions questioning this. An early dissenting view was G. Twigg, *The Black Death: a Biological Reappraisal* (London, Batsford, 1984). More recently, S. Scott and C.J. Duncan, *Biology of Plagues: Evidence from Historical Populations* (Cambridge, Cambridge University Press, 2001) have produced rather convincing evidence that none of the English epidemics that have been attributed to plague between 1348 and 1665 were, in fact, caused by that disease. Rather, they posit some now extinct infection that may have been similar to the haemorraghic fevers like Ebola. It is clearly awkward to write a survey of the literature on a topic when the prevailing orthodoxy may be about to be overthrown. In this chapter, therefore, I have adopted the policy of telling the story as if the Black Death were due to plague, but pointing out some of the difficulties with the 'plague explanation'.

highly lethal to humans, but its transmission is a complex process requiring the existence of substantial populations of rodents and an insect vector, which is described in Section 4.2. Section 4.3 then considers the origins of the Black Death, and tells the story of its arrival in England in 1348 and its spread throughout the country during the subsequent two years. The great epidemic of 1348–50 was followed by a series of major epidemics that occurred at intervals during the second half of the fourteenth century, each of which, had it not occurred in the shadow of the earlier catastrophe, would have been regarded as a demographic disaster in its own right. Section 4.4 examines the demographic consequences of the whole series of epidemics, assessing the evidence on which estimates of mortality rates may be based, and discussing the plausibility of various estimates.

It is impossible to believe that such a culling of the population could have occurred without major social and economic consequences. Section 4.5 discusses the long debate among historians about these, which has focused on the extent to which plague hastened the decline of the feudal system, and on its consequences for the standard of living of ordinary people. Of course, the Black Death is likely to have had psychological consequences as well, both at the individual level (how did different people react to the emergence of this serious threat to life?) and collectively (how were social and cultural attitudes affected?) and these are considered in Section 4.6. Finally, in Section 4.7, the question of how important the events of the second half of the fourteenth century were for the long-term development of England's population is raised.

4.2 Plague

The immediate cause of the disease that we know as plague is infection with the bacterium *pasturella pestis* or *yersinia pestis*. However, the occurrence of such an infection in humans is the outcome of a fairly involved process. The disease is not primarily a disease of humans, but of rodents. It is endemic among wild rodents in some parts of the world, such as China, central Asia, the south-western United States and parts of eastern Africa. For reasons that are not really understood, it has periodically broken out of these 'heartlands' and spread around the globe in major epidemics, or pandemics – one possible cause of these is the spread of the infection to large urban rat populations. During the last 2000 years, there have been three pandemics: the first began in the sixth century, the second in the fourteenth century and the third in the nineteenth century.

When a plague epidemic strikes a locality, it first infects the rodent population, which begins to experience heavy mortality, largely from septicaemia caused by high concentrations of the bacteria in the blood. This accounts for the observation that the first sign of a plague epidemic is the appearance of dead rats.[3] The rat flea, *xenopsylla cheopis*, which feeds on the blood of rodent populations, ingests the bacteria, which rapidly multiply inside the flea's stomach, eventually filling it completely. Fleas in this awkward predicament are said to be 'blocked'; they become ravenously hungry and seek to feed off the nearest warm-blooded creature. By then, however, the high mortality among the rat population has reduced the number of rats available, so the fleas turn to other species living nearby, such as humans.

When a 'blocked' flea bites a human, it vomits some of the contents of its stomach into the blood of its victim, thus infecting the person with the bacteria. Some authorities (anxious, perhaps, not to omit the grosser details) mention that the flea simultaneously defecates bacteria on to the skin of the victim, and that these bacteria can subsequently enter the bloodstream as the person scratches the site of the flea bite.[4] The infected person usually develops the disease within a few days. The characteristic symptoms are painful dark swellings, called buboes, in the lymph nodes, such as those under the arms and (especially) in the groin. It is these swellings that give their name to the usual description of this form of the disease: *bubonic plague*. Subsequently, the disease attacks the central nervous system, leading to coma and, in somewhat over half of untreated cases, death.

Bubonic plague cannot readily be passed directly from person to person: it requires an insect vector such as *x. cheopis*. There has been speculation about the possible role of other vectors, such as the human flea, *pulex irritans*, in human-to-human transmission, but the consensus seems to be that their role is fairly minor. *X. cheopis* does not tolerate temperatures below about 15°C (and at low humidities needs higher temperatures to be active) so in a temperate climate like that of England, the rapid spread of bubonic plague is very hard to sustain outside the summer months.[5] This means that in epidemics of bubonic plague, deaths tend to reach a peak during the late summer, a feature that has been important when using documentary evidence to infer plague years. An additional consequence of the dependence of bubonic plague on rats and fleas is that its spread depends on the movement of these creatures. Under normal circumstances, rats are relatively

---

[3]   The gradual discovery of increasing numbers of dead rats is wonderfully described in the opening pages of Albert Camus' classic story about plague in an Algerian town; see A. Camus, *The Plague*, trans. S. Gilbert (Harmondsworth, Penguin, 1960), pp. 9–21. However, the paucity of rats (alive or dead) in England in the mid-fourteenth century is one of the key problems that have led to doubts being raised about the 'plague explanation' of the Black Death.

[4]   J.F.D. Shrewsbury, *A History of Bubonic Plague in the British Isles* (Cambridge, Cambridge University Press, 1970), p. 2.

[5]   J.-N. Biraben, 'Current Medical and Epidemiological Views on Plague', in *The Plague Reconsidered: a New Look at its Origins and Effects in Sixteenth and Seventeenth Century England*, a Local Population Studies supplement (Matlock, Local Population Studies, 1977), p. 30.

immobile, but they (and their fleas) may be carried long distances over both land and sea by being attached to goods in transit.

Occasionally, the infection will enter a victim's lungs. If this happens, the victim may pass on the disease directly to other humans by coughing, in the same way as, say, influenza. This form of plague is called *pneumonic plague*; it is highly infectious and also highly lethal, causing death within three days in around 95 per cent of untreated cases. Pneumonic plague can spread rapidly without an insect vector. Though it typically arises as a complication of a bubonic case, there is evidence that pneumonic plague can exist without a simultaneous epidemic of bubonic plague.[6] Pneumonic plague is spread most effectively during the winter months.

Sometimes a third form of plague, *septicaemic plague*, is distinguished. Septicaemia can arise through high concentrations of the bacteria in the bloodstream, and may cause death even before the buboes appear. It is relatively uncommon in humans, who have a large volume of blood, but is much more common in rodents.

Surviving an attack of plague does not confer long-term immunity to further attacks in humans, though some short-term immunity is likely.

4.3 The history of the Black Death and subsequent epidemics

Though the early history of the second plague pandemic is not conspicuously clear, it seems that it began somewhere in the Far East. The disease was apparently raging in China in the 1330s, and traders who travelled overland from eastern Europe through central Asia reported it having spread to the latter area around 1339. According to Philip Ziegler it 'settled in the Tartar lands of Asia Minor in 1346'.[7] The Tartars at that time decided to attack some Genoese Christian merchants who traded locally, and laid siege to their entrepot at Caffa, in the Crimea.[8] Ziegler takes up the story:

> Their plans were disastrously disturbed by the plague which was soon taking heavy toll of the besiegers. 'Fatigued, stupefied and amazed', they decided to call off the operation. First, however, they felt it was only fair that the Christians should be given a taste of the agony which the investing force had been suffering. They used their giant catapults to lob over the walls the corpses of the victims in the hope that this would spread the disease within the city. As fast as the rotting bodies arrived in their midst the Genoese carried them

---

6 For a discussion of this issue, see L. Bradley, 'Some Medical Aspects of Plague', in *The Plague Reconsidered*, pp. 12-13. The possibility that pneumonic plague could have existed largely in the absence of the bubonic form is something which those arguing against the 'plague explanation' have, perhaps, not considered sufficiently.
7 P. Ziegler, *The Black Death* (Harmondsworth, Penguin, 1982), p. 15.
8 Ibid., p. 15.

through the town and dropped them in the sea. But few places are so vulnerable to disease as a besieged city and it was not long before the plague was as active within the city as without.[9]

The Genoese realized that the game was up. They 'took to their galleys and fled from the Black Sea towards the Mediterranean. With them travelled the plague.'[10]

Whatever the truth of this intriguing tale (and Ziegler claims there is no reason to doubt it), the plague arrived in western Europe by sea from the Black Sea or the eastern Mediterranean.[11] The first western European cities to be infected were ports trading with those areas: Messina in Sicily in 1347, and Marseilles and Genoa shortly afterwards. From the Mediterranean coast the disease spread rapidly northwards, reaching inland areas in northern France by mid-1348. Eventually, it was to spread across the whole of Europe with the exception of a few areas in what is now Poland.

The Black Death arrived in England at the south coast port of Melcombe Regis, close to what is now the resort of Weymouth, probably around the end of June 1348.[12] From there it spread generally northwards, reaching the north of England by mid-1349. By the end of 1349 all parts of England and Wales, and much of Scotland, had succumbed. The most efficient source of data for charting the spread of the disease is provided by records of the numbers of institutions to vacant benefices – that is, records of new priests taking over parishes. Clearly, one reason for a new priest taking over a parish is the death of the previous incumbent; a dramatic increase in the number of institutions in a particular area therefore suggests greatly increased mortality among the clergy. This is what happened during late 1348 and 1349. For example, in the diocese of Salisbury, between June and October the number of institutions to vacant benefices was five or fewer per month.[13] In November 1348 it rose to 17, for the next three months it was around 30 per month, and in March 1349 more than 60 institutions took place before the number fell back gradually to its pre-plague level.[14] By looking at the rise and fall of the number of institutions by diocese, a map of the spread of the disease can be constructed (Figure 4.1). The number of clergy institutions peaked in January 1349 in the diocese of Bath and Wells, March 1349 in Salisbury, April 1349 in Exeter, May 1349 in Winchester, July 1349 in Worcester, Norwich, Ely, Lichfield, Lincoln and Hereford, and August 1349 in Gloucester.[15] Thus from Melcombe Regis, the disease seems to have fanned out in all directions.

9   Ibid., pp. 15–16.
10   Ibid., p. 16.
11   Ibid., p. 16.
12   Ibid., pp. 122–5.
13   Shrewsbury, *History of Bubonic Plague*, p. 59.
14   Ibid., p. 59.
15   Twigg, *Black Death*, p. 179.

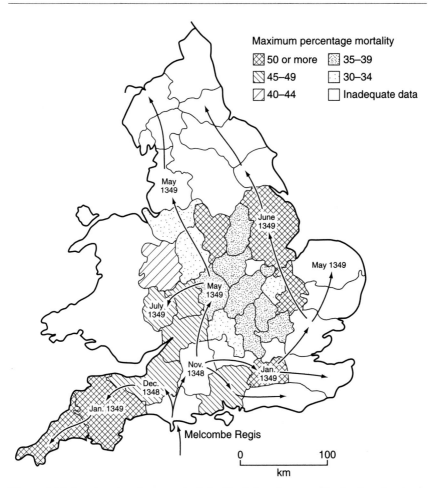

Figure 4.1 Map showing the spread of the Black Death across England and estimated percentages dying
Notes: The percentages dying are maximum estimates based on the beneficed clergy.
Source: Based on R.I. Woods, *Population Analysis in Geography* (London, Longman, 1979), p. 74; chronology from J.F.D. Shrewsbury, *A History of Bubonic Plague in the British Isles* (Cambridge, Cambridge University Press, 1971), pp. 59, 61, 64, 66, 76, 91, 99.

The arrival of the epidemic in specific communities can be identified through records of heriots, or death duties, in manorial court rolls (see Appendix I, though the effort required to produce a general picture of the whole country from this source would be overwhelming. Nevertheless, a good picture of the plague's journey through some individual manors has been drawn. For example, in the manor of Halesowen in the Midlands the plague arrived in May 1349, raged through May, June and July, and subsided in August.[16] During its visitation it killed at least 88 peasants.[17]

Urban areas fared no better, and may even have suffered more terribly. Winchester, England's ancient capital city, had a population of at least 8000 before 1348.[18] In the autumn of that year the epidemic began, and by January 1349 the cemeteries in the city's churchyards were full, and new burial ground had to be consecrated. Work on rebuilding the west end of the cathedral ceased for want of labourers; it has never been completed, and its ill-proportioned squat form stands as a monument to the ravages of the Black Death.[19] By 1377, the population of the city was probably around 3000, less than half the number in 1348.[20]

4.4 Demographic consequences

Historians have argued for years about the proportion of the population that died in the first great onslaught. Estimates have ranged from the 5 per cent of J.F.D. Shrewsbury to over 50 per cent.[21] For many years a figure of one in three was taken to be a 'best estimate' of the proportion of the inhabitants of England that perished. Recent historiography has tended to raise that figure somewhat, to perhaps 40–45 per cent.[22]

The principal source of data is, as we mentioned in the previous section, records relating to the institution of clergy to vacant benefices. The percentages of clergy dying in different regions are shown in Figure 4.1. They range from less than 35 per cent in Oxfordshire, Huntingdonshire, Shropshire and Cheshire to more than half in Cornwall, Devon, Surrey, Lincolnshire, Derbyshire and Cambridgeshire.[23] In individual places, rates could be even higher; for example, 66 per cent in Southampton and 59 per cent in Winchester.[24] Concern has been expressed about the representativeness of the clergy figures. The clergy were generally richer and probably better fed

---

[16] Z. Razi, *Life, Marriage and Death in a Medieval Parish: Economy, Society and Demography in Halesowen 1270–1400* (Cambridge, Cambridge University Press, 1980), p. 102.

[17] Ibid., p. 103.

[18] Ziegler, *Black Death*, p. 151.

[19] Ibid., p. 152.

[20] Ziegler (ibid., p. 151) quotes Russell's estimate of 2160 for 1377. For reasons given in Appendix I, however, this is likely to be on the low side.

[21] Shrewsbury, *History of Bubonic Plague*, p. 123. To be fair to Shrewsbury, his figure of 5 per cent is not meant to be an estimate of the total percentage of the population that died in 1348–50, but of those who succumbed to bubonic plague. He suggests that epidemics of typhus fever raged through the winters of 1348–49 and 1349–50, and killed substantial numbers (ibid., pp. 123–5). Nevertheless, his overall mortality estimates are generally on the low side.

[22] This is the figure quoted by J. Goldberg, 'Introduction', in W.M. Ormrod and P.G. Lindley (eds), *The Black Death in England* (Stamford, Paul Watkins, 1996), p. 4.

[23] R.I. Woods, *Population Analysis in Geography* (London, Longman, 1979), p. 74.

[24] Shrewsbury, *History of Bubonic Plague*, p. 91.

than the general population, and so might have been expected to have had more resistance to the disease and suffered lower mortality. On the other hand, they were frequently called upon to visit and minister to the sick, and therefore would have been particularly exposed to the risk of infection and would have experienced higher mortality than average. Since these two potential biases in the clergy mortality figures (relative to the population at large) act in opposite directions, there might seem to be a good argument for taking the clergy figures at face value. This would seem to place the national mortality rate at somewhere between 40 and 45 per cent.

A further factor that would seem to suggest a high death rate was the apparently unchecked spread of the disease through the winter of 1348–49 (Figure 4.1), when it would have been expected that the fleas would have been rendered inactive by low temperatures. It seems that a large proportion of cases were, by then, pneumonic rather than bubonic, and if the pneumonic form was well established, overall death rates of over 50 per cent would by no means be impossible. Pneumonic plague is spread more effectively in cold weather or cold climates, as infection is by bacteria contained in droplets, and in cold damp conditions these 'remain infective for a long time and can be inhaled so long as they are in suspension in the atmosphere'.[25]

There are, however, other sources that can be exploited. Using manorial court rolls, Razi estimates that among males above the age of 12 years in Halesowen, 430 per thousand (43 per cent) died.[26] The manorial records have the added advantage that differences in death rates by age can be analysed. In Halesowen, for example, the plague fatality rate in 1348–50 for males aged 20–29 years was only 210 per thousand, but it increased with age to 620 per thousand in the age group 50–59 years, before decreasing to 373 per thousand among those aged 60 years and over.[27] It is also likely that child mortality from plague during 1348–50 was very heavy.[28] More recently, Ecclestone has exploited the Glastonbury Abbey head-tax lists to show that on manors owned by the abbey, mortality during the Black Death among males aged 12 years and over who did not hold property was about 57 per cent.[29]

There is still greater disagreement about death rates in the subsequent

25   J.-N. Biraben, 'Current Medical and Epidemiological Views on Plague', in *The Plague Reconsidered*, p. 30. The fact that the Black Death spread unchecked in the colder months is another factor that has been seized upon by historians sceptical about whether the disease in question really was plague. There is no doubt that the uninterrupted progress of the epidemic requires advocates of the 'plague explanation' to posit that by (at the latest) the autumn of 1348 the epidemic was of the pneumonic form.
26   Razi, *Life, Marriage and Death*, p. 103.
27   Ibid., p. 109.
28   Ibid., p. 104.
29   M. Ecclestone, 'Mortality of Rural Landless Men before the Black Death: the Glastonbury Head-Tax Lists', *Local Population Studies* LXIII (1999), pp. 8, 26.

epidemics, probably because there has been less systematic analysis. Russell would have us believe that death rates in 1361–62 were scarcely lower than they were in 1348–50 (though it should be noted that his death rates for 1348–50 were lower than those quoted by most others who have worked on the subject), that in 1369 another 10–15 per cent died, and that about the same proportion died in 1375.[30]

Indeed, if the death rates quoted by Russell for the epidemic of 1361–62 are to be believed, this epidemic alone was the second most devastating demographic event since 1086, carrying off a higher percentage of the population than the famine of 1315–17 or the series of subsistence crises in 1557–59.[31] In Halesowen, however, it seems that the 1361–62 epidemic was much less severe than the original one, the death rate among males over 20 being 135 per thousand.[32] Figures from Halesowen in the 1369 and 1375 epidemics, however, compare well with Russell's, being 161 per thousand (16 per cent) and 117 per thousand (12 per cent) respectively.[33]

A disaster that carries off around two out of every five persons in the population is almost certain to have short-run effects on other aspects of a community's demography. Marriage in medieval England depended on access to land. An immediate effect of the Black Death was to make land more widely available for the survivors, and this led to both an increase in the marriage rate and a decline in the average age at marriage.[34] According to Razi, 'in the period which immediately followed the Black Death, proportionally more marriages were contracted in Halesowen than in any other three-year period in the fourteenth century', and a similar surge took place in 1361–63.[35] The increased availability of land would have led to an increase in the rate of migration between communities, as peasants moved from areas where death rates from the epidemic had been relatively low (and hence access to land was comparatively difficult) to those areas where the decrease in the population had been greater.[36]

A surge in the number of marriages is likely to have been followed by a rise in the birth rate. Though this may only have been a short-term phenomenon, it is worth pausing to consider the potential impact of a sustained increase in fertility, which might have been made possible by the improved economic position of the poor. Of course, if the general level of fertility after

---

[30] Russell, *British Medieval Population* (Albuquerque, University of New Mexico Press, 1948) pp. 216–18.

[31] Russell's death rates are reproduced in a convenient form in Twigg, *Black Death*, p. 63.

[32] Razi, *Life, Marriage and Death*, p. 128.

[33] Ibid., p. 128.

[34] Ibid., pp. 135–8.

[35] Ibid., pp. 132–4.

[36] Razi (ibid., p. 118) argues that this, indeed, was the case in Halesowen. For other suggestive evidence see P. Schofield, 'Frankpledge Lists as Indices of Migration and Mortality: some Evidence from Essex Lists', *Local Population Studies* LII (1994), pp. 23–9.

1350 had been higher than that before the Black Death, many of the 'additional' children born were destined to perish in subsequent plague epidemics. Nevertheless, the potential (at least in theory) for a population to recover even from a disaster as great as that of 1348–50 should not be underestimated. Suppose, for example, that a growth rate of 1 per cent per year could have been achieved in England after 1350; this is greater than that during the twelfth and thirteenth centuries, but does not seem unreasonable given the greater access to land and more opportunities for marriage. Then, in the absence of any further crises, the population could have regained its 1348 level by 1404.[37] The fact that it did not is due principally to the continued ravages of the plague.[38]

4.5 Social and economic consequences

Common sense suggests that in a population that, in a short space of time, experiences a catastrophe on the scale of the Black Death, things will not be the same again. However, it turns out that the impact of the plague on English society and the nation's economy is rather complex to describe. In the short term, of course, the immediate effect was to reduce the supply of labour, and to increase its cost. As the example of Winchester Cathedral shows, buildings that were under construction in 1348 and 1349 struggled to be completed for want of hands. The longer-term economic effects, however, are less certain and have been the subject of a great deal of disagreement in the literature.

Two main questions have vexed historians. The first concerns whether the decades after 1350 were characterized by 'benign economic growth', as J. Goldberg suggests, or whether England experienced overall economic decline. This question has been debated for well over a century, ever since the confrontation in the 1880s between the optimistic Thorold Rogers, and the pessimistic views of William Denton and others.[39] It was really as an attempt to reconcile the two sides in this debate that M.M. Postan produced 'the first of the general explanations of the post-plague economy'.[40] His argument, in a nutshell, was that there was an economic decline during the

---

[37] This assumes a death rate in 1348–50 of 42 per cent, distributed fairly evenly by age. It is worked out using the formula $P_t = P_0 e^{rt}$ (see Box 6.1), where the annual rate of growth $r = 0.01$, and $e = 2.718$. If we let the population in 1350 be P_0, then we want to find t such that P_t is equal to 1.72 x P_0. It is straightforward to show that, for this to be the case, $t = 54$, implying that the population will have recovered by 1404 (for the method, see Box 6.1).

[38] Some readers may have observed that the likelihood that the rate of population growth in normal years after 1348 was likely to have been greater than that in normal years before the Black Death has an effect on the calculations made in the previous chapter. The effect is to reduce the population in 1348, which is needed to correspond with any given value in 1377.

[39] Goldberg, 'Introduction', pp. 7–8.

[40] J. Bolton, '"The World Upside Down": Plague as an Agent of Economic and Social Change', in Ormrod and Lindley, *Black Death*, p. 18.

late fourteenth century, but that because there was simultaneously a decline in population numbers due to repeated plague epidemics, incomes per head did not fall. In other words, just as in developing countries during the second half of the twentieth century overall economic growth occurred even as people became poorer, because it was outstripped by rapid population growth, in late medieval England overall economic decline was outpaced by population decline, so that people still became richer. Moreover, the reduced population made access to land much easier, enabling many who had previously been wage labourers to begin farming 'on their own account', further reducing the supply of, and increasing wage rates among, those who remained as labourers. Postan's argument for overall economic decline was robustly challenged in 1962 by A.R. Bridbury, who held that the economic vitality of the towns fuelled economic growth.[41] Bridbury's dispute with Postan, though, concerned economic trends at the aggregate level: to the extent that he is right, the economic position of the average Englishman and woman improved still further.

A second debate has concerned the influence of the Black Death on the system of agriculture. Theoretically, since grain prices would have fallen as the demand for food dropped, and the wages of labourers rose because the supply of labour had fallen, the Black Death should have improved the position of peasants relative to landlords, and quickly led to the demise of the feudal system of land being held in exchange for labour services and other onerous duties, as landlords were forced to compete for tenants. In addition, it would no longer have paid landlords to farm land themselves, since their own farms would have suffered from the squeeze in profit margins caused by falling prices and rising wages. Consequently, landlords increasingly rented out their land and passed the burden to their tenants. In other words, the Black Death resulted in a monetization and commercialization of the agricultural economy.

Yet several historians have noted that this theoretical scenario of increased wages and reduced prices for agricultural products, leading to increased difficulties for landlords, does not seem to have happened in the short term. Concerning wages, there is conflicting evidence. On the Westminster manors, wages rose by 80 per cent around 1350, but on the Winchester manors they rose scarcely at all.[42] In addition, landlords were not without the power to pass laws to try to alleviate their position, and this they did, passing a Statute of Labourers in 1351 in an effort to rein in rising wage rates.[43]

The story of prices is more certain. They appear to have held up well until

[41] A.R. Bridbury, *Economic Growth: England in the Later Middle Ages* (2nd edn) (Brighton, Harvester Press, 1975).

[42] J. Hatcher, *Plague, Population and the English Economy, 1348–1530* (London, Macmillan, 1977), p. 49; J. Hatcher, 'England in the Aftermath of the Black Death', *Past and Present* CXLIV (1994), p. 28.

[43] M.M. Postan, *The Medieval Economy and Society: an Economic History of Britain in the Middle Ages* (Harmondsworth, Pelican, 1975), p. 170.

the 1370s for several reasons. First, as the incomes of the peasants increased, so their spending power grew, leading to commodity price inflation that offset the decreased demand for agricultural produce. Second, a series of poor harvests during the 1360s reduced the supply of food.[44] Third, the Black Death provided a good opportunity to reduce the area under cultivation and abandon exhausted, unprofitable lands. This, of course, would not reduce overall agricultural output pro rata, as these lands produced less than the average. The existence of a substantial cultivated area in this position prior to 1348 did mean, however, that landlords with a relatively large share of such land suffered disproportionately.

Fourth, England before 1348 was overpopulated. Population pressure was probably not as great as it had been at the beginning of the fourteenth century, but it was still substantial. Part of the effect of the Black Death, therefore, merely brought the situation back into balance. Razi, for example, argues that in Halesowen, the area cultivated did not decline as a result of the plague because many villagers were short of land before 1348 and were able to take up any land that became available.[45] Bridbury goes further, noting that '[o]ne of the most extraordinary things about the Black Death is how little effect it seems to have had on the social and economic life of the country despite the tremendous mortality . . .'.[46] The simplest explanation of this, he concludes, is that England during the first half of the fourteenth century was so teeming with people 'that the early famines and the mid-century pestilences were more purgative than toxic'.[47] It is noteworthy that on the Winchester manors, where overpopulation was probably especially severe, wages were hardly affected by the epidemic of 1348–50.

However, the 'slack in the system' caused by overpopulation was eventually taken up by successive plague epidemics, such that by the last quarter of the fourteenth century, prices were falling, wages were rising, and the end of demesne farming came rapidly.[48] Labour services were commuted to money rents, and villeins became free peasantry.[49] Even this was not sufficient to maintain landlords' incomes, however, since, as we shall see in the next

[44]   Ibid., p. 6.
[45]   Razi, *Life, Marriage and Death*, p. 113.
[46]   A.R. Bridbury, 'The Black Death', *Economic History Review*, 2nd series XXVI (1973), p. 588.
[47]   Ibid., p. 591.
[48]   Ibid., p. 586.
[49]   See P.R. Schofield, 'Tenurial Developments and the Availability of Customary Land in a Later Medieval Community', *Economic History Review*, 2nd series XLIX (1996), pp. 250–67 for a detailed study of how this happened on the Westminster Abbey manor of Birdbrook in Essex. Schofield shows how the replacement of 'a manorial economy based on labour service' by 'one in which the payment of annual money farms came to dominate' was a gradual process that started in the mid-fourteenth century but took until the early fifteenth century to complete (pp. 264–5).

chapter, further population decline meant that rents were destined to fall as land became cheaper and labour dearer.

In fact, behind these debates lies the same fundamental question raised in Chapter 3, in relation to population change. Did the Black Death mark a turning point in England's economic and social development, or did it merely accelerate pre-existing trends?[50] Since Postan first outlined his account of the medieval economy, historians have tended to try to minimize the direct impact of the epidemic, accepting that the economic turning point had come earlier, along with the demographic turning point around 1300, and although there have been recent attempts to restore the position of the 1348–50 epidemic, this is still the dominant view.[51] We return to this issue again in Section 4.7.

4.6 Psychological consequences

A calamity on the scale of the Black Death is likely to have had quite profound psychological effects on a population, even one that was as used to mortality crises as that of fourteenth-century England was. In the short term, of course, the range of possible responses was fairly limited. Boccaccio's *The Decameron*, in which ten young people fleeing from the Black Death tell tales, speaks of three. Some people believed that

> by living temperately and guarding against excesses of all kinds, they could do much toward avoiding the danger; and in forming a band they lived away from the rest of the world. Gathering in those houses where no one had been ill and living was more comfortable, they shut themselves in.[52]

If these people believed that the plague would spare the righteous they were to be disappointed, as one of its defining features (and certainly one that was well represented in contemporary art) was its randomness, striking both good and evil alike.[53] Consequently, the second short-term response – to 'eat, drink and be merry, for tomorrow we die' – may have been more rational. According to Boccaccio, those who adopted this philosophy 'went from one tavern to another, drinking and carousing unrestrainedly ... they ran wild in other people's houses, and there was no one to prevent them, for everyone had abandoned all responsibility for his belongings as well as for

---

[50] J. Hatcher, 'England in the Aftermath', pp. 3–6, describes the historiography of opinion on this question very clearly.

[51] Hatcher's article (ibid.) is one of the most important of these attempts.

[52] G. Boccaccio, *The Decameron*, trans. F. Winwar (New York, Modern Library, 1955), pp. xxv–xxvi; quoted in R.S. Gottfried, *The Black Death: Natural and Human Disaster in Medieval Europe* (London, Robert Hale, 1983), p. 78.

[53] J. Robins, *The World's Greatest Disasters* (London, Hamlyn, 1990), p. 69.

himself'.[54] The third common response was simply to run away, generally towards remote country districts. Although this may have been an effective response in sixteenth- and seventeenth-century epidemics, in 1348–50 the spread of the disease was so rapid and universal that there were very few hiding places.

The psychological consequences of the plague also made themselves felt at the societal level, though there were curious inconsistencies in the collective response. A novel feature of the pestilence was that it appears to have spared no one. Whereas the better-off tend to escape the depredations of subsistence crises, they did not escape in 1348–50. As Bridbury has put it '[p]lague broke down the barriers of class as famine could never do. Famine spared the clergy. Plague did not.'[55] Thus the prevailing view that disease was a punishment for sin took something of a knock, as the plague struck apparently at random, carrying off the virtuous and unrighteous. This led to something of a preoccupation with the vicissitudes of fate. However, the 'disease as retribution' ideas were powerfully rooted in the common culture, and after the Black Death charitable gifts went up in both number and magnitude, suggesting that a belief in justification through good works was asserting itself in the teeth of the evidence.[56] More clearly, the reputation of the Church suffered for two reasons. First, the clergy failed to offer solace or spiritual comfort, indeed many were accused of fleeing, leaving the last rites unsaid and the dead unburied. Second, physicians were at this time generally trained by the Church. These physicians were impotent when faced with the plague, and the Church had to take its share of the blame.

4.7 How important was the Black Death for England's population history?

The question of the long-term impact of the arrival of plague in the fourteenth century on England's population history is one of the most difficult, but also one of the most fascinating, to try to answer. We have already alluded to the debate among historians about the significance of the Black Death, and pointed out that despite Hatcher's recent attempt to restore the plague's reputation as an autonomous agent of change, the tendency is still

---

[54] Boccaccio, *Decameron*, pp. xxv–xxvi.
[55] Ibid., p. 587.
[56] Two recent contributions that examine the influence of demographic crises on social regulation, revealing that disease and famine continued to be seen as a punishment for sin for several centuries after the Black Death, are B.A. Hanawalt, '"Good Governance" in the Medieval and early Modern Context', *Journal of British Studies* XXXVII (1998), pp. 246–57; and K. Jones and M. Zell, 'Bad Conversation? Gender and Social Control in a Kentish Borough, c. 1450–c. 1570', *Continuity and Change* XIII (1998), pp. 11–31.

to try to minimize its impact.[57] In demography, too, there is a long tradition of regarding epidemics and other mortality crises, however massive, as temporary exogenous shocks that do not have much impact on the demographic system in the long run.[58] There are good theoretical reasons for this, as models of population dynamics demonstrate both that populations can recover from mortality crises rather quickly, and that, unless the age distribution of the excess deaths is very unlike that of the afflicted population, changes in the age structure of the population are likely to be short-lived. Indeed, a good case can be made for arguing that the decline in fertility during, say, a famine, has a more easily discernible and longer-lasting impact on the population structure than the increased mortality.

However, there are two reasons for thinking that the Black Death was an event with a greater demographic significance than this. First, the plague of 1348–50 was only the first of many epidemics that were to strike the population of England at frequent intervals until the third quarter of the seventeenth century. It is clear that repeated mortality crises can have the effect of retarding population growth, and even preventing it altogether, even after accounting for the population's ability to recover.[59] The more frequent the crises, the less severe they have to be (in terms of percentage mortality) to achieve this end. The frequency and severity of plague epidemics during the second half of the fourteenth century was certainly enough to cause population decline, as even one of the commentators most sceptical about the long-term impact of plague has acknowledged.[60] The impact of epidemic disease on the demography of fifteenth-century England will be examined in Chapter 5.

Second, J. Goldberg makes an important point when he says that 'plague was not an autonomous agent of change, but worked in tandem with other processes'.[61] The Black Death of itself may not have had the impact that historians once believed, but the epidemic of 1348 marked the arrival of a new force to which the demographic and economic system of England had to adjust. The effect of the new force in the long run was to make it harder for the population to grow rapidly, and this change in the demographic environment had implications for the working of other economic and social processes during the next 300 years.

---

[57]   Hatcher, 'England in the Aftermath'.
[58]   A well-known exposition of this view, though with respect to famines rather than epidemics, is S.C. Watkins and J. Menken, 'Famines in Historical Perspective', *Population and Development Review* XI (1985), pp. 647–75.
[59]   This was the view of two critical commentaries on Watkins and Menken, 'Famines'; see A. Palloni, 'On the Role of Crises in Historical Perspective: an Exchange', *Population and Development Review* XIV (1988), pp. 145–58; and J. Komlos, 'On the Role of Crises in Historical Perspective', *Population and Development Review* XIV (1988), pp. 159–64.
[60]   J.M.W. Bean, 'Plague, Population and Economic Decline in the Later Middle Ages', *Economic History Review*, 2nd series XV (1963), p. 436.
[61]   Goldberg, 'Introduction', p. 13.

|5|

The population of England in the fifteenth century

5.1 The last 'dark age' of demography

The Middle Ages drew to a close during the fifteenth century, a century that is also the last for which the population history of England must be written without the benefit of a sustained and reliable source of data on population totals and the trend in fertility and mortality. The absence of both census-type listings and data on births and deaths means that even gross trends are still shrouded in uncertainty, and has fuelled a long and still unresolved debate among historians about even the most basic aspects of the demography of the period. Useful sources are not completely absent: muster rolls, for example, provide an indication of the numbers of males eligible to be called up for military service, from which an estimate of the total population can be made. Yet all the extant sources require considerable processing before they can be made to yield the required demographic information, and many of them survive only for particular places, the representativeness of which is open to question.

The dearth of information is all the more frustrating because recent research suggests that the fifteenth century was a pivotal period in the history of England's population, for it marked the point at which the medieval demographic regime was transformed into the early modern demographic regime.[1] In Part II of this book it will be argued that England's population during the sixteenth, seventeenth and early eighteenth centuries had distinctive characteristics that marked it out from those of contemporary pre-industrial populations, and even from other European populations of the time. To the extent that England's demography was different, it seems that its peculiarities may have begun to emerge sometime during the fifteenth century. In demographic terms, then, the century faced in two directions: backwards to the epidemic-ridden years that preceded it, but also forwards toward the Tudor and Stuart epochs.

---

[1] M. Bailey, 'Demographic Decline in Late Medieval England: some Thoughts on Recent Research', *Economic History Review*, 2nd series XLIX (1996), pp. 1–19.

Section 5.2 considers trends in population numbers, discussing the debate about whether the century was one of population recovery after the epidemics of the second half of the fourteenth century, or whether it was a period of continued population stagnation or decline. Section 5.3 examines the components of demographic change, focusing particularly on the role of mortality and mortality crises. Section 5.4 attempts to describe what seems to be the most plausible scenario, using population estimates that link the fifteenth century to the centuries that follow it.

5.2 Population trends: recovery or stagnation?

Nineteenth-century historians generally viewed the fifteenth century as a period of demographic recovery from the drama of the Black Death and subsequent epidemics. This view was almost entirely unsupported by evidence, direct or indirect, and owed a great deal to the Victorian belief in history as a story of human progress.[2] In demographic terms, progress meant population growth, and a state of growth was therefore taken to be the 'natural' state of the population. Epidemics and famines, of course, could produce short-term periods of population decline, but as soon as a mortality crisis had run its course, it was supposed that the population would resume its growth.

There was, however, a range of opinion about economic progress, even among Victorian historians. The debate about whether there was economic growth or economic decline in the post-Black Death period encompassed the fifteenth century as well, and rumbled on through the first few decades of the twentieth century. Chapter 4 described M.M. Postan's attempt to reconcile conflicting views on the fate of England's economy during the period after the Black Death by positing a scenario of 'stagnation . . . tinged with gloom'.[3] There was economic decline, but because of continued demographic decline, real incomes among the ordinary people were high.[4] Postan applied this argument not just to the second half of the fourteenth century, but to the fifteenth century as well. His evidence for a declining population during the fifteenth century was, as ever, indirect and economic in nature. First, agricultural wages were rising in nominal terms until the first decade

---

[2]   On this belief of the Victorians, see E.H. Carr, *What is History?* (Harmondsworth, Pelican, 1964), pp. 42–3.

[3]   J. Bolton, '"The World Upside Down": Plague as an Agent of Economic and Social Change', in W.M. Ormrod and P.G. Lindley (eds), *The Black Death in England* (Stamford, Paul Watkins, 1996), p. 19.

[4]   For Postan's argument, see M.M. Postan 'The fifteenth century', *Economic History Review* IX (1939), pp. 160–7; and M.M. Postan, 'Some Economic Evidence of Declining Population in the Later Middle Ages', *Economic History Review*, 2nd series II (1950), pp. 221–46.

of the century, whence they remained high and stable.[5] Since corn prices were simultaneously falling, moreover, real wages were rising more than nominal ones (Table 5.1).[6] Alternative accounts of rising agricultural wages, such as increasing output and the migration of labour from the countryside to the cities, can be discounted.[7] As Table 5.1 shows, the wages of urban craftsmen (which were higher than those of agricultural workers) rose in parallel with agricultural wages. This suggests that large-scale rural–urban migration did not occur, since, if it had, some convergence in agricultural and urban wage rates would have been expected. The conclusion is clear: 'Labour became dear because, relatively to other factors of production, it had become scarce, and a growing labour scarcity argues for a declining population.'[8]

This conclusion can be reinforced by evidence of declining land values and a declining area under cultivation.[9] Indeed, this evidence lies before our eyes today in the form of 'ridge and furrow' lands. Medieval ploughing techniques created long parallel 'ridges' separated by 'furrows'. The survival until the present of these ridges and furrows suggests that the land in question was cultivated in medieval times, but went out of cultivation

Table 5.1 Wage trends in England, 1350–1459

Decade	Agricultural wages in silver pence	Agricultural wages in wheat	Wages of artisans in silver pence	Wages of artisans in wheat
1350–59	100	100	100	100
1360–69	128	104	109	108
1370–79			116	
1380–89	141	159	113	140
1390–99			110	
1400–09	143	142	130	141
1410–19			121	
1420–29	143	135	118	134
1430–39			128	
1440–49	142	159	138	177
1450–59			141	
1460–69	141	149		
1470–79				

Note: 1350–59 = 100.

Source: M.M. Postan, 'Some Economic Evidence of Declining Population in the Later Middle Ages', *Economic History Review*, 2nd series, II (1950), pp. 226, 233.

[5]   Postan, 'Some Economic Evidence', pp. 225–6.
[6]   Ibid., pp. 225–6.
[7]   Ibid., pp. 229–36.
[8]   Ibid., p. 229.
[9]   Ibid., pp. 236–40.

afterwards and has not been cultivated in more recent times (modern ploughing techniques would have obliterated the ridges and furrows). Closer inspection of the location of fields containing 'ridge and furrow' reveals that most are on marginal lands – for example, land prone to flooding close to rivers, exactly the sort of land one would expect to have been first to be abandoned when the demand for corn fell.

Suppose that Postan is right. An extended period of population decline requires a net reproduction rate below 1.0 (see Box 3.1). This means either that fertility must have been low, or (more likely in late medieval England) that mortality was high. The contrast between the implied demographic situation in the fifteenth century and that in the twelfth and thirteenth centuries (when population growth seems to have been steady, if unspectacular) is striking. The need for high mortality relative to fertility was recognized by some historians who wanted to argue for demographic decline.[10] As long ago as 1941, John Saltmarsh argued that repeated epidemics of plague, which continued well into the fifteenth century, led to a 'continual sapping of the human resources of England', and were sufficient to account for the extended demographic depression.[11]

Saltmarsh's thesis was not accepted universally. J.M.W. Bean, for example, argued that plague was incapable of causing such heavy mortality after 1400. He based his argument on the apparent absence of pneumonic plague in the epidemics after the Black Death, the fact that many of the plague epidemics of the fifteenth century did not affect the whole of England, and that the plague increasingly became an urban phenomenon as the century progressed, whereas the vast majority of England's inhabitants lived in the countryside.[12] Plague epidemics after 1400, therefore, were simply not frequent or widespread enough to have caused a sustained fall in population numbers.[13] Since no obvious cause of population decline could be found, and there was, indeed, no direct demographic evidence that a sustained

---

[10]   Postan is uncharacteristically reticent to ascribe the prolonged downturn to any single cause. He is not surprised that most historians lay the blame on the pestilence, but retains a belief that long swings of population growth and decline can occur in the absence of external shocks through the population-resource system. The fourteenth century, he says, would have been an era of demographic decline even had the Black Death not appeared. However, this era of decline could, under 'normal' circumstances 'be expected to correct itself by its own inherent momentum . . . in the second half of the fourteenth and in the fifteenth centuries'. That it did not, Postan thinks, is due to 'a variety of causes', including 'the continual inability of men to repair the damage done to the land in previous generations', and 'the recurrent plagues'; see M.M. Postan, *The Medieval Economy and Society: an Economic History of Britain in the Middle Ages* (Harmondsworth, Penguin, 1975), pp. 42–4.

[11]   J. Saltmarsh, 'Plague and Economic Decline in the Later Middle Ages', *Cambridge Historical Journal* VII (1941), p. 40.

[12]   J.M.W. Bean, 'Plague, Population and Economic Decline in England in the Later Middle Ages', *Economic History Review*, 2nd series, XV (1963), pp. 426–31. Of course, if a disease other than plague was responsible for the great mortalities of the fourteenth century, then the apparent absence of pneumonic plague is no longer a relevant issue.

[13]   Ibid., p. 435.

decline took place at all, Bean suggested that historians have misinterpreted the economic evidence for population decline, certainly for the later part of the century. The truth, he said, may have been that the population began to increase again.

5.3 Disease and mortality

A difficulty with the debate described in the previous section was that the protagonists were poorly equipped with empirical evidence, either about the population totals or about the components of population change: fertility, mortality and migration. Yet there are sources that can be made to yield such data, particularly about mortality. In this section we describe two attempts to produce 'hard' demographic data: the calculation of replacement rates from data on heirs to property; and the use of monastery records to estimate the mortality of monks.

Bean's scepticism about long-term population decline receives support from work on the inquisitions *post mortem* by T. Hollingsworth and J.C. Russell.[14] These inquisitions were held on the death of tenants-in-chief 'to provide royal officials with accurate evidence in dealing with certain types of feudal income'.[15] Part of the process involved ascertaining the age of the deceased man's heir (or heiress).[16] Using these data Hollingsworth and Russell calculated male replacement rates (see Box 3.1) for various periods during the 150 years after the Black Death. Their results have been synthesized by John Hatcher, and they suggest that replacement rates were below 1.0 until about the middle of the fifteenth century, but rose to levels slightly above 1.0 in the periods 1441–65 and 1466–90.[17] Of course, calculations of this kind suffer from the problem that tenants-in-chief may not have been representative of the population as a whole.

Direct estimates of mortality during the fifteenth century have been made using the records of two monasteries, at Christ Church, Canterbury, and Westminster Abbey. The Canterbury data give the names of all the monks from 1395 until 1505, the dates they entered the priory, and the dates of their death or departure.[18] John Hatcher, whose analysis of these data we draw on in this section, produces evidence from other sources that the age at entry to priory of these monks was likely to have been around 18 years,

---

[14] T. Hollingsworth, *Historical Demography* (London, Hodder & Stoughton, 1969), pp. 375–80; J.C. Russell, *British Medieval Population* (Albuquerque, University of New Mexico Press, 1948), pp. 240–2.

[15] Russell, *British Medieval Population*, p. 94.

[16] Ibid., p. 94.

[17] J. Hatcher, *Plague, Population and the English Economy 1348–1530* (London, Macmillan, 1977), p. 27.

[18] J. Hatcher, 'Mortality in the Fifteenth Century: some New Evidence', *Economic History Review*, 2nd series, XXXIX (1986), p. 23.

and not to have varied greatly.[19] Armed with this information, it is possible to produce not only annual series of numbers of deaths, but also to calculate life tables from age 18 years upwards (see Box 5.1), and hence to estimate the expectation of life at 20 years. As Hatcher says of the data, 'it is unlikely that many series of comparable quality will ever emerge'.[20] There is at least one other, however: the set of data from Westminster Abbey, which has been analysed by Barbara Harvey.[21] What is striking, and rather convincing, about these two sources is that they tell a very similar story about fifteenth-century mortality.

Box 5.1 Linking mortality estimates to population growth in fifteenth-century England

Analysis of many different sets of mortality rates from populations across the world has revealed obvious regularities in the age pattern of mortality, in the relationship of male-to-female mortality, and in the way the age pattern of mortality changes as the overall level of mortality rises and falls. Generally speaking, mortality is high in infancy and childhood, falls to a low point around age ten years, and then increases slowly at first, but more rapidly at ages over 40–50 years. Where the level of mortality is high, infant and child mortality contributes a great proportion of all deaths, but as the overall level falls, these infant and child deaths decline disproportionately, such that at low mortality levels, the mortality of infants and young children is not much greater than that of older children and adults aged under 40 years. In most populations, female mortality is slightly lower than that of males.

A *life table* is simply a description of the mortality experience of a population. It lists, for each exact age, the proportion of the persons who were born who would still be alive, under a given set of death rates at each age. Because of the regularities in the age pattern of mortality, demographers have provided sets of *model life tables* for a range of levels of mortality (defined on the basis of expectation of life at birth). Various sets of model life tables exist, and, because the age pattern of mortality does exhibit some limited variation between populations, most sets have several 'variants' to take account of this. The well-known set published in A.J. Coale and P. Demeny, *Regional*

---

[19] Ibid., pp. 26–7.
[20] Ibid., p. 22.
[21] B.F. Harvey, *Living and Dying in England 1100–1540: the Monastic Experience* (Oxford, Clarendon Press, 1993).

Model Life Tables and Stable Populations (2nd edn) (New York, Academic Press, 1983), for example, has four 'variants' (called 'north', 'south', 'east' and 'west').

To work out the fertility required to give various rates of population growth in fifteenth-century England, the stages in the calculation are as follows:

1. find the model life table that fits the expectation of life for males at age 20 years best, and note its expectation of life at birth
2. use the expectation of life at birth to find a corresponding model for females in the set of model life tables, and, from this model, evaluate the probability of a new-born girl surviving to age 28 years (see Box 3.1)
3. use the method described in Box 3.1 to find the total fertility rate required to achieve a net reproduction rate (NRR) of 1.0 under this mortality regime.

An example will help to illustrate the method. A constant population implies a net reproduction rate (NRR) of 1.0. From Box 3.1, the NRR is defined as the average completed family size, or total fertility rate (TFR) x 100/205 x l_{28}, where l_{28} is the proportion of women surviving to age 28. Rearranging this produces a formula for calculating the TFR from the NRR, which is TFR = (205/100) x (NRR/l_{28}). Now, if NRR = 1.0, the TFR can be calculated for any value of l_{28}. According to John Hatcher ('Mortality in the Fifteenth Century: some New Evidence', *Economic History Review*, 2nd series, XXXIX (1986), p. 32) the data from Christ Church, Canterbury, corresponded roughly to level 3 of Coale and Demeny's model 'west' life tables, which implies that l_{28} was about 0.4 (Coale and Demeny, *Regional Model Life Tables*, p. 43). The corresponding TFR that is associated with an NRR of 1.0 is, then, equal to (205/100) x (1/0.4), which is 5.1.

According to Hatcher's analysis, mortality during the century in Christ Church, Canterbury, fell into two phases. Until about 1450 the crude death rate (deaths per 1000 monks per year) fluctuated considerably, from below 20 per thousand in 'good' years to over 40 per thousand in 'bad' years, the 'average' being around 25–30 per thousand.[22] However, only twice between 1395 and 1450 did the death rate exceed 60 per thousand.[23] During the second half of the century, there were several years in which the crude death

---

[22] Hatcher, 'Mortality', p. 26.
[23] Ibid., p. 26.

rate rose to well above 60 per thousand, including 1457 (close to 200 per thousand), 1471, 1485 and 1504.[24] Harvey's study of Westminster Abbey reveals a cluster of crisis years between 1499 and 1508, with typical peaks of mortality in the late summer and autumn.[25] The seasonal pattern of mortality (Figure 5.1), supported by documentary evidence, suggests that the 1471 crisis was due to plague (as was, probably, that of 1457), whereas the 1485 peak was caused by the 'sweating sickness'.[26] This mysterious, but virulent, disease struck several times between 1485 and the mid-sixteenth century.[27] Contemporary reports suggest that it could cause death within a few hours, and that the disease had a marked pulmonary component.[28] Indeed, there are some similarities between it and the influenza that caused the 1918 epidemic (see Chapter 12).

Hatcher calculates that the average expectation of life at age 20 years for these monks between 1395 and 1505 was 28 years.[29] However, it was generally over 30 years for monks who entered the priory before 1435, and fell to less than 25 years among those entering the priory after about 1450.[30] This pattern is mirrored by that of Westminster Abbey, in which monks entering the Abbey during the last quarter of the century had expectations of life at age 20 years some ten years lower than those entering between 1395 and 1419.[31] The expectations of life calculated by Hatcher imply very high rates of mortality by any known standards (see Box 5.1).[32] They are similar to the values reported for the period around 1300 in Chapter 3, and that period is thought to be one of particularly high mortality, high enough to bring population growth to a halt. Moreover, it might be argued that because the monks are not representative of the population as a whole, the ordinary people might have experienced even higher levels.[33]

It is worth asking what rate of child-bearing would be required to sustain population growth under such ferocious mortality conditions. To answer

---

[24] Ibid., p. 26.

[25] Bolton, 'World Upside Down', p. 30.

[26] Hatcher, 'Mortality', pp. 28–31.

[27] The last outbreak was in 1551, and has been analysed in detail in A. Dyer, 'The English Sweating Sickness of 1551: an Epidemic Anatomized', *Medical History* XLI, pp. 362–84. Dyer's analysis is able to take advantage of the existence, by 1551, of parish registers of burials, a source unavailable before 1538 (see Appendix II).

[28] M. Taviner, G. Thwaites and V. Gant, 'The English Sweating Sickness, 1485–1551: a Viral Pulmonary Disease?' *Medical History* XLII (1998), pp. 96–8.

[29] Hatcher, 'Mortality', p. 28.

[30] Ibid., p. 28.

[31] Bolton, 'World Upside Down', p. 30.

[32] Hatcher, 'Mortality', pp. 31–2.

[33] Hatcher discusses this issue in detail (ibid., pp. 33–6) and suggests that it is not obvious that the mortality of the monks was lower than that of ordinary people. Nevertheless, the case for high mortality being responsible for the delay in demographic recovery during the fifteenth century only requires that mortality among ordinary people was not appreciably lower than that reported for the monks, and this seems plausible.

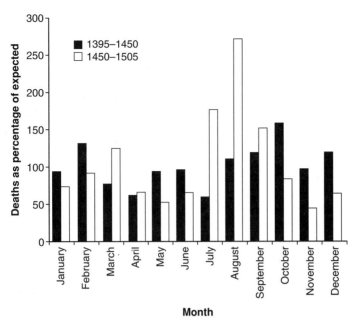

Figure 5.1 The seasonal pattern of mortality among the monks of Christ Church, Canterbury, 1395–1505

Notes: This graph plots the number of deaths in each month expressed as an index, which takes the value 100 if the observed number of deaths is equal to the number that would be expected if deaths were evenly distributed over the year. A value of 200, therefore, means that there were twice as many deaths in the corresponding month as would have been expected under the assumption of evenly distributed mortality. Some deaths due to 'sweating sickness' in September and October of 1485 have been omitted: including them would raise the values for the index for September and October during the period 1450–1505.
Source: J. Hatcher, 'Mortality in the Fifteenth Century: some New Evidence', *Economic History Review*, 2nd series XXXIX (1986), p. 26.

this question, two sets of calculations are needed. The first converts the mortality results for males over 20 years to mortality results for the whole population (both sexes, all ages). Conventionally this is done using what are called *model life tables* (see Box 5.1).[34] The results suggest that the expectation of life at birth for males in fifteenth-century England was, on average, just under 23 years, but that during the second half of the century it may have been below 20 years.[35] For females, it is likely that the expectation of life at birth was two or three years more than that of males. These are very low figures, much lower than those in sixteenth- and seventeenth-century

34 A.J. Coale and P. Demeny, *Regional Model Life Tables and Stable Populations* (2nd edn) (New York, Academic Press, 1983).
35 Hatcher, 'Mortality', p. 32.

England, and much lower than any large population in the world today.[36] A potential problem with this approach is that it assumes that infant and child mortality in fifteenth-century England bore a similar relationship to adult mortality as that obtaining in much later centuries, and we have little evidence for or against such an assumption.[37]

The second set of calculations applies demographic theory, using the 'whole population' mortality estimates to work out the rates of fertility required to produce different growth rates (see Box 5.1). The results suggest that during the early fifteenth century, the average woman would have had to have borne more than five children merely to maintain the population at a constant level. To achieve growth at 0.5 per cent per year, an average family size of almost six children would have been required.[38] This is close to the maximum prevailing today in any large population. If Hatcher's mortality figures for the second half of the century are to be believed, then even to avoid population decline, an average family size of 6.4 would have been needed. The clear implication of this is that the punishing rates of mortality the fifteenth century brought were probably the main reason for the failure of the population to grow. These mortality rates were the product, principally, of epidemic diseases, of which plague was by no means the only one. Hatcher mentions tuberculosis and other pulmonary infections as being important.[39] William Langland's description of the late fourteenth century as an age of

> fevres and fluxes,
> Coughes, and cardiacles, crampes and tothaches
> Rewmes and radegoundes and roynouse scalles,
> Byles, and bocches and brennnyng agues;
> Frenesyes, and foule yveles . . .
> . . . pokkes and pestilences[40]

could, therefore, equally well be applied throughout the century that follows.

5.4 Conclusion

English population change in the fifteenth century has been the subject of such protracted debate because of the lack of source material about either stocks or flows in the population (See Appendix I). The apparently clear

---

[36] Ibid., p. 32.
[37] M. Ecclestone, 'Mortality of Rural Landless Men before the Black Death: the Glastonbury Head-Tax Lists', *Local Population Studies* LXIII (1999), pp. 21–2.
[38] A growth rate of 0.5 per cent per year implies a net reproduction rate of 1.15. Using the formula described in Box 5.1, this leads to a TFR of 5.9.
[39] Hatcher, *Plague, Population*, p. 58.
[40] Ibid., p. 58. The quotation is from *Piers Plowman*, B Text, Passus XX, pp. 80–4, 97.

conclusions of the previous section are by no means definitive, as there are still ambiguities and difficulties with the evidence and its interpretation. For example, Hatcher's research on Christ Church, Canterbury, sits rather ill with his earlier view that the population decline was slowing and 'perhaps even being reversed' in the decade 1475–1485 or 'perhaps even earlier'.[41] For the mortality trends revealed in Canterbury suggest precisely the opposite: that the population decline should have accelerated about this time. Moreover, there is the awkward fact that the monastery data tell a different story from the inquisitions *post mortem*. One day, it may be possible to resolve some of these difficulties by using mortality data from a wider variety of populations, though extracting such information is likely to be a very slow and painstaking process.

However, it may be that a definitive description of mortality trends during the fifteenth century is unnecessary in order to reach a conclusion about overall population trends. Experience from a variety of contemporary populations suggests that average family sizes of around six children can only be achieved under conditions where marriage for women is almost universal and takes place at a young age (below 20 years). Was this true of fifteenth-century England? Although we do not know for certain, there are tantalizing fragments of evidence, which tend to suggest that marriage was delayed for both men and women until sometime in their twenties.[42] If this was so, and if the mortality rates in Canterbury are anything like the true ones, then there seems little doubt that the population would have struggled to grow at all during the century. This view is supported by the fact that L.R. Poos' study of fifteenth-century Essex produced a crude birth rate of only around 30 per thousand, whereas, according to demographic theory, if the expectation of life at birth is less than 25 years, a crude birth rate of over 40 per thousand would be required simply to maintain population numbers.[43] It is true that in Essex, it seems that the mortality regime was not quite so severe as this: Poos concludes that an expectation of life at birth of 32–34 years is 'the closest one is likely to get' to a 'realistic estimate'.[44] Nevertheless, a crude birth rate of 30 per thousand, and an expectation of life at birth of, say, 33 years are consistent with population numbers being roughly constant from year to year.[45] It seems, therefore, that the conditions in England

[41] Hatcher, *Plague, Population*, p. 63.
[42] Bolton, 'World Upside Down', pp. 34–40.
[43] L.R. Poos, *A Rural Society after the Black Death: Essex 1350–1525* (Cambridge, Cambridge University Press, 1990), p. 126.
[44] Ibid., p. 119.
[45] Demographic theory shows that in a *stationary population* (one in which the number of births each year is the same as the number of deaths), the crude birth rate is equal to the reciprocal of the expectation of life at birth (e_0). A crude birth rate of 30 per thousand would thus, if the population were stationary, equate to an e_0 of $1/0.030 = 33.3$ years. This, and the fact that Poos' estimates of the crude birth rate and e_0 were derived from separate sources suggests quite strongly that the population of late medieval Essex was approximately stationary, with a growth rate of zero.

between the Black Death and the end of the fifteenth century were much less favourable to population growth than they had been during the twelfth and thirteenth centuries.

When, then, did the period of demographic stagnation following the Black Death finally end? To answer this question, it is helpful to look forward into the sixteenth century, for from 1520 onwards, estimates of the total population start to become available. The muster rolls of 1522 and a set of tax assessments for 1524–25 can be used to provide the first snapshot of the English population since 1377. Both sources present difficulties considerably greater than the Poll Tax, but according to E.A. Wrigley and R.S. Schofield, they produce an estimate of 2.2 or 2.3 million for the early 1520s.[46] From 1541 onwards, Wrigley and Schofield's own estimates of the population trend in England become available. The method by which these were made is described in Appendix II; suffice to say here that they are probably more reliable than any estimate for any year during the medieval period. Wrigley and Schofield's figure for 1541 is 2.77 million.[47] This is still lower than the estimate for 1377 made using Postan's preferred assumptions, but is somewhat higher than Russell's estimate for 1377. Suppose we allow that the population of late fifteenth- and early sixteenth-century England could have grown at 0.5 per cent per year. Then a little arithmetic shows that even if we take a very low estimate of the population at its post-1348 nadir (say 2.0 million, which is even lower than Russell's figure of 2.1 million for 1430), this nadir could have been reached as late as 1510.[48] The evidence from fifteenth-century mortality trends, combined with these early sixteenth-century population estimates, points rather clearly to the conclusion that England's population was, at best, stagnant during the whole of the fifteenth century, and probably did not begin to recover until at least the second decade of the sixteenth century.

---

[46]   E.A. Wrigley and R.S. Schofield, *The Population History of England, 1541–1871: a Reconstruction* (London, Edward Arnold, 1981), p. 568.
[47]   Ibid., p. 531.
[48]   Russell, *British Medieval Population*, p. 270.

Appendix I
Sources and methods for learning about the population of medieval England

AI.1 Introduction and overview

Demography relies principally on two types of data. The first concerns population *stocks*, or the numbers and characteristics of the persons living in a place at a particular time; since the nineteenth century such data have been furnished principally by population censuses. The second concerns the *flows* of people into and out of the population through births, deaths, immigration and emigration. In modern times vital registration provides data on births and deaths, and a variety of other surveys is used to measure migration.

There were no population censuses in medieval England, neither were there continuous records of vital events (births, marriages and deaths). Therefore historians are obliged to make use of other documents. Although none of these was designed to provide information about population totals, or numbers of births and deaths, they may be made to yield such data with a bit of ingenuity. Two sources, the Domesday survey of 1086 and the Poll Tax of 1377, provide information about almost the whole of the English population (the 'stock') in those years. Manorial court records, on the other hand, have been used (laboriously) to chart the evolution both of stocks and flows in a particular place over a series of years. Other sources – dealing, for example, with taxation – are more patchy in their survival and difficult to use, but can provide more limited data of a similar kind, often restricted to specific areas.

This Appendix is designed to provide a brief introduction to this body of source material. It makes no claim to be comprehensive. Within the limited space available, I have concentrated on those sources referred to in the text, and aim to explain how the numbers quoted by various authorities have been arrived at. It is hoped that this will provide readers with sufficient background information to enable them to ask questions of the various estimates, and draw their own conclusions about the range of plausible demographic scenarios in medieval England. Section AI.2 describes the Domesday survey and should be read as background material for Chapter 2. Section AI.3 considers the fourteenth-century Poll Taxes, which play a central role in Chapter 3. Section AI.4 describes the manorial and other records that are referred to from time to time in Chapters 3, 4 and 5.

AI.2 The Domesday survey

The Domesday survey of 1086 is often called 'Domesday Book', but in fact it was compiled in the form of several books. The so-called 'Great Domesday' covers most of England; a separate book called 'Little Domesday' covers Essex, Suffolk and Norfolk; and entries for certain other places (such as Winchester) appear in additional 'books'. It is not clear exactly why it was written, but it was probably partly to discover the actual and potential tax revenues the land could provide for the exchequer, and partly to establish exactly who held what land, as there were numerous long-running disputes as to title.[1] An original manuscript is stored in the Public Record Office in London, but there are many facsimiles available, usually published separately by county, with translations of the medieval Latin in which the original was written.[2]

One of the most attractive features of 'Domesday Book' from the point of view of historical demographers is that most of the entries follow a standard form, giving the same kind of information. Here, for example, is a translation of two entries that relate to areas of the Wylye valley in south Wiltshire.

Land of Odo and others of the King's Thegns
Suain holds Stapleford. His father held it in the time of King Edward and it paid geld for 10½ hides. There is land for 10 ploughs. In demesne there are 2 ploughs with 1 serf; and there are 17 villeins and 10 bordars with 8 ploughs. There are 2 mills paying 30s., and 40 acres of meadow. The pasture is ½ league long and as much broad. The wood(land) is 1 league long and ½ broad. It is worth £12.[3]

---

[1]   A good general introduction to the Domesday survey is R. Welldon Finn, *Domesday Book: a Guide* (London, Phillimore, 1973).
[2]   The most widely used of these is the county series published by Phillimore under the general editorship of John Morris. There is one volume for each of the counties surveyed in 1086. See, for example, J. Munby (ed.), *Domesday Book: Vol. 4, Hampshire* (Chichester, Phillimore, 1982); and F. Thorn and C. Thorn (eds), *Domesday Book: Vol. 16, Worcestershire* (Chichester, Phillimore, 1982). In addition, information about particular places is available on the Internet. Useful websites include http://www.domesdaybook.co.uk, which has a list of all the places mentioned in the Domesday survey.
[3]   R.B. Pugh and E. Crittall (eds), *A History of Wiltshire* (London, Oxford University Press, 1955), II, p. 133.

Land of the Count of Mortain

The Count himself holds Langeford. Chatel held it in the time of King Edward and it paid geld for 5 hides. There is land for 2½ ploughs. Of this land there are in demesne 4 hides and 1 virgate of land and there are 2 ploughs. There are 2 villeins and 4 bordars with ½ plough. There is ½ mill paying 30d., and there are 20 acres of meadow land and 30 acres of pasture. It was and is worth 100s.[4]

A few points in the extracts above are worth clarifying.

- 'King Edward' was Edward the Confessor, who reigned from 1042–66.
- '. . . it paid geld for 10½ hides'. *Geld* was a form of tax. A *hide* was an area of land of variable extent, but commonly 120 acres, reckoned to be about enough for a household to live on.
- 'There is land for 10 ploughs.' By a *plough* is meant a team of oxen who would draw the plough. Since the amount of land one team could plough in a year was limited, a plough was, in effect, a measure of the amount of arable land in the place. Peasants would combine to put together plough teams. It seems that the two villeins and four bordars in Langeford could only muster half a plough between them.
- 'In demesne'. The *demesne* was the land farmed directly by the lord (Suain in the case of Stapleford, the Count of Mortain in Langeford) using labour from serfs or labour services extracted from villeins. In Stapleford, it seems that about 20 per cent of the arable land was farmed directly, with the other 80 per cent being held by villeins. In Langeford the percentages were exactly reversed (two out of two and a half 'ploughlands' were in demesne).
- '1 virgate of land'. A *virgate* was a measure of land area, probably equivalent to about 30 acres (or a quarter of a hide).
- 'The pasture is ½ league long'. A *league* was a unit of distance, of varying length, but commonly about three miles.
- 'There is ½ mill paying 30d.'. Langeford was beside the river. The mill was probably shared between it and the settlement on the opposite bank, which explains how Langeford could be recorded as possessing '½ mill'. It seems that, for the Domesday survey, the revenue to be obtained from this mill and its allocation between the two landholdings on either bank of the river were what mattered.

Now, consider what this extract tells us about the population of Stapleford. First, the number of people mentioned as being in Stapleford in 1086 is 28: '17 villeins', '10 bordars' and '1 serf'. Though Suain 'held Stapleford', it is not clear that he lived there. He may have held other land

---

4   Pugh and Crittall, *History of Wiltshire*, p. 165.

(and lived) elsewhere. In the terms of Table 2.1, Suain was a sub-tenant, whereas Odo (mentioned in the first line of the extract) was a tenant-in-chief. The process of estimating the population of England in 1086, therefore, begins with those persons recorded as being resident in each place. In Stapleford there were '17 villeins and 10 bordars', who may be presumed to have been heads of household. The chosen household size multiplier is applied to these. The 'serf' might also have been a head of household, but it is possible that he was not. In the terminology of Table 2.1, the 'serf' is a slave. Because it is not certain where tenants-in-chief and sub-tenants lived, they are treated separately in the calculations. Finally, some addition for omitted persons must be made.

The results of calculations of this kind for Stapleford and some neighbouring Wiltshire villages are shown in Table AI.1. The table shows likely minimum and maximum values for the population in 1086. Depending on the household size multiplier chosen, the treatment of the 'serf', and the proportion of the population assumed to have been missed in the survey, the population of Stapleford in 1086 could have been anywhere between 100 and 168, though a figure towards the higher end of this range seems most likely.

Although Domesday Book is a remarkably straightforward document to use compared with most other medieval sources, it is not without its difficulties. Some of these have already been mentioned. One additional problem, especially acute for regional or local demographers, is that it is not always easy to match Domesday places to present-day localities. For example, the present-day Wiltshire hamlet of Hanging Langford (Table AI.1) seems to be divided into two in the Domesday survey, the two parts being held by different persons and therefore appearing many pages apart (one of the Domesday entries is that translated above). Some present-day villages appear not to be mentioned in Domesday Book at all. Two miles to the north of Stapleford is the village of Berwick St James. It is impossible to identify any entries in the Domesday survey that relate to Berwick St James, yet it seems unlikely that there was no settlement within the area of the modern parish.

AI.3 The fourteenth-century Poll Taxes

The first of the fourteenth-century Poll Taxes was levied by King Edward III in 1377 in order to fund the long and expensive Hundred Years War with France. Everyone, male and female, aged 14 years or over was liable to pay one groat (about 1½p).[5] The only exceptions were the beneficed clergy, who

---

[5]   According to J.C. Russell, *British Medieval Population* (Albuquerque, University of New Mexico Press, 1948), p. 121, one groat was 'slightly more than a day's wage at the current rate of pay for ordinary farm labour'.

Table AI.1 Estimates of the populations of certain Wiltshire villages in 1086 and 1377

Village	Domesday population in 1086		Population in 1377	
	Assuming a multiplier of 3.5, treating slaves as individuals, and adding 5 per cent for omissions	Assuming a multiplier of 5.0, treating slaves as heads of household, and adding 20 per cent for omissions	Assuming that one-third of the population were aged under 14 years, and that 5 per cent of the population were under-enumerated	Assuming that 45 per cent of the population were aged under 14 years, and that 22.5 per cent of the population were under-enumerated
Hanging Langford	48	78	137	194
Little Langford	63	102	50	71
Stapleford	100	168	140	198
Steeple Langford	44	72	131	185

Notes: In the 1377 populations, no addition has been made for clergy and 'mendicant friars'.
Sources: R.B. Pugh and E. Crittall (eds), *A History of Wiltshire* (London, Oxford University Press, 1955), II, pp. 124, 130, 133, 139–40, 151, 165; M.W. Beresford, 'Poll-Tax Payers of 1377', in E. Crittall (ed.), *A History of Wiltshire* (London, Oxford University Press, 1959), IV, p. 308.

were to pay one shilling (equal to three groats, or 5p), and beggars and 'mendicant friars' (monks who begged for a living), who were exempt completely.[6]

The 1377 Poll Tax was collected on a county and borough basis. Each county or borough appointed *sub-collectors* who, according to J.C. Russell, went from house to house and from street to street collecting one groat from each inhabitant aged 14 or over.[7] The sub-collectors, 'when they had finished their collection, handed their money over to the collectors of the county and received an indenture as a receipt for the sum. . . . Many hundreds of the latter still remain.'[8] After a time, 'the reports of both the county and borough collectors were enrolled at the central office. . . . The enrollment has no obvious arrangement, although it may be that of order of appearance at the Exchequer.'[9] This 'Great Enrollment' forms the basis of

[6]   M.W. Beresford, 'The Poll Taxes of 1377, 1379 and 1381', *Amateur Historian* III (1958), p. 271.
[7]   Russell, *British Medieval Population*, p. 122.
[8]   Ibid., pp. 122–3.
[9]   Ibid., p. 131.

most attempts to work out the total population of England in 1377. The great advantage of the 1377 Poll Tax was its flat-rate nature, which means that the population of each county and borough can be simply worked out from the amount collected, once additions to take account of the proportion of the population that was aged under 14 years, and the proportion who escaped paying the tax for one reason or another, have been made.

Two further Poll Taxes were granted by Parliament to Edward III's successor, Richard II, in 1379 and 1381. Unlike the first, these were levied using a sliding scale, so that the better off paid more. Unfortunately, this did not mean that the poor paid less, as, compared with 1377, the sliding scale slid only upwards. In 1379 the 'average' payment was to be two groats per person, and in 1381 it was three groats per head, with a minimum of one groat. Public resistance to these increased impositions may have been one reason for the amount of evasion of the Poll Taxes of 1379 and 1381, which is thought to have been much greater than it was in 1377.[10] Discontent with the Poll Taxes is also regarded by many historians to have been a factor precipitating the Peasants' Revolt of 1381.[11]

In order to use the 1377 returns to estimate the population of England, two assumptions have to be made. The first relates to what proportion of the population was aged under 14. Russell assumes that it was one-third, implying that the 'taxed population' must be multiplied by 1.5 to obtain the total population. M.M. Postan, however, considers that 45 per cent of the people may have been aged under 14, implying a multiplier of about 1.8.[12] Under normal circumstances, we might appeal to demographic theory to help assess the plausibility of these estimates, but 1377, when England had experienced three major plague epidemics during the previous 16 years, was hardly 'normal circumstances'.[13]

The second assumption relates to the proportion who evaded paying the tax, or who did pay, but who are under-enumerated in the extant records. Again, Russell arrives at a very low figure of 2.5 per cent, whereas Postan prefers a much higher figure of 25 per cent.[14] Here, we can make some comment on these two extremes. Russell's figure is arrived at by a rather tortuous calculation involving the proportions of sums handed over to the

10   Beresford, 'Poll Taxes', p. 273.
11   See, for example, E. Powell, *The Rising in East Anglia in 1381* (Cambridge, Cambridge University Press, 1896).
12   M.M. Postan, *The Medieval Economy and Society: an Economic History of Britain in the Middle Ages* (Harmondsworth, Penguin, 1975), p. 33.
13   'Normal circumstances', in this context, means that birth and death rates have been roughly constant for a lengthy period. This is clearly not true of England in 1377, but, if we are prepared to ignore this point, R.M. Smith, 'Plagues and Peoples: the Long Demographic Cycle, 1250–1670', in P. Slack and R. Ward (eds), *The Peopling of Britain: the Shaping of a Human Landscape* (Oxford, Oxford University Press, 2002), pp. 178–9, has shown that the demographic models produce a plausible range for the proportion of persons aged under 14 in 1377 of 32–45 per cent.
14   Ibid., pp. 32–3.

collectors that were 'even shillings', or multiples of ten shillings (that is, they appear to have been rounded down by the sub-collectors).[15] In fact, his method can only possibly detect the proportion who did pay, but who are under-enumerated in the extant records (probably because of fraud on the part of the sub-collectors), and is likely to underestimate even this.[16] As Russell himself admits, 'it naturally does not include the people missed by accident or because they were too poor'.[17]

All in all, it seems that the deficiencies of Russell's method of working out the degree of non-payment are so great that we must disregard his figure of just over 2.5 per cent, and admit that it is almost certainly an underestimate.[18] Table AI.2, accordingly, which presents 'lower' and 'upper' estimates of the population of England by county in 1377, uses a minimum percentage of non-payment of 5 per cent. Totalling the county estimates produces a figure between 2.15 million and 3.03 million. To this must be added a correction to take account of the number of beneficed clergy and 'mendicant friars', and for the counties of Cheshire and Durham, which are not included in the 'Great Enrollment', because they had their own tax-collecting system.[19] Russell thinks that an addition of around 60,000 taxpayers is appropriate to account for these.[20] A further correction then needs to be made for persons under 14 in Cheshire and Durham, and the untaxed in those counties.[21] Using the 'minimum' and 'maximum' assumptions in Table AI.2, this brings the total to be added to between 78,000 and 97,000, making a total population in England in 1377 of between about 2.2 million and 3.1 million. Similar calculations have been made to estimate the populations of the Wiltshire villages listed in Table AI.1 in 1377.

---

[15] Russell, *British Medieval Population*, pp. 124–30.

[16] Since three groats made one shilling, Russell (ibid., pp. 124–30) reasoned that fraud could be detected by working out the proportion of sums handed over that were 'even shillings' (the sub-collectors having pocketed the odd groats). His calculation effectively amounts to working out the difference between the proportion of sums actually handed over that are 'even shillings' or multiples of, say, ten shillings, and the proportion that would be expected if there had been no fraud. Finding a significant excess of 'even shillings' (pp. 127–8), he then 'adds back' the minimum amount of money needed to make the distribution of what he calls 'terminal groats' (i.e. the proportion of sums that are 'even shillings') indistinguishable from one that should have obtained in the absence of fraud. The first problem with this is that it assumes that fraudulent sub-collectors were stupid enough to hand over suspiciously 'rounded' amounts. The second is that Russell only 'adds back' the minimum possible amount, and he cannot be sure that fraud was more blatant than is implied by this.

[17] Russell, *British Medieval Population*, p. 130.

[18] The results of Russell's calculations produce an estimated underpayment of 2.68 per cent (ibid., p. 130). To be fair, he eventually settles on an addition of 5 per cent 'for indigent and untaxed persons' (p. 146), but even this seems far too low.

[19] Ibid., p. 144.

[20] Ibid., p. 146.

[21] Russell (ibid., p. 146) appears to make this correction for clergy and 'mendicant friars' as well as the 'ordinary' people of Cheshire and Durham. However, since clergy and 'mendicant friars' are unlikely to have borne many children, this seems unnecessary. Moreover, the question of estimating the proportion of non-payment among 'mendicant friars' should not arise, as these were exempt anyway.

Table AI.2 Estimates of England's population by county, 1377

County	Taxed population	'Low' estimate of actual population	'High' estimate of actual population
Bedfordshire	20,339	32,034	45,301
Berkshire	22,723	35,789	50,610
Buckinghamshire	24,672	38,859	54,951
Cambridgeshire	30,974	48,784	68,988
Cornwall	34,274	53,982	76,338
Cumberland	12,519	19,717	27,883
Derbyshire	24,289	38,255	54,098
Devon	52,538	82,747	117,016
Dorset	33,251	52,370	74,059
Essex	50,917	80,914	113,406
Gloucestershire	45,344	71,417	100,993
Hampshire (including Isle of Wight)	40,566	63,891	90,352
Herefordshire	17,221	27,123	38,356
Hertfordshire	19,975	31,461	44,490
Huntingdonshire	14,169	22,317	31,558
Kent	59,701	94,029	132,970
Lancashire	23,880	37,611	53,187
Leicestershire	33,832	53,285	75,353
Lincolnshire	95,119	149,812	211,856
Middlesex	34,557	54,427	76,968
Norfolk	97,817	154,062	217,865
Northamptonshire	41,702	65,681	92,882
Northumberland	16,807	26,471	37,434
Nottinghamshire	28,885	45,494	64,335
Oxfordshire	27,339	43,059	60,891
Rutland	5,994	9,441	13,350
Shropshire	26,828	42,254	59,753
Somerset	56,074	88,317	124,892
Staffordshire	22,489	35,420	50,089
Suffolk	62,652	98,677	139,343
Surrey	18,039	28,411	40,178
Sussex	36,195	57,007	80,616
Warwickshire	30,264	47,666	67,646
Westmorland	7,389	11,638	16,457
Wiltshire	45,825	72,174	102,065
Worcestershire	16,099	25,356	35,857
Yorkshire	131,040	206,388	291,862
Total	1,362,208	2,145,478	3,034,009

Notes: The 'low' estimate assumes that one-third of the population were aged under 14 years, and that 5 per cent of the population were under-enumerated; the 'high' estimate assumes that 45 per cent of the population were aged under 14 years, and that 22.5 per cent of the population were under-enumerated.

Sources: Taxed populations from J.C. Russell, *British Medieval Population* (Albuquerque, University of New Mexico Press, 1948), pp. 132–3. Russell's figures have been used here without emendation, although M.W. Beresford, 'The Poll Taxes of 1377, 1379 and 1381', *Amateur Historian* III (1958), p. 278, points out that they include some errors of transcription.

Although the 1379 and 1381 Poll Tax returns cannot be used to estimate the total population of England because of the much greater non-payment in those years, the existence of a sliding scale led to the documents typically indicating taxpayers' occupations.[22] They, therefore, provide the possibility of examining the social structure of late fourteenth-century communities.[23] According to M.W. Beresford, the recording of occupations was less common in 1381 than in 1379.[24] However, there are some excellent examples even from 1381. E. Powell, for example, included in his study of the Peasants' Revolt in East Anglia, a transcription of the 1381 Poll Tax list for the village of Brockley cum Rede in Suffolk.[25] This lists 70 persons who paid the tax, from 'Willelmus de Walsham [William of Walsham]' and 'Elizabetha uxor ejus [Elizabeth his wife]', who paid six shillings between them (that is, three shillings, or nine groats each) down to six persons, all described as 'servientes [servants]', who paid the minimum of one groat.[26] The total paid was 70 shillings (210 groats), suggesting that the amounts had been fixed so that the payments in the village averaged three groats per person.[27] The village of Brockley cum Rede lay in the hundred of Thingo. In this hundred, a total of 870 taxpayers are mentioned in the 1381 Poll Tax returns, of whom nine were described as 'armigeri [bearers of arms]', 53 as 'agricolae [farmers]', 102 as 'artifices [makers of things]', 344 as 'laboratores [labourers]' and 362 as 'servientes'.[28] Of the 870, 487, or 56 per cent, were male, suggesting either that there had been differential out-migration of females, or (more likely) that a higher proportion of females than males did not pay the tax.[29]

AI.4 Manorial and other records

This section describes more briefly some of the other medieval source materials that have been persuaded to yield demographic information. Especially important among these sources have been the records of *manors*, or legal and administrative units over which a single lord had control. Perhaps the most widely exploited set of manorial records are the *manorial court rolls*, and the most important demographic study using these is that carried out by Zui Razi on the manor of Halesowen, in the Midlands.[30] According to Razi,

---

[22] Note that the fact that not everyone paid the same does not in principle make the 1379 and 1381 returns unusable for ascertaining aggregate population totals, as an 'average' payment of two or three groats respectively was required, and therefore the numbers of taxpayers could be worked out in aggregate from the sums collected.

[23] Beresford, 'Poll Taxes', p. 277.

[24] Ibid., p. 277.

[25] Powell, *Rising*, pp. 69–70.

[26] Ibid., pp. 69–70.

[27] Ibid., p. 70.

[28] Ibid., p. 67. A hundred is an ancient sub-division of a county. According to Powell's list, the hundred of Thingo included 18 different villages in 1381.

[29] Ibid., p. 67.

[30] Z. Razi, *Life, Marriage and Death in a Medieval Parish: Economy, Society and Demography in Halesowen 1270–1400* (Cambridge, Cambridge University Press, 1980).

Manorial courts dealt with land conveyances and transactions; disputes about inheritance, roads and boundaries; trespasses against the lord and neighbours; debts; breach of agreements, quarrels between neighbours; failures to render services, rents and other exactions; disturbances of the public order; infringement of village by-laws and the assize of ale and bread; . . . the election of jurymen, reeves and other village officials . . . deaths, marriages and pregnancies out of wedlock of bondwomen; entries into tithing groups; and departures of villeins from the manor with and without permission.[31]

Razi argues, on the basis of this extensive list of activities, that it was almost impossible for a male who lived in a village for any length of time (say, two or three years) to avoid being mentioned in the manorial court records.[32] By 'observing' the court records over a two- to three-year period, and listing every male who is mentioned, a good idea of the adult male population of a place may be obtained. This argument has not gone unchallenged. L.R. Poos and R.M. Smith have found evidence from Essex that many smallholders and landless labourers never appeared in the court rolls.[33] The debate is not yet settled, but subsequent work by Razi has confirmed the possibility of obtaining population estimates from counts of males in high-quality court records. For example, in the Norfolk manor of Gressenhall, more than three-quarters of smallholders appeared in the court in at least one in three years.[34]

Because the court records also include details of marriages and deaths, it is possible to obtain 'good data about mortality, life expectancy at 20, age at marriage, illegitimacy, male replacement rates and size of family'.[35] A limitation of the manorial court records is that women are greatly under-represented. Total populations, therefore, have to be estimated from the populations of adult males, making assumptions about the overall ratio of males to females in the population. In addition, it is clear from Razi's analysis that, despite his assertion that family size can be measured, no meaningful information about fertility can be gleaned without making heroic assumptions about the rates of infant and child mortality.[36]

One particular piece of evidence from the manorial court rolls that has been widely used to estimate mortality trends is that provided by heriots, or

---

[31] Ibid., p. 2.
[32] Ibid., pp. 2–3.
[33] See, for example, L.R. Poos and R.M. Smith, 'Legal Windows onto Historical Populations: Recent Research on Demography and the Manor Court in Medieval England', *Law and History Review* II (1984), pp. 134–6.
[34] Z. Razi, 'Manorial Court Rolls and Local Population: an East Anglian Case Study', *Economic History Review*, 2nd series XLIV (1996), p. 762.
[35] Razi, *Life, Marriage and Death*, p. 3.
[36] Ibid., pp. 139–43. A good discussion of the uncertainties surrounding all estimates of mortality from manorial records is to be found in R.M. Smith, 'Demographic Developments in Rural England, 1300–48: a Survey', in B.M.S. Campbell (ed.), *Before the Black Death: Studies in the 'Crisis' of the Early Fourteenth Century* (Manchester, Manchester University Press, 1991), pp. 52–60.

death duties. These were routinely paid by most peasants who died, and are recorded diligently and reliably in the court records. To identify mortality trends (as opposed to levels) a simple time-series of the number of heriots in successive periods will suffice. M.M. Postan and J.Z. Titow used counts of heriots in consecutive three-year time periods on the manors of the Bishop of Winchester as evidence both of the high rates of mortality prevailing in normal years in the early fourteenth century, and the excessive rates during the period 1316–18.[37]

Other manorial sources that can produce direct or indirect evidence about population numbers and trends, at least at the local level, include *customals* (lists of tenants) and *extents* (values of land, labour services and rents).[38] The proceedings of the manorial courts also included *views of Frankpledge*, a system 'by which every male member of a tithing was placed into a group of about ten who were answerable for the good conduct of, or the damage done by, any one of the other members'.[39] Views of Frankpledge and tithing-penny records for Essex have been made to reveal a great deal about the local demography of that area by L.R. Poos, and similar data have been used by J.Z. Titow to study the Somerset manor of Taunton.[40] Of course, while these kinds of sources are capable of providing excellent data for the areas for which they survive, it is always difficult to know how representative such communities are of the population as a whole, and therefore inferences about the general population made from them are bound to be problematic.

Non-manorial sources that have been used include the inquisitions *post mortem* (see Chapter 4), which deal with the aristocracy, and the thirteenth-century *hundred rolls*.[41] Other sources that could, potentially, be used include *tarrage returns* (tarrage was a ground rent paid to the King) and the *lay subsidy* (a tax on moveable items).[42]

[37] M.M. Postan and J.Z. Titow, 'Heriots and Prices on Winchester Manors', *Economic History Review*, 2nd series II (1949–50), p. 175.

[38] Hampshire Record Office, *A Guide to Sources for Archaeology and Population Studies* (Winchester, Hampshire County Council, 2002), pp. 17–18.

[39] Ibid., p. 18.

[40] L.R. Poos, 'The Rural Population of Essex in the Later Middle Ages', *Economic History Review*, 2nd series XXXVIII (1985), pp. 515–30; L.R. Poos, *A Rural Society after the Black Death: Essex 1350–1525* (Cambridge, Cambridge University Press, 1990); J.Z. Titow, 'Some Evidence of Thirteenth Century Population Increase', *Economic History Review*, 2nd series XIV (1961–62), pp. 218–24.

[41] For an introduction, see S. Raban, 'The Making of the 1279–80 Hundred Rolls', *Historical Research* LXX (1997), pp. 123–45.

[42] Hampshire Record Office, *A Guide to Sources*, pp. 21, 23. Tarrage assessments survive for the city of Winchester from 1416.

THE EARLY MODERN PERIOD

6

The Malthusian system

6.1 Population growth in early modern England

The next five chapters of this book are about population change in England from the end of the Middle Ages until around 1750, an era historians often refer to as the *early modern* period. Population growth rates in England during this period were modest (see Figure 1.1). From about 2.7 million in 1541 the population grew steadily throughout the rest of the sixteenth century to reach about four million by 1600.[1] Although growth continued into the seventeenth century, it petered out during the 1650s and the population stagnated from then until after 1700.[2] After that it resumed, though rates were modest, so that the best estimate we have of the population of England in 1750 is about 5.7 million, which is possibly less than the total around 1300 (see Chapter 3).[3] Indeed, during only eight out of 21 decades between 1540 and 1750 did the average rate of population growth in England exceed 0.5 per cent per year (a rate that is thought to have been maintained during the twelfth and thirteenth centuries) and seven of those were between 1540 and 1620. Between 1620 and 1750 population growth only exceeded 0.5 per cent per year for a single decade, and then only marginally (Table 6.1).

Why was population growth in England between 1500 and 1750 so slow? And why was growth relatively fast during the sixteenth century, very slow or non-existent for most of the seventeenth century, and modest but consistent between 1700 and 1750? These are questions that Part II of this book tries to answer. Recall from Chapter 1 that the size of a population can only change because of births, deaths and migration. If it is supposed that international migration can be regarded as a relatively insignificant component of population change during this period (its extent is discussed in Chapter 10), then the rate of population growth in early modern England was determined by variations in fertility and mortality. Slow growth, there-

---

[1] E.A. Wrigley and R.S. Schofield, *The Population History of England 1541–1871: a Reconstruction* (London, Edward Arnold, 1981), pp. 531–2.

[2] Ibid., pp. 532–3.

[3] Ibid., p. 533.

Table 6.1 Average population growth rates by decade, 1541–1750

Decade	Average population growth rate (per cent per year)
1541–50	0.83
1551–60	−0.10
1561–70	0.93
1571–80	0.93
1581–90	0.83
1591–1600	0.52
1601–10	0.70
1611–20	0.62
1621–30	0.42
1631–40	0.40
1641–50	0.27
1651–60	−0.17
1661–70	−0.32
1671–80	−0.10
1681–90	0.00
1691–1700	0.26
1701–10	0.33
1711–20	0.23
1721–30	−0.17
1731–40	0.59
1741–50	0.33

Note: The growth rates in this table have been worked out using formula (2) in Box 6.1.
Source: E.A. Wrigley and R.S. Schofield, *The Population History of England 1541–1871: a Reconstruction* (London, Edward Arnold, 1981), pp. 531–3.

fore, was due to high mortality (or, perhaps, frequent mortality crises), or to the restriction of child-bearing by some means, or a combination of the two. The next three chapters constitute an attempt to evaluate the respective contributions of high mortality and low fertility in retarding population growth, and Chapter 10 discusses the contribution of migration.

The study of the history of the English population during the early modern period is blessed by much better source materials than the medieval era. Though there are no population censuses until the nineteenth century, the establishment of the Church of England in 1538 marked the appearance of parish registers of baptisms, marriages and burials, which have been kept in many parishes in an unbroken sequence ever since (see Appendix II, for more details). The vast majority of those born in England between the mid-sixteenth century and 1750 were baptised in the Church of England, and almost all of those who died were buried there, so the baptism and burial registers function effectively as birth and death registers, and provide a continuous series of data about vital events. Moreover, if international migration can be ignored (or some assumptions made about it), then the existence of a continuous series of birth and death data means that if a single population census is available at some point during the time period covered by the series, the population at all other points can be worked out by a series of calculations. This, put in very simple terms, is the procedure used in the most important recent contribution to our knowledge of England's population history in the sixteenth, seventeenth and eighteenth centuries: E.A. Wrigley and R.S. Schofield's *The Population History of England, 1541–1871: a Reconstruction*.[4] Wrigley and Schofield used nineteenth-century census data to obtain a reliable estimate of the total population at that time, and parish register information about baptisms and burials in the preceding centuries to estimate the population using a technique known as 'back projection' (see Appendix II).[5]

In addition to the Church of England parish registers, occasional listings of the inhabitants of particular places are available for this period. Though these are rare (only about a hundred lists are known to survive) they are immensely important because they alone contain direct information about the social and familial structure of the population (see Appendix II).

The early modern period saw the birth of the serious study of vital events that has now become the modern science of demography. The pioneers were John Graunt (1620–74) whose analysis of the London bills of mortality (see Appendix II) was published in 1662, and Gregory King, who made a well-known estimate of the number of persons in England (classified by social status) in 1688.[6] But for the most important insights into the slow growth of the population of England during the pre-industrial era we had to wait, ironically, until some years after the population had been released from whatever shackles were constraining it. The ideas summarized in T.R. Malthus's *Essay on the Principle of Population*, first published in 1798, have provided a framework for subsequent analysis of the period, and the rest of this chapter is devoted to summarizing and elaborating them.[7] Section 6.2 describes Malthus's life and works, and explores the background to his writings on population. This background necessitates a

---

[4] Ibid., p. 533.

[5] J. Oeppen, 'Aggregative Back Projection', in Wrigley and Schofield, *Population History*, pp. 715–38. *Population projection* is the term used to describe the forecasting of future population totals from current population estimates and assumptions about future fertility and mortality rates. 'Back projection' is simply this process reversed, so that the forecasting moves backwards in time. See also Wrigley and Schofield, *Population History*, pp. 192–284, 527–35.

[6] J. Graunt, *Natural and Political Observations Made upon the Bills of Mortality* (London, 1662). Graunt was possibly the first to note that in London, deaths exceeded births. He also noticed that mortality among infants was high, and that females lived longer than males. On Gregory King's estimate, see D.V. Glass, 'Gregory King's Estimate of the Population of England and Wales', *Population Studies* III (1950), pp. 338–74.

[7] T.R. Malthus, *An Essay on the Principle of Population and a Summary View of the Principle of Population*, ed. A. Flew (Harmondsworth, Pelican, 1970).

discussion of the English poor laws, which, as we shall show, have an important impact on population change in the country from the sixteenth to the nineteenth centuries. Section 6.3 summarizes the Malthusian population system. Section 6.4 is a conclusion.

6.2 Background to Malthus's *Essay on the Principle of Population*

Thomas Robert Malthus was born in 1766, the second and last son of Daniel Malthus. He was educated privately before matriculating at Jesus College, Cambridge, where he read mathematics. He graduated in 1788 as ninth Wrangler, taking holy orders in the same year (his grandfather had been a clergyman).[8] In 1793 he was elected to a fellowship at Jesus College, and in 1796 he became a curate at Albury. Malthus's first and best-known work on population was his first *Essay*, published in 1798.[9] However, he also wrote several other essays on the subject, the second of which, published in 1803, was effectively a new book.[10] It was much longer than the first *Essay*, rather more moderate in its tone and circumspect in its conclusions, and contained a much greater wealth of empirical material. In 1805, having had to resign his fellowship at Jesus College the previous year because he married, he was appointed to the faculty of the new East India College as the first professor of political economy in Britain.[11] Malthus continued to write extensively on economic and demographic matters, notably revising his second *Essay* several times, until his death in 1834.

Though Malthus's contribution to our understanding of English population history has been seminal, he was not originally impelled to write about the subject by a desire to understand historical demography. His reasons for setting down his *Principle of Population* were, first, to provide a counterargument to the utopian ideas that were circulating at the time, which supposed that humans could create a 'perfect' society. Such ideas were fashionable during the early 1790s, largely inspired by the French Revolution, and chief among their proponents were William Godwin in

---

[8]   A. Flew, 'Introduction', in Malthus, *Essay*, pp. 8–9. Being a 'Wrangler' meant that he obtained first-class honours in mathematics.

[9]   T.R. Malthus, *An Essay on the Principle of Population, as it Affects the Future Improvement of Society, with Remarks on the Speculations of Mr. Godwin, M. Condorcet and Other Writers* (London, J. Johnson, 1798). Since its first publication, there have been numerous editions. Page references hereinafter are to the Pelican edition (Malthus, *Essay*, ed. A. Flew).

[10]   T.R. Malthus, *An Essay on the Principle of Population; or, a View of its Past and Present Effects on Human Happiness; with an Inquiry into our Prospects Respecting the Future Removal or Mitigation of the Evils which it Occasions. A New Edition, Very Much Enlarged* (London, J. Johnson, 1803).

[11]   Flew, 'Introduction', p. 14. Flew points out that Adam Smith, whose writings on economics predate Malthus's, was a professor of moral philosophy.

England and the Marquis de Condorcet in France. Malthus's religious beliefs would have led him to oppose the notion of human perfectibility, and it is widely believed that debates with his father provided an opportunity for him to systematize his ideas and write them down. The second contemporary development that Malthus opposed, and that provided an additional background to his first *Essay* was a change to the English poor law, which took place in 1795.

The English poor laws have their origins in the sixteenth century (see Chapter 10), and were codified during the seventeenth century.[12] They provided the system of social security that existed in England from then until the creation of the welfare state in the twentieth century. The poor laws operated at the parish level. After a gradual and rather disorganized first century, by the second half of the seventeenth century a *poor rate*, levied in the form of a property tax, was in place almost everywhere in England.[13] The money thus raised went into a parish fund to which those who were unemployed or otherwise unable to make a living for themselves and their families could apply for 'relief'. Each parish's fund was administered by *overseers of the poor* appointed by the parish. During the second half of the eighteenth century these parish funds were coming under severe strain, partly (it must be said) because of rapid population growth. As a result changes were made to the way in which the amount of relief a poor man and his family should receive was decided. One common system, which was introduced in 1795, involved calculating the amount of relief to be given according to the size of a man's family: that is, a scale was introduced which meant that additional children entitled a man to extra payments. Malthus objected in principle to the existence of the poor laws, but he regarded this particular development as singularly baleful.

Malthus started his argument with two 'postulata': first, that 'food is necessary to the existence of man' and, second, that 'the passion between the sexes is necessary and will remain nearly in its present state'.[14] From the second of these he inferred that a population, if unchecked, will increase in size geometrically. The supply of food, however, 'increases only in an arithmetical ratio. A slight acquaintance with numbers will shew the immensity of the first power in comparison of the second.'[15] The consequence of this imbalance between the 'power of population' and the 'power in the earth to produce subsistence' was that some kind of check must operate to restrict population growth.[16]

---

[12] For a good, short history of the poor laws of the sixteenth, seventeenth and eighteenth centuries, see P. Slack, *The English Poor Law 1531–1782* (London, Macmillan, 1990).
[13] Ibid., pp. 26-8.
[14] Malthus, *Essay*, ed. A. Flew, p. 70.
[15] Ibid., p. 71.
[16] Ibid., p. 71.

In his first *Essay*, Malthus described two kinds of check, which he labelled *preventive* and *positive*, and summarized them as follows:

> a foresight of the difficulties attending the rearing of a family acts as a preventive check, and the actual distress of some of the lower classes, by which they are disabled from giving the proper food and attention to their children, act [*sic*] as a positive check to the natural increase of population.[17]

The preventive check manifested itself in 'restraints upon marriage', and was felt in all classes of society, whereas the positive check manifested itself in increased mortality, and was largely confined to the poor.[18] In his first *Essay*, Malthus argued that both these checks led to unhappiness.[19] Because of this, and because it was inevitable that one or both of them must operate in any population, the perfect society could not be created.[20] Moreover, the poor laws of England, far from being a palliative, tended to make things worse. As he wrote:

> Their first obvious tendency is to increase population without increasing the food for its support. A poor man may marry with little or no prospect of being able to support a family in independence. They may be said therefore in some measure to create the poor which they maintain.[21]

This was true of poor laws in general, but *a fortiori* of the system that explicitly gave a poor man an extra allowance for additional children.[22]

It is clear that the positive check necessarily involved human misery, for it is based around increased population pressure leading to higher mortality, caused by a combination of malnutrition-induced disease and, in the limit, outright starvation. However, it does not necessarily seem to follow that the preventive check must be accompanied by misery, or that it should produce 'vices that are continually involving both sexes in inextricable unhappiness'.[23] In his second *Essay*, Malthus acknowledges this by introducing the

---

[17] Ibid., p. 89.

[18] Ibid., pp. 91–3.

[19] Ibid., p. 103.

[20] Throughout his writings, from the first *Essay* to the *Summary View*, Malthus contended that these checks were 'constantly operating' (e.g. *Essay*, ed. A. Flew, pp. 71, 242). This is clearly not the case, as a small population blessed with abundant natural resources can grow for a considerable period without any check. Indeed, one of the populations to which Malthus refers repeatedly, that of the United States of America, was in this situation during the seventeenth and eighteenth centuries. Nevertheless, it is logically true that if the population grows geometrically and the food supply grows arithmetically, then some kind of check must *eventually* operate, and that once it has 'kicked in', it will be a permanent and constant presence.

[21] Ibid., p. 97.

[22] Ibid., p. 117.

[23] Ibid., p. 92.

possibility of 'moral restraint': that people who cannot afford to bring children into the world and raise them at a decent standard of living might voluntarily delay or refrain from marriage and from alternative 'irregular gratifications'.[24]

6.3 The Malthusian system

Malthus's positive and preventive checks (whether or not the latter involves moral restraint) can be represented diagrammatically. Figure 6.1 shows a system with negative feedback, by which population growth is inevitably checked. The system works as follows. Because population growth outstrips the ability of the land to provide subsistence, it leads to an increase in the price of food and a decline in real wages (that is, money wages adjusted for changes in the prices of consumables). This decline may be reinforced if the reduced purchasing power leads to a fall in the demand for secondary and tertiary products and a decline in the demand for labour.[25] The positive check implies that the fall in real wages leads to increased mortality and therefore a reduction in the rate of population growth (and possibly even population decline), a scenario described in the outer 'loop' of Figure 6.1. This, of course, is just what M.M. Postan and his followers believe happened in England at the end of the thirteenth century. However, populations might choose to respond to a fall in real wages by restricting marriage and thereby reducing or placing limits on fertility. This would also slow down the rate of population growth. The Malthusian system, at its simplest, therefore, describes the processes by which population growth in pre-industrial societies is self-limiting. The system is self-contained, requiring no external inputs.[26]

The operation of Malthus's positive and preventive checks is predicated on a particular view about technological change, and certain beliefs about the way the world worked, which merit a little more discussion. First, consider the assumption of geometrical growth in the population. It is quite straightforward to show that this is theoretically consistent with the way in which a population with constant fertility will grow (see Box 6.1), and Malthus knew this well.[27] The geometrical growth argument, therefore, is

[24] T.R. Malthus, *An Essay on the Principle of Population: the Sixth Edition (1826) with Variant Readings from the Second Edition (1803)* in *The Works of Thomas Robert Malthus*, ed. E.A. Wrigley and D. Souden (8 vols, London, Pickering, 1986) III, pp. 465–81.

[25] Wrigley and Schofield, *Population History*, pp. 468–77.

[26] There are many variants of Figure 6.1 in the literature, most of which are considerably more complex than the system described here. See, for example, Wrigley and Schofield, *Population History*, pp. 454–84.

[27] In his *Summary View*, Malthus writes: 'all animals, according to the known law by which they are produced, must have a capacity of increasing in a geometrical progression' (Malthus, *Essay*, ed. A. Flew, p. 226).

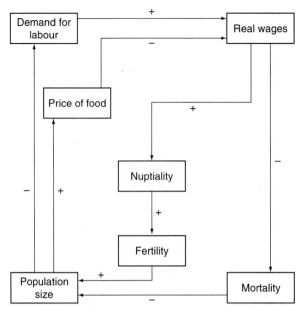

Figure 6.1 The Malthusian system

Notes: This diagram should be read starting from the box labelled 'Population size' in the bottom left-hand corner, and following the arrows. The '+' and '-' signs by the arrows relate to the direction of the relationship between the two factors in the boxes joined by the arrow. For example, population growth and the price of food are positively related, because an *increase* in population growth leads to an *increase* in the price of food; whereas the price of food and real wages are negatively related, as an *increase* in the price of food leads to a *decrease* in real wages. All complete 'circuits' in this diagram involve negative feedback, as they involve a path with an odd number of negative signs. *Nuptiality* is a technical demographic term meaning the propensity of the (females in the) population to get married. Nuptiality may change either because the average age at marriage changes, or because the proportion of the population ever marrying changes, or both.

theoretically unassailable. The same applies to his argument that if population grows geometrically and the food supply increases arithmetically, then eventually the population must grow to a level beyond the 'carrying capacity' of the land. This may be proved mathematically, and Malthus, who was a mathematician, would have known this. However, his view that the supply of food could only increase arithmetically (or linearly) rests on much less secure foundations. The arithmetical progression has no theoretical status. Though it was regarded by Malthus as probably an upper limit on the rate at which the food supply could be increased, it was a supposition, based largely on the evidence available to him about trends in agricultural production. The third point that should be stressed is that Malthus never considered it possible that married couples might wish to restrict fertility within marriage. Whether this was because he was opposed in principle to the use of birth control (classifying it under the heading of 'vice'), or whether he simply did not imagine that married people would think of it, is not clear.[28] Nevertheless, the omission of birth control from the Malthusian system does not invalidate it, for 'it is precisely, and only in order to put a check on, this formidable power to be fruitful and multiply that contraception is and has to be employed'.[29]

6.4 Conclusion

The history of research during the last 30 years or so into England's population history in the sixteenth, seventeenth and eighteenth centuries can be viewed as a project attempting to assess the operation of the Malthusian system in restraining England's population from growing rapidly. The organization of Part II of this book reflects this. In Chapter 7 the role of mortality is considered, focusing on both underlying mortality levels and on the continued importance of mortality crises. Chapter 8 discusses Malthus's preventive check, assessing the strength of the links between changing marriage patterns and fertility, and examining the relationship between marriage patterns and real wages.

Malthus did not consider that voluntary birth control within marriage played any part in restricting population growth among pre-industrial populations. However, some recent research has cast doubt on this view, and suggests that some forms of contraception may have been practised in England throughout the period. We consider this further in Chapter 9, in the context of a more general discussion of fertility patterns. Finally, in Chapter 10 the role of international migration is looked at. This provides an opportunity to contrast the demography of urban and rural areas, and, in particular, to make some comments about the singular experience of London and its impact upon national demographic patterns.

---

[28] In his second *Essay* and what is commonly called the 'sixth edition' Malthus included chapters 'On the Fruitfulness of Marriages' without mentioning birth control once (see Malthus, *Sixth Edition*, ed. Wrigley and Souden II, pp. 279–91; and III, pp. 659–66). Even modern demographers often regard birth control in pre-industrial societies as not within the 'calculus of conscious choice', to use a phrase first coined in A.J. Coale, 'The Demographic Transition', in International Union for the Scientific Study of Population, *International Population Conference, Liège, 1973* (Liège, International Union for the Scientific Study of Population), I, pp. 53–72. This view has come under attack in recent decades (see Chapter 9).

[29] Flew, 'Introduction', p. 32. We might dispute the 'is' in 'is and has to be', for in the twentieth century contraception has become widely used in rich countries to allow recreational sex without the threat of pregnancy in circumstances where it is hard to argue that extra children would seriously stretch the resources available either to the couple involved or to the population as a whole. However, Flew's general point is surely correct.

Box 6.1 Geometrical and exponential population growth

In Box 3.1 the net reproduction rate (NRR) was defined as the average number of daughters produced by a woman at prevailing levels of fertility, who survive to have children themselves. The NRR measures the size of the next generation relative to the size of the present one, therefore an NRR of, say, 1.5 means that the next generation is 50 per cent larger than the present one. The NRR depends on fertility and mortality, and if these remain constant over many generations, it allows us immediately to write down the size of any subsequent generation in relation to the present one, as follows.

Present generation (mothers)	1
Daughters	1.5
Granddaughters	1.5 x 1.5 = 2.25
Great-granddaughters	2.25 x 1.5 = 3.375
Great-great-granddaughters	3.375 x 1.5 = 5.0625

This is a geometrical progression. With an NRR of 2.0 it produces Malthus's exact series of 1, 2, 4, 8, and so on.

Geometrical growth implies that people are added to the population in discrete 'batches', once per generation or once per year. In reality, of course, population growth proceeds continuously, and it is helpful to be able to convert *geometrical growth* into growth in which people are added gradually through time. The continuous model which is related to the geometrical growth model is the *exponential growth* model, which may be expressed according to the following formula:

Population in t years' time = Population now x e^{rt},
where $e = 2.718$ and r is the annual rate of population growth.

This relationship allows us to work out the population at some future date if we know the present population and the annual rate of growth. It also can be used to estimate the rate of growth, r, if we know the population size at two points in time, and are prepared to assume that the growth rate during the intervening period is constant. To see this, denote the present population by P_0 and the population in t years' time by P_t. Then the formula above becomes:

$$P_t = P_0 e^{rt} \qquad (1)$$

Taking logarithms to base e of formula (1) produces:

$$\log_e P_t = \log_e P_0 + rt$$

and so

$$r = (\log_e P_t - \log_e P_0)/t \qquad (2)$$

Finally, suppose that a 'generation' is 28 years long. Then the NRR measures the ratio between the population now and the population in 28 years' time. In other words, if the population now is set at 1, the population in 28 years' time is equal to the NRR. Using $t = 28$ in formula (1) above, we have:

$$\text{NRR} = 1 \times e^{(r \times 28)} = e^{(r \times 28)}$$

and we can easily relate the NRR to the annual rate of population growth. This is the formula that was used in Box 3.1.

7

English mortality and population growth, 1500–1750

7.1 Introduction

Until about 40 years ago, the predominant view among historians of population was that population growth in early modern England was low because of high mortality coupled with periodic mortality crises. Even though fertility rates were high, the harshness of the mortality regime was such that rapid population growth was impossible. The dynamics of the English population were fundamentally the same as they had been in the fifteenth century, save that some reduction in mortality levels, and in the frequency and severity of crises, allowed modest population growth for much of the period. This view was doubtless influenced by the available data, which mostly related to mortality, and which naturally stressed periods of crisis and disaster. Very little was known about fertility.

With the appearance of more information about population trends, it has become clearer what historians need to be able to demonstrate in order to sustain this view. Because population growth was more rapid during the six-teenth century and the early eighteenth century than during the seventeenth century, to show that mortality levels were the main determinant of the rate of growth of the population it is necessary to show that mortality was higher during the seventeenth century than it was during the sixteenth cen-tury or the first half of the eighteenth century. This chapter examines the mortality experience of the English population during this period to see to what extent the 'mortality account' of slow population growth can be sus-tained by recent data.

Section 7.2 explains that the mortality of the English population before 1750 was the sum of *underlying mortality* levels and the effects of periodic surges in the number of deaths, or *crisis mortality*, and discusses these two components of overall mortality. The next three sections describe how parish register evidence has been used to delineate the trends over time in both: Section 7.3 explains the various methods historians have applied to the burial registers; Section 7.4 presents the history of crisis mortality dur-ing the period; and Section 7.5 the history of underlying mortality rates.

Even if we can show that fluctuations in mortality rates were the main determinants of changes in the rate of population growth in early modern England, however, further analysis is required in order to demonstrate that Malthus's positive check was operating. For Malthus's argument was that mortality rose and fell in response to changes in real wages, which in turn responded to population pressure. Mortality crises, for example, can occur for many reasons, only some of which can properly be regarded as consistent with the positive check. Section 7.6 considers these issues further, discussing the causes of mortality crises in England between 1500 and 1750.

Chapters 4 and 5 showed that the demography of late medieval England was dominated by plague. Plague continued to be a threat for much of the early modern period, too, but died out towards the end of the seventeenth century. Section 7.7 discusses the impact of plague and the reasons for its eventual decline. Section 7.8 reaches a conclusion about the role of underlying mortality and mortality crises in keeping population growth in early modern England slow.

7.2 Underlying mortality and crisis mortality

Figure 7.1 shows the number of burials recorded in the parish of Odiham, Hampshire, in each year between 1538 and 1750. The pattern is typical of pre-industrial societies, and in particular of English populations during the early modern period. In most years, there were between 20 and 40 burials, which reflects the rate of *underlying mortality*. Periodically, however, years occurred in which the number of burials was much greater than it was in surrounding years. In Odiham, such years included 1558 and 1559, 1597, 1603, 1703 and 1737. These were the years of *mortality crises*, and the additional deaths in these years (over and above the 20–40 that would ordinarily have occurred) represent *crisis mortality*. Many (and often most) deaths in crisis years were caused by whatever caused the crisis, though it should be remembered that underlying mortality was still present in those years.[1]

Figure 7.1 suggests that, in the parish of Odiham, mortality crises were rather rare during the early modern period, and that the most serious ones were concentrated in the sixteenth and early seventeenth centuries. The two obvious crises of the early eighteenth century were less severe, only resulting in a doubling of the number of burials above their 'normal' level. The number of deaths in the parish in a 'normal' year

---

[1]   This means that the deaths due to underlying mortality must be subtracted from the total number of deaths to arrive at the deaths resulting from the crisis. Thus in Odiham in 1559 there were 116 burials. However, we should have expected about 30 deaths in a 'normal' year, so the excess mortality caused by the crisis of 1559 led to about 86 additional deaths.

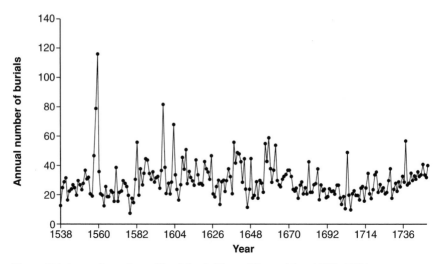

Figure 7.1 Annual number of burials, Odiham, Hampshire, 1538–1750
Notes: The totals for the following years have been adjusted because of obvious deficiencies in the registers: 1546, 1547, 1551–1554, 1564, 1586.
Source: CD-ROM available from Local Population Studies, Department of Humanities, University of Hertfordshire, Watford Campus, Wall Hall, Aldenham, Watford WD2 8AT.

does exhibit some gradual changes. It is just over 20 during the period from 1538 until around 1590, but then seems to increase to between 30 and 40 until the late seventeenth century, before falling gradually to about 20 again in the early eighteenth century, and then rising to about 40 in 1750.

Interpreting trends in the average number of burials as indicative of trends in underlying mortality, however, is problematic. If the population of Odiham were changing, then there would be changes in the number of burials even though the underlying rate of mortality remained constant. Because of the lack of census data for the early modern period, and the difficulty of estimating migration at the local level, it is hard to obtain reliable estimates of parish, or even regional, population totals, and so death rates cannot be computed. Therefore, though the pattern in Figure 7.1 suggests that underlying mortality in Odiham was higher in the early seventeenth century than in other periods, it is impossible to be sure of this. Only for the whole country, for which sensible assumptions about migration can be made, has it proved possible to estimate population totals, and therefore to convert burial totals into death rates. Figure 7.2 shows crude death rates (CDRs) in England for each year from 1541 to 1750. The influence of periodic mortality crises can be seen in the frequent peaks in the series. But there is a trend underlying these. It seems that in the late sixteenth century, the underlying CDR was around 23–25 per thousand in 'normal' years, but that it rose in the mid-seventeenth century to a level close to 30 per thousand, where it remained until 1750.

A further difficulty with using annual series of burials to examine the contribution of crisis mortality and underlying mortality to overall mortality is the subjectivity of the distinction between the two. Consider the years 1656–62 in Figure 7.1. During this seven-year period there are six years in which the number of burials was close to 40 and three in which the number exceeds 53. Does this period represent an extended mortality crisis, or simply a period during which underlying mortality was relatively high? The identification of mortality crises is considered further in the next section.

7.3 Identification of mortality crises using parish registers

To evaluate the contributions of changes in underlying mortality rates and the frequency and severity of mortality crises to changes in English population growth, it is necessary to have some means of identifying what constitutes a mortality crisis. E.A. Wrigley and R.S. Schofield, in *The Population History of England*, took the annual series of death rates,

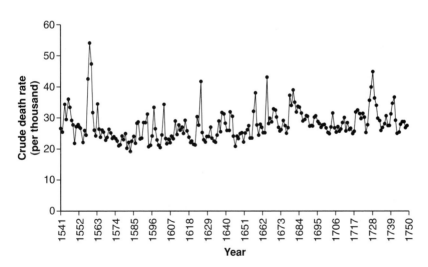

Figure 7.2 Crude death rate, 1541–1750
Source: E.A. Wrigley and R.S. Schofield, *The Population History of England 1541–1871: a Reconstruction* (London, Edward Arnold, 1981), pp. 531–3.

and calculated '25-year moving averages'.[2] They then defined a crisis year as '[a]ny year in which the death rate was at least 10 per cent above the moving average'.[3] This definition produces 37 years of crisis mortality between 1538 and 1750 (Table 7.1), some of which were consecutive, implying prolonged periods of elevated death rates. By far the most serious mortality crisis of the period was that of 1557–60. Overall, the next most important was that of 1727–30, though it was never as intense as the single-year crises of 1625–26 and 1657–58.[4]

These national-level crises are, of course, the sum of trends in individual parishes, and the relationship between national and local crises is not simple.

> A sharp rise in the national death rate . . . may result from a uniform but relatively modest increase in mortality throughout the country, or from violent surges in a few populous parishes. Again, a national crisis may reflect a country-wide peppering of local epidemics, or be widely present but only within a limited region.[5]

At the local level, crisis mortality has to be identified using frequencies of burials, as no population totals are available. The frequencies of burials can be tabulated on a monthly basis, however, which potentially allows a very detailed analysis of the seasonality as well as the overall severity of the crisis. This, as explained in Section 7.6, is important for identifying the cause of individual crises. The chief problem with enumerating local crises is that, in small parishes, random fluctuations in the number of burials from month to month may be considerable, so working out which surges in mortality are so great as not to be likely under 'normal' conditions is awkward. Wrigley and Schofield devised a criterion based on forecasting the expected number of burials in a given month for each parish.[6] They then regarded any single month with a number of burials 3.36 or more standard errors above the forecast trend, or 'any run of two or more consecutive months, each of which was at least 2.05

[2]   E.A. Wrigley and R.S. Schofield, *The Population History of England 1541–1871: a Reconstruction* (London, Edward Arnold, 1981), p. 332. A *moving average* involves calculating the average death rate in a consecutive 'window' of years, then deleting from the 'window' the earliest year, adding the next year and re-calculating the average. By moving through time in this way, a smoothed series of 'average' death rates is produced. Wrigley and Schofield worked on a 25-year 'window'.
[3]   Ibid., p. 332.
[4]   In their identification of years of mortality crises, Wrigley and Schofield use years beginning at harvest time, rather than calendar years. Thus the observation that there was a mortality crisis in the year 1625–26 means that deaths were at crisis level during the 12-month period beginning with the harvest of 1625. Using these *harvest years* makes sense for societies in which one possible cause of mortality crises is harvest failure, as it facilitates the detection of relationships between grain prices (an indicator of harvest failure) and mortality levels.
[5]   Wrigley and Schofield, *Population History*, p. 645.
[6]   Ibid., pp. 646–7.

Table 7.1 National mortality crises in England, 1538–1750

Year	Crude death rate (per thousand)	Percentage above trend	Percentage of parishes affected
1542–43	33	13	0.0
1544–45	36	23	19.6
1545–46	37	27	15.5
1546–47	33	14	11.9
1557–58	47	60	32.5
1558–59	65	124	39.1
1559–60	34	18	6.8
1587–88	31	29	16.1
1590–91	29	18	11.4
1592–93	32	30	9.1
1596–97	30	21	17.6
1597–98	31	26	18.7
1603–04	31	21	14.8
1609–10	27	11	8.6
1613–14	29	14	9.0
1623–24	30	18	16.0
1624–25	32	27	13.0
1625–26	36	43	14.6
1638–39	34	35	17.9
1639–40	29	15	8.9
1643–44	33	29	14.0
1657–58	39	43	16.8
1658–59	35	25	11.5
1665–66	37	32	9.7
1670–71	34	15	10.1
1678–79	34	12	12.4
1679–80	34	10	11.9
1680–81	41	36	16.3
1681–82	35	15	6.4
1682–83	34	12	6.9
1684–85	35	16	7.9
1719–20	34	14	15.8
1727–28	42	37	28.2
1728–29	43	41	28.5
1729–30	42	35	20.5
1741–42	40	36	17.1
1742–43	33	15	8.4

Note: Years are *harvest years* running from 1 July to 30 June.
Source: adapted from E.A. Wrigley and R.S. Schofield, *The Population History of England 1541–1871: a Reconstruction* (London, Edward Arnold, 1981), pp. 333, 653.

standard errors above the forecast trend value', as constituting crisis mortality.[7] The *standard error* depends on the population of the parish. It is larger for small parishes, because in small parishes the number of burials needs to rise relatively further above the trend than it does in larger parishes in order for a crisis to be identified. Referring back to Figure 7.1, Wrigley and Schofield's method identifies crisis years in Odiham as 1557, 1558–59, 1582, 1597, 1603–04, 1609–10, 1638, 1656, 1658, 1693, 1703, 1719, 1737 and 1750.[8] Most of these crises, however, were neither very long nor especially severe. The most severe, in terms of the excess of monthly burial totals at their peak, were those of 1558–59, 1582, 1737, 1603–04 and 1597. By far the longest was that of 1558–59, which lasted 11 months.

Applying these criteria to all the parishes for which they had data, Wrigley and Schofield were able to work out the percentages of parishes experiencing crises in the national crisis years between 1538 and 1750, and these figures are also given in Table 7.1. It is worth comparing the two indicators of the impact of a crisis (the percentage by which national death rates exceeded the 'trend', and the percentage of parishes affected). Wrigley and Schofield describe the first of these as an indicator of the 'severity' of a crisis.[9] The second is partly an indicator of its geographical extent. There is no doubt that the two indicators both agree that the worst crisis of the entire period was that of 1557–60. For three consecutive years, death rates rose more than 10 per cent above their long-term trend, and in the worst year, 1558–59, they more than doubled. At least two out of every five parishes experienced crisis-level mortality. However, apart from this episode, the correlation between the two indicators is not exact. The crisis of 1727–30 was both fairly widespread and fairly severe (though much less so than that of 1557–60), but in 1657–58 and 1625–26, when national death rates rose relatively more than in any of the years 1727–30, only 17 per cent and 15 of parishes, respectively, were affected, suggesting that those parishes that did experience a crisis in that year suffered particularly grievously. Other crises that seem to have been particularly localized or, at least, patchy in their impact, were 1592–93 and 1665–66.

---

[7]   Ibid., p. 647.

[8]   The Odiham data are available, along with data for all the 404 parishes studied by Wrigley and Schofield, on a CD-ROM from Local Population Studies, Department of Humanities, University of Hertfordshire, Watford Campus, Wall Hall, Aldenham, WATFORD WD2 8AT, for a modest charge. The CD-ROM is accompanied by a guide to the data written by Roger Schofield: R. Schofield, *Parish Register Aggregate Analyses: the* Population History of England *Database and Introductory Guide* (Colchester, Local Population Studies, 1998).

[9]   Wrigley and Schofield, *Population History*, pp. 333, 653.

7.4 The extent of mortality crises

If variations in the frequency and severity of mortality crises were a principal determinant of the slow rate of population growth in England during the sixteenth, seventeenth and eighteenth centuries, then we should expect the proportion of all deaths attributable to crisis mortality to have been considerable. However, a fairly straightforward calculation shows that, at the national level, this was not the case. If we take Wrigley and Schofield's definition, then for each of the years they define to be crisis years at the national level, it is possible to use their figures for the percentage by which the national death rates exceeded the trend to work out the number of deaths that were due to the crisis (that is, the excess of deaths over the underlying level). If we do this for all the crisis years between 1540 and 1750, we find that only 4.3 per cent of deaths at the national level can be attributed to crisis mortality. This is likely to be a minimum estimate, for even in non-crisis years at the national level (according to Wrigley and Schofield's definition) some deaths were certainly attributable to local crises. For example, in Odiham 1582 was a crisis year, but this does not appear in Table 7.1. Even, however, if an average of 5 per cent of all deaths in all non-crisis years were attributable to local crises (and this is likely to be on the high side), then the overall proportion of deaths that occurred during crises would not exceed one in ten.[10]

We can look at the percentage of deaths resulting from crisis mortality at the local level, too. Using the crisis years identified in the parish of Odiham, and making an admittedly rough calculation of the number of 'excess' deaths in each of these years, we find that there were around 500 such deaths between 1538 and 1750 out of a total of 6350 deaths, which comes to about 8 per cent. The conclusion seems inescapable, crisis mortality only contributed a small proportion of all deaths in early modern England.[11]

Moreover, when long-run changes in the frequency of mortality crises over the period are examined, it becomes clear that the relationship between these and the population growth rate is, if anything, inverse. If we divide the two centuries between 1550 and 1750 into 25-year periods, we can compare the percentage of 'crisis months' observed in Wrigley and Schofield's sample of 404 parishes during each of these periods with the average annual population growth rate (Table 7.2). The periods of slowest population growth, 1650–74 and 1675–99, were those when mortality crises were least frequent. The negative correlation between the impact of mortality crises

---

[10] The maximum proportion of deaths in any non-crisis year that is attributable to local crises cannot exceed about 10 per cent (as, if it did, the year would be in Wrigley and Schofield's list). In most non-crisis years, therefore, it is likely to have been much lower.

[11] It is likely that in some urban parishes, where epidemics were generally more severe, mortality crises were relatively more important as a component of overall mortality. England in the early modern period, however, was still predominantly a rural country.

and population growth cannot be rescued by considering the severity of the crises that did occur. Estimates of the percentages of all deaths in each quarter-century that were due to crisis mortality, using Wrigley and Schofield's national-level definition of a crisis, are also given in Table 7.2. This measure of the impact of mortality crises takes into account their severity as well as their frequency (at least at a national level). The correlation between this measure of crisis impact and the population growth rates is no better than was the correlation with frequency alone. It seems, therefore, that crisis mortality was not the main factor influencing variations in the population growth rate.

This overall conclusion, however, should not be taken to deny that individual periods of crisis were important in the short term. The most serious period of crisis between 1540 and 1750 was undoubtedly that of the late 1550s. It seems that high mortality between May 1557 and June 1559 was widely distributed across England, with only a few areas, such as Essex, the north Midlands, and the south-west, escaping.[12] The excess mortality in the year 1557–58 was around 2 per cent of the population and in the following year an additional 4 per cent died for reasons directly attributable to the crisis. This crisis was also marked by a fall in the birth rate, with the result that the total population fell from 3.16 million in 1556 to 2.96 million in 1560.[13] After 1560 there was a period of almost three decades without serious crises, until the clutch of bad years in the late 1580s and 1590s. Unlike the crises of the 1550s, these late sixteenth-century crises were concentrated in the north, the West Midlands and parts of the south-west (especially Somerset); in the south-east and East Anglia, very few parishes were affected.[14]

Table 7.2 Frequency of mortality crises and population growth

Period	Crisis months per 1000	Percentage of all deaths due to crisis mortality	Average annual population growth rate
1550–74	14.6	7.2	0.52
1575–99	13.4	4.8	0.74
1600–24	12.6	3.6	0.62
1625–49	12.9	4.4	0.38
1650–74	10.8	4.2	−0.17
1675–99	10.0	3.9	0.01
1700–24	10.4	0.6	0.29
1725–49	16.2	6.1	0.24

Source: E.A. Wrigley and R.S. Schofield, *The Population History of England 1541–1871: a Reconstruction* (London, Edward Arnold, 1981), pp. 333, 531–4, 650.

[12] Wrigley and Schofield, *Population History*, p. 670.
[13] Ibid., p. 531.
[14] Ibid., pp. 672–3.

Wrigley and Schofield's sample of parishes includes relatively few from urban areas, but there are some in Norwich, Ipswich and Shrewsbury. During the sixteenth-century crises these parishes were largely unaffected. In 1603–04, however, four of the five Norwich parishes, five of the seven Ipswich parishes, and both Shrewsbury parishes in observation suffered.[15] The geography of crisis mortality in the years 1623–26 shows that there were two distinct crises: one affected the north and north-west of England in 1623–24 and the second affected mainly the south-east and East Anglia in 1624–26.[16] The crisis of 1638–40 was similar in its geography to that of 1624–26, whereas that of 1657–59 and the protracted period of high mortality from 1678–85 were much more widely distributed, though the far north and much of the south-west escaped.[17] The geography of the crisis of 1665–66 resembled that of 1603–04, with urban parishes being heavily affected.[18] These parishes had relatively large populations, which explains why a crisis that affected fewer than one in ten of all parishes caused an increase of 32 per cent in the national death rate.

After 1685 there was an extended period without crises at the national level (apart from one relatively minor crisis in 1719–20), before the extensive and severe crisis in 1727–30. In terms of the percentage of the country affected, this was the worst crisis since 1557–60. The death rate exceeded 40 per thousand for three consecutive years, something that had not happened since the 1550s. As it had in 1558 and 1559, the birth rate fell in 1728 and 1729, and this, combined with the high mortality, led to a fall in the total population from 5.48 million in 1727 to 5.26 million in 1731.[19] Unlike in 1557–60, however, the incidence of local mortality crises varied regionally. There is very little evidence of any excess mortality at all south of the River Thames, and other areas, such as parts of Yorkshire, also seemed to have escaped, whereas the whole of the Midlands and the north-west were seriously affected.[20] We return to consider the causes of mortality crises in Section 7.6, where it is shown that the geography of a particular crisis provides one clue as to its possible cause.

7.5 Underlying mortality: trends and differentials

Mortality crises during the early modern period were neither frequent nor severe enough to retard population growth, nor is the history of their incidence correlated with population growth. But what of the underlying

---

[15] Not all 404 parishes were in observation throughout the whole period. In one Ipswich parish and two Shrewsbury parishes the registers do not start until well into the seventeenth century.
[16] Wrigley and Schofield, *Population History*, pp. 675–7.
[17] Ibid., pp. 677–81.
[18] Ibid., p. 675.
[19] Ibid., p. 533.
[20] Ibid., pp. 681–3.

level of mortality? Did this exhibit long-run trends that might have influenced population growth rates?

Consider the crude death rates (CDRs) shown in Figure 7.2. A good estimate of general trends in underlying mortality can be obtained by ignoring the most obvious crisis years and drawing a smooth line through the centre of the (fluctuating) values for 'normal' years. This exercise reveals that from a value in the high 20s per thousand in the mid-sixteenth century, the CDR gradually fell to the low 20s by the 1570s and early 1580s. As Wrigley and Schofield themselves commented, 'The middle years of Elizabeth's reign formed a period of remarkably mild mortality.'[21] From the 1580s until about the 1640s the underlying CDR fluctuated somewhat, but was not generally above 25 per thousand. In the mid-seventeenth century, however, there is a pronounced upward shift in the underlying mortality regime, such that the underlying CDR rose to close to 30 per thousand by the 1660s, where it remained until the middle of the eighteenth century.

As a summary measure of mortality, the crude death rate suffers from confounding due to differences in the population age structure. An alternative single-figure index is the expectation of life at birth, which is not subject to confounding of this sort (though care is needed in its interpretation, see Box 7.1).[22] Trends in the expectation of life at birth between 1540 and 1750 display a similar pattern to those in the crude death rate. From around 34 years in the mid-1500s it increased to around 40 years around 1580 before falling gradually to 32 years around 1660, and remaining roughly at that level until 1750.[23] The trend in underlying mortality between 1540 and 1750 is, therefore, reasonably clear: it fell until about 1580, but during the middle half of the seventeenth century it rose to levels higher than those of the sixteenth century, where it remained until 1750. The extended period during which the population grew at a rate of more than 0.5 per cent per year from 1560–1620 (see Table 6.1) was, therefore, a period of low underlying mortality, whereas the rise in underlying mortality in the mid-seventeenth century was associated with a substantial fall in the population growth rate, which, before 1750 was never again to attain its early seventeenth-century values. Population growth rates were, then, quite clearly associated with long-run changes in underlying mortality.

Evidence about what was driving these changes is not so easy to come by. One problem is that direct evidence about age-specific death rates is unobtainable from parish registers using aggregate analysis. Family reconstitution (described in Appendix II), however, can provide information about

---

[21]   Ibid., p. 413.
[22]   In a situation where fertility and mortality are constant over time, and the population growth rate is zero, the expectation of life at birth is equal to the reciprocal of the CDR, but when these rather restrictive assumptions are not met, there is no simple relationship between the two.
[23]   Wrigley and Schofield, *Population History*, p. 414.

Box 7.1 The expectation of life

The expectation of life is a useful summary measure of mortality, but is often misinterpreted. The expectation of life at any age x, e_x, is the average number of years people at that age have left to live. In order to calculate e_x, we need information about mortality rates at all ages older than x. The expectation of life at birth, therefore, reflects mortality at all ages. It is, in fact, the average lifetime that would be experienced by people living in a population with the age-specific death rates used in its calculation.

Averages, however, can mislead. An expectation of life at birth of 40 years does not mean that most, or even that many, people died at around age 40. Indeed it could be that half the people died soon after birth, and the rest lived until age 80 years, with none dying at age 40 years. However, it turns out that there are regularities in the age pattern of mortality in human populations. The table below shows the proportion of deaths in various age groups that may normally be anticipated at different values of the life expectation at birth. It has been calculated using the model 'west' tables for females in A.J. Coale and P. Demeny, *Regional Model Life Tables and Stable Populations* (2nd edn) (New York, Academic Press, 1983), pp. 44, 46, 48, 50, 52.

Age group	Percentage of deaths in age group for different life expectations at birth				
	30 years	*40 years*	*50 years*	*60 years*	*70 years*
0–4	38.8	27.5	18.2	10.2	3.9
5–19	8.2	6.7	4.9	2.9	1.0
20–39	14.4	12.8	10.0	7.0	3.3
40–59	15.9	16.9	16.2	14.4	10.9
60–69	10.7	13.8	15.7	16.7	15.9
70–79	8.9	14.6	20.4	25.9	30.3
80 and over	3.0	7.5	14.3	22.9	34.6

age-specific death rates, though this is most complete and reliable for infants and children. As infant and child deaths probably constituted around one-third of all deaths in early modern England (see Box 7.1) trends in infant and child mortality are not without interest. Taking as a measure of infant mortality the number of children per thousand born that did not survive until their first birthday, we find that this was around 160–170 throughout the period from the late sixteenth century until 1750, save for a period of heavier mortality in the 1680s and another longer period of high mortality between 1710 and 1750, when closer to 200 out of every thousand babies born failed to survive their first year.[24] A similar trend is also found among children aged 1–5 years. Relatively light mortality during the period 1580–1629 was followed by higher levels from 1630 to 1679 and another jump to a peak in the 1680s.[25] After a brief respite between 1690 and 1709 the decades 1710 to 1749 saw levels approaching those of the 1680s.[26] Adult mortality, however, followed a different trend. The expectation of life at age 25 years was around 32 years in 1600.[27] It changed little until the 1680s, when it fell temporarily to less than 28 years.[28] Recovery was rapid, though, and during the first half of the eighteenth century, adult mortality fell consistently, so that by 1750 the expectation of life at age 25 years was about 35 years.[29]

The upward shift in mortality in the middle of the seventeenth century, therefore, was largely due to increased early childhood and then infant mortality, whereas adult mortality remained roughly the same as it had been in earlier decades. After 1700, though, declining adult mortality was offset by high infant and childhood mortality, such that overall mortality changed little.

Although these national trends seem clear, mortality varied in a pronounced way from place to place. The clearest divide was perhaps between urban areas, notably London, and rural areas. There is no doubt that mortality levels in London were high: between 1650 and 1700 more than 250 out of every thousand babies born did not survive until their first birthday, and this figure rose to at least 350 per thousand in the early eighteenth century.[30] But high rates characterized other towns, too. York experienced infant mortality rates of over 200 per thousand throughout the period from 1550 to 1800, with a peak of over 250 per thousand in the late seventeenth century.[31] Assuming (and this is quite a large assumption), that the distribution of deaths by age in urban areas was similar to that in the population as a whole, infant death rates of this order imply an expectation of life at birth of well under 30 years, and those in early eighteenth-century London of under 25 years. However, not all areas of the cities were equally unhealthy. In sixteenth- and seventeenth-century London, for example, the expectation of life at birth varied from over 35 years in wealthier parishes to under 25 years in poorer, riverside parishes.[32] With the unhealthy environment of

24   E.A. Wrigley, R.S. Davies, J.E. Oeppen and R.S. Schofield, *English Population History from Family Reconstitution 1580–1837* (Cambridge, Cambridge University Press, 1997), p. 215.
25   Ibid., p. 215.
26   Ibid., p. 215.
27   Ibid., p. 283.
28   Ibid., p. 282.
29   Ibid., p. 283.
30   J. Landers, *Death and the Metropolis: Studies in the Demographic History of London 1670–1830* (Cambridge, Cambridge University Press, 1993), p. 136.
31   C. Galley, *The Demography of Early Modern Towns: York in the Sixteenth and Seventeenth Centuries* (Liverpool, Liverpool University Press, 1998), pp. 182–3.
32   R.A.P. Finlay, *Population and Metropolis: the Demography of London, 1580–1650* (Cambridge, Cambridge University Press, 1981), pp. 107–8.

most urban areas leading to excessively high death rates like these, it is unsurprising that the populations of many towns were only maintained through in-migration (see Chapter 10). The number of deaths in London already exceeded the number of births in the first half of the seventeenth century, and mortality conditions were to worsen considerably during the next hundred years.[33]

There were substantial variations within the countryside, too. Family reconstitution studies have revealed that in low-lying parishes in eastern England almost half of those born died before their fifteenth birthday, whereas the corresponding figure in drier, upland parishes in the south and south-west could be below one in five.[34] The most convincing evidence of geographical differentials in mortality within rural areas comes from Mary Dobson's study of mortality in Kent, Essex and Sussex.[35] For example, in Kent and Essex in the 1670s, crude death rates in parishes bordering the Thames estuary were a staggering 75 per thousand, whereas those in upland areas were around 25 per thousand.[36] Dobson attributes much of the extremely high mortality of marshland parishes to malaria, and her evidence, whilst not conclusive, is fairly convincing.[37] It is noteworthy, moreover, that such a contrast in mortality within the countryside dwarfed the typical differentials observed between urban and rural areas.[38] There is also evidence, discussed further in the next section, that mortality in north-western England had a distinctive pattern. For example, infant mortality in that region was in fairly continuous decline throughout the period from 1550 to 1800.[39]

7.6 Malthus's positive check

The detailed knowledge of mortality in early modern England that has been provided by the analysis of parish register data enables us to reach fairly clear conclusions about the role of Malthus's positive check. Sixteenth- and seventeenth-century England seems to have been a very different place from

---

[33] Ibid., p. 59.
[34] Wrigley, *et al.*, *English Population History*, pp. 270–1. To consider two extreme examples, in the parish of March in the fenlands of Cambridgeshire, the infant mortality rate was 311 per 1000 births, and half of those born died before attaining the age of 15 years, whereas in Odiham, the infant mortality rate was only 96 per 1000 births and four out of five of those born survived to age 15.
[35] M. Dobson, *Contours of Death and Disease in Early Modern England* (Cambridge, Cambridge University Press, 1997).
[36] Ibid., p. 139.
[37] Ibid., pp. 287–367.
[38] Ibid., p. 141.
[39] S. Scott and C.J. Duncan, 'Malnutrition, Pregnancy and Infant Mortality: a Biometric Model', *Journal of Interdisciplinary History* XXX (1999), pp. 48–9.

England at the end of the thirteenth century.[40] Indeed, one of the most striking features of early modern English demography is the absence of any convincing evidence that the positive check was in operation, save possibly in a very few localities at particular times. To begin with, the total population did not exceed 5.3 million at any time between 1500 and the 1730s.[41] Postan holds the belief of a Malthusian crisis around 1300 simultaneously with the view that this crisis was not triggered until the population total reached around six million. If the population of thirteenth-century England was allowed to rise to six million before the positive check 'kicked in', it is hard to argue that the positive check should have been in operation at lower population totals three centuries later. Moreover, the relationship between underlying mortality rates and population growth rates is not all that close. The rate of growth was slowing from the beginning of the seventeenth century, and had fallen close to zero by 1650 (see Table 6.1). After a period of population decline, growth resumed in the 1690s. Though it is clear that mortality was rising during the seventeenth century and may have contributed to the slowdown in population growth, growth was maintained during the first half of the seventeenth century despite continued high mortality.

Worse for the positive check, the crucial relationship between mortality levels and real wages is largely absent in the long run. Real wages fell rapidly during the population expansion of the Elizabethan period, reaching a nadir around 1610; they then underwent a long rise to a peak in the 1730s.[42] During the period of falling real wages, mortality was relatively low and roughly constant, whereas as mortality rose during the seventeenth century, real wages rose as well.[43] There is, as Wrigley and Schofield concluded, 'almost no sign' of the Malthusian positive check in the comparison of these two series.[44] 'It is doubtful,' they continue, 'whether the course of real wages was ever the dominant influence on mortality trends' during the period.[45]

This is not to deny the existence of subsistence crises. The most desperate years of the entire period, 1557–60, seem to have been associated with a succession of harvest failures. Real wages certainly fell in a manner consistent with this interpretation.[46] Such a calamity typically leads to a pattern of

---

[40]   This statement should not be taken to imply that there was some kind of turning point around 1500. In fact, a good case can be made for arguing that the fifteenth and seventeenth centuries were not so different from one another and that, if a turning point must be identified, it lies somewhere in the mid-fourteenth century, when the Black Death ushered in a fiercer disease environment; see R.M. Smith, 'Plagues and Peoples: the Long Demographic Cycle, 1250–1670', in P. Slack and R. Ward (eds), *The Peopling of Britain: the Shaping of a Human Landscape* (Oxford, Oxford University Press, 2002), pp. 177–84.
[41]   Wrigley and Schofield, *Population History*, p. 533.
[42]   Ibid., pp. 638–44.
[43]   Ibid., pp. 414–15.
[44]   Ibid., p. 415.
[45]   Ibid., p. 416.
[46]   Ibid., pp. 642–3.

successive years of increasingly intense crisis mortality, until a good harvest brings the episode to a close. This is precisely the pattern observed in some parishes in 1557–60.[47]

Perhaps the best evidence in favour of the operation of the positive check in sixteenth- and seventeenth-century England comes from crises of the 1580s, 1590s and 1623–24, when food prices did rise dramatically. As Andrew Appleby has shown, there is abundant evidence from parishes in north-west England that the increases in mortality in, for example, 1597 and 1623–24 were associated with malnutrition and even starvation.[48] However, as we saw earlier in the chapter, a feature of these crises was that they were not national affairs: they were concentrated in northern and north-western parishes.[49] In 1586–87, 1596–97 and 1622–23, high wheat prices coincided with troughs in the wool price in Cumberland, Westmorland and Lancashire, and it seems to have been the combination of the two that led to severe hardship.[50]

Subsistence crises in England, therefore, even in the most vulnerable localities, were exceptional events. Indeed, many, possibly the majority, of the mortality crises of early modern England were not associated in any way with subsistence crises. According to Paul Slack, of the crises listed in Table 7.1 in which mortality rose more than 20 per cent above trend, those of 1544–45, 1545–46, 1592–93, 1603–04, 1625–26, 1638–39, 1643–44 and 1665–66 were probably due to plague, or to a combination of plague and other epidemic diseases.[51] Of the remainder, only those of 1557–60, 1587–88 and 1596–98 (and, to a lesser extent, 1728–30) can convincingly be associated with temporary falls in real wages caused by high food prices.[52]

---

[47] For a good example (St Martin in the Fields, London), see P. Slack, 'Mortality Crises and Epidemic Disease in England, 1485–1610', in C. Webster (ed.), *Health, Medicine and Mortality in the Sixteenth Century* (Cambridge, Cambridge University Press, 1979), p. 30.

[48] A.B. Appleby, *Famine in Tudor and Stuart England* (Liverpool, Liverpool University Press, 1978).

[49] According to S. Scott and C.J. Duncan, 'Interacting Effects of Nutrition and Social Class Differentials on Fertility and Infant Mortality in a Pre-Industrial Population', *Population Studies* LIV (2000), pp. 71–87, in this remote part of England infant mortality may have been elevated because of nutritional deficiency. This, however, seems more likely to have been because of the poor quality of the diet than its quantity.

[50] S. Scott and C.J. Duncan, 'The Mortality Crisis of 1623 in North-West England', *Local Population Studies* LVIII (1997), pp. 21–4.

[51] P. Slack, *The Impact of Plague in Tudor and Stuart England* (London, Routledge and Kegan Paul, 1985), p. 58.

[52] For data on real wages, see Wrigley and Schofield, *Population History*, pp. 642–43. The crisis of the late 1720s was a complex one, and was associated with a series of epidemics, probably exacerbated by a deficient harvest in 1728 (Wrigley and Schofield, *Population History*, pp. 680–81).

7.7 Plague

Plague continued to afflict the country throughout the sixteenth and much of the seventeenth centuries. Its overall impact on mortality levels, though, was definitely much less than it had been in the fourteenth century, and probably substantially less than during the fifteenth century. The fact that the population of Elizabethan England expanded at a rate that may have been faster than at any time since the Romans departed is evidence that plague's demographic impact had lessened substantially, especially when it is known that epidemics of plague were taking place at this time. The declining influence of plague seems to have been a consequence of its becoming mainly (though by no means exclusively) an urban phenomenon in a still predominantly rural population, but also came about because the frequency of epidemics in any one place seems to have declined. In a study of rural parishes in Devon and Essex between 1565 and 1666, Paul Slack found that two-thirds of Devon parishes and more than four-fifths of Essex parishes furnished evidence of at least one epidemic of plague during the period, but that only 13 per cent and 30 per cent respectively provided firm evidence of more than one epidemic.[53] When plague did strike a village, however, its effect was still destructive: 'within any single parish, bubonic plague could cause greater mortality in a short space of time than any other epidemic disease', with burials frequently rising to three or four times their level in normal years, and in some parishes, such as Crediton in 1571, more than ten times.[54]

Despite the continuation of plague in the countryside, it was in towns that plague was 'an inevitable hazard', and where its impact was most impressive.[55] Almost all towns were affected, and any given town was probably affected more frequently (though not necessarily more severely) than a given village. For example, in Exeter there were plague epidemics in 1570, 1591 and 1625, which killed probably 16, 15 and 18 per cent of the population respectively.[56] In Norwich, the largest provincial town, there were severe epidemics in 1579, 1584–85, 1589–92, 1603 and 1625.[57] The 1579 epidemic was the most serious, probably causing 5000 deaths among a population of not more than 17,000.[58] Norwich was particularly badly affected by plague compared with other towns, possibly because of the large number of immigrants living in the city, or because of its poorer working-class population.[59]

---

[53] Slack, *Impact of Plague*, p. 109.
[54] Ibid., pp. 90, 108. In 1571, perhaps a quarter of the entire population of the town of Crediton perished (Slack, *Impact of Plague*, p. 96).
[55] Ibid., p. 110.
[56] Ibid., pp. 115–8.
[57] Ibid., pp. 129–30.
[58] Ibid., pp. 129–30.
[59] Ibid., p. 142.

If plague's impact was greater in the towns than in the countryside, its most spectacular manifestations, measured simply in numbers of deaths, occurred in London. As we shall see in Chapter 10, London's population increased rapidly during the sixteenth and seventeenth centuries, from 70,000 in 1550 to 575,000 in 1700.[60] Data from the London Bills of Mortality (see Appendix II) reveal that the death toll in London in the plague epidemics of 1563, 1603 and 1625 was monumental. In the 'city and liberties', there were over 17,000 plague burials in 1563, and more than 25,000 in each of the years 1603 and 1625.[61] Because of the city's dramatic growth, the largest death toll came in the most famous of the early modern London plagues, that of 1665, when around 55,000 people died (though plague deaths as a proportion of the population were fewer in 1665 than in 1563 or 1603).[62] The 'Great Plague' of 1665, though, was the last. For during the late 1660s plague abruptly disappeared from England. The causes of its disappearance have been the subject of debate among historians, and the issue merits discussion here. This is partly because the ending of the plague era could be said to mark the beginning of the secular decline in mortality, which is discussed further in Chapter 12, and partly because it provides an early opportunity to introduce the famous 'Sherlock Holmes' approach to understanding the causes of mortality decline, which was to be elaborated by Thomas McKeown in the context of the eighteenth and nineteenth centuries.[63]

The 'Sherlock Holmes' method involves drawing up a list of possible causes of the decline of mortality (or, in this case, the decline of mortality from a specific cause), and then eliminating those that conflict with empirical evidence. The remaining cause or causes are then regarded as likely to have been important. In the case of the disappearance of plague, the possible causes can be divided into those involving little or no human intervention; those that definitely required human intervention; and those that are indeterminate. The first group includes the possibility that genetic changes led to either rats or humans (or both) acquiring resistance to the disease, an argument that the rats became immune for some other reason, that some kind of change in the plague bacillus rendered it less virulent, or that the brown rat, *Rattus norvegicus* (which was less susceptible to plague) gradually invaded territory previously occupied by the black rat, *Rattus rattus*.

---

[60]   E.A. Wrigley, 'A Simple Model of London's Importance in Changing English Society and Economy, 1650–1750', *Past and Present* XXXVII (1967), p. 44.

[61]   Slack, *Impact of Plague*, p. 151.

[62]   Ibid., pp. 150–1.

[63]   See T. McKeown, *The Modern Rise of Population* (London, Edward Arnold, 1976). I should not wish to press too far the argument that the disappearance of plague marked the beginning of the demographic transition in England, even though it might be said to fit the model of the epidemiological transition proposed by Abdel Omran, 'The Epidemiologic Transition: a Theory of the Epidemiology of Population Change', *Millbank Memorial Fund Quarterly* IL (1971), pp. 509–38, in which the first stage is one of 'receding pandemics'.

The second group includes the introduction of effective quarantine measures, changes in the urban environment that led to a greater separation of rats and humans so that 'blocked' rat fleas were less likely to find nearby human hosts when the rats died (see Chapter 4), and improvements in nutrition that increased resistance to infection.

In two articles published about 20 years ago, Andrew Appleby and Paul Slack considered these.[64] Appleby dismissed the idea of genetic change, as this should have led to a gradual disappearance, whereas plague vanished abruptly.[65] The improved nutrition theory founders on the experience of France, where the nutritional status of the poor was very bad in general, and probably worse at the end of the seventeenth century than it was in earlier periods, but the plague still disappeared.[66] The value of improvements in the urban environment, and particularly the replacement of wooden buildings by stone ones, gained popular credence because of the Great Fire of London in 1666, which necessitated the rebuilding of much of the city. However, seventeenth-century plagues tended to strike most severely in the poorer suburbs of towns and cities, and, in the case of London, these were not burned down in 1666, and so were not rebuilt.[67] Of course, the fact the plague was becoming concentrated in poorer suburbs could be cited as evidence that environmental improvements were affecting its incidence, but if so, the process was very gradual, and cannot explain the rather abrupt disappearance of plague in the 1660s.[68] The spread of *Rattus norvegicus*, which may have been facilitated by the increased use of brick in construction, 'does not coincide with the known chronology for the disappearance of plague. ... The rat ... did not arrive in England until 1727, some sixty years after the plague's disappearance'.[69] Slack considers that a change in the virulence of the bacillus is unlikely, for where plague did strike after the 1660s (for example in the southern French city of Marseilles in 1720–22) it remained just as deadly and infectious as it had been during the sixteenth and seventeenth centuries.[70]

This leaves two possibilities: improved quarantine and acquired immunity among rats. Appleby regards these as both much more plausible than any of the preceding reasons. Consider quarantine first. The idea that quarantine could prevent the spread of plague was certainly current in mid-seventeenth-century England. Somewhat paradoxically, though, the most

---

[64] A.B. Appleby, 'The Disappearance of Plague: a Continuing Puzzle', *Economic History Review*, 2nd series XXXIII (1980), pp. 161–73; P. Slack, 'The Disappearance of Plague: an Alternative View', *Economic History Review*, 2nd series XXXIV (1981), pp. 469–76.
[65] Appleby, 'Disappearance', p. 165.
[66] Ibid., p. 166.
[67] Ibid., p. 166.
[68] Slack, 'Disappearance', p. 472.
[69] Appleby, 'Disappearance', p. 167; see also Slack, 'Disappearance', p. 472.
[70] Slack, 'Disappearance', p. 472.

famous example of a quarantine policy being enacted is that of the Derbyshire parish of Eyam, which was struck by plague in September 1665.[71] The inhabitants of this parish responded by erecting a cordon sanitaire around themselves to *keep the plague in* (that is, to prevent it spreading to neighbouring parishes), rather than to keep it out.[72] The result was an epidemic in the parish, and especially in the village of Eyam, of great severity: perhaps as many as 30 per cent of the inhabitants of the parish perished, and the death rate in the village was substantially higher than this, though it probably did not exceed 50 per cent.[73]

Appleby is convinced that quarantine could and did work in the long run, but is generally sceptical that it could have been introduced so completely and effectively in so short a time.[74] However, in the short run, he argues that the severity of the series of epidemics in the 1650s and 1660s, which struck most major European cities, might have eliminated almost all the rats that were susceptible to plague, allowing a temporary 'breathing space'.[75] By the time a large enough population of susceptible rats had built up again, quarantine measures, and possibly other factors, such as environmental improvements and the arrival of *Rattus norvegicus*, had begun to have their anticipated effects.[76] Slack disputes this, and argues that quarantine was working effectively in the 1660s.[77] In fact, quarantine measures were being introduced some decades before the 1660s, but they were initially not totally effective, and a single breach in the cordon could make the difference between a town escaping completely and suffering from a substantial epidemic. We should not dismiss the efforts of contemporaries to prevent the spread of plague: their failures were naturally highlighted; their successes are often invisible to us.[78]

7.8 Did high mortality keep population growth slow?

There is a sense in which mortality is bound to be related to population growth, in that, if migration is ignored, such growth can only occur as a consequence of an excess of births over deaths. It is, perhaps, better to phrase the question by asking whether changes in mortality levels were

---

71 P. Race, 'Some Further Consideration of the Plague in Eyam, 1665/6', *Local Population Studies* LIV (1995), pp. 57–8.
72 Ibid., p. 56.
73 Ibid., p. 59; L. Bradley, 'The Most Famous of All English Plagues: a Detailed Analysis of the Plague at Eyam, 1665–6', in *The Plague Reconsidered: a New Look at its Origins and Effects in Sixteenth and Seventeenth Century England*, a Local Population Studies supplement (Matlock, Local Population Studies, 1977), pp. 76–7.
74 Appleby, 'Disappearance', pp. 167–9.
75 Ibid., pp. 169–70.
76 Ibid., p. 173.
77 Slack, 'Disappearance', pp. 473–6.
78 Ibid., p. 476.

influencing changes in the rate of population growth. The data from parish registers suggest that the impact of changing mortality levels was modest, and mainly related to changes in underlying mortality. The rapid population growth of the late sixteenth century coincided with a period of low underlying mortality, and the seventeenth-century stagnation was associated with higher underlying mortality levels. Beyond this, though, the evidence suggests that mortality exercised only a weak influence on population growth. In particular, mortality crises were generally insufficiently powerful to have had more than a short-term effect on the rate of population growth, and this applied even to the most serious crisis of the period, that of 1557–60.

Given the weak impact of mortality on population growth, even in the short term, it is likely that finding evidence of Malthus's positive check in early modern England is not going to be easy. Only a minority of mortality crises were due to high food prices (and a concomitant decline in real wages).

8

The Malthusian preventive check in early modern England

8.1 Introduction

The previous chapter established that Malthus's positive check was largely absent from England, at least after 1538, and that population growth was not primarily kept in check by increased mortality due to pressure of people on the land. In this chapter, we consider the operation of the preventive check. As Malthus described it, this check arises if people delay marriage until they can afford to raise a family without risking a descent into poverty.

> [M]an cannot look around him, and see the distress which frequently presses upon those who have large families ... without feeling a doubt whether, if he follow the bent of his inclinations, he may be able to support the offspring which he will probably bring into the world. ... Will he not lower his rank in life, and be obliged to give up in great measure his former habits? Does any mode of employment present itself by which he may reasonably hope to maintain a family? Will he not at any rate subject himself to greater difficulties, and more severe labour, than in his single state? ... Does he even feel secure that, should he have a large family, his utmost exertions can save them from rags and squalid poverty? And may he not be reduced to the grating necessity of forfeiting his independence, and of being obliged to the sparing hand of charity for support?

> These considerations are calculated to prevent, and certainly do prevent, a great number of persons ... from pursuing the dictate of nature in an early attachment to one woman.[1]

Malthus believed that if this check could be operated in the absence of pre-marital sexual activity, then 'it is undoubtedly the least evil that

---

[1] T.R. Malthus, *An Essay on the Principle of Population: the Sixth Edition (1826) with Variant Readings from the Second Edition (1803)*, in *The Works of Thomas Robert Malthus* ed. E.A. Wrigley and D. Souden (8 vols, London, Pickering, 1986) II, pp. 14–15.

can arise from the principle of population'.[2] Pre-marital sexual activity was to be avoided, as when practised with birth control it tended to 'weaken the best affections of the heart, and in a very marked manner to degrade the female character', and when practised without, would 'bring as many children into the society as marriage, with a much greater probability of their becoming a burden to it'.[3] Fundamental to its successful operation, he believed, was the encouragement of young people in the poorer classes to save money, thereby accumulating the wherewithal to marry and bring up a family.[4] An implication of this view is that the time it might take a man to accumulate the required resources would depend on the economic conditions over a number of years. In hard times, it would be more difficult for young people to find spare earnings to put by than it would in more prosperous times. The result of this is that, in a society practising the preventive check, the age at marriage, and possibly the proportion of a generation who could afford to marry at all, would depend on the state of the economy during the period when that generation would have been saving up to get married.[5]

Assessing the extent to which this check operated in early modern England involves the examination of a range of issues. Section 8.2 shows that marriage in England before 1750 typically occurred late in life and that marriage was non-universal: a marriage regime that is a necessary pre-condition for the operation of the preventive check. Sections 8.3 and 8.4 discuss the structure of the English household during the sixteenth, seventeenth and eighteenth centuries. In Section 8.3 cross-sectional evidence from listings of inhabitants is presented, and in Section 8.4 we use this evidence to make inferences about the system of household formation that operated. These inferences are not straightforward, and a number of potential difficulties are discussed and resolved. Section 8.5 returns to the Malthusian model depicted in Figure 6.1, and examines the strength of the relationship between fertility and population growth. Section 8.6 shows how the prevalence of marriage (or *nuptiality*) was related to fertility. The final link in the system, that between real wages and nuptiality, is considered in Section 8.7. Section 8.8 draws on the arguments and evidence presented in this chapter and the one that precedes it to attempt an answer to the question: why was population growth in England between 1500 and 1750 so slow?

---

2   Ibid., p. 15.
3   Ibid., III, p. 475.
4   He was, for example, very keen on the idea of 'saving banks' for the poor. Ibid., p. 555.
5   Malthus was aware of this, too: 'a young man, who had been saving from 14 or 15 with a view to marriage at 24 or 25, or perhaps much earlier, would probably be induced to wait two or three years longer if the times were unfavourable' (Ibid., p. 555).

8.2 The European marriage pattern

Malthus describes his preventive check as operating through the prudence and restraint exclusively of males. For it to be effective, however, females must participate as well. In other words, the men who delay marriage must marry women who have also delayed marriage. The preventive check exercises its function as a check to population growth by removing, at any point in time, from the pool of women eligible to bear children a substantial proportion of those biologically capable of doing so. Therefore, regardless of the typical age at marriage for men, societies where the vast majority of women are propelled into teenage marriages (often by strong cultural norms) cannot be loci of the preventive check. Such societies are found, for example, in present-day south Asia, where the average age at marriage for women is well under 20 years, and marriage for women is almost universal. In contemporary sub-Saharan African populations it is common for men to delay marriage until their late twenties or early thirties, but when they do marry they typically take brides in their teens. Moreover, it is almost unknown for women never to marry.[6]

In order for the preventive check to have a chance, therefore, a society must allow either delayed marriage or lifetime celibacy for women. That this was the case in historical Europe was brought to the attention of historians by John Hajnal in his 1965 paper 'European Marriage Patterns in Perspective'.[7] Hajnal began by examining data from the period around 1900 on the proportions married among men and women in the age groups 20–24, 25–29 and 45–49 years.[8] He showed that throughout western Europe (that is, Europe west of a line running approximately from St Petersburg to Trieste), the average age at marriage for men was greater than 26 years, and that for females was less than 23 years.[9] Moreover, a substantial minority of both men and women were still single in their late forties. In the case of women, this minority comprised at least 10 per cent, and typically between 15 and 20 per cent.[10] Hajnal then presented evidence to suggest that this marriage pattern was of much earlier origin, and characterized western European populations in the seventeenth and eighteenth centuries.[11]

---

[6] We might ask how such societies manage to escape the ravages of the positive check. Generally speaking, they have done so by spacing births within marriage very widely, using the natural contraceptive effect of breast-feeding, coupled in some cases with prolonged periods of abstinence from sexual intercourse after the birth of each child. See H.J. Page and R. Lesthaeghe (eds), *Child-Spacing in Tropical Africa: Traditions and Change* (London, Academic Press, 1981).

[7] J. Hajnal, 'European Marriage Patterns in Perspective', in D.V. Glass and D.E.C. Eversley (eds), *Population in History: Essays in Historical Demography* (London, Edward Arnold, 1965), pp. 101–43.

[8] Ibid., p. 102.

[9] Ibid., p. 101.

[10] Ibid., p. 102.

[11] Ibid., pp. 106–16.

Since Hajnal's paper was published a flood of research on European marriage patterns has filled in much geographical and historical detail. In the case of England, specifically, the picture that has emerged is that a particularly extreme form of the European marriage pattern seems to have held sway throughout almost the whole country during the late sixteenth, seventeenth and early eighteenth centuries. The best evidence comes from family reconstitution studies using parish register data (see Appendix II). Essentially, these involve tracing individuals from their baptism to their marriage, and calculating the length of time elapsing between the dates of these two events. The reconstitutions carried out by the Cambridge Group for the History of Population and Social Structure indicate that, during the period 1600–1749, fewer than one in four women, of those who ever married, married for the first time before their twenty-first birthdays, around half by age 25, and three-quarters by around age 29 years.[12] For men, the corresponding figures were one or two years higher.[13] The average age at marriage in the country as a whole was between 27 and 28 years for men and between 25.5 and 26 years for women.[14] There is no discernible variation with time in these figures: during this 150-year period, the distribution of ages at marriage changed remarkably little. By contrast, geographical variations are observable, although they do not seem to have been especially significant. There are definite indications of a slightly lower mean age at marriage, at least for women, in south-east England than in the Midlands and the south-west.[15] Moreover, it seems that proto-industrial villages in the north of England were behaving in a way quite different from agricultural ones, and, indeed, that there were variations between proto-industrial villages.[16]

Unfortunately, reconstitution data is unable to shed any light on the proportions ever marrying. However, once some idea of the distribution of ages of marriage has been obtained, it is possible to combine this with information about the total number of marriages in given periods obtained from aggregative analysis of parish registers, and estimates of the size of successive birth cohorts

---

[12] E.A. Wrigley, R.S. Davies, J.E. Oeppen and R.S. Schofield, *English Population History from Family Reconstitution, 1580–1837* (Cambridge, Cambridge University Press, 1997), pp. 146–7.

[13] Ibid., pp. 146–7.

[14] Ibid., pp. 146–7.

[15] This may be illustrated by drawing an imaginary line from the Wash to the Dorset coast. For the period 1650–99, of the eight parishes south and east of this line in the Cambridge Group's data, six had a mean age at marriage for women below 25 years. Of the 13 parishes to the north and west of this line, only one did so. See Wrigley *et al.*, *English Population History*, pp. 31, 184–5.

[16] See P. Hudson and S. King, 'Two Textile Townships, c. 1660–1820: a Comparative Demographic Analysis', *Economic History Review*, 2nd series, LIII (2000), pp. 706–41. Hudson and King's work concerns the Yorkshire townships of Sowerby and Calverley. The Cambridge Group's reconstitutions only include two definitely proto-industrial parishes, Birstall (also in Yorkshire) and Shepshed in Leicestershire (though a case could be made for Gedling in Nottinghamshire). Hudson and King demonstrate that the nuptiality patterns in Sowerby and Calverley were different from those in Birstall and Shepshed.

obtained from back projection, to estimate the proportions of each birth cohort who would never marry.[17] The results are striking (Figure 8.1). Among those born in the 1550s and 1560s, fewer than 10 per cent never married. However, during the late sixteenth and early seventeenth centuries, celibacy rose dramatically, so that among those born around 1600 nearly a quarter never married. After a brief drop, the popularity of celibacy increased still further to around 27 per cent in the cohorts born during the Civil War, before a long and gradual decline to levels below 5 per cent among those born in the 1730s.

It seems clear, therefore, that late and non-universal marriage were capable of reducing fertility in early modern England to a level well below its potential (the extent of the potential reduction is described in Chapter 9). This alone, however, does not demonstrate that Malthus's preventive check was operating, still less does it explain how it worked out in practice. To understand this, we need to turn first to the topic of the structure of the English household in the past.

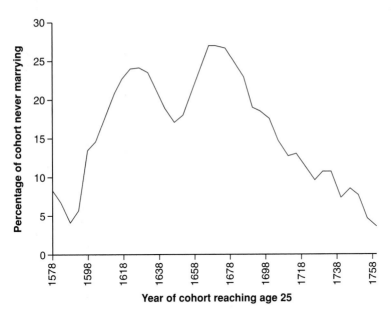

Figure 8.1 Estimated proportions of people never marrying by birth cohort in England, 1550–1750

Notes: These proportions are expressed per thousand persons aged 40–44. They are based on five-year birth cohorts. The horizontal axis shows the average year in which the cohort was aged 25 years (that is, the year around which they should have been marrying).

Source: E.A. Wrigley and R.S. Schofield, *The Population History of England 1541–1871: a Reconstruction* (London, Edward Arnold, 1981), p. 260.

17   E.A. Wrigley and R.S. Schofield, *The Population History of England 1541–1871: a Reconstruction* (London, Edward Arnold, 1981), pp. 257-65.

8.3 The structure of the English household: empirical evidence

Until the 1960s, very little was known about the size and structure of the households of ordinary English people in the past. Among many, probably most, historians, there was an assumption that households were probably large, resembling those in many parts of Asia and Africa today, with many relatives living together in extended families. To a degree, this was based on empirical evidence, but the evidence to hand related largely to the aristocracy, not to the common people.[18]

During the 1960s, however, it became clear that a number of listings of the inhabitants of English towns and villages during the early modern period survived, and that these lists could be made to reveal the size and structure of the households in the places to which they referred (see Appendix II). Historians at the Cambridge Group for the History of Population and Social Structure collected together and analysed a number of these, and came to the clear and startling conclusion that the early modern English household was not dissimilar to its 1960s counterpart. In what has been described as 'one of the most crushing and total refutations of any orthodox wisdom in recent history' the results revealed unambiguously that households were small, and that extended families were exceedingly rare.[19]

According to Peter Laslett, the average size of the English household between 1564 and 1649 was 5.1 persons, and that between 1650 and 1749 between 4.5 and 4.7.[20] The distribution of households according to the number of members they contained (Table 8.1) showed that fewer than one in ten households contained more than eight persons, and nearly half of all households contained either three, four or five persons. Viewed from a 'person' perspective rather than a 'household' perspective, we see that more than half of all people lived in households containing at least four, but no more than seven, persons.

The vast majority of households contained no more than one married couple, and that couple's own biological children. Co-resident relatives, such as brothers and sisters of the couple, or their parents, or even their grandchildren, were rare: nine out of every ten households had none at all.[21]

---

[18] This view may not have been universal. The range of multipliers used by historians to derive population totals from Domesday Book (see Chapter 2) are consistent with rather small households.

[19] F. Mount, *The Subversive Family: an Alternative History of Love and Marriage* (London, Unwin, 1982), p. 53. Mount was specifically referring to the most important collection of papers that presented the results of the analysis of listings of inhabitants; see P. Laslett and R. Wall (eds), *Household and Family in Past Time* (Cambridge, Cambridge University Press, 1972).

[20] P. Laslett, 'Mean Household Size in England since the Sixteenth Century', in Laslett and Wall, *Household and Family*, p. 138.

[21] Ibid., p. 149.

Table 8.1 Distribution of English households by size, 1574–1821

Size	Households (per thousand)	Persons (per thousand)
1	56	12
2	142	60
3	165	104
4	158	133
5	147	155
6	118	149
7	80	118
8	54	91
9	31	59
10	19	40
11	11	25
12	7	18
13 or more	13	34

Source: P. Laslett, 'Introduction: the History of the Family', in P. Laslett and R. Wall (eds), *Household and Family in Past Time* (Cambridge, Cambridge University Press, 1972), p. 77.

Only 6 per cent of households consisted of people of more than two generations.[22] By contrast, more than a quarter of households contained attached unrelated persons, most of whom were unmarried, and described as 'servants'.[23] The conclusion seemed inescapable. England was a society of nuclear families, in which each married couple had a house of its own, separated from either set of parents, in which they raised their own children. Co-resident relatives were therefore rare, whereas co-resident unrelated persons were quite common, and most of these were servants.

8.4 Family formation systems: process and form

The next stage in the argument is to use the cross-sectional evidence produced by Laslett and his colleagues to make inferences about the system of family formation that prevailed in early modern England, and to compare this system to the one advocated by Malthus as his preventive check. However, a number of issues need to be disposed of before reasonably convincing conclusions can be drawn.

First, it is sometimes forgotten how few listings of inhabitants survive. The direct evidence consists of about 100 individual listings of particular communities or parishes spanning a period of about 250 years. There were around 10,000 parishes in England, so the listings cover at most 1 per cent.

[22] Ibid., pp. 152–3.
[23] Ibid., pp. 151–3.

Doubtless there are some listings that the Cambridge Group's searches have failed to discover, but it seems unlikely that very large numbers still remain hidden. Moreover, only a minority of these lists contain data even on the ages of the persons listed; fewer still give any indication of relationships among the individuals within each household. Given the inadequacies of the evidence, then, it is a testament to the ingenuity of those who analysed them that such a clear picture has emerged.

One problem is that the nature of the criteria used by the person drawing up the list to separate the population into households is generally not known. Various possible criteria can be suggested, based on co-residence within the same building, residence in a house with a common entrance to the outside world, eating at a common table, or working together as a unit of production or consumption. The point is not so much which of these is the most useful in a historical context, but that it is not known which were used by those who drew up the disparate collection of listings that survive. The difficulties inherent in grouping the inhabitants of a place into households are not unique to the early modern period. They certainly affected the takers of the mid-nineteenth century censuses, in which many census enumerators were unable to follow detailed written instructions as to how to define the boundaries of households (see Appendix III). In the nineteenth-century censuses the problem can be solved by appealing to information given about each person's relationship to the head of household of which he or she was a member, but in the early modern listings this information is often absent.[24] Nevertheless, the listings do typically divide up the inhabitants of a place into groups, and by defining a household as consisting of 'all those who appear in the list grouped together, or in any way clearly separated from groups of others before or after', and by applying a detailed and consistent set of rules to all the hundred or so listings, a reasonably clear cross-sectional picture of the structure of the English household can be produced.[25]

However, the next inferential step presents a major difficulty, for it involves moving from the cross-sectional pattern to some conclusions about the underlying process that produced the pattern. To understand the nature of the problem, a brief theoretical digression is necessary. According to the nineteenth-century French sociologist Frédéric Le Play, there are three basic systems of household formation. The first is the *simple* or *nuclear family system*. The hallmark of this system is that only one married couple can live in each household. Upon marriage, therefore, the newly married couple sets

---

[24]   For a set of rules for interpreting nineteenth-century censuses, see M. Anderson, 'Standard Tabulation Procedures for the Census Enumerators' Books 1851–91', in E.A. Wrigley (ed.), *Nineteenth-Century Society: Essays in the Use of Quantitative Methods for the Study of Social Data* (Cambridge, Cambridge University Press), pp. 134–45.

[25]   Laslett, 'Introduction: the History of the Family', in Laslett and Wall, *Household and Family*, pp. 86–9 (the quotation is from p. 86).

up home separately from either parent (a form of marriage technically termed *neolocal*). The nuclear family is unstable: often a household will last only as long as the marriage around which it is based. A second system is the *joint family system* found in many African and Asian populations. Though variations exist, a common feature is that a household may contain two or more married couples of the same generation. This will happen, for example, if each son brings his bride into the household, and daughters 'marry out', going to live with their husbands' families.

If all that were required was to distinguish between the nuclear and joint family systems, then the cross-sectional evidence from listings of inhabitants would have been unambiguous. Indeed, evidence on the average size of households alone would probably have sufficed. However, according to Le Play, a third possibility exists, known as the *stem family system*. Under this system, one child in each generation (often, but not necessarily, the eldest son) remains living in the family home after marriage and raises his children there. The parents remain in the household, and at some point responsibility for the household passes from father to son. Those children who are not to inherit the house typically leave and seek their fortune elsewhere. The effect of this is to create a stable household that persists in the same place, often in the same building, for many generations. A feature of this system is that more than one married couple may co-reside in the same household, though each co-resident married couple must be of a different generation.

It is much more difficult to distinguish between the stem family system and the nuclear family system using cross-sectional evidence than it is to distinguish between the nuclear family system and the joint family system. If mortality were sufficiently high, it would be very rare to find two married couples in the same household even if the stem family system were in operation, simply because at least one of the parents would normally have died before the inheriting son married.[26] Moreover, the stem family system is consistent with there being few co-resident relatives, but a large number of unrelated persons.[27]

In order to dispose of this criticism, recourse was had to demographic computer simulations.[28] A world was created with fertility and mortality regimes

---

[26] This point was made originally in L.K. Berkner, 'The Stem Family and the Developmental Cycle of the Peasant Household: an Eighteenth-Century Austrian Example', *American Historical Review* LXXVII (1972), pp. 398–418. For an excellent discussion of this issue, see M. Anderson, *Approaches to the History of the Western Family, 1500–1914* (London, Macmillan, 1995), pp. 30–3.

[27] The reasons for the presence of relatives will be different in the two systems. In the stem family system, they will be there mainly because of the way in which household headship is transferred down the generations, whereas in the nuclear family system they will be present because they are providing or receiving services for reasons of family welfare (see R. Wall, 'Characteristics of European Family and Household Systems', *Historical Social Research* XXIII (1998), pp. 44–66). The key point is, though, that it is very difficult to distinguish these two processes generating co-resident relatives with the limited data available in most listings of inhabitants.

[28] See K. Wachter, E. Hammel and P. Laslett, *Statistical Studies of Historical Social Structure* (London, Academic Press, 1978).

close to those that were believed to obtain in early modern England, and with a distribution of ages at marriage typical of those reported from family reconstitutions. Into this world were inserted the stem family system's rules for the formation and dissolution of households. The simulation programme was then run until the world had attained a roughly steady state, and an imaginary household survey was then taken of this world. The results were clear. Under the demographic conditions of early modern England, the widespread operation of the stem family system could not have produced a household structure anything like that which was observed in the English listings of inhabitants: there would, for example, have been more households with two married couples than were observed.[29] Therefore, early modern England must have been a society in which the nuclear family system prevailed.

The details of this system were set out by John Hajnal, who called it the 'north-west European household formation system'.[30] Unlike the European marriage pattern, which appears to have functioned throughout western Europe, this system of household formation did not operate in Mediterranean areas, where something much closer to the stem family system prevailed. Its chief feature was that only one married couple lived in each household. It followed from this that newly married couples must form their own separate household upon marriage. The third feature followed from this neolocal marriage pattern. In order to form their own household, couples needed to accumulate the wherewithal to marry. They did this by moving out of their own home to live and work as servants in other (neighbouring) households while they were young and unmarried. Of course, the need to accumulate the resources with which to marry led to a late age at marriage. Thus Hajnal described a system ideally suited to the operation of Malthus's preventive check.

8.5 Fertility and population growth

The argument so far has shown that early modern England possessed a household formation system that could allow the preventive check to operate. The conditions were there. However, in order to demonstrate that it did function to keep population growth low, we need to show that there were associations between economic conditions (as measured by real wages) and the propensity to marry, between nuptiality and fertility, and between fertility and population growth. In this and the next two sections, we take these in reverse order.

---

[29] Ibid., pp. 89–111.
[30] J. Hajnal, 'Two Kinds of Preindustrial Household Formation System', *Population and Development Review* VIII (1982), pp. 452–3. This important paper also appears in R. Wall, J. Robin and P. Laslett (eds), *Family Forms in Historic Europe* (Cambridge, Cambridge University Press, 1983) pp. 65–104.

Box 8.1 Single-figure indices of fertility

A number of single-figure indices of fertility are in common use by demographers. Perhaps the simplest is the *crude birth rate* (CBR), which is the number of births in a given year divided by the average population (the result is usually multiplied by 1000 for convenience of presentation). The denominator of the CBR, however, includes a large number of persons who are not at risk of bearing children (men, and most females aged under 15 and over 50 years). To avoid this, an alternative index, the *general fertility rate* (GFR) divides the number of births in a given year by the average population of women of child-bearing age (usually taken to be either 15–49 years or 15–44 years). Both the CBR and the GFR are subject to distortions because of changes in the structure of the population. For example, even if each woman has children at the same rate, the crude birth rate will fall if the proportion of women in the population declines.

The total fertility rate (TFR), defined in Box 3.1, is an alternative index that is not subject to such distortions. Define an age-specific fertility rate (ASFR) for women aged x years as the number of children born per year to women aged x. Then the TFR is simply the sum of the ASFRs over the child-bearing age range. It is the number of children that the average woman would end up with if she bore children at each age at a rate given by the ASFRs used in the calculation. It may be calculated for a real group of women born in a certain period (that is, a birth cohort), or it may be calculated as a synthetic index of the fertility prevailing in a given period, by summing the ASFRs prevailing in that period. In the latter case, it measures the average number of children a hypothetical cohort of women would have if, at each age, they bore children at the rates prevailing in that period.

Finally, the *gross reproduction rate* (GRR), also defined in Box 3.1, is calculated in a manner similar to the TFR, but uses only female births. Because the sex ratio of births varies little with the age of the mother, and is normally around 100 daughters for every 105 sons, the approximation

GRR = TFR x (100/205)

is usually very good. Further details of all these measures may be found in C. Newell, *Methods and Models in Demography* (London, Belhaven, 1988), pp. 35–62; and A. Hinde, *Demographic Methods* (London, Edward Arnold, 1998), pp. 95–104, 151.

Figure 8.2 plots two single-figure indices of fertility, the crude birth rate (CBR) and the total fertility rate (TFR) (see Box 8.1), on the same graph as two measures of the population growth rate, using data taken from E.A. Wrigley and R.S. Schofield's analysis of a sample of 404 English parish registers. The two measures of the population growth rate used are the annual crude rate of natural increase (the difference between the crude birth and death rates) and the annual percentage population growth rate. The graph reveals quite a close long-run relationship between fertility and population growth. From the mid-sixteenth century until around 1660 the CBR fell from 35–40 per thousand per year to well below 30 per thousand per year, and the TFR fell from close to six births per woman to fewer than four. This decline in fertility was matched by a fall in the annual population growth rate from close to 1 per cent per year between 1550 and 1580 (ignoring the period of the severe mortality crisis in the late 1550s) to below zero by the late 1650s. After about 1660 a slow rise in fertility occurred alongside a corresponding slow recovery in the rate of population growth.

8.6 Fertility and nuptiality

The assessment of the relationship between fertility and nuptiality is not quite so straightforward. One way to consider it is to look at some measure of the evolution of nuptiality over time and compare it with the history of fertility. E.A. Wrigley and R.S. Schofield, in *The Population History of England*, present two measures: the crude marriage rate and the percentages

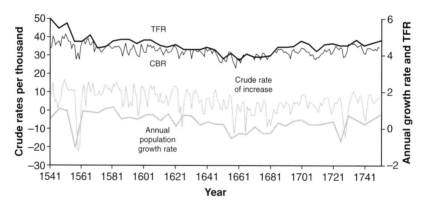

Figure 8.2 Fertility and population growth in England, 1541–1751
Notes: CBR = crude birth rate, TFR = total fertility rate.
Source: E.A. Wrigley and R.S. Schofield, *The Population History of England 1541–1871: a Reconstruction* (London, Arnold, 1981), pp. 528–9, 531–3.

ever marrying by birth cohort (see Figure 8.1).[31] These are plotted in Figure 8.3, together with the TFR.

The results of this exercise are quite striking. The decline in fertility from the mid-sixteenth century to the period of the Commonwealth was accompanied by a progressive fall in the crude marriage rate from 14 per thousand per year to around 7–8 per thousand per year. The recovery in fertility after the 1660s was associated with a similar recovery in the crude marriage rate. The percentages ever marrying show a similar trend consistent with the crude marriage rate. Figure 8.3 provides compelling evidence of a strong

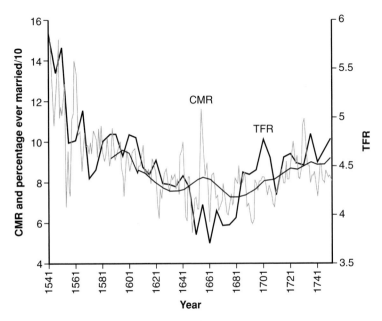

Figure 8.3 Fertility and nuptiality in England, 1541–1751
Notes: CMR = crude marriage rate, TFR = total fertility rate. On this graph, the percentages ever marrying have been divided by ten so that their scale is comparable to that of the crude marriage rate. The percentages ever marrying by birth cohort are plotted on the unlabelled line, against the year in which the cohort was aged approximately 32 years, as this is close to the mean age at child-bearing and interest in this chart is on the relationship between nuptiality and fertility.
Sources: E.A. Wrigley and R.S. Schofield, *The Population History of England 1541–1871: a Reconstruction* (London, Arnold, 1981), pp. 260, 528–9, 531–3.

---

31   Wrigley and Schofield, *Population History*, pp. 260, 262, 531–3. The crude marriage rate is the number of marriages in a given year divided by the average population in that year. It is usually multiplied by 1000 for convenience of presentation. Since the distribution of ages at marriage did not change appreciably between 1550 and 1750, the proportion ever marrying provides a good measure of overall nuptiality. For information on the distribution of ages at marriage, see Wrigley *et al.*, *English Population History*, pp. 145–7.

association of fertility with nuptiality, at least in the long run. Even so, the correspondence between the fertility and marriage series is not absolute. For example, between 1640 and 1680 fertility appears to have fallen even lower than might have been expected given the level of nuptiality. This suggests that there might have been factors other than nuptiality influencing the level of fertility, at least in the short and medium term. These factors will be considered further in Chapter 9.

8.7 Real wages and nuptiality

The final link in the preventive check model is that between real wages and nuptiality. In order to examine this, it is important to bear in mind that changes in nuptiality were almost entirely due to changes in the proportions ever marrying. The distribution of ages at marriage changed little between the end of the sixteenth century and 1750.[32] Therefore, if a decline in real wages did influence nuptiality, it seems to have done so by dissuading a larger proportion of the population from marrying at all. The median age at marriage for men in early modern England was about 26 years, and that for women was about 25 years; half of all men got married between around ages 23 and 30 years, and half of all women between ages 22 and 29.[33] Since young people were typically saving up to get married while working as servants for perhaps 10–12 years before this, then for any one birth cohort it is the real wage situation during their late teens and early twenties that is likely to have had the greatest impact on their propensity to marry.

Figure 8.4 plots real wages against the proportions ever marrying for the birth cohorts used in Figures 8.1 and 8.3. It also plots crude marriage rates. The first point to note is that the relationship between these measures and nuptiality is by no means as strong as the relationship between nuptiality and fertility. However, there is a relationship, both in relation to short-term fluctuations and in the long run. It is clear, for example, that severe temporary falls in real wages were often accompanied by similar reductions in the crude marriage rate. This occurred in the subsistence crises of the late 1550s and 1590s, and also in the late 1640s, 1661–62 and 1674–75. Temporary surges in real wages also occasionally seem to have elevated the marriage rate (for example, during the 1650s). The short-run relationship is also clearly evident in the early eighteenth century.[34] There is also a general long-run relationship, in that declining real wages during the second half of the sixteenth century and the first two decades of the seventeenth century were accompanied by generally falling marriage rates and increased celibacy,

---

[32] Wrigley *et al.*, *English Population History*, pp. 145–7.
[33] Ibid., p. 146.
[34] For a more detailed analysis of this short-run relationship between nuptiality and real wages, see Wrigley and Schofield, *Population History*, pp. 320–32 and 348–53.

whereas rising real wages after about 1680 were accompanied by a slowly increasing marriage rate and falling celibacy. However, this long-run relationship is certainly less clear than those examined in the previous two sections. Moreover, the short-run relationship also becomes much more difficult to discern between about 1660 and 1720.

Thus, although there seems to be some link between real wages and nuptiality, the mechanisms underlying this link were probably more complex than those behind the links between nuptiality and fertility, and between fertility and population growth. The Malthusian account relies on individualistic rational-choice behaviour (in other words, large numbers of individuals responding in a rational way to their economic circumstances). There certainly seems to be enough evidence to support the existence of this kind of behaviour. But there may have been other processes at work, too. In some parishes in seventeenth-century England attempts seem to have been made by parish authorities to discourage and even to forbid the marriages of paupers (that is, of those who were considered to be likely to burden the poor

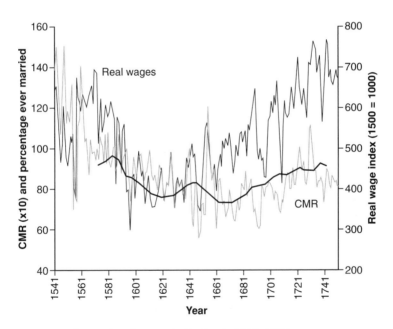

Figure 8.4 Nuptiality and real wages in England, 1541–1751
Notes: CMR = crude marriage rate. On this graph, the crude marriage rate has been multiplied by ten so that it may be plotted on the same scale as the percentages ever marrying. The percentages ever marrying by birth cohort are plotted on the unlabelled line, against the year in which the cohort was aged 20 years, as this is around the age at which trends in real wages should have most influence on the propensity of a cohort to marry.
Sources: E.A. Wrigley and R.S. Schofield, *The Population History of England 1541–1871: a Reconstruction* (London, Arnold, 1981), pp. 260, 531–3, 642–3.

rates).[35] Moreover, the extent to which pauper marriage was restricted was related to the degree of population pressure on resources: in times of 'high pressure' the incentive to restrict marriage in this way may have been greater.[36] From one point of view, the practice of forbidding pauper marriages can be seen as an example of those in positions of power deliberately imposing Malthus's preventive check in order to alleviate or to prevent the threat of the positive check. An alternative interpretation runs that when real wages were low, as they were in the seventeenth century, then pauperization will have been more prevalent, increasing the pool of persons whose marriages might have been prevented in this way. Whatever the details of the mechanism, it is possible that the prohibition of pauper marriages may have contributed to the high celibacy rate that checked population growth in the seventeenth century. This is one of the chief attractions of this theory, for, unlike the rational-choice accounts, it specifically explains why the preventive check operated through a decrease in the proportions of the population marrying, rather than an increase in the average age at marriage. However, studies of pauper populations to date suggest that they were neither numerous enough, nor generally of an appropriate age, for the practice to have made much impact on demographic trends at the national level.[37]

8.8 Conclusion

The overall theme of this chapter has been to present the formidable combination of theoretical and empirical analysis that has accumulated over the past 30 years and that forms a seemingly irresistible case in favour of Malthus's preventive check as the mechanism by which population growth in pre-industrial England was restricted. A disparate set of observations made during the 1960s about ages at marriage and the structure of the household have been gradually discovered to be early glimpses of a household formation and marriage system that was capable of adjusting quite sensitively to changes in real wages and in population pressure. England's population grew rapidly during the late sixteenth and early seventeenth centuries principally because real wages were high, it was easy for couples to accumulate the resources with which to marry, and so celibacy was low, and consequently fertility was high. During the seventeenth century real wages fell, causing celibacy levels to rise and fertility to fall. This pretty much stopped population growth in its tracks, and for a few decades after 1650

---

[35] On this practice in Fenland parishes, see S. Hindle, 'The Problem of Pauper Marriage in Seventeenth-Century England', *Transactions of the Royal Historical Society*, 6th series VIII (1998), pp. 76–8; and S. Hindle, 'Power, Poor Relief and Social Relations in Holland Fen c. 1600–1800', *Historical Journal* XLI (1998), pp. 90–2.

[36] This seems to be implied by the discussion in Hindle, 'Problem of Pauper Marriage', pp. 81–5.

[37] I am grateful to Prof. Nigel Goose of the University of Hertfordshire for this point.

the population may actually have fallen. The last two decades of the 1600s saw a slow resumption of population growth as celibacy rates fell, and this was maintained into the early eighteenth century.

So pervasive was the preventive check in England that it dominated variations in mortality as determinants of population growth. Mortality did play some part: underlying mortality rates were low in the late sixteenth century and high in the late seventeenth century. Trends in mortality, therefore, tended to reinforce the effects of the preventive check, but long-term variations in mortality rates were not the main reasons for variations in the rate of population growth.

The evidence in favour of the operation of the preventive check seems persuasive and, as a general account, it is hard to question it. However, it is worth raising a few points in this conclusion that have sometimes been overlooked by historians. First, the argument of this chapter (which reflects the literature on the topic) has relied heavily on aggregate data. Even where family reconstitution data have been employed, the tendency has been to concentrate on averages. The inevitable consequence of this is that England is portrayed as demographically homogeneous, and that differences among sub-groups of the population, both geographical and otherwise, are minimized or obscured. Perhaps this conclusion is, therefore, an appropriate place to emphasize that there were local and regional patterns to the operation of the preventive check in early modern England. For example, Steven King finds a low age at marriage among the proto-industrial manufacturing population of Calverley in West Yorkshire, and considers it clear that many brides and grooms could not possibly have been economically independent when they married.[38] There were also parts of England, notably the north-west, where (as we saw in Chapter 7) the positive check might have retained its importance longer than it did elsewhere.

The fact that Malthus's preventive check was operating so powerfully in England after the middle of the sixteenth century begs the question of why this was so. Answers to this question tend to be couched in terms of deep cultural forces at work within medieval England. One well-known argument is related to the belief that the English were, as far back as at least the thirteenth century, a particularly individualistic people and that the nuclear family system was prevalent in the Middle Ages and changed little between 1200 and 1700.[39] According to this view, had we access to better sources,

[38] S. King, 'English Historical Demography and the Nuptiality Conundrum: New Perspectives', *Historical Social Research* XXIII (1998), pp. 130–56.

[39] The most prominent exponent of this view is Alan Macfarlane. See: A. Macfarlane, *The Origins of English Individualism: the Family, Property and Social Transition* (Oxford, Blackwell, 1978); A. Macfarlane, *Marriage and Love in England, 1300–1840: Modes of Reproduction* (Oxford, Blackwell, 1986), pp. 321–44. See also R.M. Smith, 'Some Reflections on the Evidence for the Origins of the "European Marriage Pattern" in England', in C. Harris (ed.), *Sociology of the Family* (Keele, University of Keele, 1979), pp. 74–112; and P. Laslett, *Family Life and Illicit Love in Earlier Generations* (Cambridge, Cambridge University Press, 1977), pp. 47–8.

and had plague not so distorted the demographic system of England during the two centuries after 1348, we should probably have been able to trace the impact of the Malthusian preventive check during the period before 1550. This argument has been criticized by Zvi Razi, who suggests that

> ... the nuclearization of the peasant family began in the thirteenth century in East Anglia and possibly also in the south-east and south-west, and was completed in the rest of lowland England in the late fourteenth and the first half of the fifteenth centuries.[40]

Razi is not completely clear as to the reasons why this happened, but the decline in the population of fourteenth-century England, and especially the economic and demographic consequences of the Black Death, seem to have been important contributory factors.[41] They cannot have been enough alone, though, for the Black Death affected the whole of western Europe, and England seems to have experienced a much more intense nuclearization than most other countries. Razi recognizes this, and suggests that 'the serfs' determination to become free' resulted in high levels of migration in late fourteenth- and fifteenth-century England, which destroyed the extended family system.[42] This brings us back closer to a thesis of 'English exceptionalism' or 'individualism'.

---

[40]   Z. Razi, 'The Myth of the Immutable English Family', *Past and Present* CXL (1993), p. 42.
[41]   Ibid., pp. 41–2.
[42]   Ibid., p. 42.

9

Childbearing in early modern England

9.1 Introduction

The conclusion of the previous chapter was that English fertility during the sixteenth, seventeenth and early eighteenth centuries responded through the filter of the changing prevalence of marriage to fluctuations in economic conditions, and thereby the growth of the population was kept in check. The correspondence between changing nuptiality and fertility is so clear that it is tempting to conclude that little more needs to be said in order to explain fertility trends. Despite the seemingly overwhelming importance of marriage patterns for fertility in the long term, however, there are variations in fertility over time that do not seem to be explained entirely by changing nuptiality, and that must therefore be the result of changes in fertility within marriage (or possibly changes in illegitimate fertility). Moreover, although Chapter 8 discussed *trends* in fertility, it said very little about its overall *level*. Although it is clear that fertility in seventeenth-century England was lower than it had been a hundred years earlier, we might ask, for example, how levels of fertility in pre-industrial England compare with those in other populations at a similar level of development.

This chapter examines the factors affecting the fertility of English men and women during the early modern period. It uses a model of the determinants of fertility that is widely used in the demographic literature, and which is described in Section 9.2. Section 9.3 examines more fully the effect of late and non-universal marriage on fertility, comparing the fertility levels that might have been expected under universal marriage with the levels actually observed. It thus complements Section 8.6. The results of the comparisons show that the fall in fertility during the seventeenth century cannot in its entirety be explained by changing nuptiality. There was also some reduction in the rate of child-bearing among married couples.

A possible cause of this might have been a change in the impact of certain biological and behavioural factors on fertility. This is the subject of Sections 9.4 and 9.5. It turns out that in order to assess the impact of these factors with the data that are available, it is necessary to assume that deliberate birth control was not being practised. This assumption, however, is by no means unquestionable. The precise extent to which our early modern ancestors resorted to birth control has vexed historians and demographers for several decades, and is explored in Section 9.6.

In Section 9.7, we move on to examine whether social, economic and cultural factors had any direct influence on the fertility of married couples (it is already clear that they affected fertility indirectly through their relationship with nuptiality). The most well-developed body of theory in this area is the so-called 'demand' theory of fertility. This suggests that in pre-industrial populations the demand for children (assessed in economic terms) was normally at least as great as the available supply, and therefore couples had no reason to resort to fertility control. The usefulness of this theory in explaining fertility trends in pre-industrial England depends on the economic status of children: were they an asset to or a burden on their parents? It turns out that assessing the economic relations between children and their parents is extremely difficult to do, so much so that it is impossible to reach a firm conclusion about the utility of the demand theory. The concluding Section 9.8 summarizes what we know and do not know about the determinants of fertility in early modern England.

9.2 The proximate determinants of fertility

The level of fertility in any human population is, ultimately, determined by a host of social, cultural and economic factors. However, demographers have, for many years, realized that these factors can only operate through a rather small number of intermediate variables that, when taken together, completely determine the level of fertility.[1] Understanding why fertility in a particular population is at one level rather than another is, then, a matter of identifying the way in which these *intermediate variables* combine in that population to give rise to the observed fertility rate. Even if two populations share the same observed level of fertility, their intermediate variables may take on quite different sets of values that both happen to produce the same fertility outcome.

The intermediate variables are, these days, usually called the *proximate determinants* of fertility.[2] Broadly speaking, they fall into three groups.[3] The

---

[1] The first explicit recognition of this was in K. Davis and J. Blake, 'Social Structure and Fertility: an Analytic Framework', *Economic Development and Cultural Change* IV (1956), pp. 211–35.

[2] The phrase 'proximate determinants' is usually attributed to John Bongaarts; see J. Bongaarts, 'A Framework for Analysing the Proximate Determinants of Fertility', *Population and Development Review* IV (1978), pp. 105–32; and J. Bongaarts and R.G. Potter, *Fertility, Biology and Behaviour: an Analysis of the Proximate Determinants* (New York, Academic Press, 1983).

[3] The description of the proximate determinants used here is based on J. Bongaarts, 'The Impact on Fertility of Traditional Child-Spacing Practices', in H.J. Page and R. Lesthaeghe (eds), *Child-Spacing in Tropical Africa* (London, Academic Press, 1981), pp. 111–29.

first group is sometimes labelled 'exposure factors' since they affect the proportion of women of reproductive age in the population that is, at any point in time, in a more or less stable sexual relationship with a man (such a relationship being called a *sexual union*). Marriage is the most common type of sexual union, but many unions not blessed by either Church or state also fall into this category. The key issue is that women in sexual unions normally have much higher fertility than women who are not in such unions. Exposure factors include the typical age at entry into sexual unions, the extent of permanent celibacy and the proportion of the average woman's reproductive period spent between or after unions.

Men and women within sexual unions may choose to exercise control over their fertility. According to the proximate determinants framework, they do this by manipulating two 'deliberate fertility control factors': the extent to which effective contraception is used, and the use or non-use of induced abortion. These two factors are behavioural and are subject to modification by couples within sexual unions who wish directly to influence their child-bearing.

In addition, the level of fertility is determined by a third group of 'other' factors. The most important of these is the length of the period of non-susceptibility to conception after each birth. This is largely determined by the average age to which babies are breast-fed, since lactation inhibits ovulation. In addition, some populations practise lengthy periods of abstinence from sexual intercourse after each birth. Though both breast-feeding behaviour and abstinence from sexual activity are clearly subject to individual variability, demographers have for long recognized that both are usually regulated by strong cultural norms and, as such, are not commonly varied by individuals with the intention of influencing fertility. The 'other' factors also include the extent of involuntary sterility in the population, the extent to which miscarriages and stillbirths occur, and the duration of viability of ova and sperm. A final factor is the frequency of intercourse. Despite Malthus's famous dictum that 'the passion between the sexes ... will remain nearly in its present state', variations in the frequency of intercourse can have a powerful effect on the level of fertility, especially when the frequency falls below about twice per week.[4]

Variations in fertility can arise because of differences in any of these proximate determinants but, in practice, demographers have tended to stress three: the typical age at entry into sexual unions, the extent to which contraception is used, and the average length of breast-feeding (or post-partum non-susceptibility to conception). The lack of emphasis on the others has several causes. Some (for example, duration of viability of ova and sperm) are believed to be comparatively unimportant to our

---

[4] T.R. Malthus, *An Essay on the Principle of Population and A Summary View of the Principle of Population* (ed.) A. Flew (Harmondsworth, Pelican, 1970), p. 70.

understanding of why fertility varies among different populations at a given point in time, or in the same population at two closely positioned points in time, for which purposes the proximate determinants model has most often been used. In some cases measurement is very difficult. This is true, for example, of the frequency of intercourse, or the prevalence of miscarriages. In the case of frequency of intercourse, not only are accurate data hard to obtain for specific populations, but also, even when they do exist, it is very difficult to determine whether couples' adjustments to their coital frequency are made with the intention of postponing or curtailing (or possibly accelerating) child-bearing, or for other reasons.

In order to understand variations in fertility over time in England, it will be necessary to consider a wider range of determinants than is, perhaps, normally considered. The next four sections of this chapter can be viewed as an examination of the effect of the proximate determinants on English fertility during the sixteenth, seventeenth and eighteenth centuries.

9.3 The impact of the European marriage pattern

In Chapter 8 it was suggested that late and non-universal marriage had the effect of reducing English fertility substantially compared with what would have been the case under a system of universal marriage for women, such as that prevailing in South Asia today. Here, we quantify this effect, and show how it varied over time. The method used to evaluate the effect is described in Box 9.1. In brief, it involves using the age-specific fertility rates of married women – called *age-specific marital fertility rates* (ASMFRs) – to work out how many children the average woman would produce if she were married throughout her reproductive life. The ASMFRs are then adjusted using the proportions married by age, and the average completed family size recalculated using the adjusted rates. It turns out that, using an age pattern of marriage that appears to be representative of seventeenth- and early eighteenth-century England, and assuming that 15 per cent of women never married, fertility is reduced by 41 per cent from the level that would obtain under a regime of universal marriage for women. Increasing the celibacy rate to 25 per cent would lead to a fertility reduction of close to 50 per cent, and even if celibacy were only 5 per cent, delayed marriage would cause a reduction of 34 per cent.[5]

Figure 9.1 shows the results of applying the method described in Box 9.1 to examine the fertility of five-year birth cohorts of English women born between the 1550s and the 1730s. Three lines are shown. The top line (described as 'TMFR per woman') is the average number of children that

---

[5]   In fact, even if all women married, fertility would be reduced by 30 per cent through marriage delay alone.

Box 9.1 The fertility-reducing effect of late and non-universal marriage

This box describes a method which expresses the fertility that would be observed under a range of late and non-universal marriage regimes with the level of fertility in a population if all women married on their twentieth birthday and remained married until their fiftieth birthday. The method assumes that there is no child-bearing outside marriage, and that no woman marries prior to her twentieth birthday. The method makes use of age-specific marital fertility rates (ASMFRs). The ASMFR at any age x is the number of children that would be born to 1000 wives between their xth birthday and their $(x+1)$th birthday. Adding up the ASMFRs over all ages from 20 to 49 inclusive produces the total number of children that would be born to 1000 women who married at age 20 and remained married until their fiftieth birthday.

In England between 1600 and 1749 the ASMFRs were approximately as shown in the following table (based on E.A. Wrigley, R.S. Davies, J.E. Oeppen and R.S. Schofield, *English Population History from Family Reconstitution, 1580–1837* (Cambridge, Cambridge University Press, 1997), p. 355).

Age of woman	ASMFR
20–24	403
25–29	362
30–34	315
35–39	246
40–44	125
45–49	22

Summing the above figures and multiplying by five, because five-year age groups have been used, produces a figure of 7365. That is, the average woman would produce 7.365 children under a regime of universal marriage at age 20 years. This is known as the *total marital fertility rate* (TMFR).

If we then allow for late and non-universal marriage, we can multiply each ASMFR by the proportions of women married at the relevant age, and add up the results. This produces the total number of children that would be born to 1000 women who experienced the given regime of late and non-universal marriage. Suppose, for example, the proportions married in each age group were as follows (these figures are derived on the basis of the age at marriage distributions shown in E.A. Wrigley, R.S. Davies, J.E. Oeppen and R.S. Schofield, *English Population History from Family Reconstitution, 1580–1837* (Cambridge, Cambridge University Press, 1997), pp. 146–7, assuming that 15 per cent of women never married).

Age group	Proportions married
20–24	0.251
25–29	0.557
30–34	0.757
35–39	0.850
40–44	0.850
45–49	0.850

In this case, the average number of children born per thousand women would be equal to (403 x 0.251) + (362 x 0.557) + (315 x 0.757) + (246 x 0.85) + (125 x 0.85) + (22 x 0.85) = 4370. Comparing this with 7365 reveals that the regime of late and non-universal marriage produces only 59 per cent of the fertility of the universal marriage regime.

would be born to the women in each birth cohort assuming universal marriage at age 20. From about 7.6 children among cohorts born prior to about 1600 this falls slightly to just below 7.0 children among cohorts born between 1625 and 1650, before rising again to reach about 7.5 children among cohorts born after 1675. The bottom line (described as 'TFR per woman') shows the estimated average number of children per women (or total fertility rate) assuming the distributions of age at marriage obtained by E.A. Wrigley and his colleagues from family reconstitution data, and the proportions never marrying were those shown for each cohort in Figure 8.1.[6] Cohorts born during the 1550s and 1560s averaged close to five children. Subsequent cohorts born between the 1560s and 1600 had successively lower fertility, such that those born around 1600 could only muster around four children. After a brief rise, fertility then fell to reach fewer than 3.5 children on average among cohorts born around 1650. This marked the low point, and thereafter a gradual but sustained increase occurred, such that cohorts born during the 1730s were, once again, achieving an average family size of almost five children. It is worth comparing the evolution of the TFR shown in Figure 9.1 with that in Figure 8.2, which was estimated by quite a different method. The correspondence between the two sets of estimates is close, suggesting that we can be fairly confident in the results.

Figure 9.1 also depicts a third line, which shows what the average completed family size would have been if the fertility of married women had remained constant at the levels of the late sixteenth century. This third line,

---

[6]   For the age at marriage distributions, see E.A. Wrigley, R.S. Davies, J.E. Oeppen and R.S. Schofield, *English Population History from Family Reconstitution, 1580–1837* (Cambridge, Cambridge University Press, 1997), pp. 146–7.

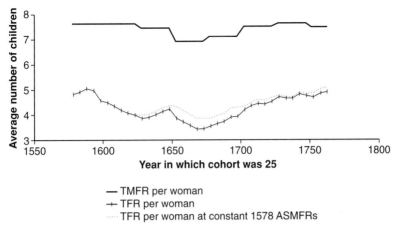

— TMFR per woman
─+─ TFR per woman
······ TFR per woman at constant 1578 ASMFRs

Figure 9.1 The impact of late and non-universal marriage on English fertility, 1575–1765

Notes: For method of calculation see Box 9.1. The top line shows the total marital fertility rate (TMFR) for women aged 20–49 years in each birth cohort from 1551–56 to 1736–41; the bottom line shows the estimated total fertility rate for each cohort; the middle line shows the hypothetical total fertility rate estimated assuming that the TMFR remained constant at its late sixteenth-century level.

Sources: E.A. Wrigley and R.S. Schofield, *The Population History of England 1541–1871: a Reconstruction* (London, Edward Arnold, 1981), p. 260; E.A. Wrigley, R.S. Davies, J.E. Oeppen and R.S. Schofield, *English Population History from Family Reconstitution 1580–1837* (Cambridge, Cambridge University Press, 1997), pp. 146–7, 355.

therefore, is an attempt to show the fluctuations in fertility that are due solely to changing proportions marrying. Although the decline in fertility within marriage does contribute to the fall and subsequent rise in the total fertility rate over the whole period, it is clear that changing proportions marrying are the main factor at work. Even if fertility within marriage had not changed over the two centuries after 1575, the average completed family size would still have fallen from 5.0 to below 4.0 by the late seventeenth century.

The calculations of the impact of the European marriage pattern in English fertility shown in Box 9.1 and reported in Figure 9.1 all make the assumption that unmarried women have zero fertility. To the extent that unmarried women also bear children, the impact of late and non-universal marriage on fertility will be attenuated.[7] The prevalence of illegitimate fertility in early modern England has been investigated by Peter Laslett, whose

---

[7]   In the limiting case, if the fertility of married and non-married women were the same, then changing ages at marriage or proportions ever marrying would have no effect on fertility at all.

data suggest that during the period from the 1550s to the 1750s, the percentage of births that were illegitimate never rose above about 4 per cent.[8] Indeed, during the mid-sixteenth century and the mid-seventeenth century it was less than 2 per cent, and although there was a slow and sustained rise after this, it had only reached 5 per cent by the 1830s.[9] There seems to have been a strong cultural belief, influenced no doubt by the Church, that bearing children outside marriage was wrong. This is not to say that unmarried women did not become pregnant; they did. In many cases, though, this occurred in anticipation of an already planned marriage, and in most of the rest social pressure was placed on couples to marry before the birth of the child. The result was that a high proportion of English brides between the sixteenth and the eighteenth centuries were pregnant. Using Laslett's figures again, we find that between 1550 and 1599 more than 30 per cent of first births took place within nine months of marriage, and though this percentage fell to just under 20 per cent in the second half of the seventeenth century, it rose again to reach about 35 per cent after 1750.[10] It seems clear, therefore, that the impact of late and non-universal marriage on English fertility was not reduced by appreciable fertility among unmarried women.[11]

9.4 Breast-feeding

After a woman has had a child, there is a period during which she cannot become pregnant again. This is known as the *non-susceptible period* and its length is determined in human populations principally by two factors: the duration of breast-feeding and the length of the period after each birth for which the couple refrains from sexual intercourse (known as *post-partum abstinence*). The contraceptive effect of breast-feeding is determined both by the length of time for which a mother breast-feeds her child, and the intensity of the feeding, since it is the action of suckling associated with infants feeding from the breast that induces the release of hormones that suppress ovulation. Generally speaking, exclusive breast-feeding (where the child is not being given any supplementation) involves frequent suckling, and the almost complete absence of ovulation. As infants are gradually weaned on to more solid food, however, the intensity of breast-feeding typically declines, and at some point ovulation is resumed, often before the infant is completely weaned.

---

[8]   P. Laslett, *Family Life and Illicit Love in Earlier Generations* (Cambridge, Cambridge University Press, 1977), p. 102.
[9]   Ibid., p. 102.
[10] Ibid., p. 130.
[11] It should be noted that none of the calculations reported in this section takes into account the impact of widowhood on fertility. Because some women were widowed during their reproductive years, the average completed family size will be somewhat lower than that reported in Figure 9.1.

Family reconstitution data (see Appendix II) provide information about fertility histories. That is, they furnish the date of marriage of a set of couples, together with the dates of birth (and, importantly, death, if they die in infancy or childhood) of all their children. If we assume that these fertility histories are complete (that is, no births are missed out), then it is in principle possible to use this information to estimate the average length of the non-susceptible period for English women in pre-industrial times. There are two possible approaches. The first compares the length of the interval between marriage and the first birth after marriage among women who were not pregnant when they married with the duration of the interval between the first and second births.[12] The rationale here is that the interval between the births of the first and second children will include the non-susceptible period, whereas the interval between marriage and the first birth will not. A second, more complex, method involves comparing the lengths of intervals following the births of children who subsequently died in infancy or early childhood with the lengths of birth intervals following the births of children who did not die.[13] The rationale here is that the lengths of the two sets of intervals being compared should differ because in the one case breast-feeding was curtailed by the death of the child, whereas in the other case breast-feeding would have continued until the 'natural', probably culturally determined, age at weaning.[14]

The results of the first approach suggest that the length of the non-susceptible period in England between 1600 and 1799 was about 11–12 months on average.[15] Assuming a gradual process of weaning, this is consistent with breast-feeding continuing until children were aged 12–18 months, and/or with a period of post-partum abstinence of just under a year. For various technical reasons, the second approach tends to produce a wider range of plausible estimates, but the results suggest that

> many women continued breast-feeding well into the second year after the
> birth of a child, and that a proportion continued until the child was past its

---

[12] This is the approach adopted in C. Wilson, 'The Proximate Determinants of Marital Fertility in England 1600–1799', in L. Bonfield, R.M. Smith and K. Wrightson (eds), *The World We Have Gained* (Oxford, Blackwell, 1986), pp. 219–20.

[13] This approach is used in Wrigley *et al.*, *English Population History*, pp. 477–92.

[14] There is an assumption here that the duration of breast-feeding, rather than the length of the period of post-partum abstinence, determines the length of the non-susceptible period. Indeed in Wrigley *et al.*, *English Population History*, I can find no mention of post-partum abstinence at all. However, in defence of the approach, it can be said that in pre-industrial populations where information on both breast-feeding durations and post-partum abstinence is available (for example, many contemporary rural African populations), it is usually the case that the duration of breast-feeding is the limiting factor. Rather few populations (mainly in West Africa) have such long periods of abstinence that the resumption of ovulation precedes the resumption of sexual relations. See R. Lesthaeghe, 'On the Adaptation of Sub-Saharan Systems of Reproduction', in D. Coleman and R. Schofield (eds), *The State of Population Theory: Forward from Malthus* (Oxford, Blackwell, 1986), pp. 212–38.

[15] Wilson, 'Proximate Determinants', p. 221.

second birthday. It was probably the case that few stopped before the end of the first year.[16]

The amount of data required for this kind of analysis meant that Wrigley and his colleagues were unable to sub-divide their data by period, so that trends over time cannot be identified.

The impact of this on fertility may be assessed by noting that the average interval between births in pre-industrial England was around 28–29 months.[17] Pregnancy occupied nine months of this, leaving 19–20 months between the birth of one child and the conception of the next. If the non-susceptible period were around 12 months, this leaves 7–8 months between the time that the woman became liable to conceive again and the time she actually did conceive. This 7–8 months is known as the 'waiting time to conception'. However, we must allow some time for miscarriages to occur, and these are common in early pregnancy. Assuming that, on average, miscarriages account for about 3–4 months of this, it seems plausible to suggest that the waiting time to conception among those women who did not experience a miscarriage was about four months. This implies a monthly probability of conception among susceptible women of about 0.23.[18] In other words, early modern English women who were having regular sexual relations with their husbands and who were doing nothing to prevent pregnancy had about a one in four chance of conceiving every month.[19]

All these figures seem very plausible, but there is a big assumption underlying them: namely that deliberate birth control was largely absent. Without this assumption, it is impossible to know whether the average non-susceptible period of 12 months or so arose entirely from lengthy periods of breast-feeding, or from shorter periods of breast-feeding accompanied by some additional efforts made by some couples to delay the next birth.

9.5 Sterility and other biological factors

Sterility is usually divided into *primary sterility*, which denotes a complete inability to bear any children, and *secondary sterility*, which is acquired after the birth of at least one child. Both primary and secondary sterility arise because of genetic factors, or as a result of acquired infections, often of sexually transmitted diseases. In addition, secondary sterility may be the direct result of complications arising from earlier births. Primary sterility is

---

[16] Wrigley *et al.*, *English Population History*, p. 492.
[17] Ibid., p. 366.
[18] This is the figure quoted by Wilson, 'Proximate Determinants', p. 218.
[19] Wilson, 'Proximate Determinants', p. 213, presents a graph that relates the monthly probability of conception to the frequency of sexual intercourse. For readers who are interested, a monthly probability of conception of 0.23 equates to sexual intercourse two or three times per week.

normally measured by examining the proportion of married women who bore no children. However, as Wrigley and his colleagues point out, in populations where late marriage is common and illegitimate fertility rare, the identification of the extent of the two types is complicated, for women who marry later in life, and produce no children (and who are therefore classed as primarily sterile) might have been able to produce some children had they married earlier.[20] One way to avoid the problem is to focus on women who marry at ages 20–24 years. The family reconstitution data suggest that only about 4 per cent of women marrying in this age group in England during the early modern period were unable to bear children at all.[21] True primary sterility must have been lower than this.

Pre-industrial England, therefore, was a low-sterility population, very different, for example, from several mid-twentieth-century tropical African populations, in which primary sterility affected more than 20 per cent of women. The high sterility rates in Africa were largely due to venereal disease, which spread rapidly among young people because of high levels of sexual activity and complex sexual networks, and which was inadequately treated. It seems unlikely that treatment of such infections was better in pre-industrial England than in twentieth-century Africa, so the most plausible conclusion is that the incidence and transmission of these infections was much lower, suggesting that sexual intercourse among young people was rare. This conclusion is supported by the very low rates of illegitimate fertility in early modern England. The absence of reliable contraception must surely have meant that, if sexual intercourse among young unmarried people had been at all common, pregnancy among young spinsters would have been fairly widespread. The logical consequence would either have been higher rates of illegitimate fertility than are observed, or, if pressure had been placed on such women to marry and legitimize their children, a lower mean age at marriage among women who were pregnant when they married. The only alternative scenario would involve high rates of induced abortion among young unmarried women, which, given the prevailing medical technology, must surely have produced horrendous complications, leading to higher rates of primary sterility than those observed.

Although outright sterility seems to have been rare, sub-fecundity may have been more common, especially in those areas of north-western England where, as we saw in Chapter 7, the nutritional status of the population was precarious. A recent study of fertility and infant mortality in the Cumbrian parish of Penrith has found evidence of greater sub-fecundity there than in southern and Midland England.[22]

---

[20] Wrigley *et al.*, *English Population History*, pp. 359–60.
[21] Ibid., p. 361.
[22] S. Scott and C.J. Duncan, 'Interacting Effects of Nutrition and Social Class Differentials on Fertility and Infant Mortality in a Pre-Industrial Population', *Population Studies* LIV (2000), pp. 77, 81–2.

According to Wrigley and his colleagues, of the women aged 20–24 who were able to bear children when they married, about 4 per cent had become sterile by their late twenties, about 13 per cent by their early thirties and about 60 per cent by their early forties.[23] Like the estimates of the average duration of breast-feeding, these estimates of 'secondary sterility' should be treated with caution, for they assume no birth control. If birth control was being practised, especially in the form of family limitation (see the next section) then these estimates will be too high.

Finally, there is some evidence that sterility varied over time. It seems that it was higher during the late seventeenth and early eighteenth centuries than it was in earlier and later periods, especially among women aged 35 years and over.[24] This is consistent with the trends in marital fertility reported in Figure 9.1. However, as Wrigley and his colleagues point out, these changes in 'sterility' need not have arisen for physiological reasons. Changes in the frequency of intercourse, or changes in the proportion of married couples abstaining from intercourse could have had an effect. Moreover, it is possible that abstinence of this sort might have resulted from couples' efforts deliberately to restrict their fertility.[25] It is time to consider this possibility.

9.6 The role of contraception

It is now 35 years since E.A. Wrigley used his pioneering family reconstitution of the parish of Colyton in Devon to suggest that married couples in pre-industrial England might have tried to limit their fertility by using some form of birth control.[26] Wrigley's evidence was based largely on the late seventeenth century, when, as Figure 9.1 shows, there was a (slight) decrease in fertility within marriage. Though it is possible that increased sterility levels or a longer non-susceptible period accounted for this fall, estimates of changes in the values of these quantities rely on the assumption that birth control was largely absent and are, in any event, very imprecise. Given this, it seems surprising that in the three decades after Wrigley's paper was published, it became almost an orthodoxy that the use of contraception in pre-industrial England was very rare.

This came about through the adoption of a peculiarly restrictive definition of what constitutes birth control, and its measurement using rather mechanistic statistical and demographic models. Birth control was equated with *family limitation*, a type of behaviour by which married couples who desired fewer children than they would ordinarily have if they did nothing

---

[23] Wrigley *et al.*, *English Population History* p. 361.
[24] Ibid., pp. 392–4.
[25] Ibid., p. 393.
[26] E.A. Wrigley, 'Family Limitation in Pre-industrial England', *Economic History Review*, 2nd series XIX (1966), pp. 82–109.

to prevent birth, allowed births to arrive in an 'uncontrolled' fashion in the early years of their marriages, and then attempted to 'stop' childbearing once they reached their desired family size by using some form of contraception. This identification of birth control with family limitation was first made by the French demographer Louis Henry in 1961, and rapidly became a crucial feature of demographers' models of fertility.[27] During the 1970s statistical methods were developed to test the extent of family limitation in a population, and it is these methods that were applied by E.A. Wrigley and his colleagues to assess the use of contraception in pre-industrial England from family reconstitution data.[28] Their conclusion was clear: in general, there is very little evidence for family limitation behaviour being practised in England at any period between the late sixteenth century and the early nineteenth century.[29] The inference was then made (implicitly at times) that, therefore, the use of contraception was very rare.

There are a number of reasons to be sceptical, both about the conclusion from the analysis, and still more about the inference. It has recently been shown that the statistical methods employed to assess the presence of family limitation are not capable of reliably identifying the practice of family limitation by minorities of the population (for example, 10–15 per cent).[30] To be fair, Wrigley and his colleagues acknowledge this. They do not 'preclude the possibility that small groups may have been practising family limitation', but they maintain that 'the reconstitution evidence suggests that such behaviour was restricted to a small minority of the population, if present at all'.[31]

However, the most serious problem lies with the inference that, if family limitation was absent, so was the use of birth control. Family limitation involves 'stopping' behaviour: the adoption of birth control once a couple has already had the number of children it desires. Yet it is quite possible, for example, that married couples used contraception to restrict fertility

---

[27] L. Henry, 'Some Data on Natural Fertility', *Eugenics Quarterly* XVIII (1961), pp. 81–91.

[28] See A.J. Coale and T.J. Trussell, 'Model Fertility Schedules: Variations in the Age Structure of Childbearing in Human Populations', *Population Index* XL (1974), pp. 185–258; A.J. Coale and T.J. Trussell, 'Erratum', *Population Index* XLI (1975), p. 572; and A.J. Coale and T.J. Trussell, 'Finding the Two Parameters that Specify a Model Schedule of Marital Fertility', *Population Index* XLIV (1978), pp. 203–13. The analysis of the family reconstitution data is most fully described in C. Wilson, 'Natural Fertility in Pre-Industrial England', *Population Studies* XXXVIII (1984), pp. 225–40; see also the summary in E.A. Wrigley, R.S. Davies, J.E. Oeppen and R.S. Schofield, *English Population History from Family Reconstitution 1580–1837* (Cambridge, Cambridge University Press, 1997), pp. 457–61.

[29] Wrigley *et al.*, *English Population History*, p. 461.

[30] B.S. Okun, 'Evaluating Methods for Detecting Fertility Control: Coale and Trussell's Model and Cohort Parity Analysis', *Population Studies* XLIII (1994), pp. 199–209.

[31] Wrigley *et al.*, *English Population History*, p. 461. In a footnote, they cite the example of Colyton in the later seventeenth century (the parish originally studied in Wrigley, 'Family Limitation'), where 'the evidence for fertility control within marriage by a part of the community is persuasive'.

by increasing the spacing between births. This could have been used systematically (that is, after every birth), as in twentieth-century African populations. But it could have been used occasionally – for example, to prevent another pregnancy too soon after a particularly difficult pregnancy and birth that drained the physical resources of the mother. It is now known that couples' behaviour in using birth control in the late nineteenth and twentieth centuries was extremely complex and varied, and, in particular, that deliberate birth spacing appears to have been quite widely practised.[32] Given this, it strains credulity to believe that contraceptive use was manifested solely as 'family limitation', or 'stopping' behaviour in earlier times.

The methods employed by Wrigley and his colleagues to measure the extent of family limitation are quite incapable of identifying the use of contraception for birth spacing unless is it widely and fairly systematically practised. Indeed, in *English Population History from Family Reconstitution*, they twice admit that they cannot exclude the possibility that birth spacing was being practised, but this admission is relegated on both occasions to footnotes.[33] Not for nothing, it seems, has Richard Vann termed birth control 'a repressed theme in the book's treatment of changes in fertility, so that it leaves the question of its prevalence still open'.[34] It is true that the results from the family reconstitution data can be accounted for without invoking such behaviour, but this does not mean that it did not occur.[35]

Birth control of some kind may, therefore, have been practised in early modern England. However, it was probably only practised by a minority of the population and its use varied over time (being higher, perhaps, between 1650 and 1700 than at other times). A question that flows naturally from this conclusion is: what methods might have been used? Those who have investigated this generally cite withdrawal, or *coitus interruptus* as the most likely candidate.[36]

---

[32]   This is demonstrated most convincingly by the work of Simon Szreter and his colleagues: see S. Szreter, *Fertility, Class and Gender in Britain, 1860–1940* (Cambridge, Cambridge University Press, 1996); and E. Garrett, A. Reid, K. Schürer and S. Szreter, *Changing Family Size in England and Wales: Place, Class and Demography 1891–1911* (Cambridge, Cambridge University Press, 2001).

[33]   Wrigley *et al.*, *English Population History*, pp. 457, 461.

[34]   R.T. Vann, 'Unnatural Fertility, or, Whatever Happened in Colyton? Some Reflections on *English Population History from Family Reconstitution 1580–1837*', *Continuity and Change* XIV (1999), pp. 91–104. Vann actually uses the phrase 'family limitation' rather than 'birth control'. I suspect he really intends to encompass 'spacing' behaviour, but, if he really means that 'family limitation' in its strict sense is 'a repressed theme', then this is true *a fortiori* of other forms of birth control behaviour.

[35]   Wrigley *et al.*, *English Population History*, p. 494.

[36]   See G. Santow, '*Coitus Interruptus* and the Control of Natural Fertility', *Population Studies* IL (1995), pp. 19–43.

9.7 The demand for children

The argument so far has been that early modern English couples tended to follow Malthus's prescription that they should not marry without the means to raise a family, but that once they married most of them, during most of the period, allowed children to arrive without even a modest amount of subsequent intervention. For many years, the standard explanation of this was couched in terms of the demand for children: in pre-industrial times, couples demanded more children than they were likely to produce during their marriage even without deliberate fertility control and that, therefore, there was no widespread economic rationale for the adoption of birth control behaviour.[37] In one of the more influential demographic theories of recent decades, J.C. Caldwell argued that fertility will be high (and uncontrolled) when the direction of the *net inter-generational wealth flow* is 'upwards' – that is, from child to parent.[38] By 'net inter-generational wealth flow', Caldwell means the balance of the whole range of goods and services that might be provided by members of one generation to members of another over the whole period from the birth of the child to the death of the parents.[39] When wealth flows 'upwards', economically rational parents will wish to have many children, therefore demand will exceed supply.

Assessing demand theories of fertility in the English context raises a host of difficult questions. First, did wealth (on balance) flow from children to parents in pre-industrial English society? J. Cleland and C. Wilson probably reflect the majority view among economic historians and demographers in their statement that there is 'overwhelming evidence that children represented a net economic loss to their parents'.[40] However, a closer examination reveals that this evidence, far from being 'overwhelming', is surprisingly thin. There are two main areas in which children traditionally provide support to their parents, the first is by contributing their earnings to the household when they are young, and the second is by providing support and security for their parents in the latter's old age. Regarding the first of

---

[37] This idea is latent in many of the early accounts of the demographic transition (see Chapter 11). It has been made explicit in more recent accounts – for example, that proposed in R.A. Easterlin, R.A Pollack and M.L. Wachter, 'Towards a more General Model of Fertility Determination: Endogenous Preferences and Natural Fertility', in R.A. Easterlin (ed.), *Population and Economic Change in Developing Countries* (Chicago, Chicago University Press, 1980), pp. 81–149.

[38] J.C. Caldwell, 'Toward a Restatement of Demographic Transition Theory', *Population and Development Review* II (1976), pp. 321–66; see, more generally, J.C. Caldwell, *Theory of Fertility Decline* (London, Academic Press, 1982).

[39] Caldwell, 'Toward a Restatement', p. 344; J.C. Caldwell, 'The Wealth Flows Theory of Fertility Decline' in C. Höhn and R. Mackensen (eds), *Determinants of Fertility Trends: Theories Re-examined* (Liège, Ordina, 1980), p. 171.

[40] J. Cleland and C. Wilson, 'Demand Theories of the Fertility Transition: an Iconoclastic View', *Population Studies* XLI (1987), p. 15.

these, Cleland and Wilson assert that children typically left home to go into service, and 'did not remit significant amounts of money back to their parents', but provide little evidence to support this statement.[41] Indeed, the 'evidence' at times seems to reduce to the assertion that because the preventive check was operating, young people cannot have been providing remittances to their parents, as they needed to save up for their own impending marriages. This is worryingly indirect, and places an enormous burden on the strong but largely circumstantial evidence supporting the preventive check, which was described in Chapter 8. However, more recently, independent evidence has come to light from qualitative sources such as diaries.[42] It seems that during the seventeenth and eighteenth centuries, parents did, on balance, provide more support for their children than children did for their parents, including, for example, help while their children were away 'in service' and economic assistance immediately after the offspring left service.[43] It seems, therefore, that the proceeds of children's labour did not, overall, benefit their parents.

But what of children's support for their parents in old age? The 'old-age security hypothesis' that demand for children is high when children are needed to provide economic security for their parents during the latter's old age has a long tradition in the demographic literature. Might not parents in early modern England have wanted to ensure that at least one or two of their offspring would have been around to care for them in their old age? There has been a tendency in the English historical demographic literature to argue that children's support for their elderly parents was not important. However, I.K. Ben Amos's diaries suggest, for example, that some children, at least, did provide this kind of support.[44] A study of Puddletown in Dorset and Terling in Essex also suggests that support was frequently given, though it was often in kind rather than in cash.[45] In the community of Ardleigh in Essex in 1795–96 'there were no pauper widows whatsoever living alone ... for they were to be found in the households of their married children'.[46]

However, it does not seem that children's support for their aged parents was universal. One reason for this might have been the existence of the Poor Law. Cash payments by the parish were vital in supporting many elderly persons, and these cash 'pensions', when combined with

---

[41]   Ibid., p. 15.
[42]   I.K. Ben-Amos, 'Reciprocal Bonding: Parents and Their Offspring in Early Modern England', *Journal of Family History* XXV (2000), pp. 291–312.
[43]   Ibid., pp. 294–5.
[44]   Ibid., pp. 297–300.
[45]   S. Ottoway, 'Providing for the Elderly in Eighteenth-Century England', *Continuity and Change* XIII (1998), pp. 391–418.
[46]   R.M. Smith, 'Transfer Incomes, Risk and Security: the Roles of the Family and Collectivity in Recent Theories of Fertility Change', in Coleman and Schofield, *State of Population Theory*, p. 202.

some additional family support in kind, would often be enough to enable old people to achieve a standard of living similar to that they attained when they were in work. Moreover, many old people, contrary to what the Poor Law advocated, supported themselves either wholly or in part.[47] Thus, although children may well have been 'one of the mechanisms by which people in England dealt with risk', they were not the only one.[48]

Taken in the round, then, the evidence in favour of an economic demand for children in pre-industrial England is not strong, but then neither is the evidence against it. There might well have been a modest demand for children, especially as a form of old age security, such that parents thought it a good idea to have at least one child alive to support them in their old age. In his analysis of the framework knitters of Shepshed in Leicestershire during the early nineteenth century, David Levine argues precisely this.[49] Even this modest demand might, given the prevailing rates of infant and child mortality, have been enough to prevent couples attempting to control fertility before they had borne about four children.[50] In other words, even this modest demand might have been enough to make fertility control within marriage a rather rare occurrence. This is an important point, because it is sometimes argued that the apparent absence of birth control in pre-industrial England, despite the fact that children were not of great economic benefit to their parents, suggests that there were other factors preventing or dissuading couples from adopting birth control.[51]

If it is not possible to assess the validity of demand theories of fertility in pre-industrial England with data available to date, can we say anything about the factors influencing fertility, and the ways in which reproductive decisions were made? There seems little doubt that children were welcomed for the pleasure they gave. They were

---

[47] The eighteenth-century Poor Law contained a clause that seemingly required families to support their indigent elderly relations, but it seems that this clause was rarely enforced; see Ottoway, 'Providing for the Elderly', pp. 397–8.

[48] A. Macfarlane, *Marriage and Love in England 1300–1840: Modes of Reproduction* (Oxford, Blackwell, 1985), p. 116.

[49] D. Levine, *Family Formation in an Age of Nascent Capitalism* (London, Academic Press, 1977), pp. 80–2.

[50] This conclusion is based on simulation of a variety of reproductive strategies using fertility and mortality rates appropriate to pre-industrial England. See P.R.A. Hinde, 'The Demand for Children in England, 1600–1900', in I. Zilli (ed.), *Fra Spazio e Tempo: Studi in Onore de Luigi de Rosa, Del Medioevo al Seicento* (3 vols, Rome, Edizioni Scientifiche Italiane, 1995) I, pp. 483–507.

[51] See, for example, Cleland and Wilson, 'Demand theories', pp. 14–7. Elsewhere, I have argued that this position is much too simplistic: see P.R.A. Hinde, 'English Fertility, 1600–1900: Is an Economic Analysis Tenable?', in R.I.M. Dunbar (ed.), *Human Reproductive Decisions: Biological and Social Perspectives* (London, Macmillan, 1995), pp. 160–79.

a psychological gratification to their parents, fulfilling their needs in various ways: the biological craving of women to reproduce, the desire of all humans to see mirrors of themselves, the desire for companions, the desire for objects to love and care for.[52]

However, in his study of the motivations for procreation in early modern England, Alan Macfarlane can find no evidence of couples manifesting a strong desire for heirs, or that children were regarded as necessary for female fulfilment, or that parents wanted to have large numbers of children because a large family was more influential within the local community, or that any social stigma was attached to childlessness.[53] We should probably not be surprised by this, as all of these motivations are usually associated with household and family systems very different from those prevailing in England. A desire for heirs (especially male heirs) is a feature of the stem family system, in which it is important to be able to pass the family property on down the generations. The influence of large families within the community tends to be most important in extended family systems.

However, according to Macfarlane there was concern if the number of children became very large (much greater than, say, five).[54] The economic costs of such large families were regarded as a problem for the father, who was expected to provide for them, and for the mother, who would be faced with the day-to-day effort of caring for and bringing up the children, which was very demanding physically. It may have been in order to avoid very large families, and particularly to avoid having a large number of young children at one time, which was the true cause of both the problems mentioned above, that some couples resorted to birth control. This is certainly the view of John Landers in his study of London Quakers between 1650 and 1849.[55] Landers found that both family limitation and birth spacing were practised by sub-groups of the Quaker population during the eighteenth century, and argues that this was done in order to minimize the 'current cost' of children, or 'the period during which large numbers are present'.[56]

9.8 Conclusion

What we know about fertility in pre-industrial England relies heavily – probably too heavily – on the results of the family reconstitutions carried out by the Cambridge Group for the History of Population and Social

---

[52] Macfarlane, *Marriage and Love*, p. 51.
[53] Ibid., pp. 61–2.
[54] Ibid., pp. 62–4.
[55] J. Landers, 'Fertility Decline and Birth Spacing among London Quakers', in J. Landers and V. Reynolds (eds), *Fertility and Resources: Society for the Study of Human Biology Symposium 31* (Cambridge, Cambridge University Press, 1990), p. 112.
[56] Ibid., pp. 106–7.

Structure. The family reconstitution data come from a sample of reconstituted parishes that never exceeds 26 out of the 10,000 or so parishes in the country; this sample was not drawn randomly but on the basis of the quality of parochial registration, and it changes over time. This problem has been recognized, and an argument supporting the representativeness of the sample has been proposed, based on a comparison of the reported fertility levels of the Cambridge Group's parishes with the fertility levels reported in the mid-nineteenth century in the registration districts in which those parishes are located.[57] The shortcomings of this comparison are rather obvious. It uses fertility levels for a period 50–250 years later than that to which the reconstitution data relate in order to validate them, and it ignores the possibility of variation within the registration districts.

Even assuming that the 26 parishes are representative of the English national experience, the analysis of fertility that is presented in *English Population History from Family Reconstitution* is relentlessly aggregative, possibly obscuring much variation in fertility behaviour. There is potentially much more work to be done on the analysis of fertility differentials by, for example, occupation.[58] It is also quite possible that geographical variations in fertility behaviour, even quite large variations, have been overlooked.[59]

The received wisdom holds that, since there is little evidence that children were an economic asset to their parents, it is unlikely that the demand for children exceeded the supply. Hence the absence of birth control behaviour can only be explained by a lack of knowledge of how to control fertility, or a lack of availability of methods, or a cultural belief that voluntary control of fertility was not 'thinkable'. Of these three possibilities, there is evidence to dismiss the first two (for example, in the case of *coitus interruptus*), and therefore the third seems most plausible. The principal thesis of this chapter is that there are good reasons to be cautious before accepting this story. Despite the declarations of historical demographers, existing analyses are unable to discount the possibility that some form of birth control was being practised. It is important to remember that, if birth control behaviour was present, it may have been practised unsystematically, by rather small groups within the population, or by people only in certain localities, or only during certain periods. It is likely that the methods used were rather ineffective compared with modern methods. Under these circumstances, the techniques that have been used to analyse fertility, even with high-quality data, are

---

[57] See C. Wilson and R. Woods, 'Fertility in England: a Long-term Perspective', *Population Studies* XLV, pp. 399–415. The fertility data for the mid-nineteenth century are based on civil registers of births and census populations (which are described in Appendix III).

[58] See, for example, Wrigley *et al.*, *English Population History*, p. 429.

[59] See D. Levine, 'Sampling History: the English Population', *Journal of Interdisciplinary History* XXVIII (1998), pp. 609–14 for more discussion of this issue. The analysis of fertility in Wrigley *et al.*, *English Population History*, is on pp. 354–511. Only pp. 501–7 deal with fertility trends in the 'individual parishes'.

simply not powerful enough to detect it, especially if, where it was practised, it took the form of deliberate birth-spacing behaviour.

Finally, the conclusion that children were an economic burden on their parents is based on rather flimsy evidence. Whereas it seems unlikely that children were seen as an enormous economic asset, the balance of the account may have been quite fine, and may have varied from time to time and from place to place. Moreover, it is at least possible to argue that children were seen as enough of an economic asset (particularly as a form of security when their parents were elderly) to have made the practice of deliberate birth control rather a risky form of behaviour. One of the most remarkable features of the Cambridge Group's version of English population history is that whereas marriage behaviour is explained using an individual rational choice framework, couples are believed to have left behind at the altar their ability to choose. Historical demographers seem to have an aversion to accounts of fertility behaviour within marriage that are based on individual economic rationality. Yet it seems at least as plausible to explain the patterns of childbearing in early modern England in these terms as it does to posit some all-powerful 'social conventions' that were capable of crushing temporal, social and regional variability.[60]

[60] Wrigley *et al.*, *English Population History*, p. 510.

10

Causes and consequences of migration

10.1 Introduction

Migration is the third component of population change, after fertility and mortality, and this chapter will assess its role in England during the sixteenth, seventeenth and eighteenth centuries. We begin by looking at the part played by international migration in population change at the national level. It is possible, at least in theory, that the slowness of England's population growth during the early modern period, and its variability over time, were due in part to changes in the magnitude and direction of international migration flows. Section 10.2 therefore examines what is known about these flows and their temporal variability.

Sections 10.3 and 10.4 turn to internal migration. It is now clear that the English population during the early modern period was highly mobile, moving frequently within the country over both short and long distances. Section 10.3 describes the main types of mobility involved, assesses their changing importance over time, and briefly examines some of their causes. Section 10.4 attempts to place this movement within a wider social, economic and demographic context, seeking to understand the extent to which increased internal migration was a consequence of rapid population growth during the late sixteenth and early seventeenth centuries. It also argues that the development of the Poor Laws to which Malthus so strenuously objected was closely connected to the processes of internal migration.

A great deal of internal migration was to or from London, and Section 10.5 examines the place of London within the English demographic system between 1550 and 1750.

10.2 International migration

The stories of the voyages made by the first migrants from England to North America are part of English folklore. Though the individual experiences of the pioneers continue to be of enormous interest to historians, our purpose here is rather more mundane: to try to establish the amount of migration to and from England that was taking place during the sixteenth, seventeenth and eighteenth centuries.

In the absence of direct records of the movements of people across international frontiers, demographers frequently resort to the indirect estimation of *net migration* as a residual from what is known as the *demographic accounting equation* (see Box 10.1). This approach can only produce estimates of the difference between the numbers of in-migrants and out-migrants but does enable the contribution of migration to overall population change to be assessed.

Use of the demographic accounting equation, however, relies on reliable population totals being available for two time points, and for early modern England this is simply not the case. However, the technique of back projection used in E.A. Wrigley and R.S. Schofield's *Population History of*

Box 10.1 Estimating net migration using the demographic accounting equation (1)

Net migration is the difference between the number of persons moving into a country or region within a given period, and the number of persons moving out.
Thus for a country:

net migration = immigration – emigration.

When direct data on migration are lacking, but the population total for a given country or region is known at two different dates, and vital registration of births and deaths is reasonably efficient for the intervening period, then net migration may be estimated. Let the population of the region or country in year t be P_t, and the population of the same country or region ten years later be P_{t+10}. Then, if the number of births registered in the intervening ten years is B and the number of deaths is D, we can write down the following *demographic accounting* equation:

$$P_{t+10} = P_t + B - D + \text{net migration}$$

and therefore

$$\text{net migration} = P_{t+10} - P_t - B + D$$

This equation may be used to estimate net migration for any geographical area for which we have details of the population at two dates, and the numbers of births and deaths in the intervening period. For more details, see A. Hinde, *Demographic Methods* (London, Arnold, 1998), pp. 1–2, 194–5.

England produces approximate estimates of net migration.[1] These estimates depend on a range of assumptions. They count as out-migrants any persons who were born in England but whose deaths were not recorded in the burial registers, which means that they probably overestimate out-migration and therefore net emigration.[2] Nevertheless, they provide the only continuous series of estimates available, and so form an obvious starting point.

According to Wrigley and Schofield's estimates, there was a continuous net outflow of people from England between the middle of the sixteenth century and the eighteenth century, but its magnitude varied over time.[3] From about 1.3–1.4 persons per thousand per year in the 1540s and 1550s it declined during the 1560s before rising steadily to a peak of about 1.7–1.8 per thousand during the 1590s.[4] A substantial fall between 1600 and 1620 was followed by an increase to a second, greater peak during the Civil War and the interregnum that followed, at which time the rate was between 2.1 and 2.4 per thousand per year.[5] The rate then declined rapidly so that by the 1680s it was less than one per thousand per year, and it remained around that level until after the middle of the eighteenth century.[6] In absolute numbers this means that during the seventeenth century, about 700,000 more persons left England than arrived there.[7] Given that this is likely to be an overestimate, it is probably safer to work on a net emigration of 500,000 people, or an average of 5000 per year. Given that the population of England at that time was about five million, this is a net emigration rate of one per thousand per year. To place this in perspective, is roughly the same as that experienced in the United Kingdom during the 1960s and rather greater than that in the 1970s and early 1980s; between 1986 and 1993 the United Kingdom gained migrants at a net rate of about 0.1 per cent per year.[8] Therefore the rate of net international migration in the early modern period was of the same order of magnitude as that in the late twentieth century. Prior to the 1630s the main destinations of out-migrants were Ireland

---

[1] For details of the back projection method, see E.A. Wrigley and R.S. Schofield, *The Population History of England 1541–1871: a Reconstruction* (London, Edward Arnold, 1981), pp. 195–207; and J.E. Oeppen, 'Aggregative Back Projection', in Wrigley and Schofield, *Population History*, pp. 715–38.

[2] '[N]ot only will those who leave to settle abroad be treated as migrants but so also will those who leave to fight abroad and fail to return, and those who take service at sea and whose ships founder taking them with them, or those vagrants who died on the road and whose burial went unrecorded. Missing deaths, in short, appear as emigrants.' (Wrigley and Schofield, *Population History*, p. 220.)

[3] Wrigley and Schofield, *Population History*, pp. 219–20.

[4] Ibid., p. 219.

[5] Ibid., p. 219.

[6] Ibid., p. 219.

[7] Ibid., p. 528.

[8] L. Bulusu, 'Recent Patterns of Migration from and to the United Kingdom', *Population Trends* XLVI (1986), p. 35; T. Champion, 'Population Review: (3) Migration to, from and within the United Kingdom', *Population Trends* LXXXIII (1996), p. 5.

and the Low Countries. After that time, though, these two places were supplanted by North America. About 380,000 people sailed across the Atlantic Ocean between 1630 and 1699, with the 1640s and 1650s seeing the largest flows.[9]

The impact of this steady, if unspectacular, net outflow on population growth can be assessed by comparing the observed population growth in England with that which would have been experienced had there been no international migration at all (Figure 10.1). The results show that from 2.8 million in 1541, the population would have reached just over seven million in 1751 if there had been no net migration, whereas it actually only reached 5.8 million. The effect of net migration was relatively modest during the second half of the sixteenth century, but became greater in the middle two quarters of the seventeenth century. However, the overall pattern of population change was not affected by migration: even in its absence, the growth rate would have been most rapid during the late sixteenth and early seventeenth centuries, and there would have been stagnation (and even a slight decline) between 1650 and 1680 before growth resumed. Out-migration, then, slowed the rate of growth during periods of expansion, and turned the period of stagnation in the seventeenth century into one of slight decline, but it did not fundamentally influence the pattern of population change, which was determined by the interplay of mortality and fertility mediated through nuptiality.

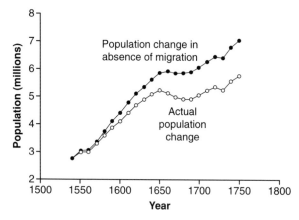

Figure 10.1 The impact of net migration on English population growth, 1540–1750

Notes: The lower line shows the actual population growth. The upper line shows the growth that would have taken place had net migration been zero.

Source: E.A. Wrigley and R.S. Schofield, *The Population History of England 1541–1871: a Reconstruction* (London, Edward Arnold, 1981), pp. 219, 531–3.

---

[9] See H.A. Gemery, 'Emigration from the British Isles to the New World, 1630–1700: Inferences from Colonial Populations', *Research in Economic History* V (1980).

The fact that net out-migration took place should not lead us to forget that many people did come to live in England during the early modern period. Many of these were refugees fleeing religious persecution in Europe. The largest single group were French and Dutch Protestants, who arrived in two waves, one in the late sixteenth century and the second in the late seventeenth century. The first of these waves numbered at least 15,000 and comprised both French and Dutch. Many of them, especially the Dutch and Walloon element, found work in the burgeoning silk industry.[10] The second wave of French Protestant refugees, or Huguenots, was even larger, probably numbering more than 20,000. Many of these also settled in London, where they made important contributions to various aspects of English economic and professional life.[11] In addition, there were migrants from Wales, Scotland and Ireland, and Jews from various parts of continental Europe.

The experiences of these groups upon arriving in England varied widely. The treatment of Christian immigrants in the seventeenth century, for example, seems to have been influenced by the general antipathy towards Catholicism in England. Irish migrants to London at that time seem, for example, to have been rather harshly treated.[12] The Protestant Huguenots, by contrast, were generally welcomed, though the linguistic barrier did fuel some suspicion against them. Jewish immigrants, perhaps, had most difficulty. Having been thrown out by James I in 1609, their commercial acumen persuaded the Commonwealth to ask them back in 1650. By the mid-eighteenth century there were about 8000 Jews in England.[13]

10.3 Internal migration patterns

Internal migration within early modern England can broadly be classified into four types. First, there was migration between the countryside and the towns (in both directions), frequently associated with the taking up of employment opportunities. Also related to the labour market was the second type: seasonal migration in search of employment. Third, especially in

---

[10] See L.B. Luu, 'French-Speaking Refugees and the Foundation of the London Silk Industry in the Sixteenth Century', *Proceedings of the Huguenot Society* XXVI (1997), pp. 564–76.

[11] The standard reference on the Huguenots is R. Gwynn, *Huguenot Heritage: the History and Contribution of the Huguenots in Britain* (2nd edn) (Brighton, Sussex Academic Press, 2001).

[12] This, for example, is the finding of K. M. Noonan, ' "The Cruel Pressure of an Enraged Barbarous People": Irish and English Identity in Seventeenth-Century Policy and Propaganda', *Historical Journal* XLI (1998), pp. 151-77.

[13] A wide variety of material on the experiences of different groups of immigrants may be found in R. Vigne and C. Littleton (eds), *From Strangers to Citizens: the Integration of Immigrant Communities in Britain, Ireland and Colonial America, 1550–1750* (Brighton, Sussex Academic Press, 2001).

the earlier part of the period, there was long-distance subsistence migration of poorer people. Finally, a great deal of local migration took place within the countryside, much of which was associated with 'life course' events, such as entering service or getting married.

The parish registers, which have provided the main data on fertility, mortality and nuptiality, are of almost no use for studying migration. Historians have, therefore, been compelled to discover other sources. Perhaps the most important body of information are the documents created as a result of the Poor Law, together with other legal records (for example, of vagrants). In addition, apprenticeship indentures shed light on migration to certain towns. Finally, use has been made of a very few listings of inhabitants that give details of places of birth. More details of all these sources are given in Appendix II.

Rural–urban migration was dominated by migration to and from London (see below). London's population grew massively between 1550 and 1700, and this growth was probably entirely sustained by net migration. It alone among English urban areas attracted substantial numbers from all parts of the country. However, most of the larger provincial towns attracted migrants from the surrounding rural areas. These migrants would often be young people looking for work or taking up apprenticeships. John Patten used apprenticeship indentures for Norwich (then England's second city) between 1510 and 1699 to show that the vast majority of apprentices from outside the city came from within a 25-mile radius, though there were relatively few from closer than eight miles.[14] There were a small number of migrants from further afield, the most important flow being that from Yorkshire.[15] It seems that other centres of a comparable size to Norwich had similar migration fields.[16]

Seasonal migration was rather rare before the mid-seventeenth century, but thereafter increased in importance. Most of it was connected to employment in agriculture. According to Peter Clark and David Souden:

> by the eighteenth century it had become widespread, helping farmers over the labour peaks and troughs of the agricultural year. People from the uplands journeyed into the south for harvesting, Londoners travelled into the home counties for hop-picking; and Welsh girls came to the nurseries and market gardens around London.[17]

---

[14]   J. Patten, 'Patterns of Migration and Movement of Labour', in P. Clark and D. Souden (eds), *Migration and Society in Early Modern England* (London, Hutchinson, 1987), pp. 87–9 (originally published in *Journal of Historical Geography* II (1976), pp. 111–29). The small number of migrants from close to the city 'might be explained by the attractions of staying as established outworkers for urban manufacture . . ., or even perhaps going into work on a daily basis' (ibid., p. 87).

[15]   Ibid., p. 93.

[16]   Ibid., pp. 101–2.

[17]   P. Clark and D. Souden, 'Introduction', in Clark and Souden, *Migration and Society*, pp. 33–4.

One possible reason for the growth of seasonal migration was that it replaced long-distance migration of a more permanent nature. The rapid population growth during the late sixteenth and early seventeenth centuries was associated not only with a general fall in real wages (see Figure 8.4) but with subsistence crises, which affected the north and west of the country particularly severely (see Chapter 7). It is argued that this led to increased migration among the poorer people, who were forced to move south and east in search of a livelihood. It certainly seems to have been the case that during this period the poor moved both more and further than those who were better off. The destinations of this class of 'subsistence migrants' were often woodland areas, where they could settle without let or hindrance, or towns. Our knowledge of this class of migrants comes largely from legal documents contingent on their being arrested as 'vagrants'. They were commonly aged between 15 and 39 years, and about half of them seem to have been single men, with a quarter being single women and the remaining quarter comprising families (including children).[18]

Long-distance migration declined after the mid-seventeenth century. There are several plausible reasons for this. First, reduced population growth may have diminished pressure on the land, leading to less of an incentive to move. Second, the implementation of the Poor Law (see Section 10.4 below), and the increasingly harsh treatment of many vagrants may have discouraged many from 'speculative' migration. Instead, as mentioned above, seasonal labour migration became more common. Seasonal migrants were going to a known source of employment, and therefore were at a much reduced risk of falling foul of the Poor Law or the vagrancy laws. Third, migration to North America and the Caribbean may have replaced long-distance internal migration as an option for the poor in depressed regions.[19]

Important though long-distance migration was in early modern England, in purely numerical terms, short-distance moves in both town and country were probably the most widespread form of internal migration. Even among the vagrants studied by Paul Slack, short-distance moves were much more numerous than long-distance ones, but vagrants only comprised a small proportion of local migrants.[20] Most moves were associated with events in the 'life course', notably entering service or getting married.[21] The great majority of moves within the countryside were over a distance of less than

---

[18] P.A. Slack, 'Vagrants and Vagrancy in England 1598–1664', in Clark and Souden, *Migration and Society*, pp. 55–6 (originally published in *Economic History Review*, 2nd series, XXVII (1974), pp. 360–79).

[19] P. Clark, 'Migration in England during the Late Seventeenth and Early Eighteenth Centuries', in Clark and Souden, *Migration and Society*, pp. 242–3 (originally published in *Past and Present*, LXXXIII (1979), pp. 57–90).

[20] Slack, 'Vagrants', p. 70.

[21] The English marriage pattern (see Chapter 8) implies that each marriage is likely to have been associated with two moves.

15 miles or so, and a large proportion of moves within urban areas were also within defined neighbourhoods, rather than between them.[22]

A listing of the inhabitants of the parish of Cardington in Bedfordshire in 1782 gives the place of birth of heads of families and their wives. Only one-third of males in this category, and 27 per cent of females (most of whom were 'wives' rather than heads in their own right) had been born in Cardington.[23] Of those born outside the parish, though, more than half of the males and almost half of the females hailed from within five miles of Cardington, and only 11 per cent of males and 18 per cent of females came from more than ten miles distant.[24] This kind of pattern is consistent with a large amount of short-distance migration from village to village. The Cardington listing also gives information about the place of residence of offspring of Cardington families who were not living in their parental home (Table 10.1). Of those not living elsewhere in the parish, most of the females were living less than five miles away. Males had moved rather further. Perhaps the most striking feature revealed by the data, though, is the large proportion of offspring who had moved to London (more than one-fifth of all those who had left the village).

Migration, therefore, for a variety of reasons, was something that most of our ancestors in the early modern period could expect to experience. The idea that early modern England consisted mainly of immobile peasants, attached for life to the parish where they were born, has long been superseded. This should not, however, be taken to imply that everybody moved.

Table 10.1 Residence of offspring absent from the parental home, Cardington, Bedfordshire, 1782

Place of residence	Males		Females	
	In service	Married	In service	Married
Cardington	18	8	5	8
< 5 miles	13	8	16	13
5–10 miles	4	5	1	6
> 10 miles (excluding London)	10	1	3	1
London	2	10	4	5

Source: R.S. Schofield, 'Age-specific Mobility in an Eighteenth-Century Rural English Parish', in P. Clark and D. Souden (eds), *Migration and Society in Early Modern England* (London, Hutchinson, 1987), p. 260.

[22] P. Clark, 'Migration in England'; J. Boulton, 'Neighbourhood Migration in Early Modern London', in Clark and Souden, *Migration and Society*, pp. 107–49.

[23] R.S. Schofield, 'Age-specific Mobility in an Eighteenth-Century Rural English Parish', in Clark and Souden, *Migration and Society*, p. 256.

[24] Ibid., p. 256.

There were some who did, indeed, spend the whole of their lives in their native villages (or, more rarely, towns). For example, a study of the large parish of Long Melford in Suffolk during the late seventeenth century revealed a substantial stable core of families who remained in the parish over several generations.[25] Population historians have reason to be grateful that there were such loyal stalwarts, as without them family reconstitution, upon which so much of our knowledge of the demography of early modern England is based, would be impossible. Nevertheless, they were, in all probability, a minority.

10.4 Internal migration and the development of the Poor Laws

Despite its centrality to the work of Malthus, the relevance of the Poor Laws to the demography of England since the seventeenth century has not always received the attention it deserves. Malthus's principal objection to the Poor Laws was that they encouraged improvident marriages and thereby fertility, but in the long run their relationship with fertility was relatively unimportant (and confined to a relatively short period at the end of the eighteenth and the beginning of the nineteenth centuries) compared with their close and complex connection to the history of internal migration. The relationship between the Poor Laws and migration worked in both directions: laws and statutes concerning the treatment of the poor were developed partly as a public response to internal migration; in turn, they influenced the mobility and migration decisions of the working classes, and the way in which migrant workers were treated. This two-way relationship developed during the sixteenth and seventeenth centuries, but, as Chapter 14 will show, it was still functioning as late as 1850.

The operation of the English Poor Laws is conventionally divided into two periods. The so-called *Old Poor Law* functioned until 1834, when it was replaced by the *New Poor Law* ushered in by the Poor Law Amendment Act. The Old Poor Law had a lengthy and complicated genesis, which lasted most of the sixteenth century. Paul Slack has pointed to nine relevant statutes between 1531 and 1576.[26] Two themes ran through these, reflecting concern about two different classes of pauper: 'sturdy vagabonds and beggars', as Thomas Cromwell's Act of 1536 described them, and the 'aged, decayed and impotent poor', a distinction that was to run through the

[25] L. Boothman, 'Mobility and Stability in Long Melford, Suffolk, in the Late Seventeenth Century', *Local Population Studies* LXII (1999), pp. 31–51. See also B. Stapleton, 'Family Strategies: Patterns of Inheritance in Odiham, Hampshire, 1525–1850', *Continuity and Change* XIV (1999), pp. 385–402.
[26] P. Slack, *The English Poor Law, 1531–1782* (London, Macmillan, 1990), pp. 59–60.

English Poor Law until the nineteenth century.[27] The 'vagabonds and beggars' were regarded as 'undeserving', and were to be both punished for their importunity and set to work. The 'impotent poor' were seen as 'deserving' of assistance, and a scheme was to be created to raise funds by which they might be supported. The system was finally put in place by two Acts of 1598, the titles of which make the distinction clear: 'For the Relief of the Poor' and 'For the Punishment of Rogues, Vagabonds and Sturdy Beggars'.[28] The poor were to be supported through a tax levied on inhabitants and landholders; vagabonds were to be whipped and sent back to their place of birth or the last place in which they had resided for a year.[29] The whole scheme was to be administered at the level of the parish by churchwardens and overseers of the poor. Thus each parish was to be responsible for supporting its own poor.

The argument that the Old Poor Law was developed as a response to internal migration is part of a wider thesis that runs as follows. The resumption of population growth in the early sixteenth century, and its acceleration after 1550, was associated with a decline in real wages. This led to an increased proportion of the population living in conditions of absolute want for all or part of the time. Moreover, the unequal geographical distribution of poverty led to the increase in long-distance 'subsistence' migration by the poor, which was described in Section 10.3. These developments demanded a response from the authorities, and this response came in the form of the Old Poor Law.

This argument has been dubbed by Paul Slack the 'high pressure' interpretation of the articulation of the English Poor Law.[30] Modern scholarship does not dismiss it, for it clearly contains some truth. Migration *was* stimulated by population pressure, and the decline in real wages must, undoubtedly, have led to the increasing visibility of want.[31] But alone, it will not account for the development of such a comprehensive structure as that created by the 1598 and 1601 Statutes. Why, for example, did the crisis of the late thirteenth and early fourteenth centuries not provoke a similar response? The answer, according to Slack, is that 'a new conception of what governments could and should do for the poor emerged during the sixteenth century', together with greater ambitions on the part of both central and local government to 'control their subjects and inferiors'.[32]

Thus it was that by the early seventeenth century the English Poor Law had reached something like its final form. However, one important piece of

---

[27]   Ibid., pp. 59–60.
[28]   Ibid., pp. 18–19, 60–1.
[29]   Ibid., pp. 60–1.
[30]   Ibid., p. 11.
[31]   R.B. Outhwaite, *Dearth, Public Policy and Social Disturbance in England, 1550–1800* (London, Macmillan, 1991), pp. 23, 34–5.
[32]   Slack, *English Poor Law*, pp. 11, 14–7.

the jigsaw was still missing, though it had been implicit in earlier legislation. Poor relief was to be financed at the parish level, each parish being responsible for the relief of its own poor. But how was a parish to decide who 'its own poor' were? Clearly, a person who had been born in a parish, lived there all his or her life, and who became indigent in old age was the responsibility of that parish. Equally clearly, also, a wandering beggar who had just arrived for the first time in a parish and made a nuisance of himself was not that parish's responsibility. But between these two examples were a multitude of cases where it was not clear which parish should support an applicant for relief. The solution to this problem was formalized in the 1662 Act of Settlement.[33] Under this Act, each person in England was to be linked to one, and only one, parish for the purposes of poor relief. If a newcomer arrived in a parish, and was thought likely to become a burden on that parish – that is, to apply for poor relief – the parish was entitled to send the person back (to *remove* the person) to his or her parish of settlement.

A person's parish of settlement was not fixed for life. Upon birth, a person took the settlement parish of his or her father, but afterwards, settlement in another parish (which superseded previous settlements) could be acquired by fulfilling certain criteria. These criteria were complex, and were changed and amended several times in later years.[34]

There has been a long debate in the historical literature about the application of the laws relating to settlement. However, the principal issue at stake for us is whether they were responsible for the decline in internal migration, and especially the decrease in long-distance migration that certainly occurred in the second half of the seventeenth century. To the extent that this long-distance migration had been from areas of labour oversupply to regions of labour scarcity it can be argued that it provided a way of correcting regional economic imbalances to the economic benefit of the country as a whole, and therefore that the settlement laws were detrimental to the economy. Evidence on this issue to date is not conclusive. A case can be made in support of the direct impact of the settlement laws on migration by considering their administrative costs. Not only did they create a huge bureaucratic burden on parishes, but parishes were also faced with the costs of legal disputes over exactly which of them was responsible for individual paupers.[35] There was

---

[33] Ibid., p. 36.

[34] According to the 1662 Act, settlement could be acquired by renting land worth more than £10 per year. An Act of 1692 added an important additional method of gaining a settlement, which involved being hired as a servant in a parish for a continuous period of one year (see Slack, *English Poor Law*, p. 36). Some parishes tried to circumvent the 1692 Act by encouraging farmers to hire servants on 51-week contracts.

[35] It is, however, an ill wind that blows no one any good. The burgeoning bureaucracy the 1662 Act created has subsequently provided voluminous and detailed documentary evidence for future historians to exploit. Perhaps the most well-known example is K.D.M. Snell, *Annals of the Labouring Poor: Social Change in Agrarian England 1660–1900* (Cambridge, Cambridge University Press, 1985), which makes extensive use of settlement records.

also the expense of physically removing persons over distances that could be hundreds of miles. Given this, it seems likely that between 1662 and 1697, parishes used the 1662 Act to remove persons whom they thought likely to need relief, and thus to pre-empt any legal disputes.[36] This should have discouraged internal migration. Reinforcing this effect was the tendency, especially in the early eighteenth century, for the treatment of vagrants to become even harsher. The growth in seasonal labour migration can also be seen as a response to the settlement laws, for parishes who might seek the removal of would-be permanent in-migrants would still be willing to admit those who were coming temporarily to meet an obvious and pressing demand for labour, such as that occasioned by the harvest.

Further, there is evidence that emigration to North America increased greatly in the seventeenth century, and that overseas migration replaced long-distance internal migration as the safety-valve for hard-pressed communities.[37] It may have been that the application of the settlement laws encouraged people to look overseas rather than elsewhere in England. The chronology of emigration suggests that the peak years for emigration to America occurred during the 1660s, which raises the possibility that it was related to the 1662 Act.

On the other hand, the direct impact on migration was probably diluted by a system which allowed parishes to issue certificates to their 'own' poor acknowledging responsibility for their maintenance if they required relief. These certificates could then be carried around the country by those seeking work as proof that they were not going to be a burden on the parishes they visited. The use of the certificates encouraged parishes to welcome able-bodied workers who might relieve labour shortages, and the evidence certainly suggests that those who were actually removed tended to be families with children rather than single adult males.[38] In other words, the settlement laws were not used to restrict the free movement of productive labour that was necessary to correct regional imbalances in labour markets. This is not to say that migrants always found it easy to settle in their destination communities. Indeed, there is considerable evidence that migrants were not always welcome in the communities they entered. Steven King's study of the proto-industrial township of Calverley in the West Riding of Yorkshire has revealed that many of those who moved into the community only stayed there a short time, and those who remained were only slowly and reluctantly assimilated into the community.[39] Indeed, it was often the case that

---

[36]   There has been a particularly intense dispute in the literature over the extent to which parishes used the settlement laws to 'monitor' migration trends. See, in particular, N. Landau, 'The Laws of Settlement and Surveillance of Immigration in Eighteenth-Century Kent', *Continuity and Change* III (1988), pp. 391–420; and K.D.M. Snell, 'Pauper Settlement and the Right to Poor Relief in England and Wales', *Continuity and Change* VI (1991), pp. 375–415.

[37]   Clark, 'Migration in England', pp. 242–3.

[38]   Slack, *English Poor Law*, pp. 37–8.

[39]   See S. King, 'Migrants on the Margin? Mobility, Integration and Occupations in the West Riding, 1650–1820', *Journal of Historical Geography* XXIII (1997), pp. 284–303.

full acceptance was only achieved by migrants' children, rather than the migrants themselves.[40]

Finally, we can return to where this section began and note that during the first half of the seventeenth century the rate of growth of the population declined, and by the mid-seventeenth century was close to zero. To the extent that population pressure in the sixteenth century led to increased subsistence migration, reduced population growth in the seventeenth century would have reduced the incentive to migrate independently of the settlement laws.

10.5 The role of London in the English demographic system

London was very much the hub of England's internal migration system, and was also the chief destination of international immigrants. It was England's largest city by far, with an estimated 200,000 inhabitants in 1600, rising to 575,000 by 1700 and 675,000 by 1750.[41] In 1650, London contained an estimated 7 per cent of England's population, and by 1750 it housed 11 per cent.[42] The dominance of London among urban centres is emphasized by the fact that only about 9 per cent of England's population in 1650, and perhaps 17 per cent in 1750, were living in towns with populations of 10,000 or more.[43] The growth of London was entirely fuelled by in-migration: the insanitary and overcrowded conditions in the capital meant that deaths exceeded births even in a normal year.

Because London was so large, the population dynamics of London affected the population in the country as a whole. E.A. Wrigley has summarized its effect as follows. Assuming that the majority of those moving to London were young, with an average age of about 20 years, then

> [g]iven the mortality conditions of the day any large group of twenty-year-olds coming into London would represent the survivors of a birth population at least half as large again. Some 12,000 births, therefore, in the rest of England and elsewhere were earmarked, as it were, each year to make it possible for London's population to grow as it did during this period . . . If the average surplus of births over deaths in provincial England was 5 per 1,000 per annum (and assuming . . . that London grew by immigration from England alone), then it follows that London's growth was absorbing the natural increase of a population of some two-and-a-half millions.[44]

[40] Ibid., pp. 294–9.
[41] E.A. Wrigley, 'A Simple Model of London's Importance in Changing English Society and Economy 1650–1750', *Past and Present* XXXVII (1967), p. 44.
[42] Ibid., p. 45.
[43] R.A. Houston, 'The Population History of Britain and Ireland, 1500–1700', in M. Anderson (ed.), *British Population History: from the Black Death to the Present Day* (Cambridge, Cambridge University Press, 1996), p. 122.
[44] Wrigley, 'A Simple Model', p. 47.

London, therefore, acted as a 'demographic sink'. People moved from the provinces to London, where they were exposed to higher death rates than obtained in the rest of the country. The population of England during the seventeenth century was between four and five million. If Wrigley is right, therefore, London was 'absorbing the natural increase' of more than half of the provincial population. The operation of London as a 'demographic sink' influenced national growth rates. It seems no coincidence that during the era in which the population of London was growing most rapidly (the second half of the seventeenth century), national population growth rates were lowest.

Appendix II
Sources and methods for studying the population of early modern England

AII.1 Introduction and overview

Recall from Appendix I that demography uses, in the main, two types of data: periodic information on population *stocks* (the population residing in a particular area at given points in time) and continuous information on *flows* (numbers of births, deaths, immigrants and emigrants). The main difference between the medieval and early modern periods in the data available to population historians is that, after 1538, the Church of England parish baptism and burial registers allow a continuous series of the numbers of births and deaths per year to be derived. In other words, regular information on some (though not all) population flows is available. Section AII.2 of this Appendix describes the parish registers, summarizes their strengths and weaknesses as demographic sources, and explains how they have been exploited by population historians in two quite different ways: aggregatively using a technique known as back projection, and at the individual level using family reconstitution.

The method of back projection was devised by population historians of this period in order to overcome the single biggest gap in the early modern data: the absence of any comprehensive source of information about population stocks. The first population census of England and Wales was not taken until 1801, and for the early modern era there are no adequate substitutes. Indeed, it is probably fair to say that there is no national source of data on population stocks in the early modern period that is as useful as either Domesday Book or the Poll Tax of 1377 described in Appendix I). Nevertheless, there are a number of potential 'census substitutes' that are useful at the regional and local levels, and these are described in Section AII.3. These include the listings of inhabitants which were used to demonstrate that households in pre-industrial England were small and 'nuclear', as well as various ecclesiastical 'censuses' and taxation documents.

Section AII.4 describes a number of sources that were not specifically designed to measure either population stocks or demographic flows but that, nevertheless, contain information from which demographic data can be extracted, mainly about migration.

AII.2 The Church of England parish registers

The registration by the Church of England of baptisms, marriages and burials began in 1538 on the instruction of Thomas Cromwell. Although only a minority of parishes obeyed Cromwell's order immediately, over the decades between 1538 and the beginning of the seventeenth century, almost all parishes in England did begin to register these events in a systematic way, and have continued to do so until the present day. There are gaps in the sequence for many parishes, and there is some evidence that the reliability of registration changed over time but, despite this, the parish registers remain 'the single most important source for historical demographers for 300 years, up until 1837 when civil registration began in England'.[1]

The information contained in the registers varies from parish to parish, at least until the nineteenth century. Baptism registers tend to give little more than the name of the child being baptized, the date of the baptism and the name(s) of the parents. Likewise, many marriage registers provide simply the names of those marrying (and perhaps their parents) and the date of the marriage. Burial registers might give as little information as the name of the deceased and the date of burial, but occasionally are much fuller. The registers are now almost all available through County Record Offices, and many of the pre-1837 registers have been transcribed by amateur historians and genealogists.

Because the Church of England parish registers are the cornerstone of empirical research into England's population history before the nineteenth century, historians have made prodigious efforts to assess their reliability. Demographers are mainly interested in baptisms and burials as proxies for births and deaths. In the case of the baptism and burial registers, therefore, two separate questions arise: first, what proportion of births and deaths, respectively, are recorded in the baptism and burial registers (this may be described as a question about the *coverage* of the registers)? and, second, how accurately do those entries that were made in the registers reflect what historical demographers are trying to measure with them (which is a question about the *content* of the registers)? For the marriage registers, only the second of these really arises – at least for the period before 1750.

There has been a long-running debate among historians about the variation in the coverage of parochial registration over time, and from place to place. Early work on both baptism and burial registers suggested that they were very reliable as records of births and deaths until the late eighteenth century (in other words, the vast majority of babies born were baptized by

---

[1]   M. Drake, 'Introduction: Local Population Studies', in M. Drake (ed.), *Population Studies from Parish Registers: a Selection of Readings from Local Population Studies* (Matlock, Local Population Studies, 1982), p. vi. This volume, and especially Drake's introduction, remains possibly the most useful general compilation about the parish registers and the variety of uses to which they can be put.

the Church of England, and the vast majority of those who died were buried by the Church, and so are recorded in the registers). The only exception to this was a period of about 20 years in the middle of the seventeenth century at the time of the Civil War and the subsequent Commonwealth period, where many registers have gaps in their coverage.[2]

During the last few decades of the eighteenth century and the first few decades of the nineteenth, however, coverage seems to have decreased markedly.[3] There were several reasons for this. Rapid population growth and increased rural–urban migration meant that Church of England clergy (especially in urban areas) became overwhelmed by the sheer numbers of baptisms, marriages and burials they had to perform, and cut corners in record-keeping. The growth of non-conformity meant that the share of events (especially baptisms) registered by churches other than the Church of England rose.[4] This decline in the coverage of the registers was not universal, and there are likely to have been many parishes where coverage remained good. Moreover, coverage probably held up better for burial registers than for baptism registers. Indeed, Peter Razzell has recently suggested that no deterioration in the reliability of burial registration can be observed during this period.[5]

But what of their content, especially when viewed as records of births, marriages and deaths? One cause of concern is the length of the birth–baptism interval.[6] There are, really, two issues to consider here. First, to the extent that the date of baptism is used to infer the date of birth, any substantial delay in baptizing new-born babies will lead to errors in dating births. Most available evidence suggests that the birth–baptism interval was very short in the sixteenth century, but that as time progressed it widened.[7] By the early nineteenth century, in the 'average' parish about half of all babies born were baptized within 30 days of birth, but around a quarter waited more than two months.[8] Intervals could be longer than this in some

[2] E.A. Wrigley and R.S. Schofield, *The Population History of England, 1541–1871: a Reconstruction* (London, Edward Arnold, 1981), p. 19.

[3] See the discussion in R. Schofield, 'History, Computing and the Emergence of *The Population History of England, 1541–1871: a Reconstruction*', *History and Computing* XI (1999), pp. 90–2. This article is an excellent summary of the research that culminated in the publication of Wrigley and Schofield, *Population History of England*.

[4] Registers of non-conformist churches do survive in places, but their survival is much more patchy than that of the Church of England registers.

[5] P. Razzell, 'Evaluating the Same Name Technique as a Way of Measuring Burial Register Reliability in England', *Local Population Studies* LXIV, pp. 8–22.

[6] The death–burial interval is not of such great concern, because burials were almost invariably carried out soon after death.

[7] E.A. Wrigley, R.S. Davies, J.E. Oeppen and R.S. Schofield, *English Population History from Family Reconstitution 1580–1837* (Cambridge, Cambridge University Press, 1997), p. 111.

[8] See B.M. Berry and R.S. Schofield, 'Age at Baptism in Pre-Industrial England', *Population Studies* XXV (1971), p. 458. According to evidence from Hampshire, this kind of distribution of ages at baptism characterized the period between 1851 and 1891; see S. Dewhurst and A. Hinde, 'Age at Baptism in Rural Hampshire in the Second Half of the Nineteenth Century', *Local Population Studies* LVII (1996), p. 74.

parishes, however. For example, in the Sussex coastal parish of St Nicholas, Pevensey, the median birth–baptism interval widened from around 25 days between 1761 and 1780 to over 50 days after 1786 and, during the last decade of the eighteenth century, at least a quarter of all babies born were baptized at ages over four months.[9]

In certain places, practices such as baptizing infants in batches on certain days led to individual intervals that were abnormally long. This brings us to the second issue that if a child died before baptism, the fact of his or her birth will be completely concealed from the demographer, unless the child was subject to an 'emergency' baptism. Since the burial of such unbaptized children was normally recorded, at least before 1700, failure to correct for this in aggregate analysis of parish registers will lead to an underestimate of fertility relative to mortality, and an underestimate of the rate of population growth.[10] In *The Population History of England*, E.A. Wrigley and R.S. Schofield make a correction to account for the 'increasing delay between birth and baptism'.[11] However, using evidence from Kent, Anthony Poole has suggested that their correction may be insufficient, especially during the late seventeenth century.[12] He is particularly worried by the practice, common at that time in his parishes in Kent, of baptizing several children in the same family together, since this inevitably meant that the older children of the group being baptized were several years old.[13] If Wrigley and Schofield's correction for delayed baptism during the late seventeenth century is too small, they will have underestimated the population growth rate during this period.

The parish registers have been exploited in two quite distinct ways. The first uses aggregative analysis, based principally on monthly totals of vital events. The most famous example of this is of course Wrigley and Schofield's reconstruction of the population history of England during the early modern period.[14] Wrigley and Schofield used data from 404 English parishes with particularly high-quality registers to estimate annual totals of births, marriages and deaths for the years 1539–1837.[15] These were then used to derive population totals for England for this period by a method known as *back projection*. *Population projection* is a well-known method

---

[9]   M.J. Saxby, 'Age at Baptism in the Parish of St Nicholas, Pevensey, 1761–1800', *Local Population Studies* LXI (2000), p. 58.

[10]   Wrigley and Schofield, *Population History of England*, pp. 96–7.

[11]   Ibid., pp. 97–102.

[12]   A. Poole, 'Baptismal Delay: some Implications from the Parish Registers of Cranbrook and Surrounding Parishes in the Kentish Weald', *Local Population Studies* LXV (2000), pp. 24–6.

[13]   Ibid., pp. 17–18.

[14]   Wrigley and Schofield, *Population History of England*.

[15]   Ibid., pp. 536–62. The original monthly number of baptisms, marriages and burials for the period 1538-1837 for the 404 parishes are available for a modest sum on a CD-ROM from the *Local Population Studies* General Office, Department of Humanities, University of Hertfordshire, Watford Campus, Aldenham, WATFORD WD2 8AT.

by which forecasts of the future population of a country, or region, are made by taking the current population and making assumptions about the numbers of births and deaths in future years, and about future migration patterns. Back projection is, effectively, this method in reverse. Starting with the 1871 census population of England, the population in earlier years was estimated by 'successively backdating and revising the known age-structure of the 1871 census, thus deriving earlier "censuses" at five-year intervals, until the first "census" of 1541 was reached'.[16] The 'backdating and revising' was done using the annual numbers of births and deaths in England estimated from the parish register, and making some assumptions about migration.[17]

The second major body of research using parish register data is *family reconstitution*. This uses individual-level data to construct genealogies of the inhabitants of particular parishes by matching entries in the baptism, marriage and burial registers. The matching procedure is often called *nominative record linkage* because it involves the linking together of information about the same person in two different records (for example, a marriage register and a burial register) by matching specific pieces of information, the most important of which is the name of the person. The details of the procedure are complex, but it involves making five types of link: between a person's baptism and his or her marriage; between successive marriages of the same person; between a person's marriage and his or her burial; between a person's baptism and burial; and between the baptism of a child and the marriage of the child's parents. The linkage proceeds by a series of logical steps that can be carried out using a computer.[18] The data that family reconstitution produces are potentially very powerful and versatile. They have been used to analyse a wide range of demographic phenomena including biological aspects of fertility and sterility, the lengths of intervals between births, the extent of birth control, the distribution of ages at marriage and levels of infant mortality.[19]

There are, however, some important caveats that should be borne in mind when interpreting results based on the technique. Family reconstitution is extremely labour-intensive, and for this reason only a small number

---

[16] Schofield, 'History, Computing', p. 93.

[17] The technique of back projection is described in J. Oeppen, 'Aggregative Back Projection', in Wrigley and Schofield, *Population History of England*, pp. 715–38.

[18] For details of the method, see E.A. Wrigley, 'Family Reconstitution', in E.A. Wrigley (ed.), *An Introduction to English Historical Demography* (London, Weidenfeld and Nicolson, 1966), pp. 96–159; on the use of computers see E.A. Wrigley and R.S. Schofield, 'Nominal Record Linkage by Computer and the Logic of Family Reconstitution', in E.A. Wrigley (ed.), *Identifying People in the Past* (London, Edward Arnold, 1973), pp. 64–101.

[19] In general, family reconstitution is more useful for analysing fertility, and about certain facets of mortality (adult mortality, for example) it reveals very little. The technique was devised by the French demographer Louis Henry in order to obtain 'pure' estimates of fertility in the absence of birth control.

of English parishes have been reconstituted. *English Population History from Family Reconstitution*, the book by E.A. Wrigley and his colleagues at the Cambridge Group for the History of Population and Social Structure in which the results of their attempts to reconstitute English parishes are presented, is based on data for only 26 parishes, not all of which provide data for the whole of the early modern period.[20] It is not clear how representative these parishes are of the population of England as a whole.[21]

The question of representativeness also arises at the 'within parish' level, for only a minority of the families in any parish can be studied using family reconstitution data. People who move from one parish to another are untraceable and therefore have to be excluded from the analysis. In most (if not all) parishes the *reconstitutable minority* of the population, which consists mainly of the 'immobile' families, is very small, and may be unrepresentative of the parish population as a whole.[22] There are, in fact, several issues here. The first is the possibility that the reconstitutable minority had a fertility, nuptiality or mortality experience that was different from that of the population as a whole. If this was the case, inferences from reconstitution data to the whole population (whether they be local inferences or national ones) will be biased. There is some, albeit limited, evidence suggesting that estimates of demographic parameters based only on non-migrants may be different from those that would be obtained if migrants could be included.[23] In a recent study of Odiham in Hampshire (one of the parishes that has been reconstituted), Barry Stapleton studied 43 families who persisted in the parish for three or more generations during the period from 1525 to 1850: these families, of course, would be more likely than the average family to be included in the reconstitution data.[24] He found that low fertility and high infant mortality, leading to a greater chance of only one son or daughter surviving their parents, helped to maintain the family property (whether farm or business) intact. If families whose property remained intact were less mobile than other families, then they will be over-

---

[20] Wrigley *et al.*, *English Population History*. There are some other reconstitutions available, either in full or in part, but the total number of parishes for which any substantial amount of work has been done is fewer than 50.

[21] There has been a lot of debate over this. Wrigley *et al.*, *English Population History*, pp. 41–53, defend the representativeness of their sample on the basis of its occupational structure compared with that of England as a whole in the early nineteenth century but others, such as D. Levine, 'Sampling History: the English Population', *Journal of Interdisciplinary History* XXVIII (1998), pp. 605–32; and S. Ruggles, 'The Limitations of English Family Reconstitution: *English Population History from Family Reconstitution 1580–1837*', *Continuity and Change* XIV (1999), pp. 106–13, are unconvinced.

[22] This criticism has been made repeatedly. For a recent example, see Ruggles, 'Limitations', pp. 114–16.

[23] See, for example, R. Bellingham, 'Age at Marriage in the Late Eighteenth Century', *Local Population Studies* LXI (2000), pp. 55–6.

[24] B. Stapleton, 'Family Strategies: Patterns of Inheritance in Odiham, Hampshire, 1525–1850', *Continuity and Change* XIV (1999), pp. 385–402.

represented in the reconstituted data, which will therefore tend to reflect their lower than average fertility and higher than average infant mortality.[25]

The Cambridge Group's response to the representativeness problem has been to compare fluctuations over time in the numbers of births, deaths and marriages in the small number of parishes for which reconstitution has been carried out with similar time series based on data for the much larger number of parishes used in the aggregative analysis.[26] The rationale behind this is that the aggregative data include all baptisms, marriages and burials in the 404 parishes, including those of migrants, and are also more representative of the national population. They observed that the two sets of series rose and fell in a similar way over time, and concluded that 'it would be surprising if the underlying demographic processes that produced totals of events in the reconstitution parishes so similar in their behaviour to those found in the aggregative sample of 404 parishes were not akin to those operating nationally'.[27]

Finally, mention should be made of the London Bills of Mortality. These were derived directly from the registers of Church of England parishes in the city by the Parish Clerk's Company of London. They comprised weekly, monthly and annual lists of the numbers of burials in each parish in the city, with the total number of baptisms also being included. From the sixteenth century, burials were typically separated into those deaths due to plague, and those due to other causes, and after 1629 a range of causes of death were given. The Bills of Mortality continue into the nineteenth century.

AII.3 Census substitutes

There was no population census of England until 1801, and the early modern period is, as has been said, devoid of alternative sources that can be used to derive national-level population totals. However, at the regional and local level there are a number of sources that can (with some ingenuity) be made to substitute for the missing population censuses, and these are described in this section. They can be classified into three broad groups: listings of inhabitants, taxation records, and ecclesiastical censuses.

---

[25] Other problems with the measurement of demographic parameters of interest from family reconstitution have been raised, many of which arise from the fact that family reconstitution does not include migrants; see, for example, S. Ruggles, 'Migration, Marriage and Mortality: Correcting Sources of Bias in English Family Reconstitution', *Population Studies* XLVI (1992), pp. 507–22; and S. Ruggles, 'The Limitations of English Family Reconstitution, pp. 105–30. See also E.A. Wrigley's response to Ruggles' criticism: E.A. Wrigley, 'The Effect of Migration on the Estimation of Marriage Age in Family Reconstitution Studies', *Population Studies* XLVIII (1994), pp. 81–97.

[26] Wrigley *et al.*, *English Population History*, pp. 53–70.

[27] Ibid., p. 70.

The *listings of inhabitants* are informal censuses of particular villages or parishes, which were conducted for a variety of purposes at different times, normally by interested residents or incumbent clergymen. Only a small number have survived. Peter Laslett's work on household structure was based on just one hundred, the earliest of which was a listing from Poole in Dorset in 1574, and the latest of which come from the early nineteenth-century censuses.[28] These do not come from a representative sample of the towns and villages of England (too few small places are included), and they were not collected according to a consistent set of rules.[29] They are independent documents, all containing broadly the same information, but gathered by different people, each of whom probably devised the exact method of collection 'from first principles'. Nevertheless, '[i]n every case ... they arranged the names of persons in blocks, which are almost always unambiguously recognizable as households, and in every case they left a clear indication of where one block ended and the next block began'.[30] They do not, typically, reveal details of within-household relationships; nor do more than a few (such as the listing of Ealing in 1599 and the very detailed list of the inhabitants of Corfe Castle in Dorset in 1790) give data on people's ages.[31] A few listings of inhabitants provide information that may be useful for the analysis of migration, such as place of birth data. Perhaps the most famous of these is the listing for Cardington in Bedfordshire in 1782, which has been analysed by Roger Schofield.[32]

The other two groups of 'census substitutes' are available for many more places and so are useful for analysis at the regional level. Among the taxation records are the Hearth Tax returns of the 1660s, the Poll Taxes of the seventeenth century and the Marriage Duty lists of the 1690s. The Hearth Tax was a tax on fireplaces, which was levied in various years after the Restoration. The surviving records are typically arranged by locality, and list the names of householders together with the number of hearths for which each was assessed. For some counties, the Hearth Tax has been published and is therefore easily accessible to historians.[33] The Poll Tax records

---

[28]   The complete list is given in P. Laslett, 'Mean Household Size in England since the Sixteenth Century', in P. Laslett and R. Wall (eds), *Household and Family in Past Time* (Cambridge, Cambridge University Press, 1972), pp. 130–1.

[29]   Ibid., p. 128.

[30]   Ibid., p. 127.

[31]   Ibid., pp. 130–1.

[32]   R.S. Schofield, 'Age-specific Mobility in an Eighteenth-Century Rural English Parish', in P. Clark and D. Souden, *Migration and Society in Early Modern England* (London, Hutchinson, 1987), pp. 253–66.

[33]   See, for example, C.A.F. Meekings, *Dorset Hearth Tax Assessments 1662–1664* (Dorchester, Longmans, 1951); E. Hughes and P. White (eds), *The Hampshire Hearth Tax Assessment 1665, with the Southampton Assessments for 1662 and 1670* (Winchester, Hampshire County Council, 1992). For more information on the Hearth Tax, see T. Arkell, 'Printed Instructions for Administering the Hearth Tax', in K. Schürer and T. Arkell (eds), *Surveying the People: the Interpretation and Use of Document Sources for the Study of Population in the Later Seventeenth Century* (Oxford, Leopard's Head Press, 1992), pp. 38–64.

relate to various periods from 1641 to 1699. Their survival is patchy, and they are often complex documents to use and interpret.[34] The Marriage Duty assessments come from the period 1695–1706. The Marriage Duty Act of 1695 imposed a tax on vital events (births, marriages and burials), and also required annual payments by bachelors aged over 25 years and childless widowers, in order to fund a war with France. 'With every vital event subject to taxation, and parishes responsible for paying the burial tax for those on poor relief, local assessors drew up purportedly complete lists of their inhabitants'.[35] Both the Poll Tax records and the Marriage Duty assessments are closer than the Hearth Tax to being a population census, and the best of them form the nearest that we have to a complete census before 1801.[36] Unfortunately, though, their survival is very patchy. A particularly good set of Marriage Duty records survives for London, and another excellent example comes from the parish of St John in Southampton.

The final group of 'census substitutes' consists of various ecclesiastical surveys conducted during the seventeenth and eighteenth centuries. The most widely used by historians has been the Compton Census of 1676. This census tried to record the numbers of men and women aged over 16 years in each parish and, of them, how many were Protestant dissenters and 'Popish recusants'.[37] By the use of multipliers to account for the population aged under 16 years, the total population of each parish in 1676 may be estimated. However, devising suitable multipliers raises the same kinds of problems as were encountered with the 1377 Poll Tax.[38] In addition to the Compton Census, useful information about population totals can be derived from the responses to Bishops' Visitations. These formed a series of questions asked of all the parish clergy in a diocese by the Bishop. The questions often asked for estimates of the parish population, average annual numbers of baptisms, marriages and burials, as well as estimates of the number of non-conformists and 'papists'.[39]

---

[34] See T. Arkell, 'An Examination of the Poll Taxes of the Later Seventeenth Century, the Marriage Duty Act and Gregory King', in Schürer and Arkell, *Surveying the People*, pp. 142–63.

[35] A. Froide, 'Hidden Women: Rediscovering the Singlewomen of Early Modern England', *Local Population Studies* LXVIII (2002), pp. 27–8.

[36] Ibid., p. 28.

[37] Schürer and Arkell, *Surveying the People*, p. 33. The Compton Census has been edited by Anne Whiteman and is published in A. Whiteman (ed., with the assistance of M. Clapinson), *The Compton Census of 1676: a Critical Edition* (British Academy Records of Social and Economic History, new series, 10) (London, British Academy, 1986).

[38] The whole question of estimating population totals from the Compton Census is considered in detail in T. Arkell, 'A Method for Estimating Population Totals from the Compton Census Returns', in Schürer and Arkell, *Surveying the People*, pp. 97–116.

[39] These questions, for example, were included in the Visitations of the diocese of Winchester in 1725, 1764–65 and 1788, the responses to which are available in the Hampshire Record Office.

In terms of accuracy, some recent investigations have suggested that the Compton Census may be rather inferior to the Hearth Tax or the Marriage Duty assessments, the other two sources available for the purposes of estimating the total population.[40] However, because of the difficulties and uncertainties attached to using all these sources, it is helpful where possible to apply the principle of 'triangulation' and to compare population estimates made for the same place using different sources.[41]

AII.4 Other sources

The Church of England parish registers provide virtually no information about migration patterns. For these, historians have turned, in the main, to four groups of sources. First, and probably least important, one or two exceptionally detailed listings of inhabitants provide information about *lifetime migration*. That is, they give details of each person's place of birth and their current place of residence. Of course, this information is only partial, and the fact that a person is not now living in his or her place of birth reveals nothing about the number of moves made in the interim. Second, apprenticeship indentures normally state the geographical origins of those who became apprentices, together with the address of their future employer.[42] This, again, is partial information about one class of moves made, typically, by young adult males.

The other two sources offer potentially much more detailed information. Church court deposition records have been used by Peter Clark for the period 1650 to 1750.[43] Clark describes them very succinctly:

[w]hen witnesses in civil and criminal actions appeared before the diocesan courts they generally prefaced their testimony with a brief autobiographical statement. From the late sixteenth century the statement normally listed name, age, occupation or status, place and length of residence, and sometimes details of previous residence.[44]

---

[40] For example, E. Parkinson, 'Interpreting the Compton Census Returns of 1676 for the Diocese of Llandaff', *Local Population Studies* LX (1998), pp. 48–57, compared the Compton Census with the Hearth Taxes and concluded that many of the Compton Census returns seemed to omit the poorer people. I.L. Williams, 'North Wiltshire Demography, 1676–1700', *Wiltshire Archaeological and Natural History Magazine*, XC (1997), pp. 113–14, concluded that, in north Wiltshire, the Marriage Duty assessment lists were more reliable than the Compton Census.

[41] See, for example, Williams, 'North Wiltshire', pp. 110–11.

[42] See J. Patten, 'Patterns of Migration and Movement of Labour to Three Pre-Industrial East Anglian Towns', in Clark and Souden, *Migration and Society*, pp. 78–81 (originally published in *Journal of Historical Geography* II (1976), pp. 111–29).

[43] P. Clark, 'Migration in England during the Late Seventeenth and Early Eighteenth Centuries', in Clark and Souden, *Migration and Society*, pp. 213–52 (originally published in *Past and Present* LXXXIII (1979), pp. 57–90).

[44] Ibid., p. 218.

They may therefore be used to chart migration patterns 'of men and women, town and countryside, different regions and varying social and economic groups'.[45]

Settlement examinations are potentially even more detailed than the Church court depositions, though for a more socially select group. They are records of the attempts by the Poor Law authorities of various parishes to establish exactly which parishes were responsible for supporting applicants for poor relief. Because settlements (rights to poor relief from a particular parish) could be acquired during the life course (for example, by working as a hired servant in the parish for a continuous period of 52 weeks), and because a newly acquired settlement superseded previous ones, deciding in which parish a person was currently settled usually involved compiling a detailed biography of the person, including (indeed, focusing specifically on) the person's migration history. Settlement examinations, of course, relate mainly to the poorer classes of society. Nevertheless, they are probably the most detailed source of data on *residential histories* (lists of the whole sequence of moves made by persons during their lives).[46]

In recent years, interest in using nominative record linkage with sources other than parish registers has been rekindled.[47] The result is a kind of 'family reconstitution plus', a database relating to a particular community, which is founded upon a standard, parish register-based, family reconstitution but which incorporates data from other sources. These other sources might include the four mentioned in this section in connection with the study of migration, but also probate records such as wills and inventories.[48] One of the best examples is the study of Calverley in West Yorkshire by Steven King.[49]

[45]   Ibid., p. 218.
[46]   The most extensive use of settlement examinations is by K.D.M. Snell, *Annals of the Labouring Poor: Social Change and Agrarian England 1660–1900* (Cambridge, Cambridge University Press, 1985).
[47]   Attempts at multi-source record linkage in early modern England go back at least to the 1970s; see A. Macfarlane, *Reconstructing Historical Communities* (Cambridge, Cambridge University Press, 1977). However, at that time the results of this extremely time-consuming exercise were felt not to be worth the work involved, and efforts focused on the much more restricted (but better defined) family reconstitution project. A key feature of family reconstitution is that the linkage process could be fully automated, vastly economizing on resources.
[48]   On the uses of probate records, see T. Arkell, N. Evans and N. Goose (eds), *When Death Do Us Part: Understanding and Interpreting the Probate Records of Early Modern England* (Watford, Local Population Studies, 2000).
[49]   See S. King, 'Multiple Source Record Linkage in a Rural Industrial Community, 1680–1820', *History and Computing* VI (1994), pp. 133–42; S. King, 'Power, Representation and the Historical Individual: Problems with Sources for Record Linkage in Two Yorkshire Townships, 1650–1820', *Local Historian* XXVII (1997), pp. 78–90. Another example is S. Ottoway and S. Williams, 'Reconstructing the Life-Cycle Experience of Poverty in the Time of the Old Poor Law', *Archives* XXIII (1998), pp. 19–29.

THE ENGLISH
DEMOGRAPHIC
TRANSITION

|11|

Population growth after 1750

11.1 The demographic transition

Part II of this book was largely an account of why population growth in early modern England was so slow. The most important reason, it turned out, was the operation of the Malthusian preventive check, which served indirectly to limit reproductivity, and to shackle the long-run rate of population growth to the long-run increase in economic productivity. Sometime during the eighteenth century, however, the English population began to increase year on year in a sustained way. The power of exponential growth is such that any sustained increase of this kind must lead to a rapid expansion of total numbers, and this chapter describes the unprecedented growth of the English population after 1750.

Demographers have for many years referred to this expansion of the population as the *demographic transition*. The set of models that has grown up around this concept form probably the best known of all demographic models: three decades ago one well-known demographer famously remarked, when giving a lecture on the demographic transition to an assembly of his colleagues, that pretty well any member of his audience was capable of giving an impromptu lecture on the subject, and the same is almost certainly true of geographers and economic historians.[1] The rapid population growth of the demographic transition is associated with a fall in fertility and mortality from the high levels characteristic of pre-industrial societies to the low levels characteristic of modern industrial countries. After an initial formulation by Warren Thompson in 1929, the first thorough accounts of the transition were written during the 1930s, 1940s and early 1950s by Adolphe Landry and Frank W. Notestein.[2]

1 A.J. Coale, 'The Demographic Transition', in *International Population Conference, Liège 1973* (3 vols, Liège, International Union for the Scientific Study of Population, 1973) I, p. 53.
2 W.S. Thompson, 'Population', *American Journal of Sociology* XXXIV (1929), pp. 959–75; A. Landry, *La Révolution Démographique: Etudes et Essais sur les Problèmes de la Population* (Paris, Librarie du Recueil Sirey, 1934); F.W. Notestein, 'Population: the Long View', in T.W. Schultz (ed.), *Food for the World* (Chicago, Chicago University Press, 1945), pp. 36–57; F.W. Notestein, 'Economic Problems of Population Change', in *Proceedings of the Eighth International Conference of Agricultural Economists, 1953* (London, Oxford University Press, 1953), pp. 13–31.

According to Notestein's model, the transition is initiated by a decline in mortality that

> is caused by the cumulative influences of the agricultural, the industrial and the sanitary revolutions which, respectively, lead to better food supplies, an improvement in the factors of production and the standard of living in general, and improvements in public health.[3]

Thus a reduction in mortality occurs because of the agricultural and sanitary improvements that accompanied the Industrial Revolution, which led to improvements in both public health and food supplies. Some time after the decline in mortality starts, there is a decline in fertility. However, the time-lag between the two declines produces a phase of rapid population growth, the length and intensity of this being to a large degree determined by the length of time elapsing between the decline of mortality and that of fertility. Eventually, fertility declines because 'the social and economic supports to high fertility are removed'.[4]

Notestein's conceptualization of the transition is depicted in Figure 11.1. The factors driving the mortality decline are all connected with economic development, and the decline in the death rate will, if all else remains the same, logically lead to an increase in the rate of population growth. However, the decline in fertility does not follow directly. Indeed, a weakness of Notestein's formulation is that there is no obvious mechanism that would propel a population right through from a situation of declining (and ultimately low) mortality to one with declining (and ultimately low) fertility.[5] Notestein himself was sceptical that economic development, at least if measured in terms of rising incomes per head, was capable of causing the decline in fertility, for, in so far as there was a direct effect of income upon fertility, it was probably weak and attenuated by the fact that increasing population size tends to retard the increase in income per head.[6] Notestein argued that the decline in fertility occurs because, as mortality falls, the rationale behind the institutional factors within society that promote childbearing is eroded. In high-mortality populations, fertility has to be high in order to sustain population growth at all, and those populations that survived the punishing rates of mortality in pre-industrial times must have such institutional mechanisms in place. The decline of mortality renders these mechanisms redundant, and allows fertility to fall. There appears to be a logical gap in this argument, in that it assumes that the 'natural' tendency is for people to want rather few children. It is only because of the need to maintain positive

[3]   R. Woods, *Theoretical Population Geography* (London, Longman, 1982), p. 161.
[4]   Ibid., p. 161.
[5]   See the discussion in Woods, *Theoretical Population Geography*, pp. 172–3.
[6]   F.W. Notestein, 'The Population of the World in the Year 2000', *Journal of the American Statistical Association* XLV (1950), p. 344.

population growth in a high-mortality environment that pre-transition populations have to be cajoled by various institutional mechanisms to have large families.

The logical gap was closed in 1963 by Kingsley Davis (Figure 11.2).[7] Davis argued that the threat to economic development caused by rising population size was critical to the whole process, as it placed at risk the newly won prosperity and led populations to make some kind of response to protect rising living standards. This response could take several forms, including a reduction of population pressure by emigration, or the control of fertility, either through an intensification of the Malthusian preventive check, or through the restriction of child-bearing within marriage. Davis therefore saw the decline of fertility as a belated consequence of the decline in mortality, establishing a direct causal link between the two declines, and, in passing, explaining why there must be a time-lag between the two declines in mortality and fertility.

In a sense, Chapters 12–14 of this book can be seen as an examination of how well the English experience fits these models of the demographic transition. This chapter sets the scene by considering the initial phases of the transition in England. Section 11.2 charts the growth of the English population during the eighteenth and nineteenth centuries. Section 11.3 focuses on the initial period of expansion and discusses whether the start of the period of rapid growth did, indeed, coincide with the beginnings of a sustained

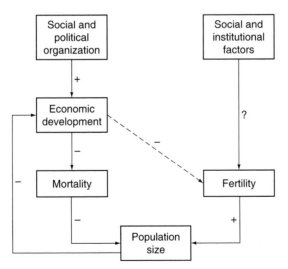

Figure 11.1 Schematic representation of Notestein's model of the demographic transition

Note: See notes to Figure 6.1 for explanation of '+' and '−' signs.

[7]   K. Davis, 'The Theory of Change and Response in Demographic History', *Population Index* XXIX (1963), pp. 345–66.

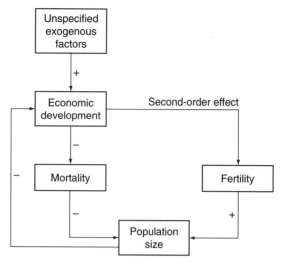

Figure 11.2 Schematic representation of Davis's conceptualization of the demographic transition

decline in mortality, as the demographic transition model would suggest it should. Section 11.4 discusses the relationship between economic development, especially as measured by real wages, and fertility and mortality during the second half of the eighteenth century. Section 11.5 summarizes the conclusions of Sections 11.3 and 11.4.

The next three chapters look separately at the three components of population change. Chapter 12 examines mortality trends in England between 1750 and the early twentieth century. Chapter 13 tells the story of fertility change in England over a similar period. Chapter 14 discusses trends in international and internal migration. In each of these chapters we elaborate on the theoretical accounts of changes in each component, and then assess them in the light of empirical evidence from England.

11.2 Population numbers

In 1750 the population of England was, according to the estimates made by E.A. Wrigley and R.S. Schofield, 5.74 million.[8] It bears repeating that this may have been no higher than the population around 1300, though it is probably not much lower. In fact, the mid-eighteenth century does not really mark a turning point, for after a 40-year period of stagnation between 1650 and 1690, population growth resumed just before 1700 (Figure 11.3).

[8]   E.A. Wrigley and R.S. Schofield, *The Population History of England, 1541–1871: a Reconstruction* (London, Edward Arnold, 1981), p. 533.

In the first half of the eighteenth century, however, growth was slow and punctuated by two short periods of population decline. The first, and most important, came at the end of the 1720s and was the result of the last great mortality crisis of the pre-industrial era, when the population fell for three or four consecutive years. The second, briefer, interruption occurred during the early 1740s, and was possibly due to epidemics of dysentery, though the harvests of 1740 and 1741 were also both deficient.[9] Thereafter, however, growth was relentless. The result was that the number of inhabitants living in England increased to eight million by 1794, ten million by 1812 and 15 million in the early 1840s (Figure 11.3). In other words, during the period 1750–1850 the population of England increased to a level more than double its previous highest value.

The rate of population growth in each year between 1650 and 1850 is plotted in Figure 11.4. During the population stagnation of the late seventeenth century, the rate was barely above zero in 'normal' years and frequently fell well below zero, especially during the 1680s. From the 1690s onwards rates just above zero were achieved in most years, and a slow but steady increase in the rate of growth is identifiable. The mortality crises of the late 1720s and early 1740s stand out as deep troughs, but thereafter the

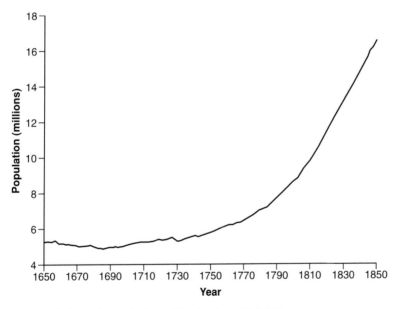

Figure 11.3 Estimated population of England, 1650–1850
Source: E.A. Wrigley and R.S. Schofield, *The Population History of England 1541–1871: a Reconstruction* (London, Edward Arnold, 1981), pp. 532–5.

9   Ibid., p. 669.

increase in the rate of population growth accelerates to reach a peak in the early nineteenth century, when the population was growing at a rate between 1.5 and 2.0 per cent per year, before declining slightly from the 1820s onwards.

The mid-eighteenth century, therefore, did witness an increase in the *rate* of population growth. However, except perhaps during the second decade of the nineteenth century, the rate of growth did not reach a level that was unprecedented, or that was different in kind from what had been experienced before during phases of growth, for example in the 1580s.[10] What was new about the second half of the eighteenth century was the *sustained nature* of the growth. According to Wrigley and Schofield's estimates, there was not a single year between 1742 and 1871 during which the population declined: during the two preceding centuries the longest continuous period for which the same could be said was 37 years (between 1560 and 1596).[11]

Population growth in England, however, was more rapid (often much more rapid) than in other large countries in western Europe (Table 11.1). During the two periods 1680–1820 and 1820–1900, the population of England increased in relative terms more than in any other country of com-

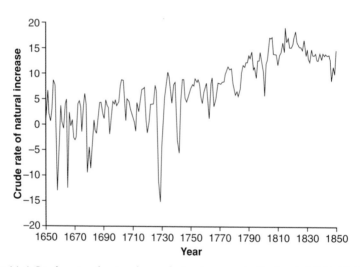

Figure 11.4 Crude rate of natural population increase in England, 1650–1850 (per thousand)

Note: The crude rate of natural increase is the difference between the crude birth rate and the crude death rate. Negative values thus imply population decline.

Source: E.A. Wrigley and R.S. Schofield, *The Population History of England 1541–1871: a Reconstruction* (London, Edward Arnold, 1981), pp. 532–5.

---

[10]   Ibid., p. 531.
[11]   Ibid., pp. 531–5.

parable size. The contrast with France is particularly striking. Whereas in 1750 there were four times as many French as English people, by 1850 the population of France was barely double that of England. However, despite being by far the most rapidly expanding of any country in eighteenth- and nineteenth-century Europe, the rate of population growth in England was well below that achieved either in the Americas at that time, or in many developing countries in the second half of the twentieth century. Malthus's famous description of the population of the United States having 'been found to double itself in twenty-five years' implies an annual rate of growth of 2.8 per cent per year.[12] The rate of population growth in developing countries since 1950 has often exceeded 3 per cent per year.

Table 11.1 Population growth in certain European countries, 1680–1900

Country	Population (millions)			Percentage growth	
	c. 1750	c. 1800	c. 1850	1680–1820	1820–1900
England	5.8	8.7	16.7	133	166
France	24.5	29.0	35.9	39	26
Germany	18.4	24.5	35.0	51	142
Italy	15.2	17.5	23.7	53	77
Netherlands	1.9	2.1	3.1	8	149
Spain	11.3	13.2	15.7	64	33
Western Europe	94.2	110.1	148.3	62	73

Note: The population figures for Germany and the Netherlands in 1750 are only approximate. The figures for Italy, Spain and western Europe for 1750, 1800 and 1850 have been estimated from figures for 1680, 1820 and 1900 by linear interpolation.
Sources: M. Anderson, *Population Change in North-Western Europe, 1750–1850* (London, Macmillan, 1988), p. 23; E.A. Wrigley, 'The Growth of Population in Eighteenth-Century England: a Conundrum Resolved', *Past and Present* XCVIII (1983), p. 122.

11.3 The demographic causes of the rise in population

A change in the rate of population growth can occur only if changes take place in fertility, mortality and migration (or possibly in all three). Since, as E.A. Wrigley has written, '[i]n the third quarter of the seventeenth century fertility and mortality were roughly in balance', with the population

[12] T.R. Malthus, *An Essay on the Principle of Population and A Summary View of the Principle of Population*, ed. A. Flew (Harmondsworth, Pelican, 1970), p. 74. Using the formula $P_t = P_0 e^{rt}$, where P_t is the population in year t, and r is the annual rate of population growth, then Malthus's observation implies that $P_{25} = 2P_0$. This means that $2P_0 = P_0 e^{25r}$, or $e^{25r} = 2$. Taking natural logarithms produces $25r = \ln 2$, or $r = (\ln 2)/25 = 0.693/25 = 0.0277$.

growth rate close to zero, and since net migration was 'not a major component of population change' during the eighteenth century, 'it must necessarily have been the case that either mortality fell very substantially or
fertility increased sharply, or both changes occurred but on a more modest
scale'.[13]

Trends in mortality and fertility between 1700 and 1850 are plotted
in Figure 11.5. Mortality, as measured by the expectation of life at
birth, rose from about 36 or 37 years in 1700 to just over 40 years by
1850. This is, by any standards, a rather modest rise. By taking 1680
(when the expectation of life at birth was around 33 years) as a starting
point, its magnitude would appear greater, but if we do this 'the gain is
somewhat exaggerated by the periodization because the 1670s and
1680s included so many years of uncharacteristically high mortality'.[14]

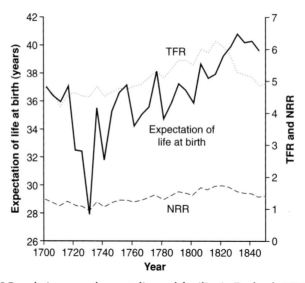

Figure 11.5 Population growth, mortality and fertility in England, 1700–1850
Source: E.A. Wrigley and R.S. Schofield, *The Population History of England 1541–1871: a
Reconstruction* (London, Edward Arnold, 1981), pp. 528–9.

---

[13] E.A. Wrigley, 'The Growth of Population in Eighteenth-Century England: a Conundrum
    Resolved', *Past and Present* XCVIII (1983), p. 126.
[14] Ibid., p. 129. An argument can also be made that the decline in mortality in the first half of
    the nineteenth century was greater than the national-level figures would indicate, because
    of the redistribution of the population from low-mortality rural areas to high-mortality
    urban areas (see Chapter 12). Even if we allow this (and there are good reasons why we
    should be careful about allowing it, since if urbanization is an intrinsic part of economic
    development it cannot be separated from the wider process leading to mortality decline), it
    is still hard to conclude that mortality decline in England between 1700 and 1850 was any-
    thing other than slow, although a definite decline did occur.

We can make the mortality decline appear substantially greater by taking the 1720s or the 1740s as the starting point (Figure 11.5), but, as pointed out above, these decades were also ones of abnormally high mortality.

Figure 11.5 also reveals that fertility showed a sustained increase from the early eighteenth century until the early nineteenth century. The total fertility rate increased from just under four births per woman in 1680, to around 4.5 births per woman in between 1690 and 1710, and thereafter rose continuously to peak at about six births per woman between 1810 and 1820. Overall, then, the English experience after 1750 was one of slowly falling mortality and rather rapidly rising fertility. It has been shown by E.A. Wrigley that between 1680 and 1820 'the fertility rise contributed about two-and-a-half times as much to the rise in growth rates as the mortality fall', or that

> if fertility had remained unchanged during the 'long' eighteenth century but mortality had fallen in the manner just described population ... would have reached a rate of growth of about 0.5 per cent per annum. If, however, mortality had failed to improve but fertility had followed its historic course, the ... growth rate would have risen from zero to about 1.25 per cent per annum.[15]

This point is illustrated in Table 11.2, which compares the observed net reproduction rate (NRR) between 1700 and 1850 with that which would have been experienced under two counterfactual scenarios: the first holds mortality constant at its level during the 1690s, but allows fertility to rise as it was observed to do; the second holds fertility constant at the 1690s level but allows mortality to fall as it was observed to do (see Box 3.1 for a definition of the net reproduction rate). The NRR actually increased from 1.12 in the 1690s to around 1.6 or 1.7 by early nineteenth century. The observed increase in fertility alone would have raised the NRR to between 1.4 and 1.55 over the same period, whereas the decrease in mortality alone could only have raised the NRR to 1.3 at the most. The growth of the English population between 1700 and 1850, therefore, was due more to increased fertility than to declining mortality.

This conclusion, based on Wrigley and Schofield's aggregative parish register analysis (see Appendix II), turned on its head the view that, consistent with the theory of the demographic transition, the initial impetus to population growth came from the onset of mortality decline. The most prominent proponent of this view was probably Thomas McKeown, whose work

---

[15] Wrigley, 'Growth of Population', p. 131.

Table 11.2 The impact of fertility and mortality on English population growth, 1696–1846

Year	Observed net reproduction rate	Expected net reproduction rate	
		Under constant 1696 mortality and observed fertility	Under constant 1696 fertility and observed mortality
1696	1.12	1.12	1.12
1706	1.22	1.15	1.19
1716	1.24	1.15	1.20
1726	1.08	1.13	1.06
1736	1.26	1.21	1.16
1746	1.20	1.16	1.15
1756	1.28	1.19	1.21
1766	1.25	1.22	1.14
1776	1.43	1.32	1.21
1786	1.41	1.34	1.17
1796	1.51	1.41	1.20
1806	1.68	1.50	1.25
1816	1.72	1.57	1.22
1826	1.68	1.47	1.28
1836	1.50	1.30	1.29
1846	1.39	1.21	1.28

Source: E.A. Wrigley and R.S. Schofield, *The Population History of England 1541–1871: a Reconstruction* (London, Edward Arnold, 1981), pp. 528–9.

is discussed more fully in Section 12.3.[16] However, although the English data do not lend much support to the simple model of the demographic transition described by Notestein, we should not fall into the trap of denying any substantial role to the decline of mortality. A more detailed exami-

[16] See, for example, T. McKeown, R.G. Brown and R.G. Record, 'An Interpretation of the Modern Rise of Population in Europe', *Population Studies* XXVI (1972), pp. 345–82. It is true that some earlier scholars had argued for a temporary rise in fertility at the end of the eighteenth century and beginning of the nineteenth century, but most such arguments foundered on uncertainty about the quality of the baptism register data during that crucial period; see, for example, J.T. Krause, 'Changes in English Fertility and Mortality, 1781–1850', *Economic History Review*, 2nd series XI (1958), pp. 52–70. Declining quality of registration means that some adjustment to the numbers of baptisms needs to be made in order to estimate numbers of births. The problem was that depending on the size of the adjustment, widely different conclusions about fertility rates between about 1780 and 1820 can be reached. The debate about the causes of eighteenth-century population growth continues to attract important contributions; see, for example, P. Razzell, 'The Growth of Population in Eighteenth-Century England: a Critical Re-appraisal', *Journal of Economic History* LIII (1993), pp. 747–71; and P. Razzell, 'The Conundrum of Eighteenth-Century English Population Growth', *Social History of Medicine* XI (1998), pp. 469–500.

nation of Table 11.2 reveals that, in the very early years of population growth (between 1700 and 1750) the contributions of declining mortality and rising fertility were about equal (though both very modest). It was only after 1750 that the rise in fertility began to dominate.

Why did fertility rise after 1750? Chapter 8 described the research that has shown conclusively that changes in English fertility before 1750 were almost entirely due to changes in nuptiality, and in particular changes in the proportions of the population ever marrying. Table 11.3 presents data on various measures of fertility and nuptiality for the period from 1700 to 1850. The data show that the rise in fertility in eighteenth-century England was due partly to changes in nuptiality and partly to a rise in fertility within marriage, but that increasing nuptiality was more important than rising fertility within marriage. A new feature of the pattern after 1750, however, was that increasing nuptiality was due both to a fall in the average age at marriage as well as decreasing celibacy. The average age at first marriage for males fell from about 27 years in 1700 to around 25 years by the 1830s; for women the corresponding fall was from 26 years to close to 23 years. Celibacy decreased from almost one in five among cohorts who were in their thirties during the first decade of the eighteenth century to about one in ten among cohorts 50 years younger, and it continued to fall after 1750.

The rise in fertility within marriage has also been studied by Wrigley. His analysis, though by his own admission somewhat speculative, suggests that the main reason was a decline in the number of stillbirths, or, more accurately, the 'conversion' of stillbirths into live births.[17] One reason for this may have been improved nutrition, though this seems more likely to have affected those areas, notably in the hills of the north-west, where nutrition-related sub-fecundity was most common during the early modern period.[18] Apart from the reduction in the number of stillbirths, early-marrying women seem to have continued childbearing for longer after 1750 than they had done in previous years, which also contributed to the increase in fertility.[19]

---

[17] This point is considered further in E.A. Wrigley, 'Explaining the Rise in Marital Fertility in England in the "Long" Eighteenth Century', *Economic History Review*, 2nd series LI (1998), pp. 435–64.

[18] For example, the parish of Penrith in Cumbria; see S. Scott and C.J. Duncan, 'Interacting Effects of Nutrition and Social Class Differentials on Fertility and Infant Mortality in a Pre-Industrial Population', *Population Studies* LIV (2000) pp. 81–2. Though the case for improved nutrition in Penrith is well made in this article, there are reasons to be sceptical about the validity of the improved nutrition argument in the rest of the country.

[19] As Richard Vann has noted, this astonishing observation immediately raises the question of why these early-marrying women did not go on having children for so long during the seventeenth century. One obvious possibility is that they were practising 'stopping' behaviour. See R.T. Vann, 'Unnatural Fertility, or Whatever Happened in Colyton? Some Reflections on *English Population History from Family Reconstitution 1580–1837*', *Continuity and Change* XIV (1999), pp. 91–104.

Table 11.3 Some components of English fertility, 1700–1850

Decade	Total fertility rate	Total marital fertility rate	Percentage never marrying	Average age at first marriage	
				Males	Females
1700–09	4.56	7.32	20.6	27.4	26.0
1710–19	4.36	7.44	17.7	27.3	26.3
1720–29	4.41	7.56	13.6	27.0	25.9
1730–39	4.65	7.61	11.8	26.9	25.5
1740–49	4.59	7.53	10.3	26.5	24.8
1750–59	4.76	7.53	8.8	26.1	25.0
1760–69	4.77	7.45	7.8	25.9	24.5
1770–79	4.92	7.49	4.3	26.5	24.3
1780–89	5.06	7.41	5.5	25.9	24.0
1790–99	5.23	7.54	6.2	25.3	24.0
1800–09	5.41	7.79	6.8	25.3	24.0
1810–19	5.69	7.67	6.9	25.1	23.6
1820–29	5.71	–	7.7	25.2	23.8
1830–39	5.13	–	9.1	24.9	23.1
1840–49	4.85	–	10.8	–	–

Notes: The total marital fertility rates reported in this table are calculated for 50-year periods centred on the decade in question, except for 1810–19, which is based on data for 1800–24. Average ages at marriage for the decade 1830–39 relate only to the period 1830–37. The total fertility rates reported in this table have been estimated from the more recent results from generalized inverse projection rather than the original back projection figures used elsewhere in this book. The figures for percentages never marrying relate to cohorts aged about 35 years during the decade in question. See Box 9.1 for a definition of the total marital fertility rate.

Sources: E.A. Wrigley and R.S. Schofield, *The Population History of England 1541–1871: a Reconstruction* (London, Edward Arnold, 1981), p. 260; E.A. Wrigley, R.S. Davies, J.E. Oeppen and R.S. Schofield, *English Population History from Family Reconstitution 1580–1837* (Cambridge, Cambridge University Press, 1997), pp. 134, 355, 450, 614.

11.4 Economic development and population growth

The beginning of the demographic transition in England, then, does not seem to fit the demographic transition model at all well. Although there was some decline in mortality after 1750, the lion's share of the growth in population happened because of a nuptially-related rise in fertility.

Why did this happen? Since the most plausible account of the late age at marriage and high celibacy during the early modern period is related to the operation of the Malthusian preventive check and the practice of using a period spent as a servant to accumulate the resources with which to marry, one interpretation of these changes is that, during the eighteenth century, the preventive check started to be applied less rigorously. The operation of the simple Malthusian model depicted in Figure 6.1 suggests that the preventive check involved several links: first, population growth would lead to a fall in real wages; second, the fall in real wages would lead to reduced nuptiality; third, reduced nuptiality would result in lower fertility; and, fourth, lower fertility would reduce the rate of population growth. The breaking of any of these links would serve to halt the operation of the preventive check. E.A. Wrigley and R.S. Schofield argue that the first link was the critical one. Comparing England in the early nineteenth century with England in the seventeenth century, they write that

> the most striking single difference ... is the complete disappearance [of] the positive link between population size and food prices, one of most fundamental and strongest of all the features of the classic pre-industrial system. Had it not disappeared, the continued existence of the rest of the preventive-check cycle would have forced down real wages.[20]

Elsewhere, Wrigley has written that in pre-industrial England '[m]arriage was the hinge on which the demographic system turned'.[21] The first sign that this 'old regime' was coming apart was the 'breaking of the link' between 'the rate of population growth and the rate of change in food prices'.[22] In other words, the preventive check was no longer needed because increased population growth no longer led to a fall in real wages. The population of England was breaking out of the Malthusian trap.

Wrigley and Schofield's account has been disputed. It has been contended that living standards in England fell, at least temporarily, between 1750 and 1810, and that rapid population growth was a cause of this, implying that the Malthusian link between population size and real wages was still intact. Evidence in support of this view has been provided by John Komlos, who argued (on the basis of the reported heights of runaway servants) that the nutritional status of English men declined in the mid-eighteenth century, as rapid population growth began, because of the pressure of population on resources.[23] However, there are several reasons to be sceptical about it. First, if living standards did fall enough to affect the heights of English men, then this implies that they fell enough to affect the health of the population. But why, then, was mortality simultaneously falling? Second, the argument for a fall in living standards in late eighteenth-century England is based on the real wage series of Phelps-Brown and Hopkins, which certainly shows a substantial fall between 1750 and 1800.[24] However, recent work has cast

---

[20] Wrigley and Schofield, *Population History of England*, p. 473.
[21] Wrigley, 'Growth of Population', p. 149.
[22] Ibid., p. 149.
[23] J. Komlos, 'On the Nature of the Malthusian Threat in the Eighteenth Century', *Economic History Review*, 2nd series LII (1999), pp. 730–48.
[24] E.H. Phelps-Brown and S.V. Hopkins, 'Seven Centuries of the Prices of Consumables Compared with Builders' Wage Rates', in E.M. Carus-Wilson (ed.), *Essays in Economic History II* (London, Edward Arnold, 1962), pp. 179–96.

doubt on this fall, and suggested that real wages were rising slowly, at least from 1770.[25]

Population growth and real wages, therefore, do seem to have become decoupled during the second half of the eighteenth century. However, this was not the whole story. Figure 11.6 plots real wages between 1700 and 1850 against the proportions never marrying. During the first half of the eighteenth century, nuptiality rose as real wages rose, just as the Malthusian preventive check model would predict. However, after about 1740, real wages fell back, yet nuptiality *continued to rise*. Moreover, if Charles Feinstein's revised real wage series for the period after 1770 is accepted, real wages began a slow recovery after about 1780 at a time when the proportions never marrying were also rising. In other words, around 1740 the relationship between real wages and nuptiality changes from being negative (the preventive check) to positive. While both series plotted in Figure 11.6 are subject to some uncertainty, they appear to show that the preventive check had been extinguished in England before any appreciable population growth took place.

Figure 11.6 Real wages and the percentage never marrying in England, 1700–1850
Notes: Real wages here relate to five-year periods. The series plotted here has been obtained by splicing E.A. Wrigley and R.S. Schofield's series to the more recent one prepared by C. Feinstein. The proportions never marrying are based on data for birth cohorts, plotted against the year in which a birth cohort attains the age of about 25 years.
Sources: E.A. Wrigley and R.S. Schofield, *The Population History of England 1541–1871: a Reconstruction* (London, Edward Arnold, 1981), pp. 260, 643; C. Feinstein, 'Pessimism Perpetuated: Real Wages and the Standard of Living in Britain During and After the Industrial Revolution', *Journal of Economic History* LVIII (1998), p. 648.

[25]   See C. Feinstein, 'Pessimism Perpetuated: Real Wages and the Standard of Living in Britain During and After the Industrial Revolution', *Journal of Economic History* LVIII (1998), pp. 625–58.

This, however, raises the question of why nuptiality in the second half of the eighteenth century continued to rise. At present, it is not possible to say for certain, but some recent local-level research raises intriguing possibilities. For example, in the Yorkshire township of Calverley, the average age at marriage remained constant (and lower than the national average) throughout the eighteenth century.[26] Calverley was a proto-industrial community, and we might speculate that the age at marriage had always been lower in such communities. The national decline in the age at marriage (and, by inference, the rise in nuptiality) might, therefore, simply have been a case of the rest of the country 'catching up' with the early industrializing areas as industrialization became more widespread. In other words, the high mean age at marriage and high celibacy in early modern England might have been an agrarian phenomenon, rather than an 'early modern' phenomenon, and it was the transformation of swathes of England from an agrarian society into an industrial society that led to nuptiality patterns changing and rapid population growth.

11.5 Conclusion

It now seems that the English population did not follow the classical model of the demographic transition. The rise in the population after 1750 was not, primarily, initiated by a decline in mortality. Though there was a fall in mortality, it was responsible for less than half (possibly much less than half) of the growth in the English population between 1750 and 1850. The main reason why the population grew was that the preventive check, which had restricted the rate of population growth in early modern England, ceased to operate. Initially, it seems that this occurred because the link between real wages and nuptiality was severed, for reasons that are not yet clear, but that may have something to do with the beginnings of the Industrial Revolution. Shortly afterwards, the Malthusian tether that bound population growth and real wages also snapped. This was undoubtedly the result of increased productivity in agriculture (and, by then, industry) arising from technological developments. These greatly increased the number of people the land could support. Economic development, therefore, did underpin the demographic transition in England, but the ways in which it affected the key demographic variables were more complex than the classical theorists supposed.

---

[26] S. King, 'English Historical Demography and the Nuptiality Conundrum: New Perspectives', *Historical Social Research* XXIII (1998), pp. 130–56.

|12|

The decline of mortality,
1750–1950

12.1 Introduction

The decline in mortality during the English demographic transition was not initiated with a fanfare. Its onset is by no means obvious, even when the time trend in a single-figure index of mortality is used to try to simplify matters. Slowly, almost imperceptibly, from the late seventeenth century, mortality began to improve. But the slowness of the amelioration was such that even by 1750 the expectation of life at birth was less than 40 years.[1] Indeed, it could be argued from the figures for the expectation of life at birth that until the second half of the eighteenth century, the trend in mortality was merely reversing the trend between the Elizabethan era and the end of the seventeenth century, during which mortality had deteriorated.

However, this argument turns out, in fact, to be a witness to the short-comings of single-figure indices of mortality, for closer inspection reveals that the eighteenth century was the harbinger of a new mortality environment. Two changes, in particular, are noteworthy. The first is the disappearance of crisis mortality. The second, which was largely hidden from historians' view until the recent work by E.A. Wrigley and his colleagues, is that the age pattern of mortality changed appreciably. Data from many countries from the late nineteenth and twentieth centuries have revealed substantial regularities in age patterns of mortality. Indeed, it is these age patterns that underlie the use of model life tables (see Box 5.1). Yet the English mortality experience of the seventeenth century was very different: adult mortality was much higher relative to child mortality than would be expected from any of the sets of model life tables in common use.[2] During the early eighteenth century, however, infant mortality became substantially worse, and adult mor-

---

[1] See E.A. Wrigley, R.S. Davies, J.E. Oeppen and R.S. Schofield, *English Population History from Family Reconstitution, 1580–1837* (Cambridge, Cambridge University Press, 1997), pp. 294–5. The 1750s were, according to Wrigley *et al.*'s figures, an abnormally healthy decade, but the average of their figures for the expectation of life at birth for the 1740s, 1750s and 1760s is 39.5 years.

[2] Wrigley *et al.*, *English Population History*, p. 284.

tality improved such that the age pattern of mortality began to resemble that of the model life tables. Therefore, 'the early eighteenth century was ... a period of transition from the old to a more modern demographic regime'.[3]

For these two reasons, it seems justifiable to place the onset of the secular decline in mortality that occurred during the English demographic transition – which we might term the *mortality transition* – somewhere in the middle of the eighteenth century. This chapter, therefore, begins in Section 12.2 by describing the course of the mortality decline over the two centuries after 1750, providing the data that will underpin subsequent sections.

Probably the best-known attempt to explain the reasons for the sustained decline in mortality after 1750 is due to Thomas McKeown and his colleagues. Section 12.3 presents the details of their argument that improvements in the standard of living were the main cause. Section 12.4 discusses the reasonableness of the McKeown thesis as an account of the English mortality decline before the middle of the nineteenth century. Section 12.5 discusses mortality differentials in England during the third quarter of the nineteenth century, taking advantage of the fact that by then both the civil registration of deaths and the taking of regular decennial censuses were established features of English administrative life. These data allow us to look in much more detail at the course of the decline in mortality after 1850 than is the case for earlier years, and this is done in Section 12.6. Section 12.7 re-assesses the applicability of the McKeown thesis for the second half of the nineteenth century in the light of recent research.

Though the nineteenth century saw substantial progress on mortality, the benefits were not felt equally by all age groups. In particular, infant mortality remained high right up until the turn of the twentieth century. Section 12.8 considers infant mortality in more detail, summarizes the most plausible explanations for its remaining so high for so long, and discusses the causes of its subsequent rapid decline.

Earlier, it was said that an important facet of the mortality transition is the disappearance of mortality crises. There is, however, normally an exception to every generalization and, in this case, the exception is the influenza pandemic of 1918, which came almost two centuries after the previous major crises due to epidemic disease. The crisis, and its effect on mortality, is described in Section 12.9, in the course of a discussion of the decline in mortality between 1910 and 1950.

12.2 Mortality trends

Figure 12.1 shows the crude death rate (CDR) in England and Wales from 1700 to 1950. The CDR series extends that shown for the early modern period in Figure 7.2. A difficulty with the CDR as a single-figure index of

---

[3] Ibid., p. 284.

mortality is its dependence on the population's age structure. Because the risk of death increases with age, the same set of age-specific death rates will produce a higher CDR in an 'older' population (that is, a population with a higher proportion of its members in older age groups) than in a 'younger' one.[4] As a population undergoes the demographic transition, the profound changes in mortality and fertility that take place lead to great changes in its age structure, which mean that the CDR series will not accurately reflect the true changes in the risk of death.[5] Accordingly, Figure 12.1 also depicts changes in the expectation of life at birth (see Box 7.1), a single-figure index that is not subject to distortions arising from the changing age structure.

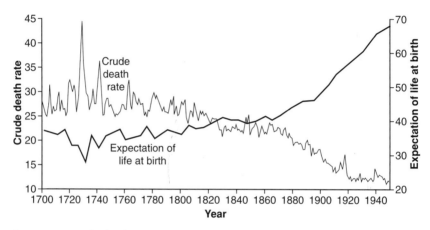

Figure 12.1 Crude death rate (per thousand) and expectation of life at birth, England and Wales, 1700–1950

Notes: Crude death rates for years before 1871 are for England only. All figures are for both sexes combined (in some cases interpolated from figures for males and females).

Sources: E.A. Wrigley and R.S. Schofield, *The Population History of England 1541–1871: a Reconstruction* (London, Edward Arnold, 1981), pp. 529, 533–5; R.I. Woods and P.R.A. Hinde, 'Mortality in Victorian England: Models and Patterns', *Journal of Interdisciplinary History* XVIII (1987), p. 33 (reprinted in R.I. Rotberg (ed.), *Health and Disease in Human History: a Journal of Interdisciplinary History Reader* (London, MIT Press, 2000), p. 67); B.R. Mitchell, *British Historical Statistics* (Cambridge, Cambridge University Press, 1988), pp. 57–9; Office of Population Censuses and Surveys, *Mortality Statistics. Serial Tables: Review of the Registrar General on Deaths in England and Wales 1841–1990* (series DH1, no. 25), (London, Her Majesty's Stationery Office, 1992), pp. 1–2.

---

[4]   See A. Hinde, *Demographic Methods* (London, Arnold, 1998), pp. 20–1 for further discussion of this point.

[5]   For an elementary introduction to the ways in which fertility, mortality and the age structure are related, see A. Hinde, 'Demographic Perspectives in Human Population Dynamics', in H. Macbeth and P. Collinson (eds), *Human Population Dynamics* (Cambridge, Cambridge University Press, 2002). For a more advanced treatment, see Hinde, *Demographic Methods*, pp. 162–7.

Both the CDR and the expectation of life at birth display marked fluctuations in the early eighteenth century, which are the result of the episodes of high mortality in the late 1720s and the 1740s. After 1750, mortality stabilized, and a sustained decline in the CDR is observed from the last two decades of the eighteenth century. This decline continued into the nineteenth century, so that by 1830 the CDR had fallen to about 22.5 per thousand. Between 1830 and 1870, however, the CDR stabilized at this level, before resuming its decline to reach about 12 per thousand by 1920. The expectation of life at birth was about 35 years in 1750. It began a gentle rise during the second half of the eighteenth century to reach about 40 years by 1830. Like the CDR, however, it then stabilized at this level until around 1870, when it commenced a second, much more rapid increase, passing 50 years during the first few years of the twentieth century and 60 years about 1930. In sum, then, the English mortality decline at the national level went through three phases: there was a definite, though rather modest, decline in mortality between 1780 and 1830; this decline was arrested for a period during the mid-nineteenth century; but a second, decisive period of decline began during the 1870s.

The overall trends reported in Figure 12.1 conceal a great deal. In subsequent sections of this chapter, a lot of this detail will be revealed, but it is helpful here to consider two aspects. First, mortality levels varied substantially between urban and rural areas for most of the period we are considering (the differentials remained substantial well into the twentieth century). In general, urban mortality was higher than rural, and the larger the urban centre, the higher the mortality (although London was an exception). The difference matters because over the period of the mortality decline, there was a massive shift of people from rural areas to urban areas (see Chapter 14). Just as trends in the CDR can be confounded by changes in the age structure, so similar distortions can occur because of shifts in the residential structure of the population. Moreover, the expectation of life at birth, which, as an index of mortality, is not confounded by changes in the age distribution, is not immune from the effects of urbanization. The issue has been examined by Robert Woods, and Figure 12.2 uses his data to illustrate the problem.[6] In the early nineteenth century, the expectation of life at birth was over 40 years in rural areas, but only about 32 years in large towns and cities. During the century there was a general improvement in mortality in both rural areas and urban areas, but there were slight setbacks in the 1840s in all urban areas. The question is whether the redistribution of population from healthy rural environments to unhealthy urban environments caused the national-level trend in the expectation of life at birth to understate the progress being

[6] R.I. Woods, 'The Effects of Population Redistribution on the Level of Mortality in Nineteenth-Century England and Wales', *Journal of Economic History* XLI (1985), pp. 645–51; R. Woods, *The Demography of Victorian England and Wales* (Cambridge, Cambridge University Press, 2000), pp. 368–71.

achieved. This redistribution was perhaps at its most rapid during the mid-nineteenth century, when the decline in mortality at the national level seems temporarily to have halted. We return to this issue in Section 12.4.

It is also worth exploring at this stage the different trends by age and sex. Accurate data on age-specific death rates are only available from the 1830s onwards, when civil registration of deaths began (see Appendix III). Table 12.1 uses data from the series of English Life Tables produced by the Registrar General to chart trends in mortality in different age groups from the 1830s to 1910–12. The pattern is fairly clear. During the nineteenth century, progress was almost entirely confined to ages between 1 and 40 years. By 1891–1900, mortality in these age groups had fallen by 30–50 per cent compared with 1838–54, with the greatest relative decline at ages 5–15 years. Infant mortality scarcely declined at all during this period (indeed it was higher in the last decade of the nineteenth century than in the period 1838–54). During the first decades of the twentieth century, the decline spread to infants and ages 40–60 years, and between about 1910 and 1950 the most rapid progress was made at younger ages, and especially among infants. By 1950, infant mortality was only 27 per cent of its 1910–12 level, and mortality at all ages below 20 years fell by more than 75 per cent during the same

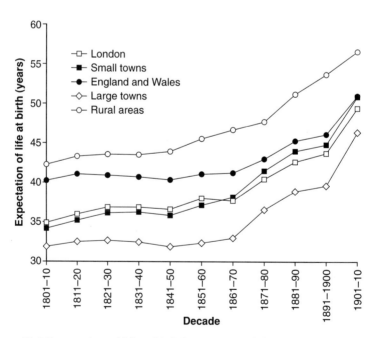

Figure 12.2 Expectation of life at birth by category of place, England and Wales, 1811–1911
Source: R.I. Woods, *The Demography of Victorian England and Wales* (Cambridge, Cambridge University Press, 2000), pp. 365, 369.

Table 12.1 Age-specific mortality, England and Wales 1838–1910

	1838–54	1871–80	1881–90	1891–1900	1901–10	1910–12
Probabilities of dying in each age group						
Males						
0	0.164	0.159	0.161	0.172	0.144	0.120
1–4	0.137	0.128	0.104	0.094	0.072	0.061
5–19	0.099	0.074	0.052	0.052	0.041	0.040
20–39	0.185	0.172	0.151	0.135	0.111	0.097
40–59	0.332	0.352	0.341	0.335	0.297	0.273
60–79	0.775	0.788	0.799	0.799	0.777	0.766
Females						
0	0.135	0.129	0.131	0.141	0.117	0.098
1–4	0.133	0.125	0.099	0.090	0.069	0.062
5–19	0.102	0.072	0.050	0.052	0.042	0.039
20–39	0.190	0.158	0.142	0.120	0.095	0.082
40–59	0.297	0.291	0.284	0.276	0.241	0.218
60–79	0.739	0.742	0.750	0.750	0.713	0.692
Trend: 1838–54 = 100						
Males						
0	100	97	98	105	88	74
1–4	100	93	76	69	53	44
5–19	100	74	52	52	42	40
20–39	100	93	82	73	60	52
40–59	100	106	103	101	89	82
60–79	100	102	103	103	100	99
Females						
0	100	96	97	104	87	73
1–4	100	94	74	68	52	46
5–19	100	71	49	51	41	39
20–39	100	83	74	63	50	43
40–59	100	98	96	93	81	73
60–79	100	100	101	102	97	94

Notes: The figures in the two upper panels are the probabilities of dying during the age group given survival to the beginning of the age group. Thus for males in 1838–54 the probability of dying before exact age five years given survival to exact age one year is 0.137. The top line in each panel is the probability of dying before exact age one year, or the infant mortality rate.
Source: R.I. Woods and P.R.A. Hinde, 'Mortality in Victorian England: Models and Patterns', *Journal of Interdisciplinary History* XVIII (1987), p. 33 (reprinted in R.I. Rotberg (ed.), *Health and Disease in Human History: a Journal of Interdisciplinary History Reader* (London, MIT Press, 2000), p. 67).

period.[7] However, mortality at ages over 60 years in 1950 was still more than half its 1910–12 level, and progress at ages over 80 years was negligible.[8]

[7] Office for National Statistics, *English Life Table No. 15* (London, The Stationery Office, 1997), p. 6.
[8] Ibid., p. 6.

12.3 The McKeown thesis

In the early 1970s, Abdel Omran described the decline in mortality as an *epidemiological transition*, which has three stages.[9] First comes an 'age of pestilence and famine', in which mortality is dominated by 'towering peaks' resulting from crises of various sorts, the majority of which involve attacks by killer epidemic diseases such as plague and typhus.[10] This stage is followed by an 'age of receding pandemics', in which mortality peaks disappear, and a decline in underlying mortality sets in.[11] The onset of this stage in eighteenth-century England can be seen quite clearly in Figure 12.1. The decline in underlying mortality comes about through the elimination of deaths from other infectious diseases, such as smallpox, measles and scarlet fever. Though their incidence is cyclical, these diseases differ from the 'true' epidemic killers in that they are ever-present in the population and confer immunity upon those fortunate enough to survive them. As a consequence, they are characteristically diseases of childhood, and become more so as population concentration increases their rate of transmission from person to person. The third stage is an 'age of degenerative and man-made diseases' in which deaths from infectious diseases have been largely eliminated and deaths from circulatory diseases and cancer dominate.[12] According to the epidemiological transition model, then, the decline in mortality is principally caused by a decline in the number of deaths from infectious diseases, of which airborne infections were most important.

The 'McKeown thesis' proposed by Thomas McKeown and his colleagues during the 1970s is an attempt to provide an account of the reasons for the conquest of infectious diseases.[13] It is probably the best example of the application of the 'Sherlock Holmes' technique described in Chapter 7. The possible causes of the decline in mortality from infectious diseases, according to McKeown and his colleagues, are as follows: advances in medical technology, improvements in the environment due to better sanitation and new public health measures, better personal hygiene (for example, more frequent washing), improvements in nutrition and the standard of living, increased resistance in the population due to the greater chance of survival to reproductive age of those with genetically induced resistance to killer diseases, and autonomous changes in the virulence or infectivity of specific diseases. Having listed these, they set about disposing of them one by one. Despite being medical historians, they began by denying that medical interventions, whether preventive or therapeutic, had very much impact prior to

---

[9]   A. Omran, 'The Epidemiologic Transition: a Theory of the Epidemiology of Population Change', *Milbank Memorial Fund Quarterly* IL (1971), pp. 509–38.

[10] Ibid., pp. 516–17.

[11] Ibid., pp. 516–17.

[12] Ibid., p. 517.

[13] T. McKeown, *The Modern Rise of Population* (London, Edward Arnold, 1976); T. McKeown, R.G. Brown and R.G. Record, 'An Interpretation of the Modern Rise of Population in Europe', *Population Studies* XXVI (1972), pp. 345–82.

the discovery of antibiotics in the twentieth century, by which time most of the decline had already occurred.[14] They were similarly sceptical of the impact of improved personal hygiene, though they were prepared to allow that improvements in public health and sanitary conditions may have played a part, but that this was most likely after 1850, when national and (especially) local governments were prepared to intervene and to invest in effective measures, and even then can only have accounted for about a quarter of the decline. Increased resistance for genetic reasons, and autonomous changes in the organisms responsible for one or two diseases might have played a minor part, the most obvious example being scarlet fever. This disease was responsible for up to one in twenty of all deaths in the 1860s, but by the early twentieth century caused almost no deaths, although its incidence did not decline until after the Second World War.[15] Again, this effect was largely felt in the second half of the nineteenth century. Together, improvements in public health and autonomous changes could not account for more than half the decline in mortality even after 1850, and were probably much less important before that.

Having assessed the impact of all the other causes, and still finding that more than half of the decline had to be explained, McKeown and his colleagues turned to the last 'suspect': improvements in the standard of living and nutrition. It is these, they argue, that formed the single most important weapon in the conquest of infectious diseases, and hence in the decline in mortality.[16]

Since the 1970s, a variety of criticisms have been levelled at the McKeown thesis, and a number of re-assessments have been made.[17] In the next four sections we use McKeown's argument as a basis on which to construct an account of the decline of mortality in England from the eighteenth century onwards. It will be convenient to consider first the period before the middle of the nineteenth century, and then to pause and look in detail at mortality patterns around 1860 before looking at the course of the decline during the late nineteenth and early twentieth centuries.

12.4 An account of the decline of mortality before the mid-nineteenth century

Studies of the decline of mortality before the mid-nineteenth century are hampered by the lack of vital registration data. Though population censuses began in 1801 (see Appendix III) it was only in 1837 that the registration of

[14] McKeown *et al.*, 'An Interpretation', pp. 349–50.
[15] R.I. Woods and P.R.A. Hinde, 'Mortality in Victorian England: Models and Patterns', *Journal of Interdisciplinary History* XVIII (1987), p. 43 (reprinted in R.I. Rotberg (ed.), *Health and Disease in Human History: a Journal of Interdisciplinary History Reader* (London, MIT Press, 2000), p. 77.
[16] McKeown *et al.*, 'An Interpretation', pp. 352–7.
[17] The most recent of these is in Woods, *Demography of Victorian England*, pp. 344–59.

deaths was introduced, and so for most of the period from 1750 to 1850, recourse must still be had to parish registers analysed through back projection, just as in the early modern period. It is particularly unfortunate in the context of the epidemiological transition model and the McKeown thesis that we do not have access to cause of death data, as both of these accounts of the decline in mortality involve changes in the distribution of causes of death. It is true that some eighteenth-century burial registers contain cause of death data (an example being that for the Hampshire parish of Odiham that was studied in Chapter 7), but even these are of limited value, as the statements of causes of death are frequently too vague to be of use in assessing the validity of models of demographic change.[18]

According to McKeown and his colleagues, an improved standard of living was responsible for the lion's share of the decline in mortality during this period. Critics of this view have, in the main, used three arguments. First, they have pointed out that the standard of living was not rising appreciably during this period. Although economic historians have debated the standard of living in England between 1750 and 1850 at great (some might say inordinate) length, until recently, it was the majority view that, over the period as a whole, there was little overall increase in real wages.[19]

The second and third reasons derive from the non-linear relationship between nutrition and mortality: it is only at very low levels of nutrition that an improved diet is likely to have an appreciable impact on mortality rates. There comes a point, as diet improves, when increased quantities of food (and even greater variety in the diet) have only a limited effect. Therefore, if an improved standard of living were mainly responsible, we might expect mortality to have fallen more among the poor than among the well off. While we lack detailed class-specific mortality data for this period, studies of long-term mortality trends among the aristocracy reveal that they benefited from reduced mortality between 1750 and 1850.[20] Since it is unlikely

---

[18] I am grateful to Mr David Bond, Hampshire Archive Education Officer for first drawing my attention to the Odiham burial register, which is to be found in the Hampshire Record Office in Winchester. Commonly cited 'causes of death' in this register are 'decline', 'fever', and even 'suddenly'! In fact, even in the early civil death registers, cause of death data are problematic. Whilst some causes (such as accidental deaths and diseases of the lung) may have been accurately reported, the early death certificates contain numerous vague diagnoses, such as 'paralysis', 'pain in the hand', and 'intestines'. All of the above are included in a sample of death certificates of members of the steam-engine makers' society who died in the 1840s and 1850s analysed in H. Southall and E. Garrett, 'Morbidity and Mortality among Early Nineteenth-Century Engineering Workers', *Social History of Medicine* IV (1991), pp. 231–52.

[19] This is reflected, for example, in the real wage series reported in E.A. Wrigley and R.S. Schofield, *The Population History of England 1541–1871: a Reconstruction* (London, Edward Arnold, 1981), pp. 643–4. On the debate, see the collection of papers in A.J. Taylor (ed.), *The Standard of Living in Britain in the Industrial Revolution* (London, Methuen, 1975).

[20] T.H. Hollingsworth, 'The Demography of the British Peerage', *Population Studies* XVIII, supplement (1966), pp. 56–7.

that the diet and standard of living of this privileged group prior to 1750 was so poor as to elevate their mortality appreciably, this suggests that some other factor was mainly responsible for the decline.

The same argument may be extended to suggest that it is unlikely that the diet and standard of living of even the poorer classes in eighteenth-century England was so poor as to be the cause of elevated levels of mortality. For, as Chapter 7 showed, the population of England during the early modern period was not constantly running up against subsistence crises. Indeed, such crises were very rare after 1600 in much of the country. Harvests varied substantially in quantity (and quality), yet there was only a weak short-term relationship between wheat prices and mortality, especially after the mid-seventeenth century.[21] It is hard to reconcile what we know of mortality in England between 1600 and 1750 with a picture of a society bedevilled by chronic malnutrition, which predisposed it to fatal infections. Consequently, it is argued that there was rather limited room for improvements in the standard of living to operate.[22]

Dismissing the standard of living hypothesis leaves us with a problem, however, since we need to replace it with something, and this implies rejuvenating one or more of McKeown's 'lost causes'.[23] In an early critique of the McKeown thesis, Peter Razzell suggested that smallpox inoculation and vaccination, which were introduced during this period, might have played a part, as might improved personal hygiene.[24] It is hard to reach a firm conclusion on the latter, but there is sufficient evidence to suggest that Razzell may be right about the former. Prior to 1750, smallpox was responsible for a large proportion of all deaths, estimated to have been as high as one in six in urban areas. Evidence that smallpox was rife in the late eighteenth century, even in smaller towns, comes from the parish of Holy Trinity, Whitehaven, where between 1750 and 1780 smallpox accounted for 597 out of 3138 deaths.[25] Though this may have been higher than average (contemporaries blamed maritime traffic for introducing epidemics to the town) it is nevertheless true that smallpox was a major cause of death during this period.

---

[21] R. Lee, 'Short-Term Variation: Vital Rates, Prices and Weather', in Wrigley and Schofield, *Population History of England*, pp. 372–84, 399.

[22] For a clear and concise exposition of the argument against the nutritional account of the decline of mortality, see M. Livi-Bacci, *The Population of Europe* (Oxford, Blackwell, 2000).

[23] This is, for example, a problem encountered by Livi-Bacci, *Population of Europe*, who, having dismissed McKeown's standard of living thesis, fails to provide a convincing alternative.

[24] P. Razzell, '"An Interpretation of the Modern Rise of Population in Europe": a Critique', *Population Studies* XXVIII (1974), pp. 5–17.

[25] See J.E. Ward, 'Death in 18th Century Whitehaven: the Mortality Records from Holy Trinity Church', *Transactions of the Cumberland and Westmorland Antiquarian and Archaeological Society* XCVIII (1998), pp. 249–61. This was another parish where cause of death data were included in the burial registers, at least for the period 1750–80. In this case, moreover, the reliability of diagnosis may be better than average, as a physician was consulted by the incumbent.

Yet by the mid-nineteenth century, immunization – first through inoculation and subsequently through vaccination – had reduced this proportion to less than one in a hundred. Though the effectiveness of inoculation and vaccination has been debated in the literature, there is no denying the fact that by the 1860s, for example, smallpox was responsible for only about one death in 200 even in unhealthy districts like the Lancashire textile towns, and in healthier rural areas, such as Devon, it had effectively been eliminated as a cause of death.

Nevertheless, we should be a little wary of immediately giving immunization against smallpox the majority of the credit for reducing mortality before 1850. The effect of vaccination on mortality levels depends on how many more years the people who no longer died of smallpox lived. Since smallpox was primarily a disease of children, it is arguable that the children who no longer succumbed to the disease might simply have died of other causes when they were not much older, and, if this was the case, the elimination of smallpox as a cause of death might have had little effect on mortality levels. At present, it seems that this question will not be easily resolved.

Let us now turn to the temporary arrest of the decline in mortality during the middle period of the nineteenth century. In 1985, Robert Woods argued that the redistribution of the population from rural to urban areas was sufficient to have brought this about.[26] Figure 12.2 shows that the decline in the expectation of life at birth at the national level between 1811–20 and 1841–50 was not reflected in declines in rural areas, small towns or London. However, there was some deterioration in what Woods has described as 'large towns', especially between 1831–40 and 1841–50. Simon Szreter and Graham Mooney explain this by arguing that 'political and administrative breakdown' in the faster growing towns, produced in large part by the very rapidity of their growth, led to a 'marked deterioration in average life expectancy during the second quarter of the nineteenth century'.[27] In other words, not only was the population being redistributed into less healthy areas, but these areas were also becoming unhealthier over time. In a recent re-analysis of his data, Woods has concluded that there is evidence that in some cities, such as Liverpool and Manchester, mortality did rise in the second quarter of the nineteenth century, but that this rise 'was due more to particular circumstances than to general administrative deterioration' – for example, the arrival of very large numbers of immigrants from Ireland and the fact that this period was when childhood diseases were most destructive of life.[28]

[26]   R.I. Woods, 'Effects of Population Redistribution', p. 649.
[27]   S. Szreter and G. Mooney, 'Urbanization, Mortality and the Standard of Living Debate: New Estimates of the Expectation of Life at Birth in Nineteenth-Century British Cities', *Economic History Review*, 2nd series LI (1998), pp. 84–112; S. Szreter, 'Economic Growth, Disruption, Deprivation, Disease and Death: on the Importance of the Politics of Public Health for Development', *Population and Development Review* XXIII (1997), pp. 701–2.
[28]   R. Woods, *Demography of Victorian England*, pp. 370–1.

The causes of the decline in mortality in England prior to 1850 are still being debated, and many of the arguments are complex, so it is perhaps worth summarizing the current state of knowledge. First, the overall magnitude of the decline in mortality during this period was rather small. However, it was not quite as small as the national-level figures would suggest, for the population was simultaneously being redistributed from regions of low mortality to regions of high mortality, and this process leads the national-level figures to understate the amount of the decline. Second, there are good reasons to be sceptical about McKeown's thesis that improvements in the standard of living were largely responsible for the decline. However, outright rejection of the role of improved nutrition requires something else to be put in its place. Although it seems likely that immunization against smallpox played some part, the lack of any obvious alternative account is still the greatest weakness of the case against McKeown and his colleagues. Third, the hiatus in the decline of mortality during the second third of the nineteenth century appears to have been due to two factors: the increasingly rapid rate of urbanization, which strengthened the pace of population redistribution from healthy to unhealthy districts, and the consequent failure of the urban infrastructure to cope with the influx of people.

12.5 Mortality patterns in mid-nineteenth-century England

Death registration was introduced in England and Wales in 1837 (for more details, see Appendix III). The deaths data thus provided can be combined with data from the decennial population censuses, which have been taken since 1801, to give a much richer picture of mortality levels and trends than is available for any preceding period. Indeed the fundamental nature of English mortality data has not changed since 1837: death rates are calculated using death registration data in the numerator and denominators based on census populations. Aggregate data on deaths were published by the government for various areal units, possibly the most useful being the registration district, of which there were around 600 in Victorian England and Wales. In the mid-nineteenth century, therefore, it is possible to present a comprehensive picture of the geography of death.

Death certificates also recorded cause of death data, and deaths by cause were aggregated for each registration district for each decade during the second half of the century and published in the Registrar General's *Decennial Supplements*. This voluminous body of data has been analysed in detail by Robert Woods and his colleagues who have thereby charted the history and geography of mortality from 1850 onwards.[29] An important conclusion of

[29] R. Woods and N. Shelton, *An Atlas of Victorian Mortality* (Liverpool, Liverpool University Press, 1997); R. Woods, *Demography of Victorian England*, pp. 170–246.

this work is that mortality levels and the distribution of causes of death varied greatly from place to place: '[w]here one lived in Victorian England critically affected not only one's life chances, but also the manner in which death might occur'.[30] In this section, we explore these geographical differentials. A knowledge of the geography of mortality around 1850 is helpful not only in identifying what progress was made in the preceding period, but also in providing a starting point for a description and explanation of the more substantial mortality decline of the second half of the nineteenth century.

The geography of mortality in mid-nineteenth-century England and Wales is shown in Figure 12.3. The expectation of life at birth ranged from under 35 years in some of the large industrial towns (for example, Manchester, Sheffield, Liverpool and Newcastle) to in excess of 50 years in some rural areas, especially in the south and south-west. The least healthy place was inner Liverpool, where the expectation of life at birth was little more than 25 years and the crude death rate approached 40 per thousand.[31] To place this in perspective, life chances in normal years in mid-nineteenth-century Liverpool were no better than those at the national level in many crisis years during the seventeenth century. The most healthy registration districts lay in north Devon.

The deaths of infants aged under one year formed a substantial proportion of all deaths, and infant mortality was an important determinant of the expectation of life at birth. The geography of infant mortality was similar in general to that of overall mortality, with very high rates in large urban areas, as well as some heavy industrial and mining areas (for example, Cornwall) and low rates in rural areas. A close relationship existed between infant mortality and population density, suggesting that environmental factors were fundamental in determining a person's life chances.[32] However, there are some apparent exceptions to this relationship, with parts of rural Norfolk and the fens around the Wash having infant mortality rates much higher than would be anticipated given the expectation of life at birth. Indeed, a zone of anomalously high infant mortality includes most of Norfolk, much of the East Midlands, Lincolnshire and East Yorkshire.[33]

If infant mortality seems to have varied greatly from place to place, the same was less true of adult mortality.[34] A major determinant of male mortality at ages over 20 years was occupation. Male expectation of life at age 20 during the 1860s varied from more than 45 years for farmers, gar-

---

[30] Woods, *Demography of Victorian England*, p. 142.
[31] Ibid., pp. 192-3.
[32] Woods and Hinde, 'Mortality in Victorian England', p. 49; Woods, *Demography of Victorian England*, pp. 190–202.
[33] Woods, *Demography of Victorian England*, p. l (between pp. 96 and 97).
[34] Ibid., p. 201.

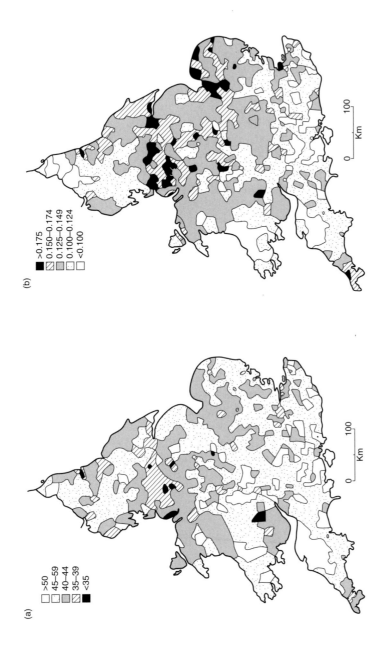

Figure 12.3 Expectation of life at birth and infant mortality, England and Wales 1861 (both sexes combined): (a) expectation of life at birth; (b) infant mortality

Source: R.I. Woods and P.R.A. Hinde, 'Mortality in Victorian England: Models and Patterns', *Journal of Interdisciplinary History* XVIII (1987), pp. 40–1 (reprinted in R.I. Rotberg (ed.), *Health and Disease in Human History: a Journal of Interdisciplinary History Reader* (London, MIT Press, 2000), pp. 74–5).

deners and clergymen to less than 35 years among a variety of occupations including the poorly paid and casual working inn and hotel servants; and certain groups working in notoriously dusty or unhealthy conditions, such as file makers, tin miners and earthenware manufacturers.[35] However, this should not be interpreted as meaning that adult males' risk of dying was entirely, or even largely, conditioned by their working environment, for 'the mortality experienced by adult men grouped in terms of occupation reflects far more than just the risks that are particular to that occupation'.[36]

In mid-nineteenth-century England death could be caused by a wide range of diseases and conditions, but four distinct groups of causes were particularly prominent.[37] First, there were the food- and waterborne diseases such as cholera, typhoid, and diarrhoea and dysentery. This group was particularly prevalent in urban environments, where it accounted for an especially large proportion of infant deaths. For example, in six Lancashire registration districts during the 1860s, 6 per cent of all deaths, and 15 per cent of infant deaths were ascribed to diarrhoea and dysentery alone.[38] The second group comprised infectious diseases of childhood, especially measles and scarlet fever.[39] These diseases caused almost no deaths at ages above 15 years, but were major killers of young children.[40] A third group of causes consisted of respiratory diseases like bronchitis and pneumonia, which were the cause of up to 20 per cent of all deaths, distributed by age in a way very similar to overall mortality.[41] The final 'group' consists of a single cause: pulmonary tuberculosis. This 'most destructive of nineteenth-century diseases', which was also known as 'consumption' or 'phthisis', was typically the cause of around 10 per cent of all deaths, though its incidence varied geographically.[42] In parts of the west of Wales, for example, it was responsible for 17 or 18 per cent of deaths, whereas in eastern England it was relatively much less important.[43] Phthisis was mainly a disease of young adults, and females were generally more susceptible than males. Among people aged 20–24, for example, it was responsible for around one-third of all deaths.[44] As Robert Woods has pointed out, three of these four groups of causes of death

[35] Ibid., pp. 224–6.
[36] Ibid., pp. 239–40.
[37] The grouping used here is that of Woods, ibid., p. 311.
[38] Woods and Hinde, 'Mortality in Victorian England', p. 43.
[39] In the 1860s, scarlet fever accounted for one in twenty of all deaths in certain areas of Lancashire, almost all of which would have been children (see Woods and Hinde, 'Mortality in Victorian England', p. 43).
[40] Woods, *Demography of Victorian England*, p. 317.
[41] Woods and Hinde, 'Mortality in Victorian England', p. 43; Woods, *Demography of Victorian England*, p. 317.
[42] Woods, *Demography of Victorian England*, p. 311.
[43] Woods and Hinde, 'Mortality in Victorian England', p. 47.
[44] Woods, *Demography of Victorian England*, p. 317.

each reflect a particular aspect of the mortality environment experienced by the population of England and Wales. Measles and Scarlet fever could be taken to reflect the effects of crowding; Diarrhoea and Dysentery, the quality of the sanitary environment; Diseases of the Lung or the Respiratory system might be used to suggest the impact of non-sanitary aspects of the environment, especially air quality and general pollution.[45]

Because of this, a study of cause-specific mortality declines after the mid-nineteenth century can potentially shed light on the ultimate causes of overall mortality decline.

12.6 The course of mortality decline after 1850

The expectation of life at birth in England and Wales as a whole in the middle of the nineteenth century was about 41 years (Figure 12.2). By the last decade of the century it had increased to about 46 years, and by 1901–10 there had been a further jump to 51 years. Therefore progress at the national level was substantially quicker during this period than in the preceding decades. Moreover, the continuing redistribution of the population from healthy rural areas to less healthy urban areas meant that the improvement made was actually greater than the national figures suggest. In 'large towns' – those with populations greater than 100,000 – the expectation of life at birth rose from 32 years at mid-century to 39 years by 1891–1900 and 47 years in 1901–10. The rate of progress in rural areas, 'small towns' and London was also greater than the national 'average' would suggest. In particular, the last decade of the nineteenth century and the first decade of the twentieth formed a period of spectacular progress in prolonging life. Despite this, the wide geographical and environmental differentials in mortality characteristic of much of the Victorian period were maintained throughout the century.[46]

If the benefits of reduced mortality were not distributed from place to place in such a way as to reduce inequalities, the same was true of their age pattern. For perhaps the most noteworthy characteristic of this period of the mortality decline was that the improvements were almost entirely confined (certainly until 1900) to ages between one year and forty years. This is clearly seen in the bottom two panels of Table 12.1, which express age-specific death rates as a percentage of their levels in 1838–54. For males, there was no improvement at all outside the age range 1–39 years before the turn of the twentieth century, whereas mortality in age groups 1–4, 5–19 and 20–39 years was 31, 48 and 27 per cent lower respectively in 1891–1900 than it had been in 1838–54. Even more remarkable progress can be observed

---

[45] Ibid., p. 316.
[46] Ibid., pp. 200–1.

within narrower age bands. For example, mortality among males aged 15–19 years fell from 7–8 per thousand per year during the 1850s to around three per thousand per year in 1900.[47] Much the same pattern is observed for females, though the relative improvement at ages 20–39 is a bit greater, and there was also a slight amelioration at ages 40–59. Though progress spills over to other age groups during the first decade of the twentieth century, it is still true that the vast majority of the decline is attributable to trends in childhood (but not infant) and early adult mortality.

12.7 An account of the decline of mortality, 1850–1910

Section 12.5 described four groups of causes of death that were especially important in mid-nineteenth-century England and, following Robert Woods, suggested that mortality from three of these four groups of causes reflected different elements of the overall mortality environment. We now pursue this theme more systematically in an effort to try to understand what was driving the mortality decline in England and Wales after 1850.

Table 12.2 presents a summary of Woods' estimates of the relative contributions to mortality change of different causes of death between the 1860s and the 1890s. As Woods admits, the interpretation of this table is beset by difficulties. The classification of causes of death used by the Registrar General changed over time, which means that the distributions for the two decades can only be compared after making a number of assumptions.[48] The way in which causes of death were classified is somewhat schizophrenic, in that it partly uses particular diseases (measles, typhus, and so on) and partly relates deaths to different sections of the body (for example, lungs and stomach). It is possible, therefore, that changes in the numbers of deaths in particular categories merely reflect reclassification of some deaths (for example, some 'phthisis' deaths being described as deaths due to 'diseases of the lung'). Even more worrying at first sight is the very large proportion of deaths in the category 'other causes'. Neither of these problems may be as serious as they seem, however. Apart from cancer (and possibly scrofula), the specific diseases listed as causes of death were, in the main, common infections of one form or another, the symptoms of which were well known and so unlikely to have been systematically misclassified, still less to have been differentially classified over time.[49] The 'other causes' category, certainly in the 1860s, tended to contain large numbers of deaths to very young infants and deaths among the elderly from chronic degenerative diseases. Moreover, to the extent that the decline in deaths from 'other

---

[47] Ibid., p. 186.

[48] These are described in detail in Woods, *Demography of Victorian England*, pp. 349; see also the table on pp. 314–15 .

[49] Scrofula was a tuberculous condition involving glandular swellings in the neck, and inflammation of the joints and mucous membranes.

causes' between 1861–70 and 1891–1900 is due to the allocation to other
categories in the 1890s of deaths that would, in the 1860s, have been placed
in the 'other causes' category, any decline in the number of deaths in those
other categories will be understated, rather than exaggerated, in Table 12.2.

Let us, then, consider the impact of the four groups of diseases identified
earlier on the decline of mortality. Measles and scarlet fever are associated
with crowding. They characteristically attack children, and cause most of
their deaths at ages between one and ten years. Mortality rates from these
causes in the mid-nineteenth century were several times higher in densely
populated towns and cities than in rural areas. Given progressive urbanization and the continued ineffectiveness of therapy, therefore, there seems no
reason why deaths from either of these causes should have declined between

Table 12.2 Contributions of different causes of death to the decline in mortality in
England and Wales, 1861–70 to 1891–1900

Cause of death	Change in number of deaths	Percentage contribution to overall change
Smallpox	–42,655	–4.27
Measles	7,370	0.74
Scarlet fever	–224,147	–22.46
Diphtheria	28,352	2.84
Whooping cough	–25,138	–2.52
Diarrhoea	–68,500	–6.86
Typhus	–212,471	–21.29
Cancer	112,765	11.30
Scrofula	67,918	6.81
Phthisis	–351,126	–35.19
Diseases of the brain	–129,774	–13.00
Diseases of the heart	93,044	9.32
Diseases of the lung	73,023	7.32
Diseases of the stomach	69,364	6.95
Diseases of the kidneys	49,374	4.95
Diseases of the generative organs	–4,541	–0.46
Childbirth, etc.	–6,242	–0.63
Violence	–81,121	–8.13
Other causes	–353,415	–35.42
Total	–997,920	–100.00

Notes: The column headed 'Change in number of deaths' is calculated by applying the age-
and cause-specific death rates in 1861–70 to the population age structure in 1891–1900, and
comparing the resulting numbers of deaths with the actual number of deaths by cause that
were observed in 1891–1900. This procedure controls for changes in the age structure of the
population during the intervening period and renders the numbers of deaths in the two
decades directly comparable.
Source: R. Woods, *The Demography of Victorian England and Wales* (Cambridge,
Cambridge University Press, 2000), pp. 350–1.

the 1860s and the 1890s. For measles, this is what is observed (Table 12.2). But with scarlet fever, things are very different. The number of deaths from scarlet fever in the 1890s was just 18 per cent of the number we would have expected if 1860s cause-specific death rates had applied, and scarlet fever was responsible for 22 per cent of the overall decline in the number of deaths during the intervening period.[50] Moreover, whereas during the 1860s and 1870s there was a clear relationship between mortality rates from scarlet fever and population density, this relationship had largely disappeared by the 1890s. Therapy was not responsible for this: scarlet fever is a bacterial infection and effective treatment had to await the discovery of antibiotic drugs. The lack of any decline in mortality from measles (which affected substantially the same people) also suggests that improved nutrition was not important. The most plausible conclusion to draw is the one reached by McKeown and his colleagues, that there was a decline in the virulence of scarlet fever. Possibly because this is not a particularly satisfying conclusion for those who wish to argue that human interventions of one form of another were largely responsible for progress in mortality, and possibly because it is 'insufficiently controversial' (almost everyone agrees with it), historians have tended to neglect the impact the decline in mortality from scarlet fever had during the second half of the nineteenth century.[51]

The next group of diseases is that associated with sanitation (diarrhoea and typhus in Table 12.2). Taken together, these had an even larger impact than scarlet fever. A feature of the decline in the number of deaths from diarrhoea and typhus was its concentration in a few geographical areas, mainly the large urban centres and especially London.[52] Indeed 53 of the 600 or so registration districts were responsible for half of all the reduction in deaths and, of these 53, 14 were in and around London, and more than 20 of the rest were in Birmingham, Cardiff, Swansea, Liverpool, Manchester, Leeds, Bradford and Sheffield.[53]. This suggests that substantial progress was being made on sanitary improvements, even in the largest towns and cities where the challenges posed to the successful provision of good public health were greatest. It is important, though, not to overemphasize the impact on mortality of environmental improvements following heavy investment by local authorities in sanitary engineering projects. Prior to 1880, the main objective of investment was the water supply, but this may not have had much of an impact on mortality because drainage and sewerage were still inadequate. It is, however, possible that major increases in expenditures after 1895 might be linked to the decline of infant mortality after 1900 (see Section 12.8).[54]

[50]   Woods, *Demography of Victorian England*, p. 350.
[51]   Ibid., p. 359.
[52]   Ibid., see map facing p. 97.
[53]   Ibid., pp. 355–6.
[54]   F. Bell and R. Millward, 'Public Health Expenditures and Mortality in England and Wales, 1871–1914', *Continuity and Change* XIII, pp. 211–49.

The story with respect to diseases of the lung is very different from that for diarrhoea and typhus. Deaths from lung diseases increased over the period. While it is likely that misclassification or changes in the way in which causes of death were classified may have been partly responsible for this, it still seems reasonable to suggest that the environmental improvements that undoubtedly lessened the impact of waterborne diseases did not carry over to airborne infections. Moreover, whereas London performed particularly well with respect to waterborne infections, it did rather badly with respect to diseases of the respiratory system. As Woods has stated, discussing the situation in London:

> the effects of the Victorian public health reforms were partial and selective prior to 1901. London was probably a substantial beneficiary as far as sanitation was concerned, but this could not be said equally of the environmental conditions that fostered the respiratory diseases. In this case not only was there little improvement, but London remained at a disadvantage.[55]

Finally, let us consider phthisis, or tuberculosis of the lung. As Table 12.2 makes clear, this was the single most important contributor to the overall mortality decline during the second half of the nineteenth century. Phthisis was a disease that characteristically attacked young adults, with death rates being highest in the age group 20–39 years. Between the 1860s and the 1890s death rates at all ages declined by around 50 per cent, the decline being somewhat greater for females (who were more seriously affected) than for males.[56] But unlike diarrhoea and typhus, the decline shows no clear association with population density. There were geographical differentials, and these were maintained over time: death rates from phthisis were highest throughout the period in sparsely populated districts of west Wales and relatively low in the areas surrounding London and parts of the Midlands. Woods argues that this creates a problem for the McKeown thesis, for it is the decline in mortality from phthisis that bears the burden of McKeown's view that improvements in nutrition and the standard of living were the most important determinants of the mortality decline. Woods suggests that the universality of the decline in phthisis mortality, and the lack of a relationship between death rates from phthisis and any identifiable measure of the quality of life, sit uncomfortably with the 'standard of living' account.[57]

> The simplest explanation is that the disease became less virulent and that this was the principal reason for a reduction in the risk of the disease developing and leading to an early death, [and] that this process occurred slowly and everywhere.[58]

---

[55]　Woods, *Demography of Victorian England*, p. 332.
[56]　Ibid., pp. 318, 334–5.
[57]　Ibid., pp. 339–40.
[58]　Ibid., p. 340.

12.8 The collapse of infant mortality

The decline in mortality after 1850 was increasingly rapid and widespread. By the last decade of the century the expectation of life at birth had risen to 44 years for males and nearly 48 years for females.[59] Yet throughout the second half of the nineteenth century one age group conspicuously failed to show any improvement at all. Whereas the mortality of children aged one to four years had begun to fall from the 1860s for the reasons described in Section 12.7, infant mortality remained high.[60] Indeed, the death rate among those aged under one year was higher during the 1890s than it had been for several decades (Table 12.2). During the late 1890s, almost one out of every six English babies born failed to survive until his or her first birthday. Geographical differentials in infant mortality remained large: in some areas of southern England and the far northern uplands more than nine out of every ten babies lived to celebrate their first birthdays, whereas some large towns – for example, Liverpool and Birmingham – still suffered from infant mortality rates in excess of 200 per thousand.[61]

The graph of infant mortality at the national level, however, shows that a remarkable and abrupt change took place as the twentieth century dawned. From 1900 onwards, the long-run trend in infant mortality is inexorably downward, despite occasional temporary reverses (Figure 12.4). Between 1899 and 1910 infant mortality, averaged over the whole country, declined by about 30 per cent. After an abrupt and temporary rise in 1911, the decline continued throughout the second decade of the twentieth century. It was not interrupted by the First World War (indeed, it has been argued that the war might even have accelerated it), nor by the influenza pandemic of 1918 (see Section 12.9).[62]

The immediate reasons why infant mortality fell precipitously after 1900 may broadly be divided into three groups: environmental and public health improvements, economic improvements, and changes in the ways in which

---

[59]   Woods and Hinde, 'Mortality in Victorian England', p. 33.

[60]   The trend in infant mortality before 1850 is rather uncertain. According to E.A. Wrigley, R.S. Davies, J.E. Deppen and R.S. Schofield, *English Population History from Family Reconstitution 1580–1837* (Cambridge, Cambridge University Press, 1997), pp. 215, 219, there was a decline during the two decades after 1780, but little change after the first decade of the nineteenth century. An alternative set of estimates made using model life tables to convert estimates of the expectation of life at birth (see Woods, *Demography of Victorian England*, pp. 253–5) suggests a slow decline in infant mortality from 1750 until about the 1840s, but this relies on the questionable assumption that the age pattern of mortality was not changing substantially over time.

[61]   R.I. Woods, P.A. Watterson and J.H. Woodward, 'The Causes of Rapid Infant Mortality Decline in England and Wales, 1861–1921: Part I', *Population Studies* XLII (1988), pp. 354, 358.

[62]   On the impact of the First World War on infant mortality, see J. Winter, 'Aspects of the Impact of the First World War on Infant Mortality in Britain', *Journal of European Economic History* XI (1982), pp. 713–38.

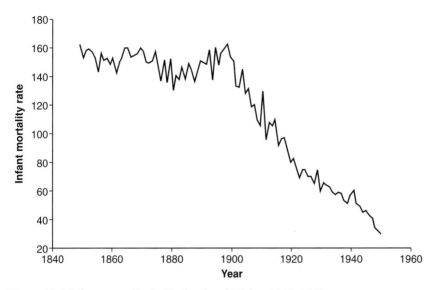

Figure 12.4 Infant mortality in England and Wales, 1850–1950
Source: B.R. Mitchell, *British Historical Statistics* (Cambridge, Cambridge University Press, 1988), pp. 57–9.

babies were cared for. Recent research has suggested strongly that environmental effects were more important than economic factors. The close relationship between infant mortality and population density persisted throughout the Victorian and Edwardian periods. The rise in infant mortality in the 1890s was largely the result of excessive rises in urban areas, and has been attributed to the increased prevalence of diarrhoeal diseases because of a succession of hot summers.[63] Indeed, it can be argued that had it not been for this temporary phenomenon, a national-level decline in infant mortality would have been observed from the late 1880s. Similarly, the fall in the number of infant deaths during the first decades of the twentieth century was associated with a big fall in the proportion of infant deaths attributable to diarrhoeal diseases from 25 per cent in the 1890s to only 10 per cent in 1920.[64] Additional evidence demonstrating the primacy of environmental factors comes from analyses of infant mortality by father's occupation. Even as late as the 1890s, the infant mortality rate among the children of agricultural labourers (whose wages were lower than almost any other large occupational group, but who lived in the healthy countryside) was lower than that of any other occupational group – even professional and managerial workers.[65] After 1900, though, all other occupational

[63] Woods *et al.*, 'Causes of Rapid Infant Mortality Decline'.
[64] Ibid., p. 360.
[65] P.A. Watterson, 'Infant Mortality by Father's Occupation from the 1911 Census of England and Wales', *Demography* XXV (1988), p. 296.

groups were rapidly catching up as improvements in the urban environment began to be effective.

Nevertheless, economic factors should not be dismissed entirely. If agricultural workers are excluded, there was a general relationship between social class (which reflected income) and infant mortality, and this persisted through the early part of the decline. In particular, the children of unskilled manual workers were much more likely to die in infancy than the children of other manual workers.[66] It is hard to believe that this differential was entirely due to the inferior residential environment that unskilled workers suffered compared with, say, semi-skilled manual workers. The low incomes and, especially, the irregularity of the incomes of unskilled workers, led to great distress among their children. Jay Winter's argument that the First World War was good for infants' survival chances is substantially based on a belief that state provision of a regular income to the wives of men serving in the armed forces actually improved the lot of the children of casual labourers, since it gave them a reliable income and a regular diet.[67]

One of the most enduring debates about the causes of the decline in infant mortality concerns the impact of child-care practices. There are two aspects worth highlighting: the effect of mothers' work outside the home, and the prevalence of breast-feeding. The negative effect of mothers working outside the home was stressed by T.H.C. Stevenson, the government statistician who analysed the responses to the fertility questions in the 1911 census. Stevenson was quite convinced that women's work was bad for babies. He drew up tables showing that infant mortality rates for working mothers were higher than those for non-working mothers. Even if this were true, however, it would only follow that changes in the prevalence of the mothers of young children working outside the home had an impact on infant mortality if those changes could be traced over time and related to the decline in infant death rates, and this dynamic comparison of the two variables turns out to be very difficult to do. Moreover, Eilidh Garrett has pointed out that Stevenson's infant mortality data relate to a period often 10–15 years before the 1911 census, whereas his data on women's employment come from 1911 itself. It seems equally (and probably more) plausible to conclude that women whose children had died had fewer survivors to care for and were thus in a better position to take up work outside the home.[68]

If changes in mothers' employment behaviour did not have much effect, it seems more likely that changes in infant feeding practices played a part. A recent study of Medical Officer of Health reports for London and other urban areas designated as 'Great Towns' in the 1911 census revealed that an

[66] Ibid., p. 296.
[67] Winter, 'Aspects of the Impact of the First World War'.
[68] E.M. Garrett, 'Was Women's Work Bad for Babies? A View from the 1911 Census of England and Wales', *Continuity and Change* XIII (1998), pp. 281–316.

improvement in the nutritional status of mothers, which rendered them better able to breast-feed, was an important contributor to the decline in mortality among infants.[69] Babies who were exclusively bottle-fed during the first weeks of life had infant mortality rates between two and eight times those of exclusively breast-fed babies. Though bottle-feeding was, therefore, not as good for babies as breast-feeding, the phasing out of the 'long tube' bottle (an excellent breeding ground for bacteria) and the introduction of dried milk helped reduce the risks of bottle-feeding.

Two final factors, which have recently been highlighted by Robert Woods, are the decline in fertility and the improvement in the education of women.[70] As the next chapter will show, fertility began to decline at a national level during the 1870s and by the turn of the twentieth century, small families were becoming increasingly common. Demographers have known for many years, largely on the basis of research in developing countries, that high fertility tends to be associated with high infant mortality through a variety of mechanisms, one being that women who do not breast-feed their babies, or who breast-feed for only a short period both damage the survival chances of their infants and increase the likelihood that they (the women, that is) will become pregnant. However, even after accounting for this, the association between fertility and infant mortality remains.[71] It is certainly suggestive that the occupational group with the highest fertility rate in the late nineteenth and early twentieth centuries, namely coal miners, also had the highest infant mortality rates.[72] The role of women's education was slightly different: it was in the background, and operated through other factors. As Woods has put it:

> Long-term improvements in levels of female education helped not only to increase the likelihood that family limitation would be attempted, but also to improve the status of women, their access to written information, the way in which they cared for their children and the way in which they were themselves cared for. They may even have encouraged more women to breastfeed.[73]

All of these effects would have helped to reduce the infant death rate.

12.9 Mortality decline, 1910–1950

Though rapid progress was made in the reduction of mortality during the

---

[69] V. Fildes, 'Infant Feeding Practices and Infant Mortality in England, 1900–1919', *Continuity and Change* XIII (1998), pp. 251–80.
[70] Woods, *Demography of Victorian England*, pp. 295–304.
[71] Various mechanisms for this have been suggested, including 'maternal depletion', by which mothers who have many children in a short space of time become exhausted and unable to care for them so well; and 'sibling competition'.
[72] Woods, *Demography of Victorian England*, p. 264.
[73] Ibid., p. 305.

last decades of the nineteenth century and the first decade of the twentieth, even as late as 1910 there was still a lot to be achieved. As David Coleman and John Salt have written: '[m]ost of the improvement in human survival since the eighteenth century has occurred within living memory'.[74] During the first half of the twentieth century, the expectation of life rose from about 47 years to 66 years for males and from about 50 years to 71 years for females.[75] Generally, progress was inversely related to age. Among infants, mortality around 1950 was barely more than a quarter of its 1910 level, among those in their twenties and thirties it was around a third, and at age 50 it was about half.[76] At ages above 60 years, there was relatively little improvement. Most of the progress during this period continued to be due to the conquest of infectious diseases, which caused a large proportion of deaths to those aged under 60. Among older people, deaths were mainly due to degenerative conditions (cancer and cardiovascular diseases) against which medicine could still do rather little in 1950. As mortality declined, the geographical variations that had been such a feature of the mid-nineteenth century were much reduced in magnitude. Among infants, where regional variations were still great, even around 1900, there was a gradual reduction in 'spatial inequality', especially after the 1920s.[77]

Though progress was great, it was not uninterrupted (save among infants aged under one year). The First World War is estimated to have caused the deaths of 723,000 servicemen, most of whom were aged between 20 and 40 years, and it did halt the increase in the expectation of life at birth.[78] As there were about 500,000 deaths in a 'normal year', then excess mortality during the war arising directly from casualties ran at an average of 35 per cent a year.[79] Shortly before the end of the war, England was struck by the 1918 influenza pandemic, which caused some 184,000 excess deaths among civilians.[80] The influenza arrived in three waves, one lasting from June to September 1918, the second (and most severe) from September 1918 to January 1919, and the third from January to May 1919.[81] It struck most

---

[74]   D. Coleman and J. Salt, *The British Population: Patterns, Trends and Processes* (Oxford, Oxford University Press, 1992), p. 238.

[75]   Woods and Hinde, 'Mortality in Victorian England', p. 33; Office for National Statistics, *English Life Tables No. 15* (Series DS no. 14) (London, The Stationery Office, 1997), p. 7.

[76]   Office for National Statistics, *English Life Tables No. 15*, p. 6.

[77]   P. Congdon, R.M. Campos, S.E. Curtis, H.R. Southall, I.N. Gregory and I.R. Jones, 'Quantifying and Explaining Changes in Geographical Inequality of Infant Mortality in England and Wales since the 1890s', *International Journal of Population Geography* VII (2001), p. 48.

[78]   Coleman and Salt, *British Population*, pp. 240–1; Office for National Statistics, *English Life Tables No. 15*, p. 8.

[79]   Assuming the 723,000 deaths of servicemen were spread evenly over the four years of the war produces about 180,000 deaths per year. 180,000/500,000 = 36 per cent.

[80]   C. Langford, 'The Age Pattern of Mortality in the 1918–19 Influenza Pandemic: an Attempted Explanation Based on Data for England and Wales', *Medical History* XLVI (2002), p. 6.

[81]   Ibid., pp. 5–6.

fiercely at young adults, and especially those aged between 20 and 35 years, among whom death rates in 1918 were more than double the average in the three preceding years.[82] Overall, the crude death rate in 1918 was 17.3 per thousand, which compares with an average over the period 1906–30 of 13.5 per thousand.[83] The crude death rate in 1918 was therefore 28 per cent above the 'normal' level. This relative increase in mortality is of a similar order of magnitude to those experienced in such notorious years as 1624–25 and 1587–88, and only four percentage points below that of 1665–66, the year of the Great Plague of London (see Table 7.1). The 1918 epidemic is a reminder that, although a principal feature of the epidemiological transition was a great reduction in the frequency and severity of great epidemics, they were not completely eliminated.

12.10 A re-evaluation of the McKeown thesis

In the 30 or so years since it was proposed, the McKeown thesis has provoked a great deal of debate, and stimulated a lot of research.[84] It might be useful, as a conclusion to this chapter, to assess what survives of McKeown's original account after the results of this research have been taken into account.

First, McKeown's assertion that medical interventions played only a small part in the mortality decline seems to have emerged relatively unscathed, with the exception of immunization against smallpox during the first half of the nineteenth century. Second, his belief that the decline of scarlet fever was caused by autonomous changes in the virulence of the causative organism seems to have been vindicated. Indeed, it seems that McKeown's account might have indirectly understressed the importance of this factor by underestimating the impact of the decline in scarlet fever mortality between 1850 and 1900. Third, his acknowledgement that sanitary reform was important, especially during the late nineteenth century, seems to have won support.

But these are just the outbuildings of McKeown's thesis. What of its central structure, that the main agent of change was a rising standard of living? It is this element of the account that subsequent research, at least until very recently, has been most emphatic in contradicting. When historians write that McKeown's account has now been superseded, and that it is probably best to 'draw a line' under it, it seems to be this core element they have in mind.[85]

---

[82] Ibid., p. 10.
[83] B.R. Mitchell, *British Historical Statistics* (Cambridge, Cambridge University Press, 1988), pp. 58–9.
[84] Indeed, Woods, *Demography of Victorian England*, p. 359, considers this its 'greatest strength'.
[85] Ibid., p. 359.

Yet we might pause before acquiescing in the almost complete dismissal of the standard of living thesis by recent historians and demographers. First, the gloomy picture painted by economic historians about real wage trends between 1750 and 1850 has been modified by recent research, which suggests that real wages only fell until about the 1770s, and then began to rise slowly, so that by 1850 they were 35–40 per cent higher than they had been at their 1775 nadir (see Figure 11.6).[86] If this revised real wage series is correct, it would increase the plausibility of some contribution to mortality decline of improvements in the standard of living prior to 1850. Second, there is no doubt that living standards rose rapidly during the second half of the nineteenth century, and that the improvements were experienced by even the lowest-paid workers. It is possible that rising living standards had an indirect effect on mortality – for example, through facilitating expenditure by local authorities on sanitation and other environmental improvements.[87] Third, and not the least important, there is the continuing problem faced by critics of the standard of living thesis of what to put in its place.

[86]   This trend is what is produced by taking the series reported by splicing the series in Wrigley and Schofield, *Population History of England*, p. 643, to the more recent one for 1770 onwards given in C. Feinstein, 'Pessimism Perpetuated: Real Wages and the Standard of Living in Britain During and After the Industrial Revolution', *Journal of Economic History* LVIII (1998), p. 648.

[87]   R. Millward and F.N. Bell, 'Economic Factors in the Decline of Mortality in Late Nineteenth Century Britain', *European Review of Economic History* II (1998), pp. 263–88.

|13|

The decline of fertility

13.1 Introduction

The decline of fertility in England and Wales lagged substantially behind the decline in mortality, permitting a substantial period of rapid population growth. From fewer than six million in 1750, the population rose to 8.6 million in 1800 and 16.5 million in 1850. Thereafter, it continued to grow, almost doubling to 31 million by 1900. The annual percentage increase in the population remained at over 1 per cent per year throughout the nineteenth century. The lengthy continuation of this period of population growth occurred because, for most of the nineteenth century, fertility remained at pre-industrial levels despite the fact that mortality had started to fall. A couple who married in mid-nineteenth-century England could still expect to bear around six children, which was roughly the same number as in the pre-industrial era. Sometime during the second half of the nineteenth century, however, the number of children born to the average English woman began to decline. Initially slow, the fall in fertility gathered pace towards 1900 and birth rates then plummeted so dramatically that by the 1920s the average family size had fallen to around two children.

This chapter attempts both to tell the story of this transformation in child-bearing patterns, and to explore the reasons underlying it. Section 13.2 describes the course of the fertility decline, using several ways of measuring fertility. It explores the timing of the decline, and shows that the fundamental reason why fertility declined was a reduction in the fertility of married couples. Given that in pre-industrial England variations in fertility were principally due to changes in marriage patterns, this fact alone marks a significant break with the past, suggesting the advent of a new situation. Demographers have given the label *fertility transition* to the supplanting of variations in nuptiality by changes in marital fertility as the immediate determinants of fertility, and to the change in behaviour this entails, and we explore demographers' conceptualization of this transition in more detail in Section 13.3.

Section 13.4 describes the two general accounts of the fertility decline that the social science literature offers. One accords primacy to the appearance of new ideas and attitudes towards child-bearing, arguing that the crucial factor was the emergence of the acceptability of family planning and choice about numbers of children. The other argues that the crucial variable was the 'demand' for children, and that fertility fell because new social and economic circumstances reduced this demand. The applicability of these accounts to the English experience are examined in more detail in Section 13.5.

In order to assess the merits of these two accounts, a number of issues have to be examined. The first of these is exactly how married couples in late nineteenth- and early twentieth-century England managed to reduce their fertility so effectively, despite modern methods of birth control not being available. The second is the extent to which there were differentials in the timing of the decline in fertility within the population. These form the subject of Sections 13.6 and 13.7 respectively, and are used in Section 13.8 to assess the competing accounts.

Traditional accounts of the fertility decline have looked forward in time and tried to establish the chronology of critical developments that led to changed behaviour. In Sections 13.9 and 13.10 we reverse this process and try to seek an understanding of the factors motivating the decline by looking at childbearing between the two world wars. The 1920s and 1930s were a period of remarkably low fertility (the same levels were not to be seen again until the late 1970s), which has been curiously neglected by demographers and historians. Fertility was not only low, but it was uniformly low, in that there seem to have been no sub-groups within the population that continued to have large families. Section 13.9 explores fertility patterns in the early years of the twentieth century, and Section 13.10 considers possible reasons for the reluctance of most English couples who married between the world wars to bear more than one or two children.

13.2 The course of the decline

Figure 13.1 shows both the crude birth rate (CBR) and the total fertility rate (TFR) in England from 1750 until 1945. Trends in the two measures are quite similar.[1] After an increase between 1750 and the early nineteenth century, fertility declined by just over one birth per woman between 1811–20 and the 1840s before holding steady at that level until the 1870s. From the mid-1870s onwards, however, a sustained decline set in, punctuated only by the distorting effect of the First World War, so that by the 1930s the average English woman was having fewer than two children. At the national level, therefore, English fertility began to fall during the 1870s, and once the decline had set in, it proceeded rapidly and relentlessly until the 1930s (with

---

[1]   This is to be expected, as the crude birth rate is only confounded to a limited degree by changes in the age structure of the population.

only a minor 'blip' in the aftermath of the First World War, caused by demobilization and the reuniting of couples separated by the war).

The TFR is the sum of the age-specific fertility rates (ASFRs) over all the child-bearing ages (see Box 8.1). Unfortunately, despite the fact that birth registration began in England and Wales in 1837, ASFRs are not available in published statistics for years before 1938. However, we do have several estimates of age-specific marital fertility rates (ASMFRs – see Box 9.1) for each census year from 1851 to 1911 inclusive, and for the years 1922 and 1933 produced by the Registrars General.[2] Figure 13.2 depicts these

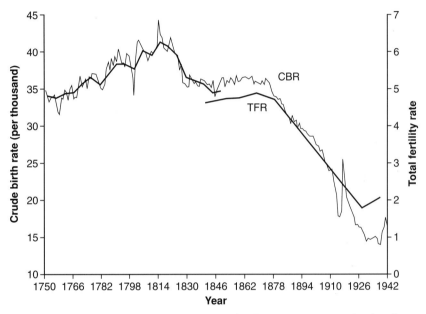

Figure 13.1 Crude birth rate (CBR) and total fertility rate (TFR), England and Wales, 1750–1945

Notes: Crude birth rates up to 1871 are for England only; those from 1872 to 1945 are for England and Wales. The total fertility rates are taken from two separate series. Those for 1750–1851 are estimated from back projection using parish register data; the series that starts in 1841 is based on civil registration and census data. The two series do not quite 'meet' in the middle, but are fairly close.

Sources: B.R. Mitchell, *British Historical Statistics* (Cambridge, Cambridge University Press, 1988), pp. 41–4; E.A. Wrigley and R.S. Schofield, *The Population History of England 1541–1871: a Reconstruction* (London, Edward Arnold, 1981), p. 529; Office of Population Censuses and Surveys, *Birth Statistics: Historical Series of Statistics from Registrations of Births in England and Wales 1837–1983* (series FM1, no. 13) (London, Her Majesty's Stationery Office, 1987).

---

[2]   These are presented in R. Woods, *The Demography of Victorian England and Wales* (Cambridge, Cambridge University Press, 2000), p. 131.

ASMFRs for selected years, together with a set of ASMFRs for the period 1800–24. Fertility within marriage declined very little, if at all, before 1871. By 1891 a modest decline is seen at all ages above 25 years, though the average completed family size of ever-married women who married at age 20 years and remained married throughout their fertile period had only fallen to 6.75 from 7.45 in 1871.[3] This decline accelerated during the subsequent two decades, being most pronounced for women in their thirties. Between 1911 and 1933 the decline continued, and now affected even women in their twenties. The average completed family size for these married women in 1933 was 3.21, barely two-fifths of its level in 1851.

Sets of ASMFRs like those depicted in Figure 13.2 are somewhat artificial, as they do not refer to any 'real' women. However, they may be used to derive approximate measures of the fertility of different groups of women born in specific periods (known as *birth cohorts* in demographic parlance). Figure 13.3 shows the ASMFRs for several such birth cohorts, and Table 13.1 the total marital fertility rates (TMFRs) for all birth cohorts from 1826–91. Women born during the second quarter of the nineteenth century could expect to have just over seven children if they married at age 20 years, and a little over five children if they married at the (more realistic) age of 25

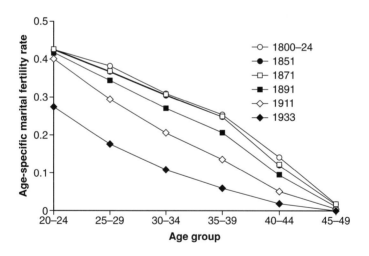

Figure 13.2 Age-specific marital fertility rates by period, 1800–1933
Source: R. Woods, *The Demography of Victorian England and Wales* (Cambridge, Cambridge University Press, 2000), p. 131; estimates for 1851 onwards originally published in Registrar General, *Statistical Review for 1938 and 1939* (London, Her Majesty's Stationery Office, 1947), p. 237; estimates for 1800–24 originally from E.A. Wrigley, R.S. Davies, J.E. Oeppen and R.S. Schofield, *English Population History from Family Reconstitution 1580–1837* (Cambridge, Cambridge University Press, 1997), p. 355.

3   Ibid., p.131.

years. The first indications of a change in behaviour can be seen in the cohort born in the 1840s, and a definite decline has set in among women born during the second half of the 1850s. This decline is maintained among all successive birth cohorts, so that a woman born during the early 1890s could expect to have around 4.2 children if she married at age 20 years, and about 2.3 children if she married at age 25 years.

Table 13.1 Average completed family size of ever-married women, birth cohorts from 1826–31 to 1891–96

Birth cohort	Assuming marriage at age 20 years	Assuming marriage at age 25 years
1826–31	7.4	5.2
1831–36	7.4	5.2
1836–41	7.3	5.2
1841–46	7.3	5.1
1846–51	7.1	5.0
1851–56	6.9	4.7
1856–61	6.6	4.5
1861–66	6.3	4.2
1866–71	6.0	3.9
1871–76	5.7	3.6
1876–81	5.4	3.3
1881–86	5.1	3.0
1886–91	4.7	2.7
1891–96	4.2	2.3

Notes: Calculated by summing the age-specific marital fertility rates over all ages from the assumed age at marriage to age 50 years (see Box 9.1).
Sources: Estimated from data given in R. Woods, *The Demography of Victorian England and Wales* (Cambridge, Cambridge University Press, 2000), p. 131.

Figures 13.1–13.3 report trends in 'average' fertility. A recent study by Michael Anderson, though, has suggested that the decline of fertility was accompanied by an increase in the variability of fertility and, in particular, the appearance of a substantial minority of married couples who stopped child-bearing after only one or two children.[4] We can address this issue by examining the distribution of completed family sizes among different birth cohorts (Table 13.2). Women born in the late eighteenth century had an 'average' completed family size of around five children.[5] This 'average' however,

---

[4] M. Anderson, 'Fertility decline in Scotland, England and Wales, and Ireland: Comparisons from the 1911 Census of Fertility', *Population Studies* LII (1998), pp. 1–20; M. Anderson, 'Highly Restricted Fertility: Very Small Families in the British Fertility Decline', *Population Studies* LII (1998), pp. 177–99.

[5] In this context, it should be noted that 'children' means 'live births'. Of course, as Chapter 12 showed, many of these children did not survive infancy and childhood.

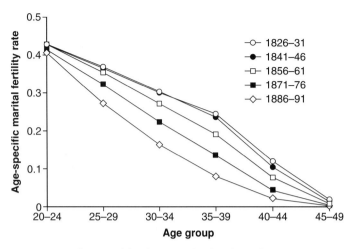

Figure 13.3 Age-specific marital fertility rates, birth cohorts from 1826–31 to 1886–91
Source: Estimated from data in R. Woods, *The Demography of Victorian England and Wales* (Cambridge, Cambridge University Press, 2000), p. 131; and originally published in Registrar General, *Statistical Review for 1938 and 1939* (London, Her Majesty's Stationery Office, 1947), p. 237.

disguises the fact that 18 per cent had fewer than two children, and 22 per cent had eight or more. Women born in the mid-nineteenth century (between 1840 and 1869) had scarcely fewer children on average, but the proportion bearing fewer than two children had risen to 24 per cent, and the proportion bearing eight or more to 25 per cent, supporting Anderson's suggestion. The onset of the fertility decline is seen in earnest among the next birth cohort, women born between 1870 and 1899, with a large increase in families of fewer than four children (and especially in the proportion of women having just one or two children), and a decrease in the prevalence of large families, with the greatest decrease being seen among the largest family sizes.

As shown in Part II, a crucial feature of English fertility during the sixteenth, seventeenth and eighteenth centuries was its dependence on nuptiality, or the prevalence of marriage. Variations over time in fertility largely reflected changes in the proportions of women marrying. Changes in nuptiality were also a major contributor to changes in fertility between 1750 and 1850, and the influence of nuptiality on fertility was still being felt in the middle of the nineteenth century.[6] However, things then changed, for very little of the massive decline in the average completed fertility between

---

[6]   On the operation of the Malthusian preventive check in nineteenth-century England, see R. Woods, *Demography of Victorian England and Wales*, pp. 71–109; and P.R.A. Hinde, 'Household Structure, Marriage and the Institution of Service in Nineteenth-Century Rural England', *Local Population Studies* XXXV (1985), pp. 43–51 (reprinted in D. Mills and K. Schürer (eds), *Local Communities in the Census Enumerators' Books* (Oxford, Leopard's Head Press, 1996), pp. 317–25).

Table 13.2 Percentages of women having different numbers of births, birth cohorts 1750–79, 1840–69 and 1870–99

Number of births	Women born 1750–79	Women born 1840–69	Women born 1870–99
0	10.0	14.9	21.5
1	8.0	8.9	17.8
2	8.3	9.1	18.2
3	8.8	9.2	13.2
4	9.5	9.1	9.4
5	10.9	8.5	6.2
6	12.1	8.0	4.8
7	10.0	7.2	3.3
8	6.9	6.4	2.2
9	4.9	5.9	1.4
10 or more	10.6	13.0	2.0
Average	5.0	4.8	2.7

Notes: The figures in this table have been estimated from data on the completed family size distribution for ever-married women, and adjusted to take account of births to never-married women, and the proportion of women in each birth cohort who never married.

Sources: Figures for women born 1750–79 were estimated from data given in E.A. Wrigley, R.S. Davies, J.E. Oeppen and R.S. Schofield, *English Population History from Family Reconstitution 1580–1837* (Cambridge, Cambridge University Press, 1997), p. 403. Figures for the 1840–69 and 1870–99 birth cohorts we estimated from data given in M. Anderson, 'Highly Restricted Fertility: Very Small Families in the British Fertility Decline', *Population Studies* LII (1998), p. 178. Data on the proportions of births to each cohort that were illegitimate were obtained for the 1750–79 birth cohort from P. Laslett, *Family Life and Illicit Love in Earlier Generations* (Cambridge, Cambridge University Press, 1977), p. 102; and for the other two birth cohorts from Office of Population Censuses and Surveys, *Birth Statistics: Historical Series of Statistics from Registrations of Births in England and Wales, 1837–1983* (series FM1 no. 13) (London, Her Majesty's Stationery Office, 1987) pp. 19–21. Data on the proportions of women ever marrying came from E.A. Wrigley and R.S. Schofield, *The Population History of England 1541–1871: a Reconstruction* (London, Edward Arnold, 1981) p. 260 for the 1750–79 birth cohort and from Office of Population Censuses and Surveys, *Marriage and Divorce Statistics: Historical Series of Statistics on Marriages and Divorces in England and Wales, 1837–1983* (series FM2 no. 16) (London, Her Majesty's Stationery Office, 1990), pp. 19–21 for the other two cohorts.

women born in the middle of the nineteenth century and women born at the end of that century can be attributed to changes in nuptiality. Table 13.3 shows how the distribution of completed family sizes among *ever-married* women born between the 1840s and 1900 changes and reveals just as remarkable a transformation as Table 13.2.[7] There was a slight fall in the

---

[7] Tables 13.1 and 13.3 have been estimated from different data sources. It is worth pausing to compare the average completed family sizes of the same birth cohorts in the two tables. Generally speaking, the estimates in Table 13.3 are rather higher than those in Table 13.1 for the 1845–54 and 1865–74 birth cohorts, but very similar for the 1875–84 and 1900 birth cohorts. One possible reason for this is that the average age at marriage of the earlier two birth cohorts in Table 13.3 was rather less than 25 years. This interpretation is consistent with a slight increase in the average age at marriage during the late nineteenth century.

proportion of women ever marrying during the second half of the nineteenth century (from about 88 per cent to 83 per cent), but this can only have accounted for a small fraction of the overall fertility decline.[8] Neither did changes in the distribution of *ages at marriage* play much of a part. An increase of about 1.5 years in the mean age at marriage for women during the late nineteenth century did make some contribution, but nowhere near enough to explain the changes in the distribution of completed fertility. Overall, then, the decline in fertility during the late nineteenth and early twentieth centuries had relatively little to do with changes in nuptiality, but a great deal to do with changes in the behaviour of married women.[9]

Table 13.3 Percentages of ever-married women born between 1845 and 1900 having different numbers of births

Number of births	Women born 1845–54	1865–74	1875–84	1900
0	8.1	10.0	11.5	15.8
1	5.4	9.5	14.8	25.1
2	7.1	13.5	18.8	25.3
3	8.6	13.5	15.6	13.9
4	9.4	12.2	12.1	7.6
5	9.5	10.0	8.2	4.7
6	9.5	8.2	6.7	2.4
7	8.9	6.5	4.5	1.9
8	8.1	5.1	3.0	1.5
9	7.7	4.0	2.0	0.8
10 or more	17.7	7.5	2.8	1.0
Average	5.8	4.3	3.4	2.2

Notes: These figures have been estimated from data for cohorts of women defined according to their age at marriage by assuming the women married at age 25 years.
Source: M. Anderson, 'Highly Restricted Fertility: Very Small Families in the British Fertility Decline', *Population Studies* LII (1998), p. 178.

13.3 Fertility decline and fertility transition

The replacement of nuptiality by fertility within marriage as the main determinant of fertility levels, then, was a key feature of the decline in fertility in late Victorian England. This change alone would be sufficient to warrant the

[8] See M.S. Teitelbaum, *The British Fertility Decline: Demographic Transition in the Crucible of the Industrial Revolution* (Princeton, Princeton University Press, 1984).
[9] Teitelbaum, *The British Fertility Decline*, pp. 79, 101, 117, calculates a summary index of the proportion of women married by age in each of the census years from 1851 to 1931, and similar summary indices of fertility within marriage and overall fertility. Between 1851 and 1931 the index of the proportion of women married hardly changes, whereas the indices of overall fertility and fertility within marriage decline after 1871.

use of the term 'fertility transition'. The eclipse of marriage as a regulator of fertility, though, was associated with a change that demographers have generally regarded as even more fundamental, specifically the adoption of birth control by married couples, and the term *fertility transition* is generally used in the demographic literature to refer to this change. According to this logic, fertility declines during the demographic transition because an increasing proportion of married couples begin to restrict their childbearing by practising contraception of one form or another – that is, by making a transition from 'natural' or uncontrolled fertility to 'controlled' fertility. It seems that once a certain proportion of couples in a population have changed their behaviour in this way, the practice rapidly spreads throughout the whole population. Figure 13.3 suggests that the transition in England and Wales began with the birth cohorts of the late 1840s and early 1850s. These birth cohorts were having the bulk of their children during the 1870s and 1880s.

Simply defining fertility transition in this way, though, begs several questions. The first relates to the nature of fertility control behaviour. Demographers have for several decades favoured a definition of 'controlled' fertility, which was first proposed by the French demographer L. Henry in 1961.[10] According to Henry, 'controlled' fertility existed where a couple's child-bearing behaviour varied according to the number of children they already had.[11] Where behaviour did not change with the number of children already born, fertility was regarded as 'natural'. The implication of this definition is that fertility control involves 'stopping' behaviour, in which couples begin to do something to inhibit future childbearing once they have achieved their desired family size. This 'stopping' behaviour was given the name *family limitation* by demographers, and a whole industry developed that tried to measure its extent in historical and contemporary populations.[12]

The second question is more specific to the English experience. If, in preindustrial England, Malthus's preventive check existed alongside a virtual absence of fertility control within marriage, was this because couples marrying at the advanced age typical of English men and women of the sixteenth, seventeenth and early eighteenth centuries did not have enough time to satisfy their demand for children before the wife's biological clock started ticking? Or was the lack of fertility control before the second half of the nineteenth

---

[10] L. Henry, 'Some Data on Natural Fertility', *Eugenics Quarterly* VIII (1981), pp. 81–91.
[11] Ibid., p. 81.
[12] See A.J. Coale and T.J. Trussell, 'Model Fertility Schedules: Variations in the Age Structure of Childbearing in Human Populations', *Population Index* XL (1974), pp. 185–258; A.J. Coale and T.J. Trussell, 'Finding the Two Parameters that Specify a Model Schedule of Marital Fertility', *Population Index* XLIV (1978), pp. 203–13; Woods, *Demography of Victorian England and Wales*, pp. 124–40; P.R.A. Hinde and R.I. Woods, 'Variations in Historical Natural Fertility Patterns and the Measurement of Fertility Control', *Journal of Biosocial Science* XVI (1984), pp. 309–21.

century determined by non-economic factors, such as lack of knowledge of how to control fertility, or a deep-seated belief that the provision of children within a marriage was 'up to God' and that couples ought not to over-ride the Divine Will? These questions will be explored in the next three sections.

13.4 The innovation and adjustment hypotheses

Nearly 30 years ago the demographer Ansley Coale laid out three preconditions for fertility transition.[13] The first of these was that '[f]ertility must be within the calculus of conscious choice. Potential parents must consider it an acceptable mode of thought and form of behaviour to balance advantages and disadvantages before deciding to have another child.'[14] The second was that the result of this balancing must be that couples consider restricting their fertility to be economically or socially advantageous. Finally, couples must know of and have access to some means of restricting their fertility, be determined to use it, and communicate sufficiently to be able to use it effectively.

For at least the last 35 years, demographers have been debating the causes of the fertility transition, and Coale's three preconditions capture very well the essence of the debate. Following Gosta Carlsson, who is generally credited with initiating the debate, the two schools of thought may be called the *innovation hypothesis* and the *adjustment hypothesis*.[15] According to the innovation hypothesis, prior to the fertility transition, the voluntary restriction of fertility within marriage did not happen either because couples lacked access to the means to do it, or because the very idea that they might be able to choose the number of children they had was alien: contraception was inconceivable. In the terms of Coale's pre-conditions, then, the innovation hypothesis considers the first and third as the determining factors. Furthermore, since it seems that access to some means of birth control (at the very least, abstinence and *coitus interruptus*) was available in the pre-industrial era, attention has focused on the first. The innovation that took place in the nineteenth century was that 'conscious choice' was applied to fertility, leading to the development of '[n]ew norms for personal behaviour' and the use of such methods of birth control as were available.[16]

---

[13]   A.J. Coale, 'The Demographic Transition', in *International Population Conference, Liège 1973* (3 vols, Liège, International Union for the Scientific Study of Population, 1973) I, pp. 53–72.

[14]   Ibid., p. 65.

[15]   G. Carlsson, 'The Decline of Fertility: Innovation or Adjustment Process?' *Population Studies* XX (1966), pp. 149–74.

[16]   See J. Cleland and C. Wilson, 'Demand Theories of the Fertility Transition: an Iconoclastic View', *Population Studies* XLI (1987), pp. 5–30; Woods, *Demography of Victorian England and Wales*, pp. 169. It is, of course, possible that the innovation was the very idea of rational decision-making about anything at all. However, there is fairly abundant evidence that English men and women were highly capable of rational economic calculations in earlier centuries (see, for example, A. Macfarlane, *The Origins of English Individualism* (Cambridge, Cambridge University Press, 1978)).

The adjustment hypothesis, by contrast, regards the decline in fertility as an adjustment to new social and economic circumstances. According to this argument, there were no restrictions, either technical or attitudinal, preventing the use of birth control in earlier centuries. However, prevailing economic and social conditions favoured high fertility and so birth control was not widely practised. In the nineteenth century, however, the economic and social environment changed, leading to changes in the relative costs and benefits of children, and couples adapted rationally to this change by having fewer of them. This hypothesis, therefore, regards the second of Coale's preconditions as the determining factor.

The adjustment hypothesis is really no more than a broader statement of the 'demand' theories of the fertility transition that were discussed in Chapter 9. It is broader in the sense that it allows for the calculation of the advantages and disadvantages of childbearing to take into account social factors, such as society's attitudes towards large and small families, as well as the traditional economic ones, such as the pecuniary costs of raising children. Kingsley Davis's account of fertility decline as a response to increasing economic strain, described in Chapter 11, is one example.

13.5 Was the English fertility transition an innovation?

Until the 1970s, the veracity of the demand theories of the fertility transition (and, hence, the adjustment hypothesis) was widely accepted, though the empirical basis for them was very weak. Yet during the past 30 years, support for the innovation hypothesis has increased markedly among demographers, at least within the social science community.[17] Two developments during the 1970s and 1980s influenced this. The first was the publication of the results of the European Fertility Project.[18] This project, based at Princeton University in the United States, comprised an analysis of the fertility decline in the whole of Europe at the level of the province (which, in the English context, meant the county). Using a standard set of indices of fertility, the project attempted to relate the timing of the decline in fertility to various social and economic factors. The conclusion was quite stark, and very bad news for the adjustment hypothesis, for there appeared to be no clear relationship between the timing of the development of an urban, industrial society and the timing of the fertility decline. The earliest fertility declines were experienced during the early nineteenth century (even the late eighteenth) in France, which was far from being the earliest part of Europe

---

[17] There are dissenting voices; for example, D. Friedlander, 'Demographic Responses and Socioeconomic Structure: Population Processes in England and Wales in the Nineteenth Century', *Demography* XX (1983), pp. 249–72, which argues in favour of Kingsley Davis's model of the demographic transition.

[18] The results are summarized in A.J. Coale and S.C. Watkins, *The Decline of Fertility in Europe* (Princeton, Princeton University Press, 1986).

to industrialize, in southern Belgium, Catalonia and parts of the Austro-Hungarian empire. By contrast, in England and Wales and Germany, where industrialization was well advanced by 1850, fertility did not decline until the last few decades of the nineteenth century. This lack of an association between any of the traditional 'modernization' variables extended to within-country comparisons, notably in Britain.[19]

By contrast, there did appear to be a relationship between the timing of the fertility decline and certain cultural variables. More specifically, the geography of fertility reflected closely the linguistic geography of the continent. Nowhere was this more apparent than in Belgium, where fertility declined earlier in the French-speaking south than in the Flemish-speaking north, despite the north being the more 'modern', to use Notestein's terminology.[20]

The conclusion that was drawn from this was that fertility decline was related to the spread of new ideas favourable to the use of birth control. The spread of these ideas was facilitated where populations spoke a common language and communicated freely with one another, and where populations were well integrated socially and administratively (for example, France and England). However, their spread was hindered by isolation, whether this arose because of physical barriers (such as the mountainous terrain in the Iberian peninsula) or cultural barriers (such as the linguistic divide in Belgium). It was also assisted by mass education.

Within England and Wales, barriers to the spread of the new ideas were few and easily hurdled. Therefore, it is not surprising that one of the most striking features of the English fertility transition is its temporal homogeneity, both socially and spatially. The decline in fertility affected all areas of the country, and all social groups, within a short time frame. The European Fertility Project measured fertility within marriage using an index of fertility that compared the observed number of legitimate births in any 'province' during any period with the number that would have been expected if married women in that province during that period had borne children at a rate equal to the highest recorded fertility.[21] Using the same index, Robert Woods has shown that, in 1861, virtually the whole of England and Wales had marital fertility greater than 60 per cent of the maximum, whereas by 1911 most of the country had marital fertility rates less than half that of the maximum, and the only areas where it still exceeded 60 per cent were County Durham in the north-east and parts of South Wales.[22]

---

[19] See Teitelbaum, *The British Fertility Decline.*
[20] R. Lesthaeghe, *The Decline of Belgian Fertility, 1800–1970* (Princeton, Princeton University Press, 1977).
[21] The index was originally proposed in A.J. Coale, 'Factors Associated with the Development of Low Fertility: an Historic Summary', in *Proceedings of the World Population Conference, 1965* (3 vols, New York, United Nations Department of Economic and Social Affairs, 1967), II, pp. 205–9. The highest recorded fertility is that of the married women from the North American Hutterites who married during the 1920s, who had an average completed family size of 12 children.
[22] Woods, *Demography of Victorian England and Wales*, map g (between pp. 96 and 97).

The second development that favoured the innovation hypothesis has been described in Chapter 9. This was the discovery that during the pre-industrial period fertility control was apparently not widely practised despite the economic and social incentives to large families being rather weak, and that fertility within marriage varied rather little from place to place, or over time. The economic benefits children accorded to their parents were not obvious, and so the fact that birth control was largely absent suggested either that in any 'calculus of conscious choice' that parents or potential parents were engaging in, non-economic factors were overriding economic ones, or that no 'calculus of conscious choice' was being carried on.

The result was a history of fertility within marriage in England of striking, almost minimalist, simplicity. For several centuries prior to the 1870s, marital fertility was universally high and fairly constant over time. Suddenly, during the last few decades of the nineteenth century, it began to decline rapidly. The decline took place in all social groups, and in all areas, within three or four decades, so that by the end of the third decade of the twentieth century, fertility within marriage was universally low.[23] The principal reason for this decline was a 'substantial and very rapid change in public opinion towards family limitation, making it both legitimate and personally acceptable', which was 'facilitated by the revolution in mass education which gathered pace from the 1840s. The effect of this was to create a largely literate society (at least among young adults) by the 1870s'.[24]

13.6 Birth control in nineteenth-century England

The change in public opinion was encouraged by the publication, between 1870 and 1900, of literature promoting family planning. There had, to be sure, been occasional attempts to promote birth control even before Victoria acceded to the throne. In 1823, for example, Francis Place had published a set of handbills entitled 'To the Married of Both Sexes', in which he recommended the use of *coitus interruptus* and the sponge as methods of birth control. These were followed in 1826 by a book entitled *Every Woman's Book, or What is Love?* by Richard Carlile. Yet it seems that these early attempts had little success, at least measured in terms of their impact on fertility within marriage.

---

[23] It is interesting to consider why this view has become so pervasive, for throughout the last 30 years there have been persistent critics. Dov Friedlander and his colleagues, for example, have presented arguments and evidence against every plank in this edifice; see D. Friedlander and B.S. Okun, 'Pretransition Marital Fertility Variation over Time: was there Deliberate Control in England?' *Journal of Family History* XX (1995), pp. 139–58; and Friedlander, 'Demographic Responses'. See also T.W. Guinnane, B.S. Okun and J. Trussell, 'What do we Know about the Timing of Fertility Transition in Europe?', *Demography* XXXI (1994), pp. 1–20. The reason, I think, is that the proponents of this view of English fertility history are largely based in England, whereas the dissenters are not (Friedlander, for example, is in Jerusalem, and Guinnane and his colleagues are in the United States).

[24] Woods, *Demography of Victorian England and Wales*, p. 165.

In the late 1830s, an American called Charles Knowlton published a book entitled *The Fruits of Philosophy: or the Private Companion of Young Married People*, in which he advocated a variety of methods of birth control, including douching with various solutions (such as alum, white oak bark, hemlock and green tea) or, if these were not available, the 'liberal use of pretty cold water'. Though this book attracted little immediate attention at the time, it was eventually to play a key part in the single event that most effectively generated publicity for the birth control movement in nineteenth-century England. In 1876 two 'freethinkers', Charles Bradlaugh and Annie Besant, decided to republish the book and distribute it in England, whereupon they were indicted on the grounds that they

> unlawfully, wickedly, knowingly, willfully and designedly did print, publish, sell, and utter a certain indecent, lewd, filthy and obscene libel, to wit, a certain indecent, lewd, filthy, bawdy, and obscene book, called 'Fruits of Philosophy' thereby contaminating, vitiating, and corrupting the morals as well of youth as of the other liege subjects of our said Lady the Queen.[25]

Bradlaugh and Besant were sentenced to six months' imprisonment, though they appealed and won on a legal technicality. From the perspective of the innovation hypothesis, however, the most important impact of the Bradlaugh–Besant trial was to greatly increase public interest in, and sales of, Knowlton's book. These had been running at a few hundred per year since its publication, but in the period during and immediately after the trial, many thousands were sold. It has often been pointed out that the Bradlaugh–Besant trial took place in the very year that fertility at the national level began its sustained decline.

During the following two or three decades, a stream of literature informing the public about birth control and promoting its use contributed to what Norman Himes has called the 'democratization' of birth control; but it was not matched by technical developments. Certainly, some methods were improved (notably condoms, which benefited from the vulcanization of rubber in 1843 and the invention of the 'seamless' condom late in the century), and others were mass-produced for the first time (for example, spermicides), but the availability of these methods to ordinary people was limited until well into the twentieth century, not least on the grounds of cost. By 1900, British couples were controlling their fertility quite effectively using methods that had been available for centuries: abstinence from sexual intercourse and *coitus interruptus*.[26]

---

[25]   Quoted in C. Wood and B. Suitters, *The Fight for Acceptance* (Aylesbury, Medical and Technical Publishing Ltd, 1970), p. 140.

[26]   One of the main contributions of Simon Szreter's recent re-interpretation of the English fertility decline is the stress he places on abstinence; see S. Szreter, *Fertility, Class and Gender in Britain, 1860–1940* (Cambridge, Cambridge University Press, 1996).

Indeed, a survey of couples married before 1910 found that only 16 per cent of those who claimed to have been controlling their fertility were using appliances, and, even among couples married during the early 1920s, the figure was fewer than one-third.[27]

Even with these traditional methods, however, by the first two decades of the twentieth century, effective birth control was widespread. The 'democratization' of birth control produced an immense and rapid social change, which was all the more remarkable for being achieved in the teeth of opposition from the 'establishment'. The Church, the legal profession, and (most notably) the medical profession, were all opposed to the promotion of birth control within marriage, and government failed to provide any support.[28] It was not until 1921 that Marie Stopes was able to open the first birth control clinic (in Holloway, North London), and not until 1930 that opposition from the Church of England was finally overcome, and the government permitted local authorities to support birth control activities financially.[29]

13.7 Differentials in the timing of the fertility decline

As we have mentioned before, a feature of the English fertility decline seems to have been its homogeneity, both geographically and temporally. The decline seems to have occurred throughout all sections of the population within four decades or so.[30] Closer examination, however, reveals that there were geographical differentials worth considerin g in a little more detail. There were certain districts where high fertility persisted into the twentieth century. At the county level, the most obvious example was County Durham in the north-east of England.[31] At the opposite end of the spectrum, districts where fertility declined earlier than elsewhere included the West End of London, the central Pennines, between Leeds and Manchester, and several areas along the south coast of England.[32]

The immediate explanation of these geographical differentials is to be found in social and occupational fertility variations. Indeed, at first sight

---

[27] E. Lewis-Faning, *Report on an Enquiry into Family Limitation and Human Fertility in the Past Fifty Years* (Royal Commission on Population, Papers, Volume I), (London, Her Majesty's Stationery Office, 1949).

[28] See R.A. Soloway, *Birth Control and the Population Question in England, 1877–1930* (Chapel Hill, University of North Carolina Press, 1982).

[29] The Anglican Church's position was outlined in the Lambeth Conference of 1930, and was typically convoluted, arguing that it was morally acceptable for couples to seek to limit their family size, and that there was a morally sound reason for married couples to avoid abstinence from sexual intercourse, and inviting interested observers to draw the logical inference!

[30] Woods, *Demography of Victorian England and Wales*, p. 122.

[31] Teitelbaum, *British Fertility Decline*.

[32] Woods, *Demography of Victorian England and Wales*, map g (between pp. 96 and 97).

it seems that occupational fertility variations coupled with regional occupational specialization might account for them almost entirely. It is certainly the case that by the turn of the twentieth century, substantial differentials in fertility had emerged. These can be examined using the 1911 census, in which, uniquely among censuses of England and Wales, questions were asked about fertility within marriage. Figure 13.4 shows the average completed family size among women aged 45 or more in 1911, classified according to the Registrar General's 'social classes' for women who married at ages 20–24 years (Figure 13.4a) and 25–29 years (Figure 13.4b). The earliest marriage cohort, that of 1851–60, represents women born in the 1820s and 1830s, before the fertility decline began. Fertility differentials between the 'social classes' in this cohort were slight, though there is evidence of slightly lower fertility among the 'upper and middle classes'. Considering Figure 13.4a, a characteristic pattern of differentials gradually appears across the first three marriage cohorts, and is clearly visible among women marrying in 1871–80, who were born between 1845 and 1860. This cohort of women were the pioneers of the fertility transition in England (see Section 13.2). The pattern of 'social class' differentials is one of low fertility among the 'upper and middle classes', and higher fertility among manual workers, especially the unskilled (category V in Figure 13.4). Categories VI–VIII in Figure 13.4 are particularly large occupational groups with distinctive fertility patterns. Textile workers (category VI) had fertility rates below all but the 'upper and middle classes', whereas miners (category VII) had the highest fertility of any group, closely followed by agricultural workers (category VIII).

The magnitude of the differentials increases still further among women marrying in the 1880s. The onset of fertility decline, therefore, was associated with a widening of social and occupational differentials in fertility, which may have been part of the reason for the increased variation noticed by Michael Anderson.[33]

In general, the pattern among women who married aged 25–29 years is similar, though average completed family sizes are between about 1.5 and 2.0 children lower for these later-marrying women in the earlier marriage cohorts, and between 1.0 and 1.5 children lower among those marrying during the 1880s. The difference in completed fertility by age at marriage is also smaller among the 'upper and middle classes' than among other groups.

It can now be seen why occupational differentials were thought to be the primary explanation of the geographical patterns described earlier. Those areas with especially low fertility by 1911 had a high proportion of either textile workers (the Yorkshire/Lancashire border) or 'upper and middle

[33]   Anderson, 'Fertility Decline'.

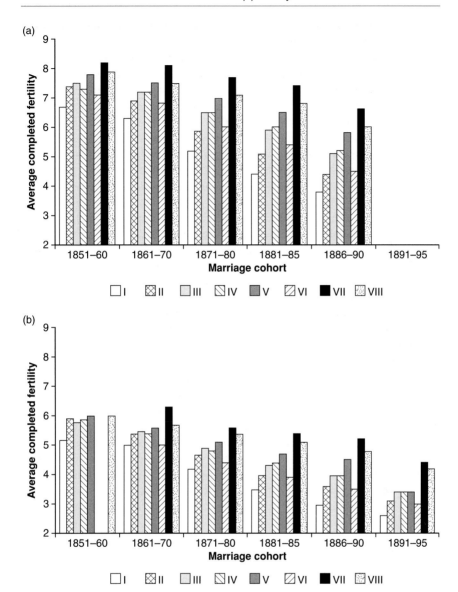

Figure 13.4 Differentials in completed fertility by 'social class', marriage cohorts between 1851 and 1896: (a) wife's marriage age 20–24; (b) wife's marriage age 25–29

Notes: The 'social classes' are defined as follows: I = upper and middle class; II = intermediate non-manual; III = skilled manual workers; IV = intermediate (semi-skilled) manual workers; V = unskilled workmen; VI = textile workers; VII = miners; VIII = agricultural labourers.
Source: R. Woods, *The Demography of Victorian England and Wales* (Cambridge, Cambridge University Press, 2000), p. 118.

classes' (the south-coast towns). Areas where fertility decline lagged typically had a high proportion of miners (for example, County Durham). To a large extent, therefore, geographical differentials in fertility arose because of a mapping of occupational differentials on to geographical space through the medium of regional variations in the occupational structure.

'To a large extent', but not entirely: recent research has suggested that the geography of the fertility transition in England is more interesting than this. Questions have been raised about the view that, before the transition, fertility was socially and geographically homogeneous. In a family reconstitution study of fertility in the Blean area of northern Kent, for example, Barry Reay argues there were small but significant variations in marital fertility prior to the fertility decline of the 1880s, and suggests that the New Poor Law of 1834 might have influenced fertility behaviour, though this suggestion is little more than speculation.[34] However, other family reconstitution-type studies of nineteenth-century populations have been carried out and, taken, together, the results do suggest that there might have been some geographical differentials in fertility within marriage. The total marital fertility rate calculated for Reay's Kent parishes between 1850 and 1864 is 8.0, which compares with 7.3 for seven Hampshire parishes between 1841 and 1891 and 7.0 for three Essex parishes between 1800 and 1880.[35]

Second, an important recent study using the 1911 census enumerators' books has revealed that fertility varied geographically even within specific occupational groups.[36] It appears that the attitudes towards family building and childbearing prevalent among the dominant occupational groups in a particular area could influence other groups within that area. So, for example, in an area where coal mining was the main industry, with its norms favouring high fertility, the fertility behaviour of the minority of middle-class couples was higher than it was in areas where the middle classes were dominant. A 'mining' effect tugged at the behaviour of the middle classes. A similar effect (in the opposite direction) was observed in areas dominated by the middle classes.

---

[34] B. Reay, 'Before the Transition: Fertility in English Villages 1800–1880', *Continuity and Change* IX (1994), pp. 91–120 (reprinted in B. Reay, *Microhistories: Demography, Society and Culture in Rural England, 1800–1939* (Cambridge, Cambridge University Press, 1996)).

[35] Ibid., p. 100; for Hampshire, see B. Eckstein and A. Hinde, 'Measuring Fertility Within Marriage Between 1841 and 1891 Using Parish Registers and the Census Enumerators' Books', *Local Population Studies* LXIV (2000), p. 47; for Essex, see C. Jarvis, 'The Reconstitution of Nineteenth Century Rural Communities', *Local Population Studies* LI (1993), p. 52.

[36] E.M. Garrett, A. Reid, K. Schürer and S. Szreter, *Changing Family Size in England and Wales: Place, Class and Demography 1891–1911* (Cambridge, Cambridge University Press, 2001). The authors of this study were, exceptionally, allowed access to the 1911 census enumerators' books for selected districts, despite the 100-year rule (see Appendix AIII.4), though personal names had been deleted from the copies given to them.

13.8 Explanations of the decline: does one size fit all?

The specific experience of certain occupational groups, particularly those with especially early or late fertility declines, has attracted the attention of historians, and a number of explanations of fertility trends within particular sub-groups have been proposed. The first, and still probably the best known, of these was J.A. Banks' study of fertility among the Victorian middle classes.[37] Banks noted that fertility declined early among the middle classes, beginning to fall as early as the 1850s and 1860s. His explanation is that during this period the middle classes were finding it increasingly difficult to maintain the trappings of 'middle class-ness' and, specifically, the status differential between themselves and the skilled working class. The incomes of middle-class families were rising more slowly than both the incomes of the skilled working class, and the costs of things like domestic servants and private education for their children, which were the features that distinguished the middle classes from those they perceived to be of inferior status. Since a major contribution to this income squeeze was the increased cost of bringing up middle-class children, the sensible response was to have fewer of them. Of course, once economic pressure led to smaller families becoming more common, it is also likely that they became more fashionable: necessity, if you like, was the mother of convention. Evidence from the 1911 census data also suggests that the low fertility behaviour of the middle classes spread to other groups within the population who were closely associated with the middle classes – for example, those employed in domestic service.[38]

However, the observed patterns do not support a more general 'social diffusion' account, whereby the 'small family ideal' (as Robert Woods puts it), which first made its appearance among the urban middle classes is transmitted down the social hierarchy and from city to countryside.[39] Ideas did spread, but within what Simon Szreter has termed 'communicating communities' – groups of people who interacted with and 'learned' from one another.[40]

Other accounts have been proposed for the high fertility of coal miners and workers in heavy industry.[41] Dov Friedlander's interpretation of the miners' position, for example, highlights the tendency for miners' brides to be young, possibly because a lack of employment opportunities for women

---

[37] J.A. Banks, *Prosperity and Parenthood: A Study of Family Planning among the Victorian Middle Classes* (London, Routledge and Kegan Paul, 1954).

[38] Szreter, *Fertility, Class and Gender*.

[39] Woods, *Demography of Victorian England and Wales*, pp. 114–16.

[40] Szreter, *Fertility, Class and Gender*.

[41] D. Friedlander, 'Demographic Patterns and Socio-economic Characteristics of the Coal-mining Population in England and Wales in the Nineteenth Century', *Economic Development and Cultural Change* XXII (1973), pp. 39–51; M.R. Haines, *Fertility and Occupation: Population Patterns in Industrialization* (New York, Academic Press, 1979).

in mining areas led to heavy sex-selective out-migration and thus a shortage of eligible women. Once married, the same absence of employment opportunities, combined with the high wages available for men, even relatively young men, created a 'male breadwinner' culture in which men provided the resources while women were expected to stay at home and raise children. The dangers inherent in coal mining, and the arduous nature of the work, meant that a miner's earning capacity was likely to diminish significantly, and maybe even to disappear entirely, at an early age (possibly in his forties), which created a strong incentive to make sure that by then he would have sons available to bring in money for the family. Given the high levels of infant mortality prevailing among miners' families many births were often required to ensure this.

The case of the textile workers is, in some senses, the reverse of that for miners. Abundant employment opportunities for women, both married and unmarried, led both to a higher average age at marriage, and (partly, though not entirely, as a consequence) women to have much greater autonomy within the home. Indeed, there is evidence that in some places, women were the main breadwinners during economic recessions when their menfolk were laid off.[42]

Moreover, closer examination of individual-level data has demonstrated clearly that the 'low fertility of textile workers' should more accurately be described as the low fertility of married women who were employed in textiles.[43] It is the women's work that determines their fertility, not the men's. However, several plausible explanations of fertility decline may be constructed from these elements. They are consistent, for example, with an 'opportunity cost' explanation, in which the availability of earning opportunities for married women indirectly increases the cost of having children and therefore makes economically rational couples have fewer of them. They are also consistent with a 'female autonomy' account, which credits work outside the home with the effect of increasing women's influence over household decision-making. However, as with the relationship between women's work and infant mortality, it is not clear in which direction causality operates in the association between whether or not a woman was working and her fertility. It may be that women who found themselves unable to bear children (or unable to bear more than one or two) sought fulfilment in work outside the home.

Despite their ambiguities, these three accounts are revealing in several ways. First, each of them contains a strong element of economic rationality. For Banks' middle classes, what economists call the 'quality' of their children was more important than the quantity. The price of child 'quality' was rising, and rather than dilute quality, couples chose to reduce the quantity of children. Indeed more than two decades after Banks' study was pub-

[42] See E.M. Garrett, 'The Trials of Labour: Motherhood Versus Employment in a Nineteenth-Century Textile Centre', *Continuity and Change* V (1990), pp. 121–54.
[43] E.M. Garrett, 'Before Their Time: Employment and Family Formation in a Northern Textile Town, Keighley 1851–81', unpublished PhD thesis, University of Sheffield, 1987.

lished, the economist Harvey Leibenstein produced a theoretical account of the fertility decline that was, in effect, a generalization of Banks' account.[44] Friedlander's coal miners saw children as a form of (in their case) not-so-old-age security. When children are valued for this reason, quantity rather than quality is important, and the miners behaved accordingly. Although the case of the textile workers is more ambiguous, the patterns we observe are consistent with an almost purely economic interpretation, based on the effect of husbands' and wives' relative wages on fertility.

Fertility trends in these three social groups, therefore, can be explained in economic terms, which suggests that the rejection of 'demand theories' by demographers has been premature. Before reinstating the demand theories, however, we might observe that the economic explanations given for fertility among these groups are all *different*. This brings us to the greatest problem with the way demographers have tried to explain the fertility transition. The innovation and adjustment hypotheses have often been presented as being in competition with one another: if one is right, the other must be wrong. There does not seem to have been much room for complex combinations of the two accounts, for a world in which new economic and social circumstances and new ideas intertwine in a complex way to produce behavioural change. This has now, belatedly, been recognized in the literature, though it should be said that it took a group of historians to 'blow the whistle', and suggest that there could have been multiple 'fertility transitions', each characterized by a different set of causative factors, operating within a population.[45]

The root cause of demographers' desire for a single explanation of the fertility transition probably lies in social scientists' wish to discover regularities and generalizations about human behaviour. In the case of the fertility transition, this very pervasive tendency has not only affected accounts of *why* fertility declined but also those of *how* it declined. For decades, the conventional view of the fertility transition was that it involved the adoption of 'stopping' behaviour, whereby couples used birth control methods to prevent further children being born once they had achieved their desired family size. Not before time, this view has come under ferocious assault during the part few years. Simon Szreter and Eilidh Garrett, for example, have argued eloquently that the evolution of English fertility over many centuries should be seen as the outcome of a changing mix of strategies adopted by couples.[46] In the nineteenth century, and especially the late nineteenth century, the spacing of births became an increasingly important component of this mix. 'Stopping' behaviour, on the other hand, only started to be significant well

---

[44] See, for example, H. Leibenstein, 'The Economic Theory of Fertility Decline', *Quarterly Journal of Economics* LXXXIX (1974), pp. 1–31.

[45] The key reference here is J. Gillis, L.A. Tilly and D. Levine (eds), *The European Experience of Declining Fertility, 1850–1950: the Quiet Revolution* (Oxford, Blackwell, 1992).

[46] S. Szreter and E.M. Garrett, 'Reproduction, Compositional Demography and Economic Growth: Family Planning in England Long Before the Fertility Decline', *Population and Development Review* XXVI, pp. 45–80.

into the twentieth century. Szreter and Garrett are probably correct to emphasize the importance of spacing behaviour, even though their argument relies heavily on analysis of the 1911 Census of Fertility, and, as Michael Anderson has shown, methods of analysis designed to uncover birth spacing from these data will overestimate the extent of spacing if a substantial proportion of couples choose to have no children at all, or only one child.[47]

13.9 Fertility trends from 1900 to 1940

The last two or three decades of the nineteenth century saw social and occupational differentials in English fertility widen, as the decline in fertility took place at different times among different groups. The first three decades of the twentieth century saw some, but not all, of the differentials contract again as the 'lagging' groups caught up with the rest. As early as 1938, David Glass was able to chart the decline in the average number of children born between 1911 and the 1930s, and a decline in the already fairly modest geographical differentials meant that by 1930 almost all of England was in the unprecedented position of not producing enough children even to replace the parental generation.[48] Even the First World War, which produced a temporary reduction in the number of births, followed by a surge after demobilization, did not have an impact on the downward trend (Figure 13.1).

Within this overall decline, however, there were subtle variations among sub-groups of the population. Table 13.4 compares fertility among three social groups: the middle classes, the 'artisan and skilled working classes', and the 'unskilled working class' using data relating to marriages in the first decade of the twentieth century (from the 1911 census) and data from a much smaller study of marriages between 1917 and 1930, carried out by 'mass observation'. The direct comparison is complicated by the different marriage durations involved, but it does seem that during the early twentieth century the fertility of the middle-class women and the skilled working-class women declined, whereas the unskilled working classes saw rather little change. The very low fertility of the middle-class women in the mass observation data probably stems from their being located mainly in prosperous boroughs of London, where fertility was, even by the standards of the 1930s, abnormally low.

The low fertility of the 1930s is not accounted for by delayed marriage or non-marriage. It was produced by the same force that had been responsible for the decline in fertility since the middle of the nineteenth century: the adoption by married couples of fertility control. The level of control

---

[47]   Anderson, 'Highly Restricted Fertility'.
[48]   D.V. Glass, 'Changes in Fertility in England and Wales, 1851–1931', in L. Hogben (ed.), *Political Arithmetic: a Symposium of Population Studies* (London, Allen and Unwin, 1938), pp. 161–212.

Table 13.4 Mean number of births by various durations of marriage: marriage cohorts of 1901–11 and 1917–30 compared

Social class	Marriage cohort of 1906–11 after 2.5 years of marriage	Marriage cohort of 1901–06 after 7.5 years of marriage	Marriage cohort of 1917–30 after 5 years of marriage	Marriage cohort of 1917–30 after 10 years of marriage
Middle class	0.81–0.95	1.78–2.22	0.66	0.93
Artisan and skilled working class	0.82–1.11	1.86–2.39	1.19	1.68
Unskilled working class	1.04–1.28	1.89–2.96	1.60	2.45

Note: All data relate only to women married at ages 20–29 years. The 1911 census data are given as the range of means of various sub-groups within each broad social class grouping. The data for the 1917–30 marriage cohorts are simple means for women in each social class. Sources. Marriage cohorts of 1901–06 and 1906–11: E.M. Garrett, A. Reid, K. Schürer and S. Szreter, *Changing Family Size in England and Wales: Place, Class and Demography 1891–1911* (Cambridge, Cambridge University Press, 2001), pp. 276–7. Marriage cohorts of 1917–30: mass observation data from the 1945 study *Britain and her Birth Rate*. The Mass Observation data are described fully in B. Eckstein, 'British Marital Fertility in the 1930s' unpublished PhD thesis, University of Southampton, 2002.

exercised was such that a large proportion of couples marrying between the wars remained childless, or had only one child. For example, among the 1925 marriage cohort, 17 per cent had no children, and 25 per cent only one child.[49] One-child families were as common as two-child families.

It was said that fertility during the early 1930s was such that the population was failing to replace itself. This was true, but only for a few years. The nadir was attained in 1933, when the total fertility rate was 1.72 and the net reproduction rate 0.74.[50] If that level of fertility had been maintained for a whole generation, then it would have meant population decline and, indeed, alarming forecasts that the population of England and Wales would shrink to below 30 million (and even to below 20 million) by the beginning of the twenty-first century were produced.[51] However, such low levels were short-lived, and on the eve of the Second World War, fertility had already begun to rise again.

[49] D.V. Glass and E. Grebenik, *The Trend and Pattern of Fertility in Great Britain: a Report on the Family Census of 1946. Papers of the Royal Commission on Population, Volume VI* (London, Her Majesty's Stationery Office, 1954) p. 87.

[50] D. Coleman and J. Salt, *The British Population: Patterns, Trends and Processes* (Oxford, Oxford University Press, 1992), p. 115.

[51] See, for example, Political and Economic Planning, *Population Policy in Great Britain: a report by PEP* (London, Political and Economic Planning, 1948), p. 56.

13.10 Why was English fertility between the wars so low?

How did such a large proportion of couples between the wars manage to restrict their fertility to one child, or even no children at all? And why did they wish to do this? Let us consider the *how* first. We are apt to forget that the English fertility decline to levels below replacement was achieved entirely without modern methods of contraception, using, for the most part, *coitus interruptus* and (probably) extended periods of abstinence from sexual intercourse, though condoms were more widely used after the First World War.

Both *coitus interruptus* and the condom are male methods rather than female methods, and therefore men's views on fertility regulation were vital. Oral history evidence gathered by Kate Fisher about attitudes towards sex and contraception among a sample of working-class couples from South Wales and the Oxford area who were married during the 1930s reveals that decisions about when to use birth control and what methods to use were largely (in many cases almost entirely) made by the husbands.[52] It seems, moreover, that women were happy to have these decisions made by their husbands: 'women successfully engineered a situation in which they abnegated responsibility for birth control and achieved their aim of remaining detached from sexual issues'.[53]

Not only was the range of methods of birth control available very limited, but access to advice about birth control was also difficult to obtain prior to 1930, when local authorities became legally able to offer it. Even then, the provision of publicly funded clinics depended on the attitudes of local Medical Officers of Health, and individuals or small groups of people who held positions of power (for example, a group of Roman Catholics on Cardiff City Council) were able to retard their introduction.[54]

The question of *why* English fertility during the 1920s and 1930s was so low is an important one, with repercussions for our understanding of fertility outside the inter-war period. 'Highly restricted fertility' – or fewer than two children – was not a new phenomenon.[55] The idea of having very small families had grown up at the end of the nineteenth century, encouraged by the separation of marriage and childbearing – or, in other words, the growth of a belief that it was acceptable to live a fulfilled married life without children. If the idea was present, what seems to have happened in the 1920s and 1930s was an increasing tendency for couples to operationalize it. David Coleman and John Salt are probably correct to cite the economic depression

---

[52] See K. Fisher, '"She Was Quite Satisfied with the Arrangements I Made": Gender and Birth Control in Britain 1920–1950' *Past and Present* CLXIX (2000), pp. 161–93.
[53] Ibid., p. 189.
[54] K. Fisher, '"Clearing Up Misconceptions": the Campaign to Set Up Birth Control Clinics in South Wales between the Wars', *Welsh History Review* XIX (1998), pp. 103–29.
[55] See Anderson, 'Highly Restricted Fertility'.

and high unemployment as one reason for this, but other factors may also have been at work.[56] A recent study by Briony Eckstein suggests that access to housing was a problem facing many young married couples, and that this discouraged childbearing early in marriage.[57] The problem of obtaining suitable housing was compounded by changing norms with respect to standards of domestic cleanliness and order. A more 'house proud' society was finding it increasingly difficult to obtain houses to be proud of. This suggestion is still tentative, and there remains much work to be done before contemporary demographers can claim to understand why their grandparents' generation was so reluctant to have children.

13.11 Conclusion

The English fertility decline looks set to be the focus of challenges to almost all the conventional ideas of the fertility transition. The old view that the fertility transition involved the adoption of family limitation expressed as 'stopping' behaviour sits very uneasily with what recent research has revealed about family-building practices among English couples marrying during the late nineteenth and early twentieth centuries. Indeed, Kate Fisher has even argued that England's married couples somehow managed to reduce their fertility to a level below replacement without seeming to have any conscious strategy at all, and without fulfilling any of Ansley Coale's three preconditions.[58] For even in the 1930s, when fertility reached its interwar nadir, 'contraceptive behaviour [was] ill-thought out, barely discussed, [and] haphazard', yet this messy, unfocused approach was enough to achieve below-replacement fertility.[59]

There is an understandable tendency among social scientists to try to explain big social changes (and the fertility transition was certainly that) by invoking 'big' theories. But it now seems clear that no single general account of the decline of fertility is likely to be found. Monocausal explanations in terms of the changing demand for children or fundamental ideational shifts are not going to be enough. Therefore, perhaps the most important conclusion of this chapter is that the English fertility decline stubbornly refuses to be characterized simply in social scientific terms. It will not fit any of the conventional models beloved of demographers. The interaction of ideational changes and economic and sociological factors was contingent on the particular circumstances facing often quite small groups of people, and this generated many different stories of fertility decline.

---

[56] Coleman and Salt, *British Population*, p. 115.
[57] Eckstein, 'British Marital Fertility in the 1930s', unpublished PhD thesis, University of Southampton, 2002.
[58] K. Fisher, 'Uncertain Aims and Tacit Negotiation: Birth Control Practices in Britain, 1925–50', *Population and Development Review* XXVI (2000), 295–317.
[59] Ibid., p. 313.

|14|

Migration patterns, 1800–1950

14.1 Introduction

This chapter describes migration patterns during the nineteenth and early twentieth centuries. The rise in England's population during the demographic transition was accompanied by a surge of emigration, mainly to North America but also to other colonies such as Australia and New Zealand. Section 14.2 describes the main trends and patterns in this exodus of Englishmen and women, examining the numbers involved, the main origins within England and destinations in the rest of the world, and the characteristics of the migrants. The majority of the out-migrants went voluntarily, and organized and paid for their own voyages. However, there was a range of schemes to assist the poor to seek a better life overseas. Some of these were funded by local authorities in England, which saw in them an opportunity to remove long-term dependants from the list of poor-relief recipients. Others were funded from abroad, in an effort to encourage certain groups of workers to make the journey. They are considered further in Section 14.3.

The nineteenth century also witnessed a great net movement of people within England from the countryside to the towns. Before 1850, most of England's inhabitants lived in the countryside; after 1850 most lived in urban areas. Section 14.4 examines the process of urbanization. Rural–urban migration was, however, only one form of internal migration, and not the most prevalent, and Section 14.5 discusses other types of mobility within rural England. Section 14.6 tries to account for the internal migration patterns, and suggests that some conventional explanations, especially those couched in terms of real wage differentials, tend to abstract from and hence to conceal important aspects of the *process* by which people made decisions to move, and then acted upon them.

14.2 International migration during the demographic transition

According to Kingsley Davis, emigration was one of several possible responses a population could make to the threat of increasing pressure on resources caused by population growth.[1] During the eighteenth century, it seems likely that emigration from England had fallen rather below the levels reported in the seventeenth century, but after 1815 it picked up.[2] According to Dudley Baines, there were 'probably more than 500,000 net English emigrants between 1815 and 1850'.[3] After 1850 there was another rise in the number of people leaving, with about 1.2 million English men and women leaving to seek a life overseas. If these figures are correct then, as Baines points out: 'there may have been as many English . . . emigrants in the two decades of the 1850s and 1860s as in the whole of the seventeenth and eighteenth centuries'.[4] Emigration continued to increase during the second half of the nineteenth century, so that by the early 1890s it was running at close to 200,000 persons per year. After a brief dip in the late 1890s it surged again, so that the first few years of the twentieth century saw the fastest rate of departure of all, with 315,000 leaving in 1912 alone, a rate of 8.7 per thousand of the population.[5]

More than half of the emigrants went to the United States. The remainder went to 'British North America' (what is now Canada), Australia and New Zealand (about 20 per cent), other British colonies and continental Europe. Of those arriving in the United States, about 80 per cent landed at New York, with 5–10 per cent heading for each of Boston and Philadelphia, and smaller numbers to Baltimore and New Orleans.[6] Taken together, these sets of figures imply that more than two out of every five persons who left England during the nineteenth century next set foot on land at New York City.

Of course, this outflow was, to some extent, counterbalanced by immigration, and not all those who left remained overseas permanently. The proportion of those who left who ultimately returned was small before the mid-nineteenth century, but rose appreciably after the 1860s, so that probably only about half of the 4.7 million people who left England and Wales between 1853 and 1900 were permanent migrants.[7] The most substantial immigration flow during the nineteenth century was from Ireland, but it was insufficient to offset the numbers departing, so that every decade from 1841–50 to 1921–30 was one of net emigration (Table 14.1). The numbers

[1] See K. Davis, 'The Theory of Change and Response in Demographic History', *Population Index* XXIX (1963), pp. 345–66.
[2] E.A. Wrigley and R.S. Schofield, *The Population History of England, 1541–1871: a Reconstruction* (London, Edward Arnold, 1981), pp. 531–4. Net emigration from England during the eighteenth century was about 519,000 persons (though this estimate is inevitably imprecise).
[3] D. Baines, *Migration in a Mature Economy: Emigration and Internal Migration in England and Wales, 1861–1900* (Cambridge, Cambridge University Press, 1985), p. 58.
[4] Ibid., p. 58.
[5] Ibid., p. 59.
[6] C.J. Erickson, 'Emigration from the British Isles to the USA in 1841: Part I. Emigration', *Population Studies* XLIII (1989), p. 354.
[7] On return migration, see Baines, *Migration in a Mature Economy*, pp. 126–40.

seem large: 600,000 in the 1880s and more than 500,000 in each of the first two decades of the twentieth century, but if emigration was a kind of response to the rapid rate of natural population growth, it was only absorbing a small proportion of the difference between birth and death rates (Table 14.1). Overall, during the second half of the nineteenth century, only about 9 per cent of the natural increase was released through net emigration.

Table 14.1 Net migration: England and Wales, 1841–1930

Decade	Net migration (thousands)	Percentage of natural increase
1841–50	–81	3.7
1851–60	–327	12.8
1861–70	–206	7.2
1871–80	–164	4.7
1881–90	–601	16.5
1891–1900	–69	1.9
1901–10	–501	12.4
1911–20	–620	21.3
1921–30	–172	7.2

Note: Net migration figures are negative, as they are calculated as immigrants minus emigrants.
Source: D. Baines, *Migration in a Mature Economy: Emigration and Internal Migration in England and Wales, 1861–1900* (Cambridge, Cambridge University Press, 1985), p. 61.

If nineteenth-century emigration was largely a 'safety valve', then we might have expected to it be concentrated among the poor. Yet, at least until the mid-nineteenth century – at the time when the economic conditions in England were most likely to have been affected to some degree by rapid population growth – the evidence suggests that the migrants were not drawn from the poorest sections of society. Charlotte Erickson's study of the characteristics of migrants to the United States in 1841 has revealed that migrants were, as might have been expected, drawn disproportionately from the age group 20–39 years, whereas those aged 50 or more were seriously under-represented.[8] However, the sections of the English population that were suffering most from overpopulation in the regions where they lived, the agricultural workers of southern England, were also under-represented, whereas non-agricultural labourers and those in 'industry' formed more than their 'fair' share of emigrants (at least relative to the occupational structure of the 1841 census).[9] Nor were declining crafts conspicuously well represented. On the other hand, a feature of the emigration in the first half

---

[8]   C.J. Erickson, 'Emigration from the British Isles to the USA in 1841: Part II. Who Were the English Emigrants?', *Population Studies* XLIV (1990), p. 23.
[9]   Ibid., p. 25.

of the nineteenth century was the large proportion of family groups. For example, it has been estimated that about 70 per cent of English emigrants in 1841 left with their families, a figure much higher than that in the late eighteenth century, or for the second half of the nineteenth century. It seems, therefore, that the emigrants, at least prior to 1850, were not primarily drawn from the poorer sections of society, and chiefly comprised people from the middling ranks who wished to improve their chances of prosperity and to fulfil the ambition of owning land. As Erickson concludes:

> the English had as much choice as regards destination, if not more, as did people in other parts of the United Kingdom and Europe. They could obtain assistance or cheaper passages if they had chosen to go to parts of the Empire. Yet those who emigrated went mainly to the U.S.A., probably because the opportunity to secure freehold title to land, even if they arrived with little or no capital, was greater there . . . than anywhere else.[10]

After 1850, however, the characteristics of the migrant flows changed. During the second half of the nineteenth century a much greater proportion of the emigrants came from the worst-paid occupations. Dudley Baines argues that the declining cost of – and reduced time taken by – ships travelling from England to North America might have contributed to this, though he also suggests that the idea of emigration might have diffused down the social hierarchy.[11] However, the idea that this marked the appearance of emigration as a safety valve is hard to sustain in the light of Baines' evidence about the regional distribution of those who emigrated. For he found that geographical and temporal variations in conventional 'economic' variables like wages, the percentage of the population that was urban or the percentage in agriculture, could not explain differentials in emigration rates.[12] It is more likely, he suggests, that

> the answer to the question why more people went from some counties than others was partly because there were special circumstances in particular villages and (parts of) towns and partly because the quality of hard information about emigration was very varied.[13]

Some sources of local-level variation are considered in the next section.

As has been said, the large amount of net emigration should not be allowed to hide the fact that there was a substantial amount of immigration to England during the nineteenth and early twentieth centuries. The vast majority of immigrants came from Ireland, and a large proportion of these

[10] Ibid., p. 40.
[11] Baines, *Migration in a Mature Economy*, pp. 77–80.
[12] Ibid., p. 172–7.
[13] Ibid., p. 176.

came in a single surge in the aftermath of the Irish potato famine of the 1840s, settling principally in the towns and cities of the north-west of England and in London.[14] Many of the Irish immigrants to England typically lived in crowded and insanitary conditions, and often had poorly paid, casual employment.[15] One reason for this was that the passage across the Irish Sea to England was very cheap compared with the passage across the Atlantic. Among those fleeing the famine, therefore, those who could afford to bought a ticket to North America, leaving those who could not to settle in England. Not all the Irish immigrants were, however, confined to the poorer sections of major cities. In some smaller towns, such as Stafford, where there had been a tradition of Irish immigration, the assimilation of Irish migrants into English society was much easier and more thorough. The dominance of the Irish among the immigrant population was such that in the early twentieth century they numbered more than all the rest put together. Apart from the Irish, Germans were most numerous before 1891, but they were then overtaken by Polish and Russian Jews.

14.3 Assisted and voluntary emigration

We have cited Erickson's conclusion that emigration to the United States principally consisted of 'economic migrants' anxious to improve their lot. The vast majority of these people funded their own costs. Migrants to other destinations, however (especially the British colonies), were able to benefit from a range of schemes offering financial assistance, which burgeoned during the second half of the nineteenth century. Some of these schemes were aimed at removing the poor from the relief rolls of English communities; others were organized from the colonies by those anxious to attract labour.

Some of the earliest attempts to assist emigration followed the introduction of the New Poor Law (NPL) in 1834. For example, in 1836, 3069 poor people from Norfolk were assisted to emigrate to North America.[16] The NPL replaced the Poor Law against which Malthus had railed (see Chapter 6). Its cornerstone was that poor relief was only to be given to able-bodied persons in workhouses. The parish authorities reasoned, probably correctly, that the workhouse test could potentially result in increased expenditure, especially if whole families had to be accommodated in the workhouses. Consequently, they made use of the provision in the NPL to assist emigration, particularly of whole families, and most notably of families with young

---

14   On the experiences of the Irish migrants, see, for example, L.H. Lees, *Exiles of Erin: Irish Migrants in Victorian London* (Manchester, Manchester University Press, 1979); and D.M. MacRaild, *Irish Migrants in Modern Britain, 1750–1922* (Basingstoke, Macmillan, 1999).
15   Studies of the Irish population of specific localities include J. Farrell, 'The Irish in Hammersmith and Fulham in 1851', *Local Historian* XXIX (1999), pp. 66–75.
16   G. Howells, 'Emigration and the New Poor Law: the Norfolk Emigration Fever of 1836', *Rural History* XI (2000), p. 145.

children. These pauper emigrants, however, were not just pushed out, but typically left after a process of negotiation with local Poor Law authorities, occasionally laced with a threat that unless they were assisted to emigrate, they would continue to burden the rate payers of their native parishes for years to come.[17]

Although there was a risk that assisted emigration would be selective of the most ambitious and energetic members of the labouring classes, those responsible for administering poor relief believed that, provided the labour supply could be reduced so that it balanced the available work, unemployment would be reduced, to the general benefit of the community: '[t]hus it did not matter who left, as long as some people left'.[18] Indeed, there is some evidence that, contrary to a widely held belief, assisted emigrants were not drawn from the poorest and least able members of society.[19] Assisted emigration continued well into the twentieth century. For example, several thousand pauper children and orphans were helped to travel to Canada between 1870 and 1928 by the Poor Law authorities, and various religious and charitable organizations.[20]

Perhaps the key point to emerge from this discussion in this and the preceding section is that emigration from nineteenth-century England cannot be understood simply (or even mainly) as a matter of people being pushed out by poverty. It has been well known for many years that a 'friends and relatives' effect operates to encourage the migration of those familiar to previous migrants, a process often termed chain migration. A recent study of the parish of Melbourn, Cambridgeshire, shows that it also worked in origin communities to influence emigration patterns.[21] The whole process by which migration was instigated, and by which decisions were made, needs to be analysed in context. For example, in the case of assisted migration, the energy and enthusiasm of the person charged with recruiting potential emigrants was a significant factor.

14.4 Urbanization

Until fairly recently, the analysis of internal migration has been primarily conducted at the aggregate level, and has adopted one of two major approaches. The first uses place of birth data from the published census

---

[17] G. Howells, '"For I Was Tired of England Sir": English Pauper Emigrant Strategies, 1834–60', *Social History* XXIII (1998), pp. 181–94.

[18] Howells, 'Emigration', p. 160.

[19] See R. Haines, M. Kleinig, D. Oxley and E. Richards, 'Migration and Opportunity: an Antipodean Perspective', *International Review of Social History* XLIII (1998), pp. 235–63.

[20] P. Horn, 'The Emigration of Pauper Children to Canada 1870–1914', *Genealogists' Magazine* XXV (1997), pp. 393–9.

[21] P. Hudson and D. Mills, 'English Emigration, Kinship and the Recruitment Process: Migration from Melbourn in Cambridgeshire to Melbourne in Victoria in the Mid-Nineteenth Century', *Rural History* X (1999), pp. 55–74.

reports to identify the magnitude and direction of lifetime migration streams; the second estimates net migration for specific areas (usually either the 50 counties or the 600 or so registration districts) using the demographic accounting equation (see Box 14.1).[22] This line of research is responsible for much of the received wisdom about internal migration in nineteenth-century England. Rural areas were losing population through migration for much of the century, but the rate of depopulation accelerated after 1851. By contrast, urban areas in general were gaining. There were differences within rural and urban areas in the rate of loss and gain. In particular, rural areas in southern England were experiencing a slightly greater loss, relative both to their population and to the rate of natural increase, than were rural areas in the north.[23] Industrial towns in the north of England and old established towns throughout the country were not gaining anywhere nearly as much as London, certain port towns and the residential towns of the south.[24]

Box 14.1 Estimating net migration using the demographic accounting equation (2)

The demographic accounting equation says that the change in the population of any place between two dates is accounted for by births, deaths, in-migration and out-migration. For example, if the population of a place at two successive censuses is known, then

population   population
at second   =   at first   + births − deaths + in-migrants − out-migrants
census   census

The difference between births and deaths is known as *natural increase*, and the difference between in-migrants and out-migrants is *net migration*. If the numbers of births and deaths in the place are also known (from ecclesiastical or civil registration data) then net migra-

---

[22] Important specific works include J. Saville, *Rural Depopulation in England and Wales, 1851–1951* (London, Routledge and Kegan Paul, 1957); Baines, *Migration in a Mature Economy*; D. Friedlander and R. Roshier, 'A Study of Internal Migration in England and Wales', *Population Studies* XIX (1966), pp. 239–79; R. Lawton, 'Population Changes in England and Wales in the Later Nineteenth Century: an Analysis of Trends by Registration Districts', *Transactions of the Institute of British Geographers* XLIV (1968), pp. 55–74; and C.T. Smith, 'The Movement of Population in England and Wales in 1851 and 1861', *Geographical Journal* CXVII (1951), pp. 200–10. Many studies of this type are reviewed in G.R. Boyer and T.J. Hatton, 'Migration and Labour Market Integration in Late Nineteenth-Century England and Wales', *Economic History Review*, 2nd series L (1997), pp. 697–734, and interested readers are referred to their excellent bibliography.

[23] Boyer and Hatton, 'Migration and Labour Market Integration', p. 705.

[24] Lawton, 'Population Changes', p. 70. Indeed, Lawton's results indicate that the industrial towns and several old established towns actually lost population through net migration over the period 1841–1911.

tion may be estimated indirectly as the difference between the observed population change and the observed natural increase. The procedure may be applied at the national level, or at the local level, provided the population data and the births and deaths data all relate to the same geographical area.

For example, the resident population of the Wiltshire parish of Berwick St James in 1851 was 284, whereas in 1861 it was 248. During the intervening decade there were 82 recorded births and 50 deaths. The population change was therefore 284 - 248 = -36 and the natural increase was 82 - 50 = 32. Net migration was therefore -36 - 32 = -68; that is, there were 68 more out-migrants than in-migrants. (For further details of this analysis, see P.R.A. Hinde, 'The Population of a Wiltshire Village in the Nineteenth Century: a Reconstitution Study of Berwick St James, 1841–71', *Annals of Human Biology* XIV (1987), pp. 475–85.)

Important though net migration was, it did not dominate population change in most areas (Table 14.2). Even the large towns grew much more between 1841 and 1911 by natural increase than by net in-migration. In urban areas as a whole, net migration was only responsible for one-sixth of the overall population increase. The impact of net migration was, arguably, greatest on the population of the countryside, where it almost counterbalanced the natural increase.

Table 14.2 Population change in England and Wales, 1841–1911, by type of district (all figures in millions)

Type of district	Population		Natural increase 1841–1911	Net migration 1841–1911
	1841	1911		
All towns	8.7	23.8	12.7	2.6
London	2.3	7.3	3.8	1.3
Other large towns	1.5	5.2	2.7	0.9
Industrial centres	0.9	2.5	1.8	–0.2
Residential towns	0.9	2.3	0.9	0.5
Colliery districts	1.3	5.3	3.4	0.7
Rural areas	6.2	7.0	5.3	–4.5

Source: R. Lawton, 'Population Changes in England and Wales in the Later Nineteenth Century: an Analysis of Trends by Registration Districts', *Transactions of the Institute of British Geographers* XLIV (1968), pp. 55–74.

Migration to the cities tended to be a step-by-step process, people moving from remoter rural areas to less remote parts closer to the principal urban areas to take the place of the inhabitants of those less remote parts that had moved into the cities.[25] Thus it was thought that individual moves tended to be short, and people who ultimately moved long distances tended to achieve these long moves by a series of shorter moves in the same general direction. Finally, most migration tended to involve young people, especially those in the age groups 15–29 years. Local studies using the census enumerators' books in conjunction with other sources to analyse population turnover (see Appendix III) have confirmed that out-migration from rural England was characteristic of young people. They have also shown that a very large proportion of those native to English villages, especially in southern England, had left by the time they were 25 years of age.[26]

Of course, a change of residence between two time points may hide a great many moves. Moreover, it is possible that a person whose residence appears not to have changed may have moved away and back again. It has long been believed that many, probably a majority, of actual moves are thus concealed from the historian's view by reliance on census and registration data to measure net migration at the regional level or population turnover at the local level. In recent years, an effort has been made to obtain data relating to actual 'moves'. The best-known study of this type has been carried out by Colin Pooley and Jean Turnbull.[27] They obtained a sample of over 16,000 residential histories from family historians, and used these to chart the often complex paths traced across England by individual men and women. Their results confirm the suspicion that a large number of short-distance moves are missed by conventional forms of analysis. More than half of all moves were over distances under ten kilometres, and after 1840 more than two in five were of distances under one kilometre, the majority of which were clearly within the same settlement (Table 14.3). Only about one in ten moves were of over 100 km, and the destination of many of these was London.[28] The trend towards urbanization is evident in their data, with a larger proportion of moves being 'up' the urban hierarchy (to a larger place) than in the opposite direction.

---

25 Boyer and Hatton, 'Migration and Labour Market Integration', pp. 703–4.

26 For example, in the Wiltshire village of Berwick St James, almost all the females, and three-quarters of the males born between 1841 and 1851 had left the parish by the time they were aged 25 years; see P.R.A. Hinde, 'The Population of a Wiltshire village in the Nineteenth Century: a Reconstitution Study of Berwick St James, 1841–71', *Annals of Human Biology* XIV (1987), pp. 481–2.

27 See C.G. Pooley and J. Turnbull, 'Migration Trends in British Rural Areas from the 18th to the 20th Centuries', *International Journal of Population Geography* II (1996), pp. 215–37; C.G. Pooley and J. Turnbull, 'Migration and Mobility in Britain from the Eighteenth to the Twentieth Centuries', *Local Population Studies* LVII (1996), pp. 50–71; and C.G. Pooley and J. Turnbull, *Migration and Mobility in Britain since the Eighteenth Century* (London, UCL Press, 1998).

28 Pooley and Turnbull, 'Migration Trends' pp. 234–5.

Table 14.3 Internal migration patterns in England, 1750–1919

	1750–1839	1840–1879	1880–1919
Percentage of moves by distance moved			
Under 1 km	24.5	40.5	43.7
1–10 km	28.8	22.6	19.7
10–50 km	27.7	19.3	16.5
50–100 km	8.6	7.2	7.7
More than 100 km	10.4	10.5	12.4
Mean distance moved (km)	37.7	33.7	38.4
Percentage of moves			
Within same settlement	27.5	45.1	47.9
To new settlement in same size category	49.8	25.9	16.9
To settlement in larger size category	13.8	16.3	17.8
To settlement in smaller size category	8.9	12.6	17.4

Notes: The following population size categories were used: under 5,000; 5,000–9,999;
10,000–19,999; 20,000–39,999; 40,000–59,999; 60,000–79,999; 80,000–99,999; 100,000
and over. Settlement sizes were determined in 1801, 1851 and 1891 for the three periods.
Source: C. Pooley and J. Turnbull, 'Migration and Mobility in Britain from the Eighteenth to
the Twentieth Centuries', *Local Population Studies* LVII (1996), pp. 55, 63.

Just as emigration was assisted under the New Poor Law, migration
from the overpopulated countryside of southern England to the manufacturing towns and cities in the north was supported. However, it was
limited in extent, possibly because the experiences of those who moved
were by no means all favourable. A minority of migrants did prosper and
settle permanently in the north, but many were struck down by smallpox
upon arrival in the cities, or suffered discrimination by mill owners and
employers.[29]

14.5 Internal migration within the countryside

Although rural–urban migration remains the paradigmatic type of internal migration taking place in nineteenth-century England, it should not
be allowed to obscure the enormous amount of local-level movement that
took place within rural areas, at least during the second half of the century. English villages of the Victorian era were far from being static communities; indeed, English villages probably had never been static.

---

[29] V. Worship, 'Cotton Factory or Workhouse? Poor Law Assisted Migration from
Buckinghamshire to Northern England, 1835–1837', *Family and Community History* IV
(2000), pp. 33–48.

Virtually all local studies reveal a great deal of short-distance, circulatory migration within the countryside, which increased in volume as the century progressed.[30] Most of the movement observed by Pooley and Turnbull did not involve movement to or from a town (Table 14.3). Moreover, the majority of moves in all three periods were either within the same settlement or to another settlement of roughly the same size (that is, they did not involve movement from a 'rural' to an 'urban' area).[31] Between 1750 and 1839 nearly half of all moves were to another settlement of the same size. Since England was predominantly rural during this period, most of these moves represented circulatory movement within the countryside. As we pointed out earlier, urbanization, according to this analysis, is measured by the difference between the proportion of moves 'up' the urban hierarchy (to a larger settlement) and moves 'down' the urban hierarchy (to a smaller settlement). Prior to 1879, this difference is positive, implying population concentration, but in the context of all moves, the moves giving rise to urbanization were a relatively small proportion. After 1880, it is not clear that migration was responsible for urbanization at all.

It is sometimes argued that migration within the countryside was at a lower rate during the late eighteenth and early nineteenth centuries than in earlier or later periods. There is rather little direct evidence to back up this argument, though a very few extant studies of population turnover in the late eighteenth and early nineteenth centuries do show relatively low rates. On the basis of a large number of studies, M. Kitch has reckoned that there was an annual turnover in village populations of 4–6 per cent between the sixteenth and the nineteenth centuries.[32] A study of Swinderby in Lincolnshire between 1771 and 1791 produced a figure of 3.8 per cent, which is rather lower than Kitch's range but not conspicuously so.[33] It is also not dissimilar to figures obtained from a variety of villages between

---

[30] See, for example, D.G. Jackson, 'Short-Range Migration and the Parish of Borden, Kent, from the 1851 Census Enumerators' Books', *Local Population Studies Society Newsletter* XXIII, (1998), pp. 3–10; and A. Perkyns, 'Migration and Mobility: Six Kentish Parishes 1851–1881', *Local Population Studies* LXIII (1999), pp. 30–70. Data on the percentages native-born in mid-nineteenth-century rural parishes will be found in D. Mills and K. Schürer, 'Migration and Population Turnover', in D. Mills and K. Schürer (eds) *Local Communities in the Census Enumerator's Books* (Oxford, Leopard's Head Press, 1996) pp. 221, 223. See also N. Goose, *Population, Economy and Family Structure in Hertfordshire in 1851. Volume 1: the Berkhamsted Region* (Hatfield, University of Hertfordshire Press, 1996).

[31] The fact that in the two later periods the proportion of moves within the same settlement was much higher than the corresponding proportion in 1750–1839 probably reflects the fact that there were many larger settlements in the latter two periods.

[32] M. Kitch, 'Population Movement and Migration in Pre-Industrial Rural England', in B.M. Short (ed.), *The English Rural Community: Image and Analysis* (Cambridge, Cambridge University Press, 1992).

[33] R. Tinley and D. Mills, 'Population Turnover in an Eighteenth-Century Lincolnshire Parish in Comparative Context', *Local Population Studies* LII (1994), p. 36.

1851 and 1871.[34] Pooley and Turnbull state, on the basis of their residential history data, that '[t]here is little evidence that the level or nature of mobility changed dramatically in the two centuries after 1750; patterns of mobility show a high degree of stability over time and space'.[35]

Some of these short-distance moves within the countryside were associated with stages in the life course – for example, the movement of young women into domestic service – which remained important throughout the nineteenth century. Others, especially among young men, were prompted by economic opportunities (attracting migrants), or the lack of opportunities (encouraging out-migration). In general, during the second half of the nineteenth century, and especially after 1870, there was a movement out of agriculture into other occupations, and this was frequently associated with short-distance migration.[36]

In Chapter 10 we explained that the Poor Laws and migration were closely related in the early modern period. This relationship extended well into the nineteenth century, but it is complex. Accounts of population change at the parish level often contrast 'open' and 'closed' parishes. So-called 'closed' parishes were those in which one or two powerful landowners and occupiers were able to influence population growth by the simple expedient of limiting the supply of housing. Their motivation for doing this was normally to keep the poor rates low. In 'open' parishes, in contrast, land was in the hands of many small proprietors, and it was rational for any individual proprietor to build (often ramshackle) cottages on his or her small plot of land that he or she could let to labouring families. Of course, the families who took the cottages might become a charge on the parish, but if they did the extra burden would fall on all the rate payers of the parish, not just the proprietor of their cottage. The result of this calculation was that the poor who were excluded from 'closed' parishes crowded into large 'open' parishes.[37]

The main element of the Poor Laws affecting migration were the settlement laws. It is believed, for example, that the slowing down of circulatory migration within the countryside in the late eighteenth and early nineteenth centuries took place in part because changes to the settlement laws made it

---

[34] In village populations in the mid-nineteenth century, it was typical for about half the inhabitants listed in a census not to have been present in the previous census. The data for Swinderby, 1771–91, imply turnover of about this level; see Tinley and Mills, 'Population Turnover', pp. 35–6.

[35] Pooley and Turnbull, 'Migration and Mobility', p. 65.

[36] Perkyns, 'Migration and Mobility'; see also D.G. Jackson, 'The Impact of the Agricultural depression of the Second Half of the Nineteenth Century on the Parish of Borden, Kent', *Local Population Studies Society Newsletter* XXV (1999), pp. 4–8.

[37] There is a large literature on the 'open' and 'closed' parish dichotomy. For a recent critique of the model, and a good bibliography, see D. Spencer, 'Reformulating the "Closed" Parish Thesis: Associations, Interests and Interaction', *Journal of Historical Geography* XXVI, pp. 83–98.

increasingly difficult for people to leave their parishes of birth. However, though most commentators agree that the role of settlement in labour migration was important, there is disagreement over whether the impact of the Law of Settlement on the amount of migration was always negative. For example, B.K. Song has argued that in late eighteenth- and early nineteenth-century Oxfordshire, local policies on pauper settlement and migration were selective, allowing movement that would benefit the local economy by redistributing labour to where it was most needed.[38] The Poor Law was therefore a most important tool by which landlords were able to retain control over labour mobility within groups of parishes in the countryside between 1750 and 1850.[39]

14.6 Conclusion

The rates of both international and internal migration were greater during the nineteenth century than they had been during the preceding period. Ultimately, the explanation for this probably lies in a combination of economic development and the decreased cost of moving. Except in a few selected cases, most of which relate to internal migration out of poverty-stricken regions of the country, migration was not principally caused by people being 'pushed out' of their native parishes. To be sure, at the macro level, it seems clear that migration within England during the demographic transition was primarily economically driven; but the influence of economic factors is probably better seen in a positive light, in which people moved to take advantage of perceived economic opportunity, rather than being forced to move in their desperation to escape poverty. This applies both to emigration and to most internal migration flows.[40] Recent studies of internal migration in the late nineteenth century have highlighted the major determinants of migration flows to be the perceived benefits to be obtained from moving, the costs of the move itself, and the amount of information available about urban employment opportunities.[41] In other words, the overall patterns of internal migration can be explained satisfactorily by the 'human capital' models of migration, which suggest that migration is a function of the difference between perceived economic prospects in potential destination areas and origin areas, adjusted to take into account the costs of the move.

---

[38] B.K. Song, 'Agrarian Policies on Pauper Settlement and Migration, Oxfordshire 1750–1834', *Continuity and Change* XIII (1998), pp. 363–89.

[39] See B.K. Song, 'Landed Interest, Local Government, and the Labour Market in England, 1750–1850', *Economic History Review*, 2nd series LI (1998), pp. 465–88.

[40] Exceptions might include the migration of those in obsolete craft industries, such as hand-loom weaving, in the early nineteenth century.

[41] Perhaps the most thorough of these is G.R. Boyer and T.J. Hatton, 'Migration and Labour Market Integration in Late Nineteenth-Century England and Wales', *Economic History Review*, 2nd series L (1997), pp. 697–734.

At the micro level, however, satisfying accounts of the movement of individuals and groups of people demand a detailed knowledge of local economic and social conditions, as well as of the contexts in which migration decisions were made.[42] Simple models of 'push' factors and 'pull' factors, still less the rather mechanistic human capital model, fail to take into account the contingent nature of people's decisions about whether or not to move.[43] There is a great deal of research yet to be done at the local level to illuminate these issues.

[42] For example, in the northern Pennines, Christine Hallas has shown that migration was an integral part of the population's successful response to poverty, but that its role can only be understood in the context of a local economy characterized by non-agricultural by-employments; see C. Hallas, 'Poverty and Pragmatism in the Northern Uplands of England: the North Yorkshire Pennines c. 1770–1900', *Social History* XXV (2000), pp. 67–84.

[43] Song, 'Agrarian Policies'.

|15|

England's demography since the Second World War

15.1 Introduction

The English demographic transition was effectively over by the Second World War, in that falling fertility had led to population growth rates returning to levels close to zero. The 'classical' model of the demographic transition suggests that once this has happened a population will from then on experience very modest rates of growth overall (under 0.5 per cent per year), though these may vary with time, principally because of fluctuations in fertility.[1] Mortality rates will continue to be low, and will probably decline slowly, as the desire to prolong life creates a natural incentive for human societies to invest in improvements in health.

This is, essentially, what has happened in post-war England. The population has continued to rise (from 41 million in 1950 to 50 million in 2000), but annual growth rates, which were close to 0.5 per cent during the 20 years after the Second World War, have gradually fallen. Section 15.2 describes the evolution of mortality since 1950, emphasizing that the expectation of life has continued to advance. We discuss changes in the age pattern of mortality, and note that two new features have been the slowing of the decline among young adults because of increased numbers of accidental deaths, and the belated appearance of progress among the elderly. Section 15.3 turns to examine fertility trends, revealing that these have fluctuated much more erratically than mortality. However, behind the time series of single-figure indices of fertility lurks a complex story, with important new elements such as the increase in fertility outside marriage. These new elements have been significant enough in the eyes of some demographers to encourage them to talk of a 'second demographic transition', a concept we discuss briefly in Section 15.5. In the meantime, Section 15.4 describes trends in international and internal migration since the Second World War.

---

[1] F.W. Notestein, 'The Population of the World in the Year 2000', *Journal of the American Statistical Association* XLV (1950), pp. 338–40.

This chapter does not claim to be comprehensive, and there are other works in which the material covered here is presented in much more detail.[2] It aims to view recent trends in mortality, fertility and migration in the light of the past experience of the population of England, and to distinguish developments that are genuinely new from those that are continuations of previous patterns.

15.2 Trends in mortality

The history of English mortality since the Second World War has been one of continued improvement. At 1930–32 age-specific death rates, English males could expect to live about 59 years, and females about 63 years (Table 15.1). By 1990–92, the expectation of life at birth for males had increased to 73.4 years and that for females to 79 years. The rate of progress has been somewhat uneven, though. During the 1930s and 1940s the average length of life rose at about 0.4 years per year for both sexes. In the following two decades progress was much slower, especially for males. Indeed during the 1960s the expectation of life at birth for men rose by just 0.09 per year. The result of this was an increase in the difference between male and female mortality (Table 15.1). Since around 1970, the rate at which mortality has been falling has increased slightly, and the rate of progress for males has risen above that for females, leading to a reduction in the sex differential.

The increased longevity has been accompanied by a continued decline of mortality from infectious diseases. By the late twentieth century infections had almost been eliminated as a cause of death among people aged under 60 years, save for a few exceptions within specific sub-groups of the population,

Table 15.1 Expectation of life at birth, 1930–32 to 1990–92

Years	Male	Female	Difference between male and female
1930–32	58.7	62.9	4.2
1950–52	66.4	71.5	5.1
1960–62	68.1	74.0	5.9
1970–72	69.0	75.3	6.3
1980–82	71.0	77.0	6.0
1990–92	73.4	79.0	5.6

Sources: Office of Population Censuses and Surveys, *English Life Tables No. 14* (series DS no. 7) (London, Her Majesty's Stationery Office, 1987), p. 6; Office for National Statistics, *English Life Tables No. 15* (series DS no. 14) (London, The Stationery Office, 1997), p. 7.

[2]   See, for example, D. Coleman and J. Salt, *The British Population: Patterns, Trends and Processes* (Oxford, Oxford University Press, 1992).

the most obvious of which is Acquired Immune Deficiency Syndrome (AIDS).[3] Among the elderly, however, opportunistic chest infections are still the immediate cause of a substantial proportion of deaths. The most common causes of death overall are now heart disease, cancer and cerebro-vascular diseases (in that order). England in the late twentieth century, therefore, was firmly in the final stage of the epidemiological transition, which Omran described as the age of 'degenerative and man-made diseases'.[4]

The figures for the expectation of life quoted in the previous paragraph are artificial, in the sense that they are obtained from age-specific death rates relating to specific periods (for example 1950–52 and 1990–92). Because death rates have been changing over time, no real persons experience these sets of death rates, and the expectations of life given in Table 15.1 are better viewed as a reflection of the 'healthiness' of the population at the relevant dates than as estimates of the average lifetimes of any group of 'real' people (see Box 15.1). If we turn to look at the experiences of specific *birth cohorts* (sets of people born in particular years), then a man born in 1891 could expect to live about 49 years, and a woman born in the same year about 55 years.[5] Among the 1911 birth cohort, the corresponding figures were 54 years and 62 years, and for those born in 1931, 67 and 72 years.[6] For later cohorts, figures must be estimated as many of them have not yet died, but it looks as if men born in the early 1950s can expect to live at least 75 years and women more than 80 years.[7]

Mortality improvements during the second half of the twentieth century varied substantially by age. Table 15.2 shows age-specific death rates at particular ages for males and females, and charts the relative improvement during each decade since 1950. For both sexes the greatest relative improvement has been at the younger ages. At age 20 there is a large disparity between the rate of improvement for males and females, as males' progress was slowed by an increased number of accidental deaths. At age 30 years males' improvement continues to lag behind that of females. Accidents are probably also part of the reason for this, though the slight rise in male mortality at age 30 during the 1980s is probably due to AIDS. Reductions in male mortality at ages 50–70 years have been influenced by mortality from lung cancer. The prevalence of lung cancer among men in England

3   In England, AIDS deaths are still largely confined to certain specific sections of the population, such as homosexual males and intravenous drug users. Other examples might include the increasing incidence of tuberculosis among the very poor, especially those of South Asian origin.
4   A. Omran, 'The Epidemiologic Transition: a Theory of the Epidemiology of Population Change', *Milbank Memorial Fund Quarterly* IL (1971), p. 517.
5   Office for National Statistics, *English Life Tables No. 15* (series DS no. 14) (London, The Stationery Office, 1997), p. 9.
6   Ibid., p. 9.
7   Ibid., p. 9.

Box 15.1 Fertility and mortality by period and cohort

Both the fertility and the mortality experience of a population can be looked at from either a period or a cohort perspective. The *period perspective* uses data for a given period to calculate birth or death rates. Age-specific birth and death rates, therefore, relate to people of different ages in that period. For example, the age-specific death rates (ASDRs) reported in Table 15.2 relate to people of those ages in given three-year periods: 1950–52, 1960–62, and so on. When these ASDRs are used to calculate a summary index of mortality, such as the expectation of life at birth, the resulting index is measuring the mortality experience of a hypothetical person who, at each age, experiences the mortality of persons of that age during the period in question. Similarly, period indices of fertility, such as the total fertility rate (see Box 8.1) represent the fertility experience of hypothetical women. Period indices are useful to identify trends in mortality and fertility that are related to social, economic and technical developments that occur at specific points in time.

The *cohort perspective* examines fertility and mortality by considering the experience of successive generations of real people, born in different periods. Expectations of life and total fertility rates may be calculated using ASDRs and age-specific fertility rates for the cohort, and have the advantage over period indices that they relate to real people. A disadvantage of the cohort perspective, however, is that the data needed to calculate such measures are not available until the cohort has completed the necessary events (which, in the case of ASDRs, may mean over 100 years after its birth), rendering cohort fertility and mortality data inherently out of date.

varies by cohort, increasing steadily among cohorts born during the late nineteenth century, reaching a peak among those born in 1895–1900, and then gradually declining among more recent cohorts. The slow progress in reducing male mortality at ages 60 and 70 between 1950 and the early 1970s reflects the fact that the cohorts who suffered most from lung cancer were then at the ages at which deaths from lung cancer are most common. Once these cohorts had passed through, improvements during the 1980s and 1990s at ages 60 and 70 were more rapid.

At the oldest ages, females' mortality seems to have declined faster than that of males. An important (and new) feature of mortality trends since the Second World War is that more progress has been made in reducing mortality at very advanced ages than during the earlier stages of the mortality transition. Medical technology is now better able to prolong the lives of

Table 15.2 Mortality at specific ages, 1950–52 to 1990–92, and relative improvement

Age	1950–52	1960–62	1970–72	1980–82	1990–92
Age-specific death rates					
Males					
0	0.0326	0.0250	0.0198	0.0127	0.0081
10	0.0005	0.0004	0.0003	0.0002	0.0002
20	0.0013	0.0012	0.0011	0.0009	0.0008
30	0.0016	0.0012	0.0010	0.0009	0.0009
40	0.0029	0.0024	0.0023	0.0018	0.0017
50	0.0085	0.0073	0.0074	0.0062	0.0046
60	0.0237	0.0229	0.0208	0.0184	0.0139
70	0.0565	0.0557	0.0555	0.0470	0.0393
80	0.1363	0.1275	0.1202	0.1133	0.0962
90	0.2926	0.2559	0.2408	0.2269	0.2047
Females					
0	0.0251	0.0190	0.0152	0.0098	0.0063
10	0.0004	0.0002	0.0002	0.0002	0.0001
20	0.0008	0.0004	0.0005	0.0004	0.0003
30	0.0013	0.0008	0.0006	0.0005	0.0004
40	0.0023	0.0018	0.0016	0.0013	0.0011
50	0.0052	0.0044	0.0045	0.0038	0.0029
60	0.0127	0.0109	0.0103	0.0099	0.0083
70	0.0353	0.0310	0.0278	0.0244	0.0219
80	0.1050	0.0911	0.0801	0.0698	0.0596
90	0.2415	0.2213	0.1981	0.1847	0.1555
Trend: 1950–52 = 100					
Males					
0	100	75	61	39	25
10	100	75	65	46	35
20	100	92	82	72	65
30	100	73	62	56	58
40	100	81	78	63	59
50	100	86	87	72	55
60	100	97	88	78	59
70	100	98	98	83	70
80	100	94	88	83	71
90	100	87	82	78	70
Females					
0	100	76	61	39	25
10	100	69	66	51	37
20	100	53	54	42	37
30	100	59	47	41	34
40	100	79	70	56	47
50	100	84	86	72	56
60	100	86	81	78	65
70	100	88	79	69	62
80	100	87	77	67	57
90	100	92	82	76	64

Notes: The age-specific death rates given in this table are probabilities of dying within one year assuming survival to the specific ages. The rates have been rounded to four decimal places, but the trends have been calculated from the original data and therefore may show some small (apparent) inconsistencies with the rates.
Source: adapted from Office for National Statistics, *English Life Tables No. 15* (series DS no. 14) (London, The Stationery Office, 1997), p. 6.

elderly persons suffering from various diseases of old age (such as cancer and some forms of heart disease). One consequence of this decline in old-age mortality has been a rapid increase in the number of people at very advanced ages living in England: during the last few decades, the most rapidly increasing section of the population has been those aged 85 years and over.

15.3 Trends in fertility

The hint of an increase in fertility in the years just before the Second World War was prescient, for fertility did not return to its 1930s levels for three decades. There was a short-lived 'baby boom' immediately after the war, associated with demobilization, and a much more substantial increase in fertility during the late 1950s and early 1960s. Calculated on a period basis (see Box 15.1) the total fertility rate (TFR) rose from around 2.2 in the early 1950s to about 2.9 in the mid-1960s. It then fell sharply (save for a brief hiatus in 1970–71) to a record low of just under 1.7 in 1977. Since then, it has been fairly constant at about 1.8. Looking at the fertility of real birth cohorts, some of the short-term period fluctuations disappear, but the rise in fertility during the 1950s and 1960s remains clear. Women born during the first decade of the twentieth century could expect to bear an average of around 1.8 children, whereas those born in the 1930s had close to the '2.4 children' familiar to the advertisers of breakfast cereals.[8] This level of fertility, though, was not maintained, and subsequent birth cohorts have had fewer children.

Trends in single-figure indices of fertility often mask changes taking place in the distribution of completed family sizes or the age pattern of fertility, and this is certainly true of post-war England. Demographers analyse the distribution of family sizes using what are called parity progression ratios (PPRs), or the proportion of women with a given number of children who go on to have another child. Just as the age-specific fertility rates for a given period can be combined to give the TFR, the PPRs for a given period can be used to work out the proportions of women who would end up with no children, one child, two children, and so on, if the PPRs of that period remained constant for a child-bearing generation (Figure 15.1).[9] The 1950 PPRs suggested that 16 per cent of women would have no children, 27 per cent of women only one child, 28 per cent two children, 13 per cent three children and 16 per cent four or more children. This was a clear continuation of the inter-war pattern (see Chapter 13) in which a large proportion of women had fewer than two children. The rise in fertility between 1950 and the

[8] Coleman and Salt, *British Population*, p. 114.
[9] For more details on parity progression ratios, see A. Hinde, *Demographic Methods* (London, Arnold, 1998), pp. 109–18.

mid-1960s was associated with a dramatic fall in the prevalence of 'highly restricted' fertility (to use Michael Anderson's terminology).[10] The proportion of women having fewer than two children almost halved, and there was an increase in families of three or more children. Since the mid-1960s there has been an increase in the proportion of women having exactly two children. The proportion of women remaining childless or having one child has also risen, but has not returned to inter-war levels. By contrast, the proportion of families of three or more (and especially of four or more) has fallen.

The age pattern of fertility has also changed (Table 15.3), especially since the 1970s. The fertility of women in their twenties, and especially their early twenties, has fallen, whereas that of women in their thirties has risen. A common explanation of this trend cites the increasing tendency of women, including married women, to participate in higher education and then to take paid employment and wish to pursue careers. For such women, postponing childbearing until they are fully qualified and have a secure position in the labour market is clearly economically rational.[11] The average interval between marriage and first birth, which was about 18 months in the 1950s, rose to almost two and a half years in the 1980s.[12]

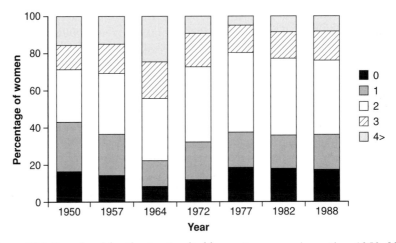

Figure 15.1 Completed family sizes implied by parity progression ratios, 1950–88
Source: J. Hobcraft, 'Fertility in England and Wales: a Fifty Year Perspective', *Population Studies* L (1996), p. 512.

---

[10] M. Anderson, 'Highly Restricted Fertility: Very Small Families in the British Fertility Decline', *Population Studies* LII (1998), pp. 177–99.

[11] As is having two children close together when they do finally start child-bearing: see M. Ní Bhrolcháin, 'The Interpretation and Role of Work-Associated Accelerated Childbearing in Post-War Britain', *European Journal of Population* II (1986), pp. 135–54.

[12] J. Hobcraft, 'Fertility in England and Wales: a Fifty Year Perspective', *Population Studies* L (1996), p. 499.

Table 15.3 Age-specific fertility rates by period, England 1960–94

Age-group	Period 1960–64	1965–69	1970–74	1975–79	1980–84	1985–89	1990–94
15–19	0.040	0.049	0.045	0.030	0.030	0.031	0.033
20–24	0.175	0.165	0.130	0.108	0.095	0.094	0.088
25–29	0.183	0.164	0.135	0.125	0.127	0.125	0.120
30–34	0.105	0.090	0.067	0.065	0.075	0.084	0.087
35–39	0.049	0.040	0.025	0.020	0.024	0.030	0.033
40–44	0.015	0.010	0.007	0.005	0.005	0.005	0.006
TFR	2.84	2.59	2.05	1.77	1.78	1.85	1.84

Note: The total fertility rates (TFRs) are obtained by summing the age-specific fertility rates in each column and multiplying by five (since five-year age groups are used).
Source: Derived from data in Office of Population Censuses and Surveys, *Birth Statistics* (series FM1 no. 13) (London, Her Majesty's Stationery Office, 1987), p. 54; *Population Trends* LX (1990), p. 50; and *Population Trends* LXXXIII (1996), p. 64.

However, viewed in a historical perspective, what might be as important is the dissociation of childbearing from marriage that the twentieth century has produced. For centuries, the timing of marriage and the start of child-bearing were closely related. The fact that marriage determined the start of a woman's childbearing period was the basis of the preventive check. The late nineteenth and early twentieth century saw the emergence of 'birth spacing after marriage', by which newly married couples sought to postpone the onset of child-bearing for a few more years. Thus marriage could now take place without the children necessarily following in short order. During the second half of the twentieth century, the association between marriage and childbearing was broken from the other direction by the increase in fertility before or outside marriage. The proportion of births that were 'extra-marital' had been under 10 per cent throughout the early modern period, and remained at this level until the 1960s. But it then increased to 12 per cent by 1980, 25 per cent by 1988 and over one in three by the 1990s.[13] We return to this issue in Section 15.5.

15.4 Migration patterns

According to David Coleman and John Salt, international migration since the Second World War can be understood by considering three migration systems:

---

[13] Ibid., p. 497.

[t]he first is a 'settlement system' which strongly reflects old colonial ties, and is centred on the Indian subcontinent at present . . ., [t]he second is a 'labour system' which has long been selective in the levels of skill of those involved but is now very much concerned with highly skilled workers often moving between advanced economies. . . . Finally there is a 'refugee system' which involves a small number of troubled countries sending an increasing number of asylum seekers.[14]

The first two of these systems combined during the 1950s when, faced with the need to recruit additional labour, England turned to the 'New Commonwealth' countries of the Indian sub-continent and the Caribbean. During the late 1950s, net inward movement from the West Indies was running at 15,000–30,000 per year, and in 1961 it reached a peak of 66,000.[15] Subsequently immigration from the Caribbean declined, and the Indian sub-continent took up the slack, so much so that by the time of the 1971 census there were twice as many residents from the 'Asian and Oceanic Commonwealth' (618,000) as there were from the Caribbean (302,000).[16] Initially, the majority of migrants from the Indian sub-continent were single men, but as time went on they were joined by their wives and families in a long wave of settlement migration. This continued into the 1970s, when it was temporarily boosted in 1973 by the expulsion of Asians from Uganda.

Despite this large net inflow of migrants from the New Commonwealth and Pakistan, overall net international migration during the 1960s and 1970s was fuelled by the large number of emigrants leaving for Australia, Canada and New Zealand – the so-called countries of the 'Old Commonwealth' – the inverse aspect of Coleman and Salt's 'settlement system'. The net outflow was between 50,000 and 100,000 per year between 1965 and 1970 but gradually reduced so that by the late 1970s the inflow and the outflow were almost in balance. The driving force behind this reduction was a fall in the net emigration to the Old Commonwealth countries, which were responsible for almost the whole of the net difference between immigration and emigration during this period. The contribution of net international migration to overall population growth during the 1960s was to attenuate the amount of growth that would have occurred because of the high fertility of the period. In the 1970s, a combination of net emigration and a slower rate of natural increase led to very low overall growth: only 400,000 people being added to the population of England during the entire decade.

After a brief resumption of net out-migration during the early 1980s, the net balance turned positive from 1983 onwards, and between 1983 and the early 1990s, net international migration continued to be responsible for a

---

[14] Coleman and Salt, *British Population*, p. 435.
[15] Ibid., p. 449. The peak in 1961 arose because of foreknowledge of the impending restrictions on immigration in the 1962 Commonwealth Immigrants Act.
[16] Ibid., p. 452.

substantial part of overall population growth, though its magnitude fluctuated from year to year.[17] About 25 per cent of immigrants and emigrants were travelling to or from the countries of the European Union.[18] With other parts of the world, the inflow and outflow were not in balance: there was a net gain of migrants from the New Commonwealth countries, and a continuing net loss to the traditional destinations of Australia, Canada and New Zealand, though the most popular single destination was still the United States.[19] Increasingly, as restrictions have been placed on immigration from the New Commonwealth countries and Pakistan, the 'labour system' has come to dominate international migration flows, and especially flows to and from other European Union countries. The largest of these flows continues to be that between England and the Irish Republic, though because of the lack of data its precise magnitude is hard to measure. There is no doubt, though, that Irish nationals constitute the largest single group of foreign nationals working in England, comprising probably around 30 per cent.[20]

Historically, England has a long tradition of accepting refugees fleeing from persecution in their home countries. It is in the nature of refugee migration that it occurs in short, often unpredictable, bursts, and since the Second World War England has seen flows from Poland and eastern Europe in the late 1940s, Hungarians in 1956, Czechs in 1968, Ugandan Asians in 1972–73, and the 'boat people' escaping from Vietnam in the 1970s. Alongside these short-lived movements of people facing an emergency, there has been a relatively continuous – but small – flow of 'asylum seekers'. During the 1980s, for example, applications for asylum in the United Kingdom ran at between 3000 and 5000 per year.[21] As a component of overall international migration, the 'refugee system' has, at least until very recently, been much smaller than the other two systems.

Internal migration within England since 1945 is perhaps best understood in four phases. From 1945 to the mid-1960s the dominant flow was, as in the latter part of the inter-war period, from the north of England to the south, and population movement was related to the changing regional distribution of employment prospects. The most important foci of in-migration were new towns such as Harlow and Basildon in Essex, and Crawley in Sussex, and there was a striking correlation between the places with greatest population increase and those with most rapid growth in employment.[22]

---

[17] T. Champion, 'Population Review: (3) Migration To, From and Within the United Kingdom', *Population Trends* LXXXIII (1996), p. 5.

[18] Ibid., p. 6.

[19] Ibid., p. 6.

[20] Coleman and Salt, *British Population*, p. 459.

[21] Ibid., p. 466.

[22] Between 1951 and 1961 the five places experiencing most rapid population growth were, in order, Harlow, Crawley, Basildon, Stevenage and Hemel Hempstead. These same five places, *in the same order*, topped the employment growth table during the same period.

By contrast, those places losing population were also those in which employment was falling, and these were mainly located in Lancashire and Yorkshire. During the early 1960s these two counties continued to experience population loss (though the rate of net out-migration was still greater in Northumberland and Durham) whereas the East Midlands, East Anglia and the whole of the south of England all gained.

The whole of the south of England, that is, except for Greater London. The emergence of population decline in London through net migration marked the onset of the second phase of post-war internal migration, which was characterized by an increasingly urgent exodus of people from England's major cities, superimposed on a continued north–south movement. Between 1961 and 1971 London, Manchester and Liverpool all featured among the ten areas losing population most rapidly, whereas none of them had been in the same category during the previous decade. The 'flight from the cities' was at its most intense in the central areas of these conurbations. For example, net out-migration from inner London gathered pace throughout the 1960s, eventually peaking around 1970 at a rate of almost three per thousand per year, whereas outer London almost held its own.[23] This phenomenon, which has been termed *counterurbanization*, was not new (central London was losing population through net migration at the end of the nineteenth century and during the early decades of the twentieth century as the development of suburban railways allowed Londoners to seek more salubrious accommodation in Essex and areas such as 'Metroland' to the north-west), but it became more widespread than it had been in previous decades.

The counterurbanization of the 1960s and early 1970s, however, was attenuated from the mid-1970s onwards, when a third phase saw the restoration of north–south movement. Net migration from the 'north' (defined as all of northern England plus the West Midlands) to the 'south' increased from barely 10,000 in 1973 to close to 50,000 per year between 1977 and 1982, and around 70,000 in 1985.[24]

The fourth phase witnessed a second change in the balance in favour of counterurbanization, starting in about 1987 and continuing until the late 1990s. The pattern of net population loss was similar to that of the second phase, with the inner areas of major conurbations losing population most rapidly. The central areas of Leeds, Manchester and Newcastle all experienced a net loss of more than ten per thousand during the year 1990–91, for example.[25] However, the distribution of areas experiencing the greatest net

---

[23]   T. Champion and P. Congdon, 'Recent Trends in Greater London's Population', *Population Trends* LIII (1988), p. 8.

[24]   T. Champion, 'Internal Migration and the Spatial Distribution of Population', in H.E. Joshi (ed.), *The Changing Population of Britain* (Oxford, Blackwell, 1989), p. 118. These figures include migration from Scotland and Wales to the 'south' of England.

[25]   Champion, 'Population Review', p. 10.

gain from migration was rather different, with rural areas, and especially peripheral rural areas such as the south-west, being (relatively) the greatest net recipients.

The description in this section has been framed mainly in terms of net migration, which is the difference between in-migration and out-migration. Of course, all areas of England experienced flows in both directions throughout the period, and the absolute numbers of persons moving into an and out of a region were usually both greater than the difference between them. Finally, though the geographical pattern of migration flows has undergone considerable change since the Second World War, some characteristics of internal migration have changed little. It remains the case, as it was during the nineteenth century, that young people are the most prone to change their place of permanent residence. Migration rates are highest among young people in their twenties, and decline rapidly after age 30 years.[26]

15.5 Conclusion: what is new?

The population of England at the turn of the twenty-first century has moved back into a kind of demographic equilibrium, occupying a position in fertility–mortality space close to the zero growth line where it was located throughout most of the period before 1750. Yet it is a different kind of demographic equilibrium to that which prevailed in pre-industrial times. Fertility and mortality are, roughly, in balance, but at levels very different from those that prevailed even as recently as the late nineteenth century. Figure 1.3 reveals that during the last hundred years, the English population has journeyed as far through fertility–mortality space as it did during the eight preceding centuries. The rapid pace of change during the twentieth century means that certain characteristics of the population now have a very different appearance from that at any time in the past. Chief among these is the age composition. In 1901, almost a third of those enumerated in England and Wales were aged under 15 years, and fewer than 5 per cent were aged 65 years and over; in 1991, fewer than one in five were aged under 15, and more than 15 per cent were aged 65 or more.[27] This transformation has, of course, major implications for many aspects of social and economic life, especially the provision of care for the elderly.[28]

It is, however, not the only major new development of the twentieth century. The other has already been mentioned: the dissociation of childbearing and marriage. This change, combined as it is with the increasing fluidity of marital relationships, the surge in the divorce rate and the

[26] Ibid., p. 13.
[27] Coleman and Salt, *British Population*, p. 544.
[28] Ibid., pp. 541–56.

contraceptive revolution of the 1960s, is sufficiently great for some demographers to have labelled it a 'second demographic transition'.[29] According to Dirk van de Kaa, one of the proponents of this idea, the 'second demographic transition' is distinguished from the first by an 'overwhelming preoccupation with self-fulfilment, personal freedom of choice, personal development and lifestyle, and emancipation, as reflected in family-formation, attitudes towards fertility regulation and the motivation for parenthood'.[30] In other words, whereas variations in fertility in previous centuries could be understood in terms of social and economic forces acting on individuals, the greater economic security brought about by economic prosperity has meant that individuals have been set free to make their own decisions about with whom they will live and form partnerships, and how many children they will have – or, indeed, whether they will have children at all.

There is no disputing the *degree* of freedom that English men and women now have to exercise personal preferences of this nature, but a look back over the centuries at the population history of England leads me to be rather sceptical that the 'second demographic transition' heralds a new *kind* of society. For it seems to me that the people of England have always tried to make their own decisions about these matters, but for the majority of the last thousand years their freedom was curtailed by the overwhelming need at the individual level to ensure their own economic welfare, and at the aggregate level to maintain the balance between population and resources. And, apart from a few exceptional periods, they have been remarkably successful in achieving this.

---

[29]   See, for example, D. van de Kaa, 'Europe's Second Demographic Transition', *Population Bulletin* XLII (Population Reference Bureau, Washington, 1987); and R. Lesthaeghe, 'The Second Demographic Transition in Western Countries: an Interpretation', Inter-University Programme in Demography Working Paper 1991–92 (Brussels, Inter-University Programme in Demography, 1991).

[30]   D. van de Kaa, 'Anchored Narratives: the Story and Findings of Half a Century of Research into the Determinants of Fertility', *Population Studies* L (1996), p. 425.

Appendix III
Sources and methods for studying the population of nineteenth- and early twentieth-century England

AIII.1 Introduction and overview

It was not until the nineteenth century that regular, 'official' data about demographic stocks and flows became available in the form, respectively, of decennial population censuses and the civil registration of births, marriages and deaths. The censuses were the first to appear, beginning in 1801. Civil registration followed in 1837, and by the 1840s a system for collecting demographic data had been put in place that was still fundamentally unaltered at the end of the twentieth century. From the middle of the nineteenth century, therefore, it is possible to calculate, both for England as a whole and for a variety of regions and sub-regions, a wide range of demographic measures of fertility, mortality and nuptiality.

Both civil registration and the population censuses provide data in two forms, at least in principle. First, their outcomes are published in a regular series of reports, giving summary statistics for a range of population aggregates at national, county and registration district levels. The data were, though, originally collected from individuals, and some information, particularly from the nineteenth-century population censuses, is available for individual, named persons. Sections AIII.2 and AIII.3 of this appendix consider the aggregate-level data from civil registration and the population censuses respectively, and Section AIII.4 the individual-level data that are now available from the population censuses from 1841 to 1901. Unfortunately, individual-level civil registration data are not, under normal circumstances, available to researchers.[1] Section AIII.5 briefly describes some other nine-

---

[1] Members of the public may obtain copies of particular birth, marriage or death certificates. There are also indexes to the registers of births, marriages and deaths, which may be consulted at local record offices. However, the indexes contain little information that is of use to population historians, and access to large batches of the original registers is still denied. The restriction is an administrative one, not a legal one, and there is therefore no bar to historians asking for large numbers of, say, death certificates, provided that they ask separately for each individual one! This was done, for example, in one study: H. Southall and E. Garrett, 'Morbidity and Mortality among Early-Nineteenth Century Engineering Workers', *Social History of Medicine* IV (1991), pp. 231–52.

teenth-century data sources that have been of use for the study of the period's demography.

AIII.2 Civil registration

The system of civil registration for births, marriages and deaths, which was set up in 1837, was a considerable improvement over the ecclesiastical registration that had preceded it. First, it dealt directly with births and deaths rather than baptisms and burials. Second, it was designed to include the whole population, not just those who attended the Church of England. By the fourth decade of the nineteenth century, Anglicans still formed the majority of the population overall, but their majority was gradually being eaten away by non-conformity and by the increasing secularization of the population.[2] The data collected included almost everything that had been collected by the ecclesiastical registration system, together with some additional items. Because the main interest of those who were administering the registration system was mortality, rather than fertility, the range of information on death certificates is wider than that on birth certificates. Thus we have, for the first time in English population history, detailed cause of death data, and information about the place of death and the occupation of deceased persons, as well as age at death and the sex of the deceased. By contrast, birth data, which modern demographers would regard as essential, such as the age of the mother and the number of children she already had, were not routinely collected. This means that it is possible to calculate age-, sex- and cause-specific death rates for a variety of population aggregates from the mid-nineteenth century onwards, but age-specific fertility rates, even at the national level, must be estimated indirectly.[3]

Coverage of civil registration in the early years was incomplete. The problem was more serious for births than deaths or marriages. A number of attempts have been made to assess the degree of under-registration and the consensus seems to be that in the 1840s (the first full decade of registration), about 6 to 8 per cent of births were unregistered, a figure that declined to fewer than 2 per cent by about 1870.[4] The level of under-registration of deaths was less than that of births, but it seems that there was a particular problem with infant deaths.[5] Other doubts about the quality of the data concern age reporting in the death registers (people did not always know the

---

[2] For the geography of religious attendance in the mid-nineteenth century, see K.D.M. Snell and P.S. Ell, *Rival Jerusalems: the Geography of Victorian Religion*, (Cambridge University Press, Cambridge, 2000).

[3] R. Woods, *The Demography of Victorian England and Wales* (Cambridge, Cambridge University Press, 2000), p. 111.

[4] Ibid., p. 42.

[5] See D.V. Glass, 'A Note on the Under-Registration of Births in Britain in the Nineteenth Century', *Population Studies* V (1951), pp. 70–88.

ages of their deceased relatives), and the reporting of causes of death, especially in relation to infant deaths.[6]

The civil registration data for the nineteenth and early twentieth centuries are available for various sub-divisions of the population in two forms. First there are the *Annual Reports of the Registrar General*, which provide a summary of the numbers of births, marriages and deaths in each year. These may be found among the Parliamentary Papers. Second, there are decennial supplements to the annual reports, which provide more detailed analysis, especially about mortality by cause and occupation. The geographical subdivisions used were based on the *registration district*. There were just under 600 of these in England, based on the Poor Law unions defined by the Poor Law Amendment Act of 1834. They were amalgamated into 43 *registration counties* (similar to, but not always coterminous with, the ancient counties).[7] There were also *registration sub-districts*, but the amount of information provided at this level of disaggregation is limited. The registration districts were used in the *Annual Reports of the Registrar General* until 1911, when they were replaced by local government administrative areas.[8]

Using the annual reports and the decennial supplements can be a tedious exercise, especially if information is desired for a run of years. Fortunately, most of the information has been extracted and made available in electronic form. A particularly important collection is that deposited in the United Kingdom Data Archive at the University of Essex by Robert Woods. This consists of the number of deaths classified by age, sex and cause for each registration district in England and Wales for each decade from 1851–60 through to 1891–1900.[9] Other electronic abstracts of the material exist, such as the database compiled by David Gatley mentioned in Section AIII.3. In addition, the Office for National Statistics (formerly the Office of Population Censuses and Surveys) has produced a number of volumes of historical statistics that stretch back in time to the beginning of the civil registration era.[10]

AIII.3 The population censuses: aggregate data

The first population census was taken in 1801, and was little more than a count of heads. However, the information gained was sufficiently useful

---

6   Woods, *Demography of Victorian England and Wales*, p. 68. Typically, large proportions of infant deaths were ascribed to 'other causes'.
7   Ibid., p. 37.
8   Ibid., p. 37.
9   The catalogue of the UK Data Archive may be consulted on-line at http://www.data-archive.ac.uk.
10 See, for example, Office of Population Censuses and Surveys, *Birth Statistics: Historical series of Statistics from Registrations of Births in England and Wales, 1837–1983* (series FM1, no. 13) (London, Her Majesty's Stationery Office, 1987); Office of Population Censuses and Surveys, *Mortality Statistics 1841–1985: Serial Tables* (series DH1, no. 19) (London, Her Majesty's Stationery Office, 1989).

that the exercise was repeated in 1811 and a census has been taken every decade since then, except for 1941 during the Second World War. The censuses of 1801 to 1831 used the overseers of the poor to collect a rather limited range of information about the people of their parishes. The advent of civil registration, however, allowed the population censuses to be reorganized so that the data collected on population stocks could be meshed with the newly available data on population flows. Thus from 1841 onwards, the population censuses, too, were organized on the basis of registration districts. The use of the same geographical units for collecting both types of data is important, for it ensures that when demographic rates are calculated the *events* (births, deaths or marriages) in the numerator correspond with the population exposed to the risk of experiencing those events. The range of questions asked was also expanded. The 1841 census asked about address, name and surname, age (in exact years for children and to the nearest five years for adults), and occupation. It also collected limited information on birthplace.[11]

In 1851 the range of questions was extended to include relationship to the head of household, marital status, age in exact years for everyone, a more comprehensive description of each person's 'rank, profession or occupation', much more detail about 'place of birth' (which normally included both parish and county for persons born in England and Wales), and some information on physical or mental disability. This set of questions remained the same until 1891, when questions were added about the status of each occupied person ('employer', 'employee' or neither), and the number of rooms in the house, if this were fewer than five. In 1911 questions were added about marriage and fertility, collecting data from married couples on the date of their marriage, the number of children born and the number of children still alive.

The responses to these questions were aggregated over registration districts, counties and regions, and the results published in a series of census reports, all of which are, like the Registrar General's annual reports and decennial supplements, published among the Parliamentary Papers. Using the published census reports can often be difficult and frustrating, not least because the tables seem to be slightly different in each census year, so that making comparisons across time is complicated.[12] Some useful compilations of aggregate census data by county and registration district have been made available to historians in machine-readable form. An example is the set of registration district data taken from the 1861 census, which has been

---

11   The birthplace information indicated whether each person had been born in the county in which he or she was enumerated, and, if not, whether he or she had been born in Scotland, Ireland or 'foreign parts'.
12   A guide to exactly what tables are in each census report is to be found in M. Drake, 'The Census, 1801–1891', in E.A. Wrigley (ed.), *Nineteenth-Century Society: Essays in the Use of Quantitative Methods for the Study of Social Data* (Cambridge, Cambridge University Press, 1972), pp. 37–46.

distributed by David Gatley of the University of Staffordshire. This includes information on the total population of each district, the ages and marital status of the population, occupations of males and females aged 20 years and over, and birthplaces.[13] It also includes some related civil registration data – for example, on the numbers of births, marriages and deaths in each district.[14] The Victoria County Histories also usually contain summaries of the population enumerated in each of a county's parishes in the censuses from 1801 onwards.

AIII.4 The census enumerators' books

In order to take the population censuses from 1841 onwards, each registration district was divided into *enumeration districts*, the latter being small enough so that one man could visit each house in one day. In rural areas, the typical enumeration district would include a single parish; in urban areas it might cover several adjacent streets. For each enumeration district, an *enumerator* was appointed, whose responsibility it was to distribute the census forms to householders and to collect them in shortly after the night of the census. The data from the forms were then copied into *census enumerators' books* (CEBs), in which all the information about each person was written on a single line, before being forwarded to the registrar. The CEBs have survived, and are accessible to researchers in the Public Record Office in London, and in local record offices. They form a vitally important source of individual-level population data. For reasons of confidentiality, however, the CEBs are closed to researchers for a period of 100 years after each census is taken. Therefore, at present, the latest census for which they can be consulted is that of 1901.[15]

The CEBs have attracted a great deal of attention, and have been the focus of countless local studies. In part, this stems from their being relatively easy to use compared with other manuscript sources. Their simple structure, with each person's details forming one row, and the different pieces of information the columns, also lends itself naturally to computer analysis. They are also relatively straightforward to interpret.

There are, however, a number of challenges that are worth mentioning briefly. Victorian enumerators found it hard to follow the instructions given

[13]   D.A. Gatley, 'Computerising the 1861 Census Abstracts and Vital Registration Statistics', *Local Population Studies* LVIII (1997), p. 41.

[14]   Ibid., p. 41. Copies of the data can be obtained through the Local Population History Book Club, 46 Fountain Street, Accrington, Lancashire BB5 0QP.

[15]   For further details of the census enumerators' books, see E. Higgs, *A Clearer Sense of the Census: the Victorian Censuses and Historical Research* (London, Public Record Office, 1996); D. Mills, M. Edgar and A. Hinde, 'Southern Historians and their Exploitation of Victorian Censuses', *Southern History* XVIII (1996), pp. 61–86; and P.M. Tillott, 'Sources of Inaccuracy in the 1851 and 1861 Censuses', in Wrigley, *Nineteenth-Century Society*, pp. 82–133.

them on what constituted a separate household. Different enumerators adopted different conventions, with the result that, unless some common set of rules is used, comparative work on the structure of the household is likely to be confounded. Fortunately, Michael Anderson has provided a set of rules, which covers most eventualities.[16]

The column in which the relationship of each person to the head of the household is given rarely poses too many problems of interpretation. One issue that sometimes causes problems relates to the existence of 'kin servants', these being persons described in the 'relationship to head of family' column of the CEBs as kin, but who, according to the 'occupation' column, were working in domestic service. One study of these people has found that the proportion of all domestic servants who were 'kin servants' varied from about 20 to 40 per cent (30 to 50 per cent if only servants aged 20 years and older were considered).[17]

The reporting of ages in the nineteenth-century censuses has often been questioned. Certainly, when individuals are traced through successive censuses using nominative record linkage, a large percentage of persons do not 'age' by ten years between each census. There was, therefore, a certain inaccuracy in age reporting. However, the percentage of people manifesting gross errors in age reporting is rather small. Most of those who are not reported as being ten years older at one census than they were at the preceding censuses have ages nine or 11 years apart, and few report age differences of less than eight or more than 12 years. The place of birth data are often considered to be fairly accurate, but record-linkage exercises sometimes reveal a substantial number of inconsistencies. The most common problem seems to be that persons who were not native to a place, but who had lived there for a long period of time would state that they had been born there. The existence of this error means that studies of internal migration using the place of birth data in the censuses have a tendency to underestimate the true extent of mobility.

Possibly the most problematic column is that relating to 'rank, profession or occupation'. This is one piece of information that can be checked against 'independent' sources. Unfortunately, when such checks are made, there is often a large difference between the numbers listed in the CEBs as being employed in a particular industry, and those listed, for example, in contemporary company records, trade directories and newspapers.[18] But the most serious and widespread charge that has been laid against the Victorian censuses' recording of occupation is that the employment of women, especially

---

[16] M. Anderson, 'Standard Tabulation Procedures for the Census Enumerators' Books 1851–91', in Wrigley, *Nineteenth-Century Society*, pp. 134–45.

[17] R. Hancock, 'In Service or One of the Family? Kin-Servants in Swavesey 1851–81, Ryde 1881 and Stourbridge 1881', *Family and Community History* II (1999), pp. 141–8.

[18] See, for example, F.W.G. Andrews, 'Employment on the Railways in East Kent, 1841–1914', *Journal of Transport History* XXI (2000), pp. 54–72; and P. Jennings, 'Occupations in the Nineteenth Century Censuses: the Drink Retailers of Bradford, West Yorkshire', *Local Population Studies* LXIV, pp. 23–37.

married women, was routinely and systematically understated. According to Michael Anderson, 'it is fast becoming a new orthodoxy' that 'the reporting of married women's employment in the CEBs is so bad that the data are almost useless for serious analytical purposes'.[19] Yet things might not be as bad as this view suggests. Anderson's own study of data from Lancashire and Cheshire on textile employment and the employment of wives of craftsmen, traders and labourers leads him to conclude that 'the census enumerators' books must remain, for many parts of the country at least, the best indicator that we have of variations in married women's gainful work activity in the mid-nineteenth century'.[20] The one contribution women made to the labour supply that is universally agreed to be under-recorded is seasonal work in agriculture.

The considerable discussion about the recording of women's work in the census has focused largely on their work in the 'formal' economy. Yet it has become clear that women without husbands, or in households with very low incomes, resorted to a great variety of 'informal' methods of earning a few extra pence: in Leicestershire, for example, these ranged from the taking in of washing to the embezzlement of material supplied to out-workers.[21] These activities, which were probably of considerable economic importance to poor households, are almost entirely missed by the census.

Because occupational variations in aspects of the demography of nineteenth-century England are frequently of interest, the classification of the occupations recorded in the Victorian CEBs is important. The most detailed scheme currently available is that described by W.A. Armstrong, and is based on a classification schedule drawn up by Charles Booth in 1886.[22] The so-called 'Booth–Armstrong scheme' works well for urban and industrial areas, but has been found less helpful in rural areas, where many of its industrial categories are largely redundant and it does not allow sufficient differentiation of agricultural occupations.[23]

It was recognized long ago that harnessing the power of computers would greatly facilitate work using the CEBs. More than 20 years ago a 2 per cent sample of the CEBs of the 1851 census was put together by Michael Anderson. With the advent of greater computing power, the possibility of

[19] M. Anderson, 'What Can the Mid-Victorian Censuses Tell Us about Variations in Married Women's Employment?', *Local Population Studies* LXII (1999), p. 10. On the under-recording of middle-class women's occupations, see E. Gordon and G. Nair, 'The Economic Role of Middle-class Women in Victorian Glasgow', *Women's History Review* IX (2000), pp. 791–814.

[20] Anderson, 'What Can the Mid-Victorian Censuses Tell Us?', p. 27.

[21] See P. Lane, 'Work on the Margins: Poor Women and the Informal Economy of Eighteenth and Early Nineteenth-Century Leicestershire', *Midland History* XXII (1997), pp. 85–99.

[22] W.A. Armstrong, 'The Use of Information about Occupation', in Wrigley, *Nineteenth-Century Society*, pp. 191–310.

[23] For further discussion of the merits of occupational classification schemes, see D.R. Mills, *A Guide to the Nineteenth-Century Census Enumerators' Books* (Milton Keynes, Open University Press, 1982), pp. 19–27.

making the CEBs for larger areas available in machine-readable form has emerged, and during the last few years a major development has been the publication of the entire set of 1881 CEBs (with individual-level data on about 30 million people) in machine-readable form. This was made possible by the Genealogical Society of Utah, who transcribed the data in every CEB for that census and then made the resulting files available to researchers through the History Data Service at the United Kingdom Data Archive at the University of Essex.[24] Researchers can now order the data from the CEBs on this census in the form of spreadsheet or database files for a variety of geographical units. These will lead to research on topics that have hitherto remained off limits to population historians – for example, the study of the destinations of persons moving out from specific areas (as opposed to the origins of persons moving in to a specific region, which the place of birth data reveal).[25] An index to the 1901 census (containing some of the information in the CEBs) is also available on-line from the Public Record Office, though, as with the indexes to the birth, death and marriage certificates mentioned earlier, it is not very useful to academic researchers.

There is insufficient space here to list the whole range of topics that have been analysed using CEB data. Readers are referred to the excellent bibliography by Dennis Mills and Carol Pearce, and to a recent collection of papers edited by Dennis Mills and Kevin Schürer.[26] It is, however, worth describing some of the more important uses to which they have been put. When the CEBs first attracted the attention of demographers and historians in the 1960s, work focused on the analysis of aspects of the population structure, including household and family structure (most notably in Michael Anderson's classic study of Lancashire), and social structure.[27] Since then they have been used to analyse fertility, marriage patterns and migration (through the use of the place of birth data).[28] Research using the CEBs has

---

[24]   See the on-line catalogue at http://www.data-archive.ac.uk.

[25]   The study of destinations is achieved by sorting the machine-readable file on the basis of place of birth, to obtain a list of all persons living in a region (or even in the whole country) who were born in a particular place.

[26]   D. Mills and C. Pearce, *People and Places in the Victorian Census: a Review and Bibliography of Publications Based Substantially on the Manuscript Census Enumerators' Books 1841–1911* (Historical Geography Research Series no. 23), (Cheltenham, Department of Geography, College of St Paul and St Mary, 1989); D. Mills and K. Schürer (eds), *Local Communities in the Victorian Census Enumerators' Books* (Oxford, Leopard's Head Press, 1996).

[27]   M. Anderson, *Family Structure in Nineteenth-Century Lancashire* (Cambridge, Cambridge University Press, 1971); W.A. Armstrong, 'Social Structure from the Early Census Returns: an Analysis of the Census Enumerators' Books for the Censuses after 1841', in E.A. Wrigley (ed.), *An Introduction to English Historical Demography* (London, Weidenfeld and Nicolson, 1966), pp. 209–37.

[28]   For work on fertility, see R.I. Woods and C.W. Smith, 'The Decline of Marital Fertility in the Late Nineteenth Century; the Case of England and Wales', *Population Studies* XXXVII (1983), pp. 207–25. For marriage, see P.R.A. Hinde, 'The Marriage Market in the Nineteenth-Century English Countryside', *Journal of European Economic History*, XVIII (1989), pp. 283–92.

analysed migration in two ways. First, the birthplace data has been used to chart the extent of lifetime in-migration to particular places, and to chart the geographical origins of the in-migrants.[29] Second, record linkage of successive censuses for a particular place, together with Church of England burial registers, has permitted some limited analysis of out-migration.[30] Using the other information provided in the CEB for the earlier of the two censuses, out-migration can be analysed for different age, sex and occupational groups.[31]

The last example also illustrates a more general point, namely that the greatest insights are often gained when the CEBs are used in conjunction with other sources. Because the CEBs, in principle, list every inhabitant of a place by name, they provide a base population. The information about individuals given in the CEBs can be augmented by searching for and finding these same persons in other sources, and then linking together all the data about the same person, a process known as nominal record linkage. For historians of population, the parish registers provide the most obvious other source to use (since the required access to the civil registers is not possible).[32] For example, Briony Eckstein and I have shown how family reconstitution-type rules for analysing fertility might be extended to incorporate data from the CEBs, allowing the measurement of fertility within marriage during the second half of the nineteenth century using a much larger proportion of marriages than would be possible with conventional family reconstitution.[33]

---

[29] For examples, see D. Mills and J. Mills, 'Rural Mobility in the Victorian Censuses: Experience with a Micro-Computer Program', *Local Historian* XVIII (1988), pp. 69–75; and W. Turner, 'Patterns of Migration of Textile Workers into Accrington in the Early Nineteenth Century', in Mills and Schürer, *Local Communities*, pp. 246–52. A general discussion of the use of the CEBs for the analysis of local migration will be found in D.R. Mills and K. Schürer, 'Migration and Population Turnover', in Mills and Schürer, *Local Communities*, pp. 218–28.

[30] See, for example, J. Robin, *Elmdon: Continuity and Change in a North-West Essex Village 1861–1964* (Cambridge, Cambridge University Press, 1980); P.R.A. Hinde, 'The Population of a Wiltshire Village in the Nineteenth Century: a Reconstitution Study of Berwick St James 1841–71', *Annals of Human Biology* XIV (1987), pp. 475–85; B. Wojciechowska, 'Brenchley: a Study of Migratory Movements in a Mid-Nineteenth Century Rural Parish', *Local Population Studies* XLI (1988), pp. 28–40 (reprinted in Mills and Schürer, *Local Communities*, pp. 253–66); and J. Robin, 'From Childhood to Middle Age', Cambridge Group for the History of Population and Social Structure working paper no. 1 (Cambridge, 1995).

[31] Wojciechowska, 'Brenchley'; Robin, 'From Childhood to Middle Age'.

[32] Although increasing non-conformity and secularity mean that the Church of England parish registers suffer from poor coverage in many parts of Victorian England this is not universally true. In rural areas, especially in southern and eastern England and the Midlands, over 90 per cent of births were recorded in the baptism registers; see Hinde, 'Population of a Wiltshire Village'.

[33] B. Eckstein and A. Hinde, 'Measuring Fertility within Marriage between 1841 and 1891 using Parish Registers and the Census Enumerators' Books', *Local Population Studies* LXIV (2000), pp. 38–53.

AIII.5 Other sources

Many other sources, such as trade directories and Poor Law records, can be used to shed light on particular aspects of England's population history during the demographic transition. Often, the most valuable insights are gained when these sources are used in conjunction with census data, perhaps through the application of nominal record linkage.[34]

Trade directories can be used to complement the information about occupation given in the CEBs. In rural areas they are usually arranged on a parish-by-parish basis, and include lists of the 'gentry and clergy, farmers, and tradesmen and craftsmen'.[35] For the analysis of migration, Poor Law settlement examinations continue to be a rich source of data of the migration histories of the poor well into the nineteenth century (see Appendix II). The settlement examinations are, of course, heavily concentrated on the poor, and are therefore not socially representative. They may be complemented by other sources that represent other sections of the population. Quaker removal certificates, for example, record all moves that involved persons changing the location of their Quaker meeting.[36] A recent study of internal migration in England and Wales makes use of detailed residential histories of their ancestors compiled by family historians.[37] This source has the great advantage over sources (like the population censuses) conventionally used for the analysis of internal migration in that it records actual moves rather than 'transitions' and thus allows a much richer picture of the 'migration fields' of individuals to be painted. Its disadvantage is that it tends not to be representative of the population as a whole (people with 'interesting' lives tend to be over-represented, while those who did not leave descendants are not represented at all).

For the analysis of international migration, the place of birth data in the population censuses provide details of the numbers and origins of immigrants. Emigration must normally be tackled using other sources and methods. One ingenious method for measuring the *amount* of emigration by county was devised by Dudley Baines. It is, essentially, an application of the

---

[34] For an example of this kind of analysis, see C.A. Crompton, 'An Exploration of the Craft and Trade Structure of Two Hertfordshire Villages, 1851–1891: an Application of Nominal Record Linkage to Directories and Census Enumerators' Books', *Local Historian* XXVIII (1998), pp. 145–58.

[35] D.R. Mills, *Rural Community History from Trade Directories* (a *Local Population Studies* supplement) (Aldenham, Local Population Studies, 2000, p. 12); for a guide to trade directories in urban areas, see G. Shaw, 'The Content and Reliability of Nineteenth-Century Trade Directories', *Local Historian* XIII (1979), pp. 205–9.

[36] See B. Dackombe, 'A Quaker Perspective on Migration: Ampthill and Hitchin Preparative Meetings, 1811–1840', *Family and Community History* III (2000), pp. 49–64. Because Quaker meetings were often several miles apart, many short-distance moves would not have been recorded, as they would not have required a change of meeting.

[37] C. Pooley and J. Turnbull, *Migration and Mobility in Britain since the Eighteenth Century* (London, UCL Press, 1998).

demographic accounting equation described in Boxes 10.1 and 14.1. Baines describes it thus:

> It consists of estimating the number of deaths of natives of each of the fifty-two counties of England and Wales distinguishing those that occurred in the county in which the individuals had been born and those that occurred in the other counties of England and Wales. Since the number of births, the number of natives still living in their place of birth, and the number living in the other counties is known, we can calculate migration of natives out of each county and the migration into the other fifty-one counties in each decade. The difference between the two flows must be the number of natives of each county who went overseas.[38]

Baines' method, of course, tells us nothing about *where* the migrants went. For that information, historians have tended to rely on various sets of government migration statistics. Data on the characteristics of emigrants, on the other hand, tend to come from passenger manifests, records of organizations that assisted or subsidized emigration, or records in destination countries.

---

[38] D. Baines, *Migration in a Mature Economy: Emigration and Internal Migration in England and Wales, 1861–1900* (Cambridge, Cambridge University Press, 1985), p. 5.

Index of names and places

Subject index